The Impact of the
Spanish Civil War
on Britain

Sussex Studies in Spanish History

General Editor: José Alvarez-Junco, Universidad Complutense, Madrid

Advisory Editors:
Nigel Townson, Universidad Complutense, Madrid
Pamela Radcliff, University of California, San Diego

This authoritative series provides a forum for critical and scholarly debate on a wide range of topics and themes in Spanish History. Forthcoming volumes will be developed not only from original, critical work, but from newly translated studies that have only been available in the Spanish language, but which are recognized by the Editorial Board as adding substantially to knowledge and debate of Spanish history issues in the English-speaking world.

Published

The Emergence of Mass Politics in Spain: Populist Demagoguery and Republican Culture, 1890–1910
José Alvarez-Junco

The Impact of the Spanish Civil War on Britain: War, Loss and Memory
Tom Buchanan

Constancia de la Mora in War and Exile: International Voice for the Spanish Republic
Soledad Fox

The Quest for Survival after Franco: Moderate Francoism and the Slow Journey to the Polls, 1964–1977
Cristina Palomares

The Crisis of Democracy in Spain: Centrist Politics under the Second Republic, 1931–1936
Nigel Townson

Forthcoming

The Spanish Right and the Jews, 1898–1945: Antisemitism and Opportunism
Isabelle Rohr

The Impact of the Spanish Civil War on Britain

War, Loss and Memory

TOM BUCHANAN

sussex
ACADEMIC
PRESS

BRIGHTON • PORTLAND

2 4 6 8 10 9 7 5 3 1

First published 2007 in Great Britain by
SUSSEX ACADEMIC PRESS
PO Box 139
Eastbourne BN24 5BP

and in the United States of America by
SUSSEX ACADEMIC PRESS
920 NE 58th Ave   Suite 300
Portland, Oregon 97213–3786

British Library Cataloguing in Publication Data
A CIP catalogue record for this book is available from the British Library.

Library of Congress Cataloging-in-Publication Data
Buchanan, Tom, 1960-
  The impact of the Spanish Civil War on Britain : war, loss, and
  memory / by Tom Buchanan.
    p. cm.
  Includes bibliographical references and index.
  ISBN 1-84519-126-9 (h/c : alk. paper)
  ISBN 1-84519-127-7 (p/b : alk. paper)
    1. Great Britain—Social life and customs—20th century.
  2. Spain—History—Civil War, 1936–1939—Foreign public
  opinion, British. 3. Spain—History—Civil War, 1936–1939—
  Influence. 4. British—Spain—History—20th century.
  5. Spain—History—Civil War, 1936–1939—Participation,
  British. 6. Great Britain—Politics and government—
  1936–1945. I. Title.

  DA566.4.B793 2007
  941.084—dc22   2006020739

Typeset and designed by SAP Editorial, Brighton & Eastbourne
Printed by TJ International, Padstow, Cornwall
This book is printed on acid-free paper.

Contents

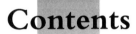

Series Editor's Preface

Studies of the relationship between Britain and Spain in the modern era have inevitably tended to revolve around the pivotal event in the history of twentieth-century Spain: the Civil War of 1936–39. Certain aspects have, understandably, received particular scholarly attention, above all the policy of Britain's Conservative-led "National" government during the conflict and its pursuit of appeasement via the so-called strategy of 'non-intervention'. Likewise, the material and ideological contribution of the British International Brigaders to the Republican war effort has generated enormous and lasting interest. Over the last fifteen years, Tom Buchanan, starting with his pioneering account of the British labour movement's reaction to the Civil War, has considerably enriched our knowledge of the political and diplomatic links between Britain and Spain during this crucial period. That reputation is confirmed and enhanced by this collection not only by making available in book form articles which have previously appeared in academic journals but also by furnishing seven entirely original pieces. In this book Buchanan continues to broaden our vision of Britain's involvement in the Spanish Civil War by tackling a range of new questions, such as the response of journalists and artists to events in Spain. Furthermore, the author has also taken the subject forward, both chronologically and thematically, by addressing post-war issues such as the memory of the 1930s, changing perceptions of Spain during the Franco dictatorship, and the importance of the Civil War as a point of ideological reference in British politics since 1939.

No doubt the friendship of my family with John Langdon-Davies, the protagonist of the chapter 'My country right or left', and his family, which included summer holidays at their delightful Catalan villa, Casa Rovira, played a part in fostering my own interest in Spain, and for that reason it gives me particular pleasure to present this wide-ranging and extremely stimulating collection of essays by Tom Buchanan.

NIGEL TOWNSON
Series editor of Sussex Studies in Spanish History

Acknowledgments

This book contains three of my published articles and seven new essays. Chapter 1 was first published in *Twentieth Century British History*, 4, 1, 1993; chapter 4 in *History Workshop Journal*, 54, 2002, and chapter 6 in *The Historical Journal*, 40, 2, 1997. Chapters 1 and 6 have only been slightly edited in order to prepare them for this volume. However, chapter 4 has been more heavily revised to take account of significant new archival material. Chapters 1 and 4 are reprinted by permission of Oxford University Press; Chapter 6 is reprinted with permission of the editors of *The Historical Journal*. Of the new chapters, a number were initially given as seminar or conference papers; chapter 5 at the University of Sheffield History Department seminar in December 2003; chapter 8 at the conference of the Anglo-Catalan Society in Oxford, 2001; chapter 9 at a conference organised by the Cervantes Institute in Manchester, 2001, and chapter 10 at the History Department seminar, De Montfort University in 1998. In each case I was grateful for the opportunity to present my research and found the discussion helpful.

I am grateful to the following for permission to make quotations from manuscript sources: The Master and Fellows of Trinity College Cambridge (Julian Trevelyan papers); UCL Library Services (Haldane papers); the Bodleian Library and the Dawson family (Dawson papers); the Society of Authors (Rosamond Lehmann papers); Christopher Whittick (Ron and Percy Horton papers); Dr Charlotte Townsend-Gault (William Townsend papers); Scottish National Gallery of Modern Art (Roland Penrose papers); and the Archivist, Times Newspapers Limited. The quotation on page 95 is reproduced by permission of the Henry Moore Foundation. The letters from Wogan Philipps form part of the Rosamond Lehmann collection at King's College, Cambridge; I am grateful to the Archivist, Dr Patricia McGuire, for facilitating my access to them. The jacket design and figures 1 and 4 were first published in *Drawings by Felicia Browne* (Lawrence & Wishart). Figures 2 and 3 are reproduced by permission of Mrs Lin Lobb.

I am indebted to the many archivists, colleagues and friends who have kindly assisted me while researching this book, and I have singled out a number of individuals for particular thanks in the notes at the end of this volume. I would also like to thank Dr Nigel Townson, Advisory Editor of Sussex Studies in Spanish History, and Anthony Grahame, Editorial Director at Sussex Academic Press, for all of their support and encouragement over the last three years. Finally, all of these essays have benefited enormously from discussion with my wife, Julia. As ever, her contribution, has been invaluable.

TOM BUCHANAN
Oxford
July 2006

Abbreviations

AIA	Artists International Association
CCA	Churchill College Archive, Cambridge
CPGB	Communist Party of Great Britain
DMP	David Murray papers, National Library of Scotland
IBA	International Brigade Association
IBD&WAC	International Brigade Dependants and Wounded Aid Committee
ILP	Independent Labour Party
JRL	John Rylands Library, Manchester
LDV	Local Defence Volunteers
MML, IBMA	Marx Memorial Library, International Brigade Memorial Archive
MRC	Modern Records Centre, University of Warwick
NJCSR	National Joint Committee for Spanish Relief
NLS	National Library of Scotland
NMLH	National Museum of Labour History, Manchester
POUM	Partido Obrero de Unificación Marxista
RGASPI	Russian State Archive of Social and Political History, Moscow
SMAC	Spanish Medical Aid Committee
TNA	The National Archives, Kew
TNL	Times Newspapers Limited
TUC	Trades Union Congress

The Impact of the Spanish Civil War on Britain

War, Loss and Memory

Chapter 1

'A far away country of which we know nothing'?

British perceptions of Spain and its civil war, 1931–1939

On 27 September 1938 Prime Minister Neville Chamberlain made a radio broadcast during the Sudetenland crisis which has become immortalized as the embodiment of isolationist appeasement: "How horrible, fantastic, incredible it is that we should be digging trenches and trying on gas masks here because of a quarrel in a far away country between people of whom we know nothing." It is inconceivable that a similar comment could have been made about the Spanish Civil War which broke out in July 1936, partly because no one had any intention of going to war over Spain, but also because no politician could pretend that the British people were as ignorant about Spain as they were about Czechoslovakia. Indeed, there was considerable awareness of Spain's political problems prior to the Civil War, and, once it had begun, British spectators found an easy frame of reference for understanding the conflict in the history and national character of the Spanish people. Both the right and the left in British politics, however, faced difficulties in presenting their respective views of the Civil War, and differed diametrically over how Spanish history, politics and culture should be interpreted. This introductory chapter will elucidate the mental framework within which British politicians and journalists looked at the Spanish Civil War, and show how left and right came to develop contrasting accounts of the war for public consumption.

British political responses to the Civil War were conditioned by the decision of Stanley Baldwin's Conservative-dominated administration to sponsor an international policy of "non-intervention", whereby the means of making war would be denied to both the Spanish Republican

1

forces and their rebel (Nationalist/Francoist) opponents. It is now well known that the agreement was a sham which worked to the advantage of the rebels, aid for whom from Germany and Italy outweighed Soviet assistance to the Republic. This was not, however, immediately apparent, and the Labour Party (which sided with the Republicans) initially backed non-intervention, slowly reversing its decision between the autumn of 1936 and the summer of 1937. The smaller Communist Party of Great Britain (CPGB) and Independent Labour Party (ILP) both opposed non-intervention more consistently. Thus, all the parties of the left came to share a commitment to building public support for the Republic and to seeking a change in government policy towards the war. The mass of the Conservative party, however, took little interest in the conflict beyond backing non-intervention. The focus, therefore, will be primarily with the left-wing parties mentioned above, and with a group of politicians and journalists on the Conservative right wing who identified with the Nationalists on ideological grounds and, like the left, sought to influence public perceptions and official policy.[1]

Spain had entered a period of prolonged political unrest in 1931 following the overthrow of the monarchy and its replacement by the reforming Second Republic. Thereafter, power swung between governments of the centre-left and centre-right against a background of mounting social conflict and political violence. In October 1934 the Spanish Socialist Party (PSOE) led an unsuccessful rebellion against the elected centre-right government, fearing that it was acting as a Trojan horse for fascism, and initiated two weeks of bloody conflict in the coal-mining region of Asturias. The deployment here of colonial Moroccan troops, used for the first time to suppress workers within Spain, caused considerable international disquiet. When the left was again elected to office in February 1936, having formed a wide-ranging Popular Front alliance, there was a further spate of assassinations, culminating in the rebellion by elements of the army that began on 17 July. The outbreak of some form of civil conflict in Spain would not have surprised many British commentators, even though its eventual scope may have done. Indeed, as early as 11 October 1934 the communist *Daily Worker* was employing the headline "Spanish Civil War" to describe the relatively limited conflict in Asturias. The communist writer Ralph Bates, whose book *The Olive Field* was published in early 1936 and dealt with the years 1932–4, stated firmly: "This is a novel of *the Spanish Revolution*."[2] For the right-wing *Morning Post*, meanwhile, the ill-starred history of the Second Republic had been a "violent see-saw", punctuated by rebellions and strikes – "that Spanish plague".[3]

By the 1930s Spain occupied a rather peculiar position in the British world view. While the British public was aware of Spain, if for no other reason than its historic rivalry with England,[4] the introverted Spain of the early twentieth century had been of relatively little concern to Britain, especially in the light of its neutrality during the First World War. However, in the 1930s the creation of the Republic crystallized a revival of British interest in Spain for political, economic and cultural reasons. The Foreign Office displayed an obsessive concern in these years that Spain would form the next, and strategically significant, target for communist revolution.[5] This belief was shared by those sectors of British business that had important interests in mining and agriculture, and followed Spanish developments keenly.[6] The Republic also revived the spasmodic interest that the British left had taken in Spain ever since the judicial murder of the Anarchist educationalist Francisco Ferrer in 1909 had sparked a considerable protest movement, echoes of which were still heard in the 1930s.[7] The triumph of the Popular Front made Spain attractive not only on narrowly political grounds, but also as a counterweight to the rise of European fascism. Indeed, Spain was already a centre of British left-wing attention in July 1936 because the "People's Olympiad", the Socialist riposte to the Berlin Olympics to which the British Workers' Sports Association sent a team of forty-four competitors, was scheduled to take place in Barcelona from 19 to 26 July. The British team arrived just in time to form a valuable pool of eye-witness accounts of the street-fighting at the start of the Civil War.[8]

Personal and cultural links were also developing in these years. For individual travellers Spain's neutrality during the First World War could prove attractive. The writer Gerald Brenan, for instance, who lived in Spain intermittently between 1919 and 1936 and received visitors from the Bloomsbury circle in his remote Andalusian village, wrote that "my choice of Spain rather than of Greece or Italy was not due to any special feeling that I had for it. Almost all I knew about that country was that it had been neutral in the war and would therefore, I imagined, be cheap to live in."[9] Spain was also well known to members of the upper and middle classes who chose to retire there, and was just beginning to become accessible to working-class tourists through the Workers' Travel Association.[10] The Republic, indeed, sought to stimulate foreign tourism, and in the early 1930s there was no shortage of brochures and guidebooks advocating holidays in Spain on the grounds of romance, adventure, health (for "jaded nerves and tired constitutions") and, as ever, cheapness. Whereas Gage's *Autumn Tour to Spain* in 1901 had advertised conducted tours as the best way to see Spain, given "the undoubted difficulties of Spanish travel, the language, the coinage and the peculiar characteristics of the people", Southern Railways' 1933 brochure on "How to get to Spain" by rail suggested a new era of uncomplicated, unescorted travel to a fellow European country. In fact, within a few years such rail routes would be the preserve of volunteers for the International Brigades rather than independent-minded tourists.[11]

Despite such areas of special interest and knowledge, however, British perceptions of Spain remained rooted in (often crude) ideas about national character which were to some degree shared by both right and left. Nor was the frequent resort to such stereotypes during the Civil War simply the result of ignorance. The fact that even sophisticated commentators on Spanish affairs tended to rely heavily on clichés about the "Spanish character" was attributable not only to the ubiquity of such stereotypes of the Spanish within British culture, but also to the fact that the British public was thought likely to find many aspects of the Civil War alien, incomprehensible, and even repugnant, and would have need of such aids to interpretation. The most significant of these stereotypes were those that saw the Spanish people as, first, incompetent and lazy; second, cruel and violent; and, finally, highly individualistic.

The first of these assumptions was commonplace at the time. Herbert Morrison, a strong supporter of the Spanish Republic within the Labour Party leadership, commented in August 1936 that Spain's main problem was failure to control its army: "a reflection upon the capacity of the Spanish people for self-government and good public administration".[12] Victor Schiff, an exiled German Social Democrat who acted as Spanish correspondent for the labour movement's *Daily Herald*, wrote in October 1936 that the poor air defence of Madrid (especially the fact that street lights were left on) was "so stupidly illogical that I should be inclined to suspect Fascist sabotage, if I did not know by many other examples that Spanish military incompetence has no limits and is perfectly genuine".[13]

The idea of good-natured Spanish inefficiency, characterized by such immutable customs as the siesta, and by the *mañana* attitude, was a recurrent theme, implying that the Civil War was too important to be left to the Spanish. Rather comically, for instance, the Trotskyists Mary Low and Juan Breá, visiting Barcelona in August 1936, were horrified when they discovered from a resident that the siesta still survived:

> *"Surely you don't still have the siesta here?"*
> *He looked surprised.*

"Why not?" he said.

"Do you mean to say that you shut up everything and go to sleep from one till four during the revolution and the civil war?"

He stared at us from large languid eyes as if the sun had struck us."[14]

The concept of the Spanish as bound by peculiar customs was rooted in British popular culture. The term "old Spanish customs" was well known in London's Fleet Street to describe workers moonlighting on their printing jobs – indeed, the *Daily Worker* made pointed reference to this in a cartoon claiming that Spain's United Front of working-class parties was "the new 'Spanish custom' – and it wins!"[15]

Cruelty and violence were also thought to be "old Spanish customs" – due in equal part to the legacy of the Inquisition and the bull ring. Consul-General King of Barcelona believed that the "atrocities" in Spain were proof that "the Spaniards are – for the most part – still a race of blood-thirsty savages, with a thin veneer in times of peace".[16] Conversely, a romantic gloss was placed on the Spanish Anarchists' propensity for political violence by Sir Peter Chalmers Mitchell in his introduction to the Penguin edition of Ramón Sender's *Seven Red Sundays*, written before the war began in January 1936:

May it be worth while considering if what are certainly the legal crimes of the 'Reds' are an inevitable reaction to the tremendous forces of repression with which science has armed authority . . . And above all, is there not a flicker of hope for humanity, if it be the case that a selfless love and a generous purpose glow through the cloudy dreams of the 'criminals'?[17]

Even so acute an observer as the Austrian-born sociologist Franz Borkenau, on his arrival in Barcelona in August 1936, ventured to suggest that it was "not so much an anarchist but a Spanish habit to massacre one's enemies wholesale".[18] Such was the extent of this stereotype that in May 1936, following the Popular Front's election victory, the official journal of the British Trades Union Congress (TUC) felt compelled to reassure readers that: "The average Spaniard, despite his sometimes ferocious appearance, his devotion to his spectacular national blood sport and the fact that his country still breeds anarchists, is a very ordinary, kindly-disposed human being, heartily sick of the disorder which exists on his doorstep."[19]

Finally, as we shall see, Spanish individualism was alluded to by both left and right in Britain in order to explain the phenomenon of Spanish Anarchism and to show that Spain would never succumb to an externally imposed communist or fascist dictatorship.

These perceptions of the Spanish character were fixed not only in relation to assumptions about the British character (as moderate and competent) but also in relation to the regional diversities of character within Spain itself. This was especially true with regard to the Basque country, where an intensely Catholic region, dominated by the conservative Basque Nationalist Party, chose to side with the Republic against the Nationalists in pursuit of the goal of autonomy. Basque resistance was brutally crushed in the summer of 1937. However, the sufferings of the Basque people, widely seen as an innocent party to the Civil War, heightened the perception that they were fundamentally different from the Spanish and, indeed, shared many common characteristics with the British. The view was expressed, at the highest level in government, that the Basques were a moderate, pious and hard-working people who had managed to avoid the excesses of the rest of Spain and wanted only to be left alone.[20]

In addition to these perceptions of the Spanish character, other characterizations profoundly influenced British views of Spain in the 1930s. The foremost (and by no means incorrect) of these was that Spain remained a fundamentally rural nation. Different lessons were, however, drawn from observing different parts of Spain. By those on the right, the small farmers of central and northern Spain were upheld as a prime example of sturdy conservatism, contrasting with the "ignorant" proletariat and the decadence of the big cities. For one Conservative MP, Barcelona, the centre of Anarchism, had "for thirty years been the political cesspool of Europe".[21] Likewise, it was the apparently timeless struggle between the landlords and peasants on the great estates of Andalusia and Estremadura which caught the imagination of the left in Britain, receiving much more attention than the development of industry in the Spanish regions. Spanish rural life had recently been lovingly described from a left-wing viewpoint in Ralph Bates' quasi-anthropological novel *The Olive Field*, published immediately prior to the Civil War. On a smaller scale, a correspondent told the *Daily Herald* that he had been moved to write a 45-minute playlet on rural life during the war and wanted it performed during fund-raising collections for the Republican side.[22] The Scottish socialist David Murray found it particularly easy to relate the Spanish conflict to the people of the Outer Hebrides while on a speaking tour in January 1938: "He showed the parallel between the fight of the Spanish workers and peasants for Land, Liberty and Education against the forces of Landlordism and reaction, and the long drawn out struggle of the crofter and fishermen of the Long Island for the same things."[23]

These characteristics reinforced the tendency to see Spain as a fundamentally different kind of society from the modern, industrial Britain of the 1930s. In particular, it contributed to a sense that Spain was starkly divided between the 'old Spain' of rigid hierarchy (and, for the left, oppressed masses) and the 'new Spain' which was challenging it. Both right and left shared these categorizations, though they would draw very different conclusions about which side best embodied them during the Civil War.

For the British left, the 'old Spain' of landlords, army and clergy was clearly the fundamental evil in contemporary Spain (at least until external fascist intervention in the Civil War became the left's main target). The attempt by these atavistic forces to hinder the legitimate agents of progress was widely taken as the main cause of social conflict. In 1935, for instance, the sometime Labour MP Leah Manning visited Spain as part of a committee investigating the suppression of the 1934 Asturias rising. In a subsequent book she confessed to having several "preconceived notions of Spain" – romantic images of gipsy girls and bull fights jostled in her mind with school history of "a Spain that specialized in torture and inquisitions and *autos da fé*", as well as with recent ideas of an industrial Spain "where the upsurging organized workers were fighting for economic freedom and liberty of conscience, but were for ever held down by a savage capitalist system reinforced by the iron hand of the Church". She sadly concluded that modern Spain had not lost "its taste for torture and inquisitions".[24] The *Daily Worker* greeted the formation of the Spanish Republic in April 1931 with equally vivid language, although seeing Spain as still in the grip of pre-capitalist forces. The Republic was a blow against the "medieval state structure" – but Spain was "still dominated by parasitical aristocratic castes of a feudal type. Its great landowners hold the peasantry in an intolerable servitude [aided by the clergy and army]".[25] A cartoon in the *Daily Herald* following the 1934 Asturias rising showed the figures of clerical reaction and fascism (in a military uniform) swinging the clock back to the year 1400.[26] The most lurid invocation of the dead weight of the past was a parliamentary speech by the ILP MP John McGovern in October 1937. Himself a Catholic, McGovern was keen to challenge the view that the Civil War was in essence an attack on the Catholic religion:

> *For some time people have said that this was a war between religion and Communism, but they forget that years ago people were suffering under the Inquisition in Spain. They forget the ticking clock that slowly penetrated the bridge of the nose until the eyes were torn out . . . [A litany of other tortures followed] . . . People who say that there is terror and cruelty in Spain should remember that Spain has been gradually emerging from the cruelty, terror and tor-*

ture of the past. . . My sympathies are with the common people every time because they are down in the gutter striving for expression and for a way out.[27]

Prior to the outbreak of the Civil War, therefore, the most common interpretation on the left was that the 'new Spain' of the Republic (and, latterly, of the Popular Front government) was set on reducing the powers of the 'old Spain' – ultimately allowing Spain to "take her place among the free and progressive nations of Europe".[28] In the months of peace between the February 1936 elections and the outbreak of the war, the *Daily Herald* ran two series of articles on the 'new Spain'. One series by the writer Geoffrey Brereton looked, for instance, at the slow emancipation of Spanish women ("Economically they are independent, socially they are bound by the conventions of a bygone age") and the attempts to reduce the powers of the Church.[29] Another, written by the Labour MP Ellen Wilkinson, reported on the wave of strikes afflicting the government. An interview with a waiter from the Socialist UGT union struck a hopeful note: "'The time has gone now for bombs' he said, 'people want to vote. The women want to vote. They like voting. Direct action, huelgas [strikes] are necessary, yes. But bombs, no.'" Even when peasants resorted to using force to seize land, Wilkinson justified these actions as motivated by idealism rather than self- or class-interest – the peasants were inspired because they had caught a glimpse of "the Spain that might be".[30] The left wanted to see itself as supporting the sane, idealistic, and unthreatening agents of change in the 'new Spain'.

There was, however, little that was sane, idealistic or unthreatening in the opening phase of the Civil War. In fact, the left faced severe problems of presentation in the process of building support for Republican Spain. The military rising of July 1936 was greeted by weeks of anarchy and disorder, in which, even in areas that stayed loyal to the Republic, power slipped into the hands of ill-controlled militias. The massacres of supposed enemies and the burning of churches by anarchists and others was deeply offensive to British opinion. Within the labour movement many working-class Catholics doubted whether they could tolerate any degree of support for a Spanish Republic which appeared to condone such acts (and which were, of course, also deplored by the many non-Catholic workers who respected law and order).[31] Anarchism, which had played such an important role in recent Spanish history, and was so little understood in Britain, presented particular problems to left-wing journalists and politicians, who often fell back on the idea of the "Spanish character" to explain it. American journalist Walter Duranty, with the Anarchist leader Durutti outside Saragossa, wrote for the *Daily Herald* that: "They are strange soldiers, these militia, who make a boast of their virtues of 'indiscipline', by which they really mean what Americans would call individual initiative."[32] Leah Manning spoke for many in explaining the influence of anarchism on the grounds that "by temperament and tradition the Spaniard is strongly individualist".[33] Indeed, one perceived benefit of anarchism was that the very 'individualism' from which it sprang would insulate Spain against the dangers of Soviet-style communism. As the Liberal MP Wilfrid Roberts put it: "The individualism of the Spanish character, the love of individual liberty, has sunk very deep into the people and I do not believe that the rigid type of Soviet Communism can ever fasten itself upon the people of Spain."[34]

Similar problems of presentation attended the well-publicized phenomenon of women fighters joining the Republican militias in the early months of the Civil War. Where Geoffrey Brereton had noted the absence of a Spanish 'suffragette' movement and the slow entry of women into Spanish public life, a few months later his newspaper was running captions such as this: "Gone are all thoughts of gay dresses and shawls so much in evidence on festive occasions – instead rifles and cumbersome military equipment." However, change was not allowed to go too far – the caption ended: "On the left a woman soldier's aid is sought to replace a button"![35] The presence of women on the front line in Spain struck a highly ambiguous note in Britain. (Indeed, official British Union of Fascists speakers' notes, under the heading of 'atrocities', appeared to find such women combatants the worst atrocity of all).[36] In general, women fighters injected a note of exotic interest, and even titillation, into coverage of the conflict. The *Daily Herald* ran a short story entitled 'The Spanish Amazon' (a term first coined in the newsreels[37]) about a Spanish dancer who joins the Republican forces and finds herself having to shoot her fascist brother in a firing squad. However, the concept of women fighters would have been unlikely to enthuse supporters within a male-dominated British labour movement. It contrasted uneasily with the scene in Epping Forest where a branch of the tailors' union held a mass picnic to raise money for a Spanish ambulance, and where female members were encouraged to join a 'Bathing Belles' contest.[38] The London taxi drivers' section of the Transport and General Workers' Union (T&GWU) responded to the Rothermere press 'lies' on Spain by forbidding their wives to purchase any goods advertised in the *Daily Mail*.[39]

The outbreak of the Civil War, therefore, undermined the concept of the new Spain, peacefully and democratically displacing the old. Instead, many British observers saw a confused conflict of almost indiscriminate savagery, and a Spain distinct from the rest of industrial Europe in its 'backward', 'feudal' society and in the harshness of its social relations which sparked forms of resistance that were quite *sui generis* and outlandish – lawless anarchism and women on the barricades. The TUC journal *Labour* was able to note smugly that, thanks to trade unionism and democracy, the British workers and their families had avoided the "beastlinesses against which the Spanish peasantry have at long last taken arms".[40] The opening phase of the Civil War reinforced prejudices against the Spanish as violent and undisciplined, and did much to obscure the legitimacy of the elected government's cause.

In this situation a new basis of solidarity with the Spanish people had to be rapidly constructed – one that would show them as the victims of unprovoked external aggression and uncivilised attack rather than as a leaderless and factional mob. In the later stages of the war this image was provided by the well-documented involvement of Nazi and Fascist forces from Germany and Italy and the terror bombing of urban centres such as Guernica, Barcelona and Madrid. In the short term, however, the left ruthlessly exploited the racial scare associated with General Franco's use of Moorish soldiers to spearhead his invading army. These soldiers had originally been raised to hold down Spain's Moroccan Protectorate, and an estimated 60,000–70,000 served in Spain during the Civil War. It was common for these forces to be rewarded with rape and looting while on service in Morocco, and this practice was readily extended to the Spanish mainland by officers who saw little difference between the 'Reds' and the colonial enemies in the Rif.[41]

Interestingly, Franz Borkenau on his arrival in Barcelona in August 1936 noted that: "Nobody seems to think that the landing of the Moors in the South may be a serious matter. The English papers, before my departure, were full of it, but here hardly any foreign papers are available, and the local Press does not even mention the matter."[42] Franco's use of Muslim Moroccan troops did indeed have a profound effect in Britain. Clearly it made sound political sense to point up this central contradiction in the Nationalist Catholic 'crusade' at a time when opinion in Britain was still deeply troubled by the church burnings within the government zone. However, the phenomenon is more interesting than that, not least because there was no common agreement on why the use of Moroccans was in fact so hateful. There were at least four distinct arguments advanced on this point. First, the Moroccans were Muslim. One correspondent to a trade union journal feared a rebel victory because "the Moors have been promised mosques in various towns which suggests that Mahommedanism will be officially recognised in a European country".[43] Another stated simply that the Moors were "anti-Christ".[44] Second, the Moors were mercenaries. According to Labour MP E. J. Williams, "never in the history of the world has there been such a display of cruelty and barbarity by a ruling class in the ruthless use of mercenaries against the people".[45] Third, in the words of the London Trades Council, use of the Moors was a "crime against civilisation and a violation of international law".[46] Ernest Bevin made a similar point at the 1936 TUC Conference. He said that he resented the use of the Moors "to kill the Spanish people . . . as much as we resented the putting of black troops into the Rhineland during the [French] occupation". Moreover, they had been brought over in violation of a treaty which specified that "before a Moor can be recruited to fight in Europe the international law lays down that there must be consultation with the Sultan of Morocco".[47]

Finally, and most significantly, the Moors were singled out because they were 'black'. As one correspondent put it, the rebels' "most heinous crime, in British eyes, was that of using a horde of black troops to crush the white inhabitants of Spain".[48] The Moroccans were regularly referred to as 'black' in Britain, and the confusion as to who they were was not confined to a hapless volunteer in O'Duffy's pro-Franco Irish Brigade who thought that the Moors were in fact Mormons.[49] The point was made visually with striking clarity by the *Daily Herald* in a series of cartoons. In one a gas-masked Italian soldier going to Abyssinia says "I'm spreading civilisation in Africa", passing a Negro soldier going to Spain who says: "Dats all right – I'm spreading it in Europe." In another, two blacks are shown. One wears a fashionable suit and holds a card saying "Negro vote may decide presidential elections [in the USA]", while another is swapping his tribal grass skirt for an Italian uniform in Mussolini's "enormous black army", while black troops charge into the smoking ruins of Spain. The caption runs:

> *"Big Boy, I may decide who rules de United States of America!"*
> *"Big Boy, I may decide who rules de Disunited States of Europe!"*

In a third cartoon, depicting the "Fascist Front", a black soldier identified as "Franco's own" is saying "Yow hi! Brudder Europeans."[50]

Such cheap propaganda, far removed from the noble sentiments so commonly identified with the Civil War, doubtless served a useful purpose in building popular sympathy for Republican Spain. Moorish savagery and attacks on women were particularly emphasized. The Labour MP John Dobbie, back from a visit to Spain, said: "How are the Moors paid? When they take a town or village they are allowed two hours to loot and murder. Seventy-five per cent of Franco's army are Moors and members of the Foreign Legion, and they are being let loose among the white women of Spain."[51] Yet some critics felt that this card had been overplayed. At a Spanish Medical Aid rally in late1936 a friend of the *New Statesman* editor Kingsley Martin commented: "I liked [Viscount] Churchill best – he spoke of Moors as human beings . . . the Left in Spain has always extolled the Moors in the past as a race cruelly persecuted by the Catholics. Now the Moors are just part of the Fascist devil."[52] A letter to a trade union journal about the "bogey" of the Moors noted that "incidentally, many of your readers must have fought side by side with black troops not so long ago and were not ashamed".[53] Such arguments were dismissed by the respected radical writer Henry Nevinson in a hysterical article entitled "This crime calls to high heaven." He argued that Franco's "crime" in importing Moors ("semi-savages") to fight Spaniards was comparable to British fascists importing "an armed force of Zulus to overthrow our Constitution and established Government". This was different from British use of Indian troops and the French use of Senegalese during the First World War because they

> *were imported to fight against the common enemies of the countries which commanded them. General Franco is bringing the Moors over to fight against his own people. He is himself responsible for all the bloodthirsty and shameful abominations practised upon Spanish men and women by the savage hordes whom he has called to his assistance.*[54]

The most direct use of this tactic came at the Edinburgh Labour Party conference in October 1936, where the Labour leadership had managed to persuade sceptical delegates to accept the policy of non-intervention. Two days later, however, two fraternal delegates from the Spanish Socialist Party addressed the conference to dramatic effect. One of them, Jiménez de Asúa, had to be translated and was heard with respect as he detailed violations of the non-intervention agreement at great length. But Isabel de Palencia, who spoke good English, made a passionate speech which was probably the single most important element in the discrediting of non-intervention within the labour movement. At the heart of her speech lay an appeal to precisely the kind of images referred to above:

> *We are suffering the most terrible, the most cruel attack that any civilised nation could suffer, at the hands of the Moorish troops which have been brought over. The Catholics know that it took eight centuries for Spain to free the country from the Moors – from the infidels – and now they are bringing those infidels back into the country to kill us.*

She then absolved rebel Spanish troops of rapes and atrocities. "Not a woman is respected, not a church is respected. The plunder of the churches in Spain is being done by the Moors, and it is against these forces that the loyal forces of Spain are fighting."[55] This speech, so well-received by the audience that they rose spontaneously to sing the Red Flag, was the cause of great discomfort to Labour leaders in private as they contemplated the ruin of their carefully-crafted support for the policy of non-intervention.[56]

Moral outrage at the use of Moorish troops, and the side which employed them, thus formed a crucial element in the reconstitution of support for the Spanish Republic in the summer and autumn of 1936, at a time when external fascist intervention was nowhere near its peak. This issue, above all else, dispelled the very negative images associated with the Republican side in the early months of the war, and placed Spain firmly within the comity of 'civilized' nations threatened by the most ancient of foes. With the Moors at the gate there could be no doubt that the boundary of 'civilisation' rested on the Spanish, rather than the French, side of the Pyrenees. In the following months and years of the Civil War the left was remarkably successful in portraying the Spanish Republican government as the only true representative of the Spanish people. Indeed, the word 'Spain' came to represent one side in what was, after all, a civil war, and the Spanish people were seen as the victims of a handful of disloyal generals, commanding a mixture of Moors, Italians, Germans and the "dope fiends and dregs of humanity in the Foreign Legion"[57] – anyone, in fact, other than fellow Spaniards. Moreover, the Republican regime was successfully presented as the inheritor of the progressive and democratic mantle of the pre-war 'new Spain'. The best known popular account of the Civil War, the Duchess of Atholl's *Searchlight on Spain*, for instance, stressed the Republic's continuing achievements in education, land reform, women's liberation, science and culture against the savagery and philistinism of Franco's rule.[58] Another well-known text, Gannes and Repard's Left Book Club offering *Spain in Revolt*, concluded that: "The supporters of the government took up arms in defence of their Republic and for the fulfilment of its promises." They depicted the conflict thus: "Out of the carnage and wreckage of civil war, a new Spain had to emerge. The choice lay between the brutalising and violent enslavement of fascism and the liberating, progressive developments which a democratic victory could make possible."[59]

The power and essential simplicity of this image has suffered with hindsight. In the acrimonious aftermath of the Civil War it became clear that Republican unity had, to a degree, served to obscure the growth of communist political control over the government and armed forces and, in particular, the suppression of the Marxist POUM party following the May 1937 fighting in Barcelona. Moreover, many historians of the Civil War emphasize the discontinuity between the pre-war and the wartime versions of the Republic, stressing the degree to which the military rising had triggered a social revolution in many of the remaining parts of Spain (and especially in Catalonia). A semblance of political continuity was only restored by the Communist Party, acting on Stalin's orders, at the cost of popular disillusionment with the Republican cause.[60]

The modern perception of the Civil War is, therefore, seriously at odds with the prevailing contemporary view. The liquidation of the POUM, for instance, caused little concern to British left-wingers at the time (other than in its sister party the ILP) and George Orwell's *Homage to Catalonia*, destined to be the most influential account of communist wrongdoing, was, in his lifetime, his least successful book. More generally, apart from the ILP, the concept of workers' revolution played no part in mainstream left-wing perceptions of the Civil War. This was not simply the result of communist manipulation, but reflected at least two other factors. First, British left-wingers did not see a revolution unfolding in Spain, but rather an inevitable period of weakened state authority (with attendant abuses) which would have to be reversed if the Spanish Republic were to survive. Such a view was of a piece with the overall perception that the Civil War represented a defensive struggle against military aggression, and allowed even the worst revolutionary excesses to be glossed over. For instance, Gannes and Repard's comments on the church-burnings are instructive: "Atrocity stories are the easiest to make and the hardest to prove . . . At any rate, it must be remembered that the burning of churches in one country may be the most common and traditional channel of popular resentment while in others it may amount to the most horrible kind of desecration."[61] The burning of churches was therefore reduced from a revolutionary act to yet another 'old Spanish custom'. Secondly, the very language of revolution had been debased by the British left in analysing Spain's politics. The events of 1931 and 1934 had both in turn been greeted as 'revolutions', and the whole of the Second Republic could be seen as one long 'revolution' against Spanish feudalism. For instance, the POUM supporter Edward Conze, the bulk of whose book *Spain Today* was written before the military rising, concluded in 1936 that "the present [Spanish] revolution is five years old, and shows no signs yet of old age or decay".[62] In a country where all change was routinely hailed as 'revolutionary' it is not surprising that the confused events of the summer of 1936 were seen as just that, and not as a 'real' revolution.

In interpreting left-wing perceptions of the Civil War, then, historians should be aware of the enduring power of what I have termed the ideal of the 'new Spain', and the degree to which it was forged anew to suit the needs of a very difficult situation in the summer and autumn of 1936 when international solidarity with the Republic was by no means assured. In fact it was a major achievement to persuade so many British people that the Spanish Republic was worth supporting – indeed, that it was the heir to the principles of peaceful, democratic progress, confronting the most atavistic and anti-national forces in Spanish society. It is noteworthy that George Orwell, whose *Homage to Catalonia* did so much to mould post-war perceptions of Republican politics as communist-dominated, was himself far from immune to the idea of the 'new Spain.' In an article published in 1939 he wrote:

> *In Government Spain both the forms and the spirit of democracy have survived to an extent that no one would have foreseen; it would even be true to say that during the first year of the war they were developing . . . the civil war, amid all its frightful evil, was acting as an educational force. Scores of thousands of ordinary people had been forced into positions of responsibility and command which a few months earlier they would never have dreamed of . . . There was a huge intellectual ferment, a sudden expansion of consciousness. It must be set down to the credit side of the war, a small offset against the death and suffering, and it is doubtful whether it can be completely stamped out, even under a dictatorship.*[63]

Right-wing opinions and perceptions of the Civil War are less easy to delineate than those of the left. The main reason for this is that the Conservative-dominated British government was a strong supporter of non-intervention in Spain, and rallied support on the right for a policy that was seen increasingly to favour Franco's side. Accordingly, right-wing Conservatives were content to follow the government lead, even though they may have been fervent supporters of the Spanish Nationalist rebels. There were, of course, even within the government, divisions of opinion over the Civil War. Foreign Secretary Anthony Eden came increasingly to believe that British interests would not be served by a Franco victory, while, conversely, Sir Samuel Hoare, as First Lord of the Admiralty, conceived a visceral hatred of the 'Reds' following the lynching of Spanish naval officers at the outbreak of the war. Such a degree of interest in the Civil War was, however, unusual. Neville Thompson has shown that for most Conservatives the Civil War was, at best, a 'distraction' from the more pressing problems of keeping the European peace – Tories could not understand "why their opponents were so exercised over the war", and a wedge was driven between antiappeasement backbenchers and the Labour Party.[64] According to Leo Amery, the mass of Conservatives, both in government and out, remained emotionally unengaged with the Spanish conflict: "[They] found little to choose between both sides, either on the merits of the case or in the ferocity of the methods. In any case no national or even party interest was directly involved."[65]

This view is, however, somewhat disingenuous. Whatever the mass of Tories thought about Franco's methods, he was consistently seen as preferable to communism and anarchy, which appeared to be the only alternative. Only in a few interesting cases, notably that of Winston Churchill, can one observe real changes in attitude during the conflict.[66] The Duchess of Atholl was alone on the right in moving from die-hard anti-Bolshevism and opposition to Indian self-government to becoming a leading campaigner for the Spanish Republic. Her main motivation, however, remained the defence of the Empire.[67] On the far right, Oswald Mosley's British Union of Fascists (BUF) took little official interest in the Civil War, although on the local level BUF members worked closely with rebel agents in escapades such as seizing impounded Spanish ships from British ports.[68]

Nevertheless, the lack of interest taken in the Civil War by mainstream Conservatives should not hide the very real interest shown by the vocal group of British right-wingers in Parliament and elsewhere. Here I shall follow G. C. Webber's definition of this group as a disparate "collection of anti-Liberals who disliked Socialism and despaired of official Conservatism with varying degrees of intensity"; it included both the right wing of the Tory party as well as elements of the fascist and anti-Semitic right. The presence of some Catholics on the right (qualified by their hostility to Nazism) gave additional impetus to right-wing interest in Spain, although Webber has concluded that the Civil War "was in general less of an issue for the Right than it was for the Left".[69] It would certainly be wrong to over-estimate the degree of right-wing support for Franco: there was a core of some twelve Conservative MPs who spoke out strongly for Franco and the rebels in Parliament, and received backing from right-wing organs such as the *Morning Post*.[70] Many of these individuals were associated with the two most prominent pro-Franco pressure groups, the Friends of National Spain and the Basque Children's Repatriation Committee (set up following the evacuation of 4000 Basque children to Britain in May 1937).[71]

Right-wing interest in Spain, like that of the left, had been triggered by the fall of the monarchy and the creation of the Republic in 1931. Douglas Jerrold, who was later to fly Franco from the Canary Islands to

Morocco to begin his revolt, formed a small study circle with Sir Charles Petrie and the Marquis del Moral in 1933, convinced that there was a communist revolutionary plot afoot.[72] Similarly, Wyndham Lewis's novel *The Revenge for Love* is of interest in its use of Spain as the scene for a political thriller as early as 1935, again envisaging it as the arena for communist subversion. However, although the Nationalist rebellion was envisaged as a pre-emptive strike against a communist conspiracy, the actual conditions in which the Civil War broke out gave the right, like the left, severe problems in presenting their case. Instead of seeing a repeat of October 1934, when the Spanish government had moved to crush a left-wing revolutionary provocation, the British right was now forced to respond to an old-style military *pronunciamento*. Moreover, this was a military coup that had gone badly wrong, and had resulted in a civil war in which the Nationalists could be branded as rebels against the legitimate civil power.

The right's response to the Civil War came in two distinct phases. Initially it sought to present the rebels as defenders of the true Spain against the demonic forces of external subversion; later, as Franco consolidated his power, it would seek to give the Nationalists a positive image, as the makers of their own 'new Spain'. As the writer Eleanora Tennant put it, she felt that on her visit to the rebel zone she had been "'in at the birth' of a nation".[73]

In almost a mirror image of the left's view, the right glorified the 'old Spain' and presented it as a haven of lawfulness and natural hierarchy. Any problems associated with it were due purely to the imposition of non-Spanish ideas and institutions following the fall of the monarchy. Tory MP Anthony Crossley traced the origins of the Civil War to "the Spanish character itself. If government is not autocratic it is despised and disobeyed. Spain has had four years of so-called Democratic Government. At the end it was appallingly bad government."[74] Sir Henry Page Croft, in particular, emphasized that the root of Spain's problems lay in the abandonment of the monarchy. Democratic institutions did not thrive in Spain – and could never do so when thrust on "untrained peoples, or on nations who have not acquired the sense of corporate assent to chosen leaders".[75] Speaking at the end of the Civil War, Croft predicted a return to the old-style government in Spain "before they unwisely and rashly experimented in forms of democracy in their later years, and we shall find emerging in Spain something very similar to the old government, a people under a monarchy".[76] For Tory MP Charles Emmott, parliamentary government was contrary to the "genius, the history and the contemporary conditions of the Latin peoples".[77] The

Lisbon correspondent of the *Morning Post* compared Portugal to Spain, and noted that in both agrarian-dominated countries the majority of people "asked only for independence and secure possession of their small properties. It is the politicians, theorists, and intellectuals who insist that the people should have something more than this." Spanish liberals, he continued, were susceptible to foreign beliefs – and by attacking the Church and monarchy were placing themselves at odds with the "Spanish nation".[78] Similarly, for Catholic intellectual Bernard Wall, who travelled widely in Nationalist Spain, the Civil War was a struggle to save Spain from "foreign and secularist ideas".[79] There were, however, variations on this theme. The Tory MP Wing Commander James, for instance, who had also visited Nationalist Spain, had no hesitation in placing the Civil War within the long Spanish history of struggle between indigenous forces of conservatism and liberalism, dubbing the conflict a "Third Carlist War".[80]

By contrast with the values espoused by the right, the Republican system was reviled for allowing the rise of subversive elements within Spanish society. The pre-civil war Republic was accused of failing to govern and of allowing, if not condoning, attacks on churches and right-wing politicians. Winston Churchill said that parliamentary government had been used as a "mere mask" to cover the "swift, stealthy and deadly advance of the extreme Communist or anarchist factions, who saw, according to the regular programme of Communist revolutions, the means by which they could obtain power".[81] The regime that emerged following the military revolt was seen as weak, fragmented and at the mercy of the worst elements of society. A British resident of Spain, writing in December 1936, depicted the Republican zone as dominated by the "fear of the riff-raff of society, which, like mud on a stormy day, has risen to the top and stained the social stream".[82] Ian Colvin ridiculed Scottish socialist supporters of the Republicans such as James Maxton – would they approve of the "arming of the 'low Irish' of Glasgow to loot Sauchie Hall Street and burn down the Cathedral"?[83] One *Morning Post* writer, from the safety of Perpignan, paid particular attention to the fact that women in the Republican zone were "playing a grim part in the horrible business", revelling in "the sight of priests and Conservatives being shot and of churches being destroyed".[84]

The right was understandably cagey about trying to define Franco's movement politically and consistently denied that he was a "fascist". Instead, it sought to portray the Nationalists as defenders of "all that is traditional in Spain",[85] with the relatively limited aim of restoring unity and the authority of government. The *Morning Post* characterized

Franco's goal as "a national and constructive dictatorship which would establish order, protect industry and commerce, both national and foreign, and put an end to gun play in the streets".[86] More simplistically, Tory MP N. Stewart Sandeman would offer this definition of Franco's intention: "I call it putting things right."[87]

For many on the right, Franco's authoritarianism, guaranteeing as it did the safety of business interests, was sufficient justification for supporting him. However, as the war progressed some of Franco's enthusiasts began to look with approval at his supposed social reforms, and, indeed, began to challenge the left for the use of the term 'the new Spain'. As early as October 1936 the *Morning Post* was publishing adulatory articles on Franco's social policy by the American journalist James Abbe, who quoted Franco as saying that "workmen and peasants will take an important and integral part in the future life of the country".[88] The author Florence Farmborough, who visited Spain in 1938, was clearly swept up with the 'new Spain' that she had witnessed – and not just because as an ardent anti-communist she saw Franco's regime as a 'National Crusade' against the 'Red Infidel'. She noted the way that the war had affected the position of women ("A young girl has duties to perform, public duties outside her home") and hoped that Franco's ambitious 'New State' would satisfy the working classes – "class-strife will be completely suppressed and strikes and lock-outs will disappear". She was also optimistic for the land worker, who was enjoying "a solicitous attention such as he has never before experienced".[89] In February 1939 Tory MP Patrick Donner welcomed the British government's recognition of the Franco regime, just as he welcomed the "social reforms which General Franco has already inaugurated. I welcome the better conditions for the people of Spain – the new houses, the raising of wages."[90] Franco's social reforms were greeted particularly warmly by some Catholics. As early as October 1936 a letter to the *Christian Democrat*, organ of the Catholic Social Guild, was claiming that Franco had excellent credentials in this area (he "had run workmen's restaurants and other things himself in Oviedo") and praising the recent achievements in the rebel-held area – "cheap workmen's houses have been built by public subscription, free dinners have been served to poor children, crèches are soon to be opened . . . ".[91]

While seeking to portray the rebels in a more positive light, the right also had to respond to the left's criticisms, especially over the use of Moorish troops. The right was unabashed on this point, and a number of lines of justification became clear. The first was that such criticism was hypocritical. According to Sir Arnold Wilson, both British and French governments "are fortunate in the possession of more loyal Moslem troops and citizens than any other countries. They have steadily supported us for over a century."[92] A further line of defence was that there was nothing shameful in the use of the Moors because they "are part of Southern Spain and their blood is the blood of Spain".[93] Eleanora Tennant challenged the racial attacks by the left – the Moors were "not a black race, and have no racial connection whatsoever with the Abyssinians or negroes . . . Nearly all Spanish families have Moorish blood and are proud of it."[94] Irrespective of these claims, however, the right's approval of Franco's use of Moroccan soldiers owed most to their deep hatred, and demonization, of the Spanish 'Reds'.

Thus, the right, as defined above, was happy to identify with Franco's regime. Unencumbered by a doctrinaire commitment to parliamentary government, it saw Franco as defending the essential principles of conservatism – in the words of Henry Page Croft, in Spain "everything that we hold most dear is being assailed, whether it be law and order, liberty of conscience or even the right to worship God".[95] Anthony Crossley, a Catholic Tory MP, expressed broadly similar views on his return from Nationalist Spain in 1937:

> It does seem to me both petulant and misguided to challenge the bona fides of those people who are fighting for their religion against atheism, for their right to hold property against compulsory impoverishment, for a military dictatorship against a Communist dictatorship, for their country against Internationalism. If they are not fighting for those objects, at least they profoundly believe they are. After my visit to Spain, I am inclined to be of their opinion.[96]

When right-wing Tory MPs praised Franco as a "gallant Christian gentleman",[97] as "the Leader of our cause today",[98] or even as "an angel",[99] they were doubtless enjoying baiting their left-wing opponents, but they were also expressing a genuine admiration for Franco's strength of purpose in defending the 'true Spain' against external threat.

In the crude words of Randolph Churchill, on meeting Arnold Lunn in Avila: "A few excitable Catholics and ardent Socialists [in Britain] think that this war matters, but for the general public it's just a lot of bloody dagoes killing each other."[100] This view proved to be unduly cynical. However, it is important to bear in mind the strong negative factors which initially hindered public identification with either side in the Civil War. On the Republican side there was the appalling factionalism, the chaotic bloodletting of the early months, and the twin spectres of communism and anarchism. On the Nationalist side there was the rebellion against legitimate authority, the use of non-Spanish soldiers, and the prospect of a pro-fascist regime threatening Gibraltar. In the background loomed deep-seated preconceptions according to which the Spaniards were inherently cruel, incompetent and politically unstable. Both right and left were forced to produce a manicured picture of the Spain that they were defending, suitable for public consumption. Each sought to portray its side in the Civil War as the representative of the real Spain, threatened by external forces. However, such was the thrust of British government policy that the right, in practice, never had to seek to build a real popular following for its views in the country at large. This was in marked contrast with the left. Out of office and ill-placed to influence government policy, the left was still remarkably successful in constructing an acceptable image of the conflict and building a preponderant degree of at least passive public support for Republican Spain.[101]

In the process, both left and right were forced to work with and, on occasion, to challenge the prevailing stereotypes associated with Spain and the Spanish people. Having established the frame of reference that stereotypical images of Spanish history and culture provided for politicians and journalists as they struggled to come to terms with Spain's Civil War, it is clear that clichéd ideas about the Spanish character formed a convenient vehicle for explaining a savage and complex conflict. The consequence was frequently to exaggerate the image of Spain as unique, exotic, and remote from the rest of Europe. In this sense, British knowledge of Spain and the Spanish proved to be almost as harmful (at least to Republican interests) as British ignorance of the Czechs during the Munich crisis. For in the crucial early stages of the Civil War the idea that the conflict was somehow typically Spanish played into the hands of a British government which sought to divorce it from the wider political crisis within Europe.

However, there was nothing immutable about the stereotypes involved. It is apparent that the British perceptions of Spain did (at least at the level of propaganda) begin to change in the course of the Civil War; indeed, that political transformation was seen as bringing with it changes to national character. The favoured sides of both right and left offered heroic images of moral certainty and martial vigour which contrasted starkly with the perceived languor of the National Government at home. Moreover, the interpretations offered by right and left alike came to challenge the images of the Spanish prevailing at the start of the war. Both, for instance, emphasized the more efficient forms of government in their respective zones and the creation of formidable military machines; both emphasized the birth of political unity and a new collective will in place of rampant individualism, Anarchism, or regionalism; and each emphasized the degree to which 'its' side, when victorious, would exercise mercy over the vanquished. Perhaps these more positive images failed to convince or to strike deep roots. Perhaps, also, they were too closely tied to support for the Republican side to survive Franco's victory, given that the mass of the British people saw that victory as a triumph for the old Spain over the new. Yet, although it is probably fanciful to argue that a Republican victory would have brought immediate changes in British perceptions of Spain, the decades of post-Civil War isolation for Franco's Spain merely reinforced the traditional stereotypes, a topic to be taken up later in chapter 9.

Chapter 2

Journalism at war

*George Lowther Steer, Guernica and the
resistance to fascist aggression*

In the early morning of 27 April 1937 George Steer and two other journalists, Noel Monks and Christopher Holme, entered the still burning
ruins of Guernica. For three hours during the late afternoon and early
evening of the previous day the Basque town had been bombed and set
ablaze by German aircraft of the Condor Legion, in the service of Franco.
Hundreds of civilians had perished. The three men, all hardened professional reporters, were appalled by the destruction and human suffering
that they encountered. Monks of the *Daily Express* later wrote that
"whenever I think of it, and often the memory haunts me, [it] makes my
blood boil".[1] The journalists then returned to Bilbao where, in the course
of the day, they began to file their reports. In the event, the story of
Guernica was broken by another British journalist, Keith Scott Watson,
who had been an eyewitness to the bombing. His unattributed story,
accompanied by Holmes' Reuter's dispatch, was published in the London
Star on the evening of 27 April.[2] However, a far greater impact was made
by Steer's account in *The Times*, also unattributed, which was published
on the morning of 28 April. His masterful, understated, language brought
home the horror of the attack while making clear its historic significance:
"In the form of its execution and the scale of the destruction it wrought,
no less than in the selection of its objective, the raid . . . is unparalleled
in military history . . . The object of the bombardment was seemingly
the demoralization of the civil population and the destruction of the
cradle of the Basque race." Steer's dispatch, which was also published in
the *New York Times*, made a powerful impression on international
opinion. In Britain, news of the destruction of Guernica came to
symbolise the wanton aggression of Franco and his foreign allies, and

tipped many from neutrality into overt sympathy for the Spanish Republic. The civil war was no longer an incomprehensible struggle between factions, but could now be presented as a violent assault on civilised values.

Not surprisingly, the British journalists' account of Guernica did not go uncontested. Indeed, Franco's officials initially claimed that they had no planes in the air that day due to bad weather. They soon withdrew to a more defensible position: that the town had been intermittently bombed, but that it was a legitimate military target, and that the devastating fires had been started by retreating Republican soldiers rather than by aerial bombardment. In the ensuing war of words the Nationalists' position was greatly strengthened by the fact that the ruined town fell to their forces on 29 April, allowing them to present their version of events to parties of journalists (subject to fierce censorship and control) and visiting Franco sympathisers. The other strand of Nationalist damage limitation was to seek to discredit the British journalists. Steer, in particular, was vilified by Franco's supporters in Britain and North America, not only because of the power of his original dispatch, but also because of the vigour with which he defended it, most notably in his book *The Tree of Gernika* (published in January 1938). Right-wing critics such as the Conservative MP Sir Henry Page Croft and Robert Sencourt emphasised that Steer was not an eyewitness to the bombing, as *The Times* had wrongly claimed, and that he was not an impartial commentator. Page Croft described Steer's story as "flimsy" and unconfirmed.[3] Sencourt wrote that Steer was a "gifted, sensitive and imaginative artist", who had "deep emotional reasons" for writing as a partisan of the Basque cause and lacked the objectivity to report the story accurately.[4] In 1939 Steer went as far as to threaten a libel action against one of his detractors – presumably Sencourt – who had insinuated that Steer had parted company with *The Times* over his coverage of the Civil War.[5]

Although Steer's case never reached court, his account of the bombing of Guernica has been broadly vindicated by historians, notably through the painstakingly detailed research of the American writer Herbert Rutledge Southworth.[6] There is now no question that German aircraft perpetrated an atrocity at Guernica, although there is still debate about the exact reason for the raid and the degree to which the Nationalist high command was implicated in it. Steer's report has also weathered more recent criticism, notably the argument advanced by Phillip Knightley that Steer misinterpreted what he had seen and "overreacted", thereby turning an everyday bombing attack into an icon of modern warfare.[7] It is certainly true that Steer and his colleagues were journalists with an eye for a story. Noel Monks recalled his initial reaction on the evening of 26 April as: "Here, I thought, is a story that will shock the world. Guernica bombed! In flames! That peaceful town! Those devout people massacred!"[8] Yet they were also professionals who re-checked their stories and were careful only to report what they could justify from the limited available evidence. Hence, in his dispatch Steer gave no estimate of casualties, and repeated – albeit sceptically – a Basque government statement that they were "fortunately small". Likewise, he made it clear that his claim that the raid was intended to terrorise the civilian population was based purely on what he had observed – notably that Guernica's arms factory had been left unscathed – and on what he was able to glean from survivors. A separate criticism, levelled by historian Franklin Reid Gannon, was that *The Times'* coverage of Guernica was "unusual and controversial"[9] because it was the only newspaper to identify German aircraft as responsible from the outset, thereby inviting the storm of criticism that broke over it in Nazi Germany in May 1937. This, however, was clearly not the case. Scott Watson's eyewitness account in the *Star* stated that German planes had carried out the bombing, and a number of other newspapers made similar claims. The Nazis were outraged not because *The Times* had made an ill-founded allegation, but because it was seen as a highly influential (and semi-official) newspaper that had briefly but damagingly departed from its appeasing path.

However, while Steer's account of the destruction of Guernica has stood the test of time, the one question raised by his critics that continues to perplex is that of his objectivity. In a sense, there is no mystery here, as it was well known at the time that Steer sided wholeheartedly with the Basques, just as he had previously sided with the Abyssinians during their war with Italy in 1935–6. Yet how far did he take his support for the Basques, what was his political motivation, and to what degree did his commitment to the Basque cause cloud the objectivity of his reporting? In many respects Steer remains a somewhat elusive and puzzling figure. A man who wrote copiously during his short life – Steer died in a car crash in India while on active service in 1944 – left surprisingly little evidence as to his personality and political beliefs. Nicholas Rankin, who has recently written an excellent biography,[10] relied heavily on Steer's journalism and books, supplemented by a few family papers relating to the last years of his life. This chapter offers an interpretation of Steer's activities in the 1930s in the light of a number of archival sources that have not previously been consulted, notably his correspondence with the Labour politician Philip Noel-Baker. It will be argued that – even more than other journalists of a politicised generation – Steer felt himself to be personally at war with Fascism during the 1930s. As his father-in-law Sir Sidney Barton wrote in 1942, Steer was "at the front in the Second World War ever since this began in fact with the Italian invasion of Abyssinia on 1 October 1935".[11] In other words, Steer was not merely covering one of the greatest international stories of the late 1930s, but was also an active participant in it, and this participation was nowhere more intense than during the crisis in the Basque country during April–June 1936. In his introduction to *The Tree of Gernika* Steer wrote that, just because he identified with the Basques, it should not be inferred that "I participated in any way in the struggle". Rankin correctly observes that Steer's comment was "disingenuous", but it is only in the archival record that the full extent of his disingenuousness becomes clear.[12]

■ ■ ■ ■ ■ ■ ■

George Lowther Steer was born in East London, South Africa, on 22 November 1909, the only child of Bernard Steer, chairman of and a substantial shareholder in the *Daily Dispatch*, who had moved to South Africa six years previously. Although he had a lifelong commitment to Africa, Steer was mainly educated in England at St Peter's, Seaford (1921–3), Winchester College (1923–8) and Christ Church, Oxford (1928–32). He was, therefore, perfectly placed to be at the same time an outsider and a part of the British elite. His identity was essentially English, although he was aware that his origins in the South African "wilderness" made him far more appreciative of all that England had to offer.[13] He retained a somewhat idealised vision of "English" values of fair-play, integrity and support for the underdog. Both in Abyssinia and the Basque country his moral anger was fuelled by a sense that Britain had turned its back on those who had placed their trust in these very values.

Steer was a highly successful student at Oxford, where he obtained a Double First in Greats. (He told a prospective employer that he was "the best ancient historian in Christ Church").[14] He was also closely involved in establishing two societies on African affairs. The first, *Saamwerk* ("working together" in Afrikaans), was established in March 1930 in response to the escalation of racial segregation in South Africa. Steer had been one of 16 signatories to a letter of support from Oxford to the newly-founded Non-Racial Franchise Association in December 1929.[15] He was also involved in the Africa Society (founded in 1931), of which he was University Secretary. These societies allowed Steer to deepen his knowledge of contemporary Africa, but also brought him into contact with influential men in public life, some of whom he carefully cultivated as potential patrons.[16] While at Oxford Steer also took every opportunity to return to Africa. In 1930 he toured the native territories of the Transkei "to study native education and encourage a stiff resistance to the proposals of the Nationalist Government", and in the winter vacation of 1930–31 he made a study trip to the Gold Coast with the aid of a grant from the Rhodes Trust. He later recounted that he "saw many kings and chiefs, stayed with African lawyers and in African hotels, travelled 2nd class to see how so-called 2nd class officials behaved and thought".[17] His predilection for journalism was also clear from an early stage: he edited *The Wykehamist* at Winchester and regularly wrote letters on "native policy" to the British press while at Oxford.

Steer was a self-confident and ambitious undergraduate who, during his final year at Oxford, 1931–2, was eager to make his mark. He applied for a League of Nations post as a "white advisor" in Liberia with, as he put it, "the support of Lord Olivier, Mr Philip Noel-Baker, General Smuts, Lord Cecil, the Archbishop of Cape Town and soon of Lord Lugard".[18] In 1932 he attempted to win financial backing from the *Manchester Guardian* for a visit to Manchuria, which had recently been seized by Japan from China in defiance of the League of Nations. Steer had the support of Lord Olivier, who wrote that he was "a remarkably able and promising fellow: and I should like to see him do as well for himself as he can". However, the editor Ted (E.T.) Scott who interviewed Steer was more discerning. He recognised a young man of "obvious ability and enterprise", but went on to say that

> he did not seem to me to have much political sense (he thought Gt. Britain ought to have declared war on Japan) and his general manner did not inspire confidence. Indeed so little do I feel we could trust his judgment and his capacity for reporting impartially on what he sees that I am afraid it will be quite doubtful whether we shall be able to use his stuff if he sends any.[19]

Scott offered Steer an advance of £50, but Steer was unable to guarantee repayment and eventually abandoned his journey to the Far East due to pressure from his family. Instead he worked as a crime and baseball reporter for the Capetown *Argus* (1932–3) and then joined the London staff of the *Yorkshire Post* (1933–5).[20]

Steer's breakthrough as a journalist came with his appointment in May 1935 as a special correspondent for *The Times* at £60 per month,[21] with a brief to cover the Italo-Abyssinian dispute from Addis Ababa. Steer later wrote that he had been "free-lancing the plebiscite" in the Saarland (in January 1935) when he decided to go to Abyssinia as he "wanted a holiday in Africa".[22] In truth, however, the looming war in Abyssinia was one of the major issues of the day and Steer must have seen the chance to prove himself in the field. *The Times* was taking something of a gamble on an inexperienced, if clearly talented and eager, journalist, and during Steer's first months in Africa the foreign news editor Ralph Deakin had to remind him that his newspaper was not interested in "rumour" or "prediction". However, Deakin was clearly impressed with the quality of Steer's work, which had provided *The Times* with a "long series of pioneer dispatches" and aroused the interest of other papers. In September he raised Steer's salary to £80 per month.[23]

Steer's working practice followed the same, highly distinctive, pattern in both Abyssinia and Spain: he always sought to forge the closest possible relations at the highest possible level. By late July 1935 he was able to report to Deakin that he had been granted the longest interview on record with Emperor Haile Selassie, and that the Emperor had broken with precedent in inviting Steer to interview him. Steer added that "he has given me the free run of his ministries".[24] A month later he was able to claim that he was "now on more friendly terms than any other journalist" with the Emperor, and the only one allowed to see him privately.[25] While Steer clearly respected a ruler that he later affectionately termed "the little man", there was also mutual benefit in the relationship. When Steer was permitted to travel to the Ogaden in September (where it was anticipated that the first Italian blow would fall) on his return he reported his findings directly to the Emperor. Once this trip had cemented his relationship with Haile Selassie, Steer was confident that when war came "unlike other journalists I shall be able to go where I wish".[26] Steer was certainly not exaggerating his relationship with the Emperor, as the two men remained in close contact during the Emperor's exile in Britain (1936–40), as well as during the military campaign that resulted in his restoration to the throne (1940–41). The Emperor even acted as godfather to Steer's son in June 1940. Likewise, in the Basque country Steer would establish a close and privileged relationship with the Basque President José Antonio de Aguirre, based on mutual respect, which lasted beyond the end of the conflict. In June 1940, during the Nazi assault on western Europe, it was Steer who was able to provide Aguirre's address in Belgium to the British government, although in the event Aguirre was forced to make his own way to safety.[27]

Steer viewed the Abyssinian conflict as a victory for a modern European power over an African army that was superior only in bravery. According to one colleague, Steer warned at the outset that there would be a massacre as: "These people are still living in the spear age. That's all they've got – spears."[28] The war, which began in October 1935, illustrated both the strengths and weaknesses of Steer's journalism. He was extremely brave, if at times reckless (such as his decision to remain in Addis Ababa once the Emperor and his remaining troops had left the capital). He also cut a dashing figure, courting and marrying the Spanish journalist Margarita Herrero in the British Legation in May 1936. His reporting was passionate and informed by a deep sympathy for the Abyssinian cause. Although he had not personally witnessed Italian use of poison gas, he did his best to bring the allegations to international attention. However, his military punditry was at times questionable. For instance, he misread Italian strategy and as late as February 1936 remained convinced that the main offensive would come in the south.[29] Even in 1939 he was arguing that the Emperor could still have won the war by defending the capital against Italian forces which were now at the end of lengthy and precarious supply lines. More realistically, in the same article he argued that prolonged Abyssinian resistance would have made Italy's intervention in the Spanish Civil War impossible in 1936.[30] Maybe: but such considerations meant nothing to a defeated Haile Selassie.

On 16 May 1936 Steer was expelled from Addis Ababa by the occupying Italian troops, and he arrived back in Britain just in time to greet the exiled Emperor on 3 June. He maintained a keen interest in Abyssinia, as we shall see, but with the outbreak of the Spanish Civil War in July, his attention was about to be captivated by another foreign cause. Between 8 August and 14 September 1936 he served as *The Times'* correspondent on the Spanish frontier and from the safety of Hendaye was able to observe the Nationalist capture of the Spanish border town of Irun. This defeat completed the isolation of the Republican enclave in Northern Spain, which was already cut off from the principal territory administered by the government in central and eastern Spain. Soon afterwards Steer ended his arrangement with *The Times* to finish work on his first book *Caesar in Abyssinia*, although in the autumn he made a journey into Nationalist Spain. (Indeed, the introduction to this book is dated "Burgos [the temporary Nationalist capital] 1936.") He was eventually "expelled by Franco as the result of an Italian report on his activities in Abyssinia".[31] It remains unclear whether this was a mere journalistic foray, or indeed which paper he was working for. It is striking that he makes no mention of this visit in his account of the Basque campaign, nor does he appear to have mentioned it to close journalistic colleagues while in Bilbao.[32]

Steer made his first visit to Bilbao in January 1937, but only stayed for six days as his visit was cut short by the appalling news – received on 30 January – that his wife had died in childbirth. Even so, as in

Abyssinia, Steer used this brief time to make contact with the Basque leadership. He was highly impressed by Aguirre, who struck him as an "idealist first and last". The Basque President reminded him of the captain of a soccer team who "even if they lost . . . were going to obey the whistle and the rules".[33] It was presumably during this visit that the foundations were laid for Steer's opinion of the Basques as a democratic, orderly and humanitarian people who were crushed between the pressures of "military Fascism from without, and proletarian pressure from within". Many in Britain would express this view over the coming months, but none more eloquently or with greater conviction than Steer in *The Tree of Gernika*.[34] Steer appears to have made an equally good impression on his hosts, and the captain of HMS *Echo* reported that – on hearing of his bereavement – the Basque authorities had placed a trawler at his disposal to take him to Bayonne, and paid his hotel bill in Bilbao.[35] Steer's grief at the death of his wife and child was intense, as we can see in his letter to Lints Smith of *The Times* in which he wrote of the loss of "my little fellow soldier . . . How cruel was the bullet that laid her in this muddy trench."[36] Yet his grief was hardly disabling, as, having embalmed Margarita's body to await the arrival of his mother, he embarked on a series of visits to brief government officials and other interested parties on the situation in Spain. The funeral took place on 4 March and the burial, in Biarritz, on 2 April. As was frequently the case in Steer's life the personal and the political were closely intertwined. As Rankin points out, the intensity with which Steer flung himself into the Basque cause in the next few months, combined with his disregard for his own safety, suggests a man who almost wanted to die.[37]

Before Steer could return to the Basque country a crisis developed in Abyssinia that complicated his relations with *The Times*. On 19 February there was a grenade attack in Addis Ababa on the Italian military ruler Marshal Graziani, and in retaliation thousands of Abyssinians were slaughtered. Steer wrote an account of the massacres in the *Spectator* (12 March 1937), but was appalled to see a report in *The Times* on 13 March which, in his view, exonerated Graziani of any responsibility for the violence. On 20 March Steer wrote to *The Times* setting out eye-witness evidence of the atrocities (his main informant was Konstantin Trage in Djibouti) and calling for an international committee of enquiry to be established into "a brutal massacre of dimensions unparalleled since the burning of Smyrna [in 1922]". According to his sources Graziani had to carry his share of the blame as "his wounds were not grave enough to prevent him remaining in control of the civil and military authority throughout the period". Deakin's reply was that "we hardly think that it is advisable to revert to the Addis Ababa incidents in such a letter as you have suggested". This decision "horrified" Steer's close ally Philip Noel-Baker, who felt that *The Times'* behaviour was "really unheard of" given that Steer had been their correspondent throughout the Abyssinian war. He consoled Steer with the thought that his information had been put to good use in the recent parliamentary debate. At Steer's request Noel-Baker also undertook, unsuccessfully, to attempt to place the article in another national newspaper such as the *News Chronicle*. Interestingly, *The Times* was described as "a bit sticky" on this issue, as Deakin and his deputy believed that Steer had sent his report in "the ordinary course of his correspondent's duties" and that it should not be published elsewhere.[38] Meanwhile, on 30 March *The Times* published a further article which reported that Graziani was still in hospital and had not learnt of the reprisals for 48 hours. Steer was by now *en route* to Spain with his wife's body: it was evident that, even before the bombing of Guernica, there were tensions between his ardent anti-fascism and the editorial policy of *The Times*.

In early April 1937 Steer returned by boat to Bilbao, where, according to *The Times*, he "acted on his own initiative as an occasional correspondent from April to June, 1937".[39] He immediately became embroiled in a serious crisis. Nationalist forces under General Mola had launched their offensive against the Basque country on 20 March, and introduced two new weapons. One was the heavy bombing of undefended civilian populations (notably the raid on the village of Durango on 31 March and subsequent days); the second was the declaration of a blockade of the port of Bilbao in an attempt to prevent the arrival of British ships carrying food. The British government was bamboozled by the illegal blockade, and on 11 April warned shipping not to proceed to Bilbao. Steer accepted the Basque assurances that the approaches to Bilbao had been swept clear of mines and that their shore batteries could easily protect shipping within the three-mile territorial limit. It was, therefore, up to the Royal Navy to prevent Nationalist warships interfering with British ships on the high seas. He told the Basques "in a patriotic flush that in England the truth usually wins: this blockade will not last".[40] While no complete record of his activities survives, the gist is captured in his telegram to Noel-Baker on 19 April, in which he argued that the blockade existed only in the "hopes" of the Nationalist capital Salamanca and the "imagination" of Whitehall. Steer was busily briefing Noel-Baker and encouraging him to make representations at the highest level. "Don't use my name," he added, "except in private with your friends and Eden [the foreign secretary] [.D]escribe me as an observer in

Bilbao [. A]m here as Times correspondent [. T]ell Eden this too serious an injustice done to a decent orderly democratic people too flagrant to be treated as a party issue."[41] In the event the blockade was broken by the bravery of individual British captains, with Captain Roberts of the *Seven Seas Spray* the first to enter Bilbao on 20 April. Steer, who had sailed out to meet Roberts, was on board as his vessel entered the city amidst great celebrations. He had done his best both to discredit the blockade and to create the political pressure in Britain that forced the government to protect British shipping in international waters. He later commented that "I take to myself the credit that I, before anyone else, exposed the fake in the blockade and recovered the truth . . . I did not rest until I had torn this falsehood to pieces."[42]

The crisis affords some insights into Steer's conception of his role as a journalist. "A journalist", in his view, "is not a simple purveyor of news, whether sensational or controversial, or well-written, or merely funny. He is a historian of every day's events, and he has a duty to his public." If as a historian he must be filled with "the most passionate and most critical attachment to the truth, so must the journalist, with the great power that he wields, see that the truth prevails".[43] Yet alongside this apparently straightforward credo, we also have to take into account the fascination that Steer felt for the French agent Robert Monnier, who became his closest colleague in the Basque country. Monnier worked under the pseudonym "Jaureghuy", and was officially the Special Correspondent of *Blood and Fire*, the newspaper of the Salvation Army. However, Steer suspected him of having come to sell arms. Monnier, a former French army officer, already knew the Basque front "better than all the staff officers combined"[44] and regularly advised Aguirre and the Basque high command. Ironically Steer, whom the other British journalists regarded as having the keenest nose for a story, was himself somewhat in awe of Monnier and later wrote that he followed him "around like a dog because he always knew the smartest sectors of the front".[45] He admired his friend's military knowledge, but also his glamour and insouciance, and his belief that war was a game – "to be executed as near the touchline of danger as possible".[46] Steer was never an adventurer like Monnier, but there was much in the Frenchman's character that he found attractive, and he paid heartfelt tribute to him following his death in November 1939.[47] Above all, as the crisis in the Basque country demonstrates, Steer was never happier than when traversing the narrow "touchline" between journalism, politics and diplomacy.

Steer's approach was not party-political, but rather sought to mobilise influential politicians across the internationalist centre of British politics.

Where the British left relied heavily on protest meetings and demonstrations during the Spanish Civil War, Steer still believed that Parliament should act as the focus for moral outrage. His principal ally was Noel-Baker, who at one point stated that he was receiving messages "almost every day" from Steer.[48] At least some of these messages were sent in code via the Basque government. Noel-Baker was an independent-minded Labour MP who had recently returned to the Commons following the Derby by-election in July 1936 and, from 1937, sat on the Labour Party's National Executive Committee. He had worked for the League of Nations in the early 1920s, and was prominent in both the League of Nations Union and the International Peace Campaign. Through him Steer was put in contact with radical internationalists on the League's staff such as Konni Zilliacus and Ludwik Rajchman. Within Britain, Noel-Baker disseminated Steer's information to prominent politicians in both the opposition and government. As he wrote to a senior Spanish Republican minister in May: "Direct messages from Bilbao have brought the matter very closely before the leaders here who are most anxious for your victory."[49] Amongst those receiving such information were the Liberal party leader, Sir Archibald Sinclair, the Foreign Secretary Anthony Eden, and David Lloyd George (who had spoken powerfully against the blockade of Bilbao). In mid-May Lloyd George stated that he would like to meet Steer, although there is no evidence that a meeting took place.[50]

Barely a week after the triumphant entry of the *Seven Seas Spray* into Bilbao, the event occurred that would define Steer's reputation and career: the bombing of Guernica. This was no mere scoop, as Steer must also have been aware of the wider ramifications of his story. Above all, he had given valuable political ammunition to his allies in Parliament and helped to shift British opinion irrevocably against the Nationalists and their foreign supporters. Politicians and churchmen who had previously equivocated about the Spanish Civil War now spoke out clearly against the iniquities of Franco's side. On 6 May 1937 Noel-Baker told Steer that " . . . no article in modern times has made so deep an impression throughout the whole country as your dispatch about the bombing of Guernica . . . I have quoted the dispatch at length in at least ten big meetings . . . and it everywhere makes a tremendous impression."[51] In an earlier letter he had written that the report had probably been the "decisive factor" in securing a change in government policy (presumably a reference to the decision by the Home Office on 29 April to allow 4000 Basque children and their teachers to come to Britain and thereby avoid the dangers of bombing).[52]

However, Steer was soon mired in controversy. The story of Guernica was simply too powerful to remain uncontested and in the short term Franco's supporters were able to sow serious doubts in the public mind. While the counter-arguments of Steer's Francoist critics now often seem laughable, it must be recalled that the serious diplomatic issues at stake between Britain, Franco and Nazi Germany gave them considerable force at the time. Newspapers and cinema newsreels, for instance, were unwilling to follow *The Times* and the *Star* in identifying the aircraft that destroyed Guernica as German.[53] Moreover, Steer's critics had sheer incredulity on their side, as it was far easier (and more comforting) to believe that the town had been destroyed by incendiarists than by bombers. Henry Page Croft argued that Steer's story could not be true because, if it were, "a bombardment of such accuracy and intensity" would surely have triggered a profound rethinking of British defence policy.[54] Meanwhile, Steer's pro-Basque sympathies (as well as his previous "form" in Abyssinia) were so evident that during the subsequent controversy his own objectivity inevitably became part of the story. It would, of course, have saved Steer and his supporters a great many problems if he had actually witnessed the bombing. As late as 1990 Peter Kemp, one of the few Britons to fight for Franco, could write that "I know of no published account of the Guernica bombing by an eyewitness; all have come to us second hand."[55] Indeed, it is interesting to note that in late May Noel-Baker wrote to Sir Walter Layton of the *Star* to establish the identity of the author of the "first and most vivid" dispatch from Guernica, which he had quoted many times at public meetings. Noel-Baker hoped that Steer and Keith Scott Watson could take part in a joint public meeting, although he added that he would be happy to go ahead *without* Steer. The implication is that Noel-Baker realised that, as an eye-witness, Scott Watson was politically far more useful than Steer.[56]

Despite these considerations, there is no evidence to support the contention that *The Times* was reluctant to publish Steer's first dispatch.[57] Indeed, the report was supported by an editorial which went even further than Steer in stating that the aim of the raid "was *unquestionably* to terrorize the Basque Government into surrender".[58] The editor Geoffrey Dawson, an ardent appeaser, seems to have been genuinely puzzled by the hostile reaction that the report encountered in Germany. On 11 May he wrote to *The Times* correspondent in Berlin: "I do not quite know why there is all this excitement about Guernica, but the Dictators seem to be very touchy. The news reported in *The Times* is confirmed in every detail by an independent eyewitness in the *Daily Express* today." On 23 May he added that the "essential accuracy" of Steer's report "has never been disputed, and there has not been any attempt here to rub it in or harp upon it".[59] Admittedly, matters were somewhat complicated on 5 May when *The Times* published a report by James Holburn, its temporary correspondent with the Nationalist forces, which seemed to endorse claims that the destruction had partly been caused by retreating Republican forces. However, buried within the report was a Nationalist admission that the town had been bombed "intermittently over a period of three hours". Holburn later recalled that "from that moment every day everyone, particularly Captain Bolin [the Nationalist press officer] was very angry and abusive towards me", and he was glad to be allowed to return to his post in Berlin soon afterwards.[60] In the prevailing circumstances of censorship and intimidation, Holburn's dispatch had been a brave one that substantiated much of Steer's story, although it was often to be cited by his detractors. In any case, on the following day (6 May) *The Times* published a further dispatch by Steer in which he defended his original account. Tellingly, Steer had actually submitted this report on 29 April, copied to Noel-Baker with instructions to inform Lloyd George, Eden and the French politician Pierre Cot if *The Times* would not use it.[61]

There seems little doubt that *The Times* came under acute pressure from a variety of sources, ranging from Catholic prelates to senior British diplomats, over its Guernica story.[62] While it never publicly repudiated its correspondent, Steer (who did not write for *The Times* again after 22 June 1937) was increasingly on his own.[63] For example, on 30 July 1937 he abandoned anonymity to defend himself in the *Spectator* against the attacks of the Catholic writer Douglas Jerrold. Franco supporters later boasted that *The Times* had become more "'impartial' and 'neutral'" in its coverage of the Civil War "about a month after the exposure of the Guernica swindle".[64] This perception was shared by some on the left. On 14 December 1937, for instance, *The Times* published an article by the right-wing MP Wing Commander James which referred casually to "the destruction of many places upon evacuation, such as Guernica". According to Kingsley Martin of the *New Statesman* a fellow journalist wrote a letter of complaint to *The Times*, but Dawson refused to use it on the grounds that it raised "controversial issues on the position in Spain". Martin's interpretation of this incident was that *The Times* had "accepted Franco's victory as desirable and regards any reply to Franco's propaganda as undesirable".[65] This probably overstated the case, but it seems clear that, as previously over Abyssinia, *The Times* editorial policy and Steer's personal views had eventually parted company. Certainly, when Steer's solicitor was preparing his libel case in 1939, *The Times* had to be prompted on a number of occasions to provide evidence. (However, it did eventually confirm that his report on Guernica had no connection to the "cessation of his service"). Steer undoubtedly felt that he had been poorly treated. In January 1938 he wrote that "I don't suppose that the Times will be too nice to my book [*The Tree of Gernika*]. They have a bad conscience over the suppression of news from Bilbao."[66]

Although the defence of his Guernica story now overshadowed Steer's journalistic career (and he became increasingly aware of his notoriety[67]), he remained heavily engaged in the final, desperate campaign to defend Bilbao. On 8 May he predicted that the "badly led wretchedly staffed [Basque] militia" could not hold out for more than a few days. However, he believed that the Basque capital could be successfully defended if more aircraft (even as few as 15 or 20) and 200 machine guns could be supplied either by France or by the Spanish Republican government, and he deluged Noel-Baker and his other contacts with messages to that effect. He asked Noel-Baker to put pressure on Pierre Cot, the French Air Minister, and to reassure him that if he "has any fears of English I.S. [Intelligence Service?] men reporting his naughtinesses in Bilbao, they will be idle. I am the only trusted one here, and when the time comes I can deny it all more than thrice."[68] Sadly for the Basques, when Republican planes did attempt the difficult passage to Northern Spain on 9 May, they had to land at Toulouse and were stopped by British officials of the Non-Intervention Committee. Undeterred, Steer took the Basque case to the League of Nations Assembly in Geneva in late May. Noel-Baker was unable to attend, but told Steer that he could "do more with Eden" in his absence.[69] Steer also visited the US Consul, to whom he offered further proof of the German involvement in the destruction of Guernica, and – having failed to catch Eden – Walter Roberts of the Foreign Office. He gave Roberts a message from the Basque government that they would not surrender and was "satisfied to find that [Roberts] liked the Basques and admired their struggle".[70] However, he came away from Geneva disillusioned with the League and fully aware that it was only Britain that could now save the Basques.

Even so, Steer remained remarkably optimistic. On 31 May he wrote privately that if the Nationalist command were "as intelligent as the material which it uses is powerful, it ought to have taken Bilbao April 27/28 and again May 9/10". He concluded that a rebel defeat at Bilbao would be the beginning of the end of Mussolini, and would force Germany to pull out of Spain. Accordingly, France should "send real aid to Vizcaya".[71] On 4 June Steer wrote to Noel-Baker that the Basques had been given a "breathing space" by the death of the rebel commander

Mola in an air crash, and took heart from the stiffening of Basque resistance in Bilbao's defensive perimeter (the *cinturon*). He predicted that if the Basque capital had not fallen by the end of the month it would not fall at all, as Franco had already "muffed" two chances to take it.[72] However, both these letters were written from Toulouse, as Steer made his way back from Geneva. By the time of his return to the Basque country the defences of Bilbao were close to collapse. Steer was the only foreign correspondent left to witness the city's last hours and the decision of the Basques on 19 June to evacuate westwards. With a typical flourish Steer claimed to have "looted" a pen and notepad from President Aguirre's office to begin work on *The Tree of Gernika*, the great vindication of the Basque cause.[73]

Steer made one more foray to Spain in August 1937, "to get material for my book", much to the consternation of his mother.[74] On 18 August he flew to Santander shortly before it fell to Nationalist forces. He was in time to report that the remnants of the Basque army had chosen surrender on 26 August in preference to a further withdrawal west into Asturias. He was beginning to turn away from pulling diplomatic and political strings towards mythologizing the Basques as gallant warriors struck with "an over-mastering melancholy" at the destruction of their homeland.[75] In fact, with the Basque surrender Steer's active involvement in the Spanish Civil War had largely come to an end, although he continued to view it as the epicentre of the struggle against fascist aggression until the Munich crisis in the autumn of 1938. In January 1938 he wrote that "Spain is the main issue of today. The Spanish war *must* be won."[76] As late as October 1938 he was still hoping to be able to "take part in any negotiations for mediation in Spain, my object being to press Basque claims . . . I don't think anybody could press these points better on the War Office and the Air Ministry than I can."[77] He also remained active in the Abyssinian cause during this period. For instance, at the same time as preparing to visit Santander he was also helping, anonymously, to draw up a "white book" of Italian atrocities in Abyssinia to present to the League Assembly in September. This document would deal not only with the Addis Ababa massacres of February, but with "unrest and repression all over the country". It was "a fight not to be refused".[78]

Steer's interests were now revolving far more around Africa and the danger posed to British interests by Germany's demands for the return of its former colonies. In November 1937 he sailed for South Africa asking Noel-Baker to "flash" him "if you want me for any really major crisis of a warlike kind". He sketched in an ambitious programme: "I shall remain in South Africa for about six months, I think, then do a journey north, studying Protectorates, ex German colonies, Abyssinian refugees, Italian frontiers, British French and Egyptian defences for another six months, and perhaps Palestine." His friend's rather troubled reply was that he should rest as he was "using up [his] youth much too fast".[79] Steer largely fulfilled this programme over the next 18 months,[80] in the process writing two further books, on the former German African colonies and French–Italian North Africa, as well as contributing to British newspapers and weeklies.

Although he spent 1938 in Africa, Steer remained principally concerned with the threat of European fascism. He was appalled by the Munich agreement in late September 1938 and wrote to Noel-Baker that: "Henceforward, I feel, our main job is not to save Spain or Ethiopia or China or even democracy, but something far more material – to get [Prime Minister Neville] Chamberlain out . . . It is above all things essential to see our prestige as a nation restored again by a vigorous . . . foreign policy."[81] Tellingly, his private denunciations of Chamberlain were now regularly seasoned with attacks on his former employer, Geoffrey Dawson, and the rest of "the Times gang". After Munich Steer felt torn between returning to Spain, where he believed that there might soon be a mediated settlement of the civil war, and embarking on a tour of the ex-German colonies. By 18 October 1938 he had decided to pursue the latter course on the grounds that "it is vital to our interests, to Native African interests, and to world democratic interests . . . to keep the Nazis out of Africa". He also confided to Noel-Baker, with surprising indiscretion, that "I should be working professionally for S.African military intelligence on the trip."[82] Briefly, Steer believed that his efforts in Africa might even galvanise cross-party opposition to Chamberlain within parliament. Following the "Crystal Night" anti-Semitic violence in Nazi Germany in early November, Steer urged Noel-Baker to propose the large scale settlement of expelled Jews in Tanganyika, a former German colony, accompanied by the territory's permanent association with the British crown. Such a policy would, he believed, force a rupture in Britain's relations with Germany and fatally weaken Chamberlain's political position.[83]

Steer had clearly lost none of his energy, but his later writing and journalism lacked the impact or the intensity of his initial work in Spain and Abyssinia. Above all, he seemed to have lost his instinctive feel for the most important story of the moment. The threats that he identified in Africa came to nothing in 1939–40, and the actual war in North Africa was very different from that which he had envisaged. After returning to Europe and covering the "Winter War" between Finland and the USSR in early 1940 for the *Daily Telegraph*, the final phase of his career was determined by Mussolini's ill-starred decision to join the war on Hitler's side in June 1940. Suddenly the British government, which had recognised Italy's conquest of Abyssinia in November 1938, saw the advantage of encouraging the Abyssinian resistance. On 24 June 1940 Steer found himself, with the rank of captain, accompanying Haile Selassie to Egypt and, eventually, participating in the campaign to free Abyssinia from Italian rule. Once the campaign was under way, and later on in the Far East, where he was a member of the Special Operations Executive (SOE), Steer emerged as a talented and innovative proponent of offensive field propaganda. At the time of his death, on Christmas Day 1944, he held the rank of Lieutenant Colonel in the Intelligence Corps.

■ ■ ■ ■ ■ ■ ■

To his detractors, of course, a propagandist is what George Steer had always been. Indeed, criticism of Steer was re-ignited by his ill-judged admission in his book *Sealed and Delivered* (1942) that he had employed deliberate falsehoods during his propaganda work against the Italians in 1940–41.[84] Bolín, the Nationalist press officer, later commented that Steer was thereby "self-convicted as the author of mendacious propaganda",[85] which discredited his Spanish Civil War journalism. The conventional defence is that mounted by Southworth: that there was a world of difference between Steer's independent journalistic duties in Spain and his wartime military work in the service of his country. However, Steer's open admission of links with military intelligence in 1938 suggests that this distinction between the independent journalist and the servant of government cannot be drawn quite so sharply. Moreover, his active political commitment to the Basque cause added a further layer of complexity. There is no question that Steer was one of those journalists who reported the war in the Basque country (in the telling words of Noel Monks) "factually and, as far as was possible, objectively".[86] Even so, it is now clear that Steer worked assiduously behind the scenes in support of the Basques, in collaboration with the Basque government. While it would be an exaggeration to suggest that Steer choreographed the British response to the Basque crisis, there is no doubt that his private briefings influenced political opinion just as his newspaper dispatches influenced public opinion. Such interventions could be highly effective. To take one example, in March 1937 Steer had briefed the National Joint Committee for Spanish Relief (NJCSR) on the possibility of evacuations from the Basque country; in late April his "Guernica" dispatch played a significant role in the Home Office decision to allow just such a mass evacuation; while in early May Steer wrote that Noel-Baker and Wilfrid Roberts (Liberal MP and chairman of the NJCSR) should "keep up the evacuation of women and children from Bilbao at high pressure. It is the British contribution to the defence of Bilbao . . . ".[87]

Franco's supporters had every reason to fear and dislike Steer, and had they had evidence of his activities they could surely have embarrassed both him and *The Times*. Yet, interestingly, they *did* have some evidence, captured when Bilbao fell. In August 1937 the right-wing author Major Yeats-Brown reported that he had been shown captured documents, including "a correspondence between an English M.P. and a journalist in Bilbao who excelled himself in describing the Guernica affair".[88] Over time this material leaked out into Francoist publications, but it was fairly innocuous. (For instance, a telegram from *The Times* asking Steer to furnish further evidence on Guernica was published in North America).[89] Why then was more damage not inflicted on Steer? Maybe the Nationalist counter-propaganda machine was simply as incompetent as many suspected. However, another possibility is that the most incriminating papers had gone: maybe Steer took away more than a pen and a notepad when he "looted the rooms of the President, his Secretaries and the Secretary-General of Defence" during the fall of Bilbao.

George Steer described himself in 1938 as a "political amateur . . . a straightforward sort of citizen without strong party ties, but with a real desire to see an organised peace in the world".[90] Unlike so many of his generation and background he was not attracted to the left during the 1930s. The consequences were most visible in his hostility to the intolerance of the Spanish left (both Marxist and Anarchist) and his admiration for the moderation of the Basque nationalists. Instead, his natural rebelliousness and sympathy for the oppressed produced a most original outlook on life. After Spain and Abyssinia he cared little for a world in which the political rewards seemed to go to those who "batter the unarmed".[91] Perhaps Kingsley Martin captured it best when he wrote of Steer's "thoroughly, indeed I might say vehemently, democratic outlook".[92] Indeed, at a time when many on the left were mouthing democratic platitudes in a highly instrumental manner,[93] Steer was unusual in desiring to see not only the triumph of democratic forms but also of democratic values and practices. Yet this was intercut with a highly personal approach to politics. Steer's profound respect for Haile Selassie, Aguirre and even Monnier was understandable: more disconcerting was the admiration that he expressed for Italo Balbo, Italian ruler of Libya during his visit in 1939.[94] Yet in each case

Steer was responding to what he saw as "manly" virtues of honesty, frankness and compassion.

Steer's views on race could be equally disconcerting. He was no racist, and had developed his early political views in opposition to racial segregation in his native South Africa. His admiration for the valour and independent spirit of the Abyssinians was genuine, although somewhat patronising to the modern eye. Steer's *Caesar in Abyssinia* was dedicated to the memory of Afewerk, the commander in the Ogaden, a "great soldier and a noble spirit".[95] Yet in most respects his views did not transcend the progressive imperialism of his day. For instance, he saw the British and French mandates in Africa as an immeasurable improvement on German colonial rule, and noted that in the Cameroons the British used the whip "as little as possible".[96] With regard to his proposal for Jewish settlement in East Africa he commented in private that: "Actually I believe that Tanganyika [should] always remain a native country where the African [should] have room to develop under control of experts, and it [would] be criminal to push too many whites into the country – whether Jew or Gentile."[97] In Tunisia he noted that the Arab – rather than French rule – was "himself the cause of his own poverty". In Libya he was intrigued by the sight of Italian peasants working the African soil without recourse to native labour, and speculated on whether this would lead to "wealth or degeneration".[98]

Steer's correspondence contains one further, disconcerting, twist. In a letter written in January 1938, Steer welcomed the fact that the Spanish "Government aviation is figuring much more in the news as we receive it here [in South Africa]. It was good to hear that they had raided Salamanca [Franco's capital] at last – unpleasant though it is, reprisal is the only sound method in war, and they have held off Salamanca too long."[99] Such sentiments are hardly surprising, but perplexing when coming from the pen of George Lowther Steer. A man whose writings showed how "aerial bombing . . . would magnify in the imagination, becoming the presiding terror"[100] of the modern era, and who captured the horror of the bombing of Guernica, had come to realise that such devastation would have to be repeated many times in the tit-for-tat savagery of total war. At almost the same moment as Steer was writing this letter, George Orwell's review of *The Tree of Gernika* was being published. It contained the following comment: "The horror we feel of these things has led to this conclusion: if someone drops a bomb on your mother, go and drop two bombs on his mother. The only apparent alternatives are to smash dwelling houses to powder, blow out human entrails and burn holes in children with lumps of thermite, or to be enslaved by people who are more ready to do these things than you are yourself . . . ".[101]

In December 1937 Steer wrote to his mentor Philip Noel-Baker that "the condition into which the world is now drifting is one of *chronic local wars*. Where there is no limit to military objectives, and where wars are fought for the total destruction of the administrative system and personnel of the enemy, and no peace treaties are signed, *local wars never end*". The only way forward was to "protract the conflict and to call on all the resistance of the victim and eventually to bankrupt the aggressor and involve everybody".[102] George Steer was perfectly equipped to be a warrior in this new era of warfare. Throughout his career he not only displayed a clear understanding of the specific situation in, say, Abyssinia and the Basque country, but also of how these local conflicts related to each other and to the wider pattern of fascist aggression. He was not only a fine journalist – there were many in Spain during the civil war – but also one who understood that passionate, incisive reporting could rally world opinion, prolong resistance, and inflict severe damage on the aggressor. Above all, he appreciated that informal networks of influential politicians, suitably briefed, could greatly magnify the political impact of print journalism. For George Steer, the arch-combatant of the "chronic local wars" of fascist aggression, there was no question that the truth would prevail.

Chapter 3

The masked advance

Politics, intrigue and British medical aid for the Spanish Republic

> . . . these men whom we nurse are fighting to drive the foreign invaders from Spain, whilst those in the rearguard are building a new Spain; slowly and surely in spite of the war, education is coming to the Spanish people and health services and better conditions too. No wonder, when we see this, we believe our work here is worth while. Our aim is to send men from this hospital with healthy bodies and healthy minds.
>
> (Ann Murray, 1938)[1]

The achievement of the Spanish Medical Aid Committee (SMAC) during the Civil War was remarkable. A small, primarily voluntary, organisation raised substantial sums of money from sympathisers in Britain, recruited and sustained some 150 personnel in Spain (more than a third of whom were women), and operated a variety of hospitals and other medical facilities on behalf of the Spanish Republic. Convoys of ambulances and lorries plied ceaselessly between London and Barcelona, laden with drugs and equipment for distribution at the front. Despite the relative inexperience of the medical staff (some of whom were not yet fully qualified) their pioneering work in areas such as mobile blood trans-fusion and triage had, by the end of the war, caught the attention of the medical establishment in Britain. However, the volunteers' achievements came at a heavy price. At least five personnel were killed in action, another died in an accident,[2] and many more suffered physical and mental wounds. Those on the front-line often faced almost overwhelming demands, working in conditions that one volunteer likened to a "butcher's shop".[3] Nurse Molly Murphy later wrote that "many of these harrowing and horrible scenes have haunted my nights for years", while ambulance driver Sir Richard Rees described how his capacity for sympathy "almost atrophied" in Spain.[4] Inevitably, comparisons were drawn with the British volunteers in the International Brigades. As Peter Kerrigan wrote in April 1937, "the British Medical Unit has in its sphere created a similar record . . . for courage and heroism" to that of the British Battalion.[5] It is tempting, therefore, to present the work of the British medical volunteers as a straightforward story – as nurse Ann Murray's statement cited above suggests – of political commitment to the ideals of the Spanish Republic combined with compassion for the suffering of its soldiers and citizens.

And yet, the record of both the SMAC and of the British Medical Unit in Spain is also one of intrigue and of intense personal and political infighting. As we shall see, evidence of this abounds in memoirs, in recorded interviews and in such archival material as survives.[6] All historians of the SMAC and its work in Spain have had to decide what use to make of this difficult, often treacherous, material. When Jim Fyrth was writing the history of the British Medical Unit, Bill Alexander (the former commander of the British Battalion) encouraged him never to lose sight of the Republic's principal accomplishment: "the creation of a medical service almost from nothing."[7] In the event Fyrth devoted much of a chapter to the "shadows of suspicions, accusation and espionage", but concluded that none could "dim the brilliance of the work which the SMAC performed".[8] More recently, Angela Jackson has warned against some historians' emphasis on "disorder and conspiracy" in their accounts of the British medical unit, and a "retrospective 'cherry-picking' of instances of discord" from archival sources.[9] Jackson, whose work on British women in the Spanish Civil War inevitably deals extensively with medical aid, concluded that these women were motivated primarily by a practical desire to help the victims of fascist aggression. "[F]ew British women played an active role in the factional conflicts of the Left in Spain, many were manifestly uninterested in these party political struggles and others rejected involvement in such matters entirely."[10] The view of both of these authors is that politics was marginal to the work of the medical volunteers. Where there was political discord it occurred in the heat of the moment and had little lasting significance.

Part of the problem was that three highly articulate and competitive young doctors played a pivotal role within the British medical unit (Kenneth Sinclair-Loutit, Archie Cochrane and Alexander Tudor Hart), and their feuds in Spain were perpetuated long after the end of the civil war. Moreover, Viscount Churchill, the SMAC's representative in Spain during the first sixteen months of its work, displayed a remarkable appetite for intrigue and dissimulation. However, there was more at stake here than the conflicts between these four men. Questions of politics and political control, far from being marginal, were integral to the SMAC and its work in Spain. This was inevitable given the tension between the Popular Front ideals which the SMAC represented and the Communist Party's desire, in practice, to exercise influence and authority over its activities. While it is true that some of the British nurses' political views conformed to the model suggested by Jackson, the intensely political environment in which they worked impinged on all of the medical personnel. This chapter surveys the work of Spanish Medical Aid in the light of these questions. It begins with an analysis of the origins of the SMAC and the nature of its work in Spain.

■ ■ ■ ■ ■ ■ ■

The Spanish Medical Aid Committee was the first significant voluntary organisation to be created in Britain in response to the military rebellion in Spain.[11] It represented a collaboration between members of the Socialist Medical Association (SMA) and left-wing political activists (most notably Isabel Brown of the Relief Committee for the Victims of Fascism). The committee met for the first time at the National Trade Union Club on 8 August 1936, where Dr Charles Brook of the SMA was, reluctantly, elected secretary. Dr Hyacinth Morgan, medical adviser to the TUC, became Chairman and proved, in Brook's phrase, an "extremely able and tactful negotiator".[12] Viscount Churchill and Viscountess Hastings (neither of whom had a medical background) became joint-Treasurers alongside Professor J. R. Marrack, a Cambridge biochemist. There were two further senior – if, in the long term, less influential – appointments: Dr Somerville Hastings of the SMA (as vice-chairman), and Lord Addison, a former Liberal minister of health and now a Labour peer, as President. Much of the daily work of the committee was carried out by small sub-committees for "Equipment and Personnel" and "Finance and Propaganda". These were later heavily crit-icised for meeting "informally round the lunch table" and leaving no written record of their decisions.[13]

The main committee, which was composed of left-wing politicians and progressive members of the medical profession, had a cross-party, "people's front character".[14] In practice, this meant that there was an uneasy and often fractious relationship between the Communists and their allies and the more moderate members of the committee. A number of senior figures did not conceal their willingness to work closely with the Communists. For instance, Leah Manning, an elemental former

Labour MP who served as Honorary Secretary of the SMAC from December 1936, wrote in her memoirs that while many chose to join the Communist Party in the 1930s, "many more joined broad-based institutions, in which they were happy to work with the Communists. I did myself".[15] Despite a number of internal crises, however, unity was maintained for the duration of the civil war. One important point of agreement was that the committee should be avowedly apolitical and humanitarian in its goals, although it was also quite clearly intended to assist the Republican side. Much was made, therefore, of an early incident in which the British unit cared for a wounded Nationalist Moroccan soldier as proof of its impartiality.[16]

The SMAC caught the initial wave of solidarity with the Spanish Republic, and almost immediately took the decision to send an "Ambulance Unit" to Spain. A meeting on 14 August raised £500, and advertisements were placed for volunteers in the medical press. In addition, the TUC was persuaded to provide £1000, although it eventually severed relations with the SMAC on political grounds.[17] The committee dispatched its first unit amidst considerable publicity on 23 August, barely a month after the outbreak of the civil war. The party was led by Viscount Churchill and by Kenneth Sinclair-Loutit, a 23-year old medical student, who was appointed as the unit's administrator. The Party members in the group met as a secret "fraction" prior to their departure and were instructed by Isabel Brown to "do everything to conceal their party-membership". Sinclair-Loutit alone, who had not disclosed that he was a Communist to the SMAC, was given credentials to allow him to make contact with the Spanish Communist Party.[18] The volunteers – four doctors, three unqualified doctors working as dressers, six nurses, six drivers, two administrative staff and three quartermasters – paused for a week in Paris to purchase equipment and vehicles. It soon became apparent that the unit had been assembled too hastily and lacked experienced medical staff – above all, trained surgeons – and Churchill was soon cabling urgently for reinforcements.[19] While in Paris, where the volunteers were fêted by the French Popular Front, the political dynamic within the unit became more apparent. Archie Cochrane, a young trainee doctor, was appalled to learn that the Communist quartermaster Hugh O'Donnell, who had made a "stupid speech" on the unit's behalf at a Paris rally, was to be their "chief political administrator" in Spain.[20] The volunteers were also joined at this point by Tom Wintringham, the *Daily Worker* journalist, who quietly pointed out to Sinclair-Loutit, that, once in Spain, "unless the unit is right with the Party you'll be lost".[21]

A British woman who met the volunteers in Paris was alarmed by their combination of "unbounded enthusiasm" and "not nearly enough experience". Were they aware, she added, that it was no "garden-party down there"?[22] Indeed, when the unit arrived in Barcelona at the end of August 1936, the political situation was still highly volatile. Relations were tense between the Communist-Socialist PSUC party, with which the unit was affiliated, and the Anarchists. Sinclair-Loutit and Churchill set out to reconnoitre by car and found a dead man, shot through the head by anarchist gunmen, on the edge of town. When the young doctor thought to stop and offer help, their Catalan political attaché screamed at him: "Get the hell out of here, you'll have us all shot."[23] The two men eventually identified a site for a hospital in a farm house at the Anarchist village of Grañen, 18 kilometres behind the front line in Aragon and comfortably distant from the violence in Barcelona. Once the filthy building had been cleaned the British volunteers created an effective evacuation hospital, which not only cared for the wounded on a fitfully active front but also offered general medical care to the local population. Grañen was a backwater in the civil war, but the work could still be highly demanding and dangerous when fighting flared up. Ann Murray, who arrived with the reinforcements in September, wrote home that she was "seeing war at its worst".[24] An Australian nurse, Margot Miller, was shot in the legs while visiting the front line, and SMAC platform speakers were encouraged to emphasise her "heroism". In late November she was presented, still limping, to a rally at the Albert Hall.[25] Emmanuel Julius, who was a quartermaster with the unit, joined a militia column and was killed.

The opening of the siege of Madrid in November, as well as the first appearance of the International Brigades in defence of the capital, appeared to confirm that the medical unit was in the wrong place. The SMAC expressed private concern that the "drama" of a rival Scottish ambulance unit based in Madrid was detracting from the "more steady, persistent, consistent work" of Grañen. One committee member, Professor Marrack, publicly conceded that the Aragon front had been an "unfortunate" choice for the hospital's location.[26] Moreover, by late November the British unit was descending into political and personal acrimony and a round-robin letter, highly critical of Sinclair-Loutit's leadership, was supported by seventeen of the staff. There was considerable personal resentment of the administrator's cliquish style and his "obsession for political manoeuvring and intrigue", but criticism was also directed against the amount of influence given to Barcelona-based Communists such as O'Donnell, Wintringham and the writer Ralph Bates, who had oversight over the unit.[27] The tendency of the Communist "fraction" in Grañen to meet secretly was also bitterly resented, especially as two members of this group, Sinclair-Loutit and nurse Thora Silverthorne, were involved in a very public relationship. Cochrane – the principal critic – was eventually invited to participate in these meetings, albeit without a vote.[28] However, the crisis was by no means a direct clash between the Communists and their opponents, as the signatories included the staunch Communist Ann Murray. Many of the grievances were practical (concerning, for instance, the poor quality of staff and equipment), and the main demand was for a more transparent and "democratic" administration. The document concluded that: "Most of us have come here because of political ideals. We want to feel that our unit is acting as a lever for moving public opinion in Britain, and we want also to maintain a unit here which will act as an example of efficiency . . . to our Spanish comrades."[29] For Communist apparatchiks such as O'Donnell in Barcelona, however, the British unit must have appeared to be slipping out of their control.

In the short term, Sinclair-Loutit was forced to return to London, and his place was taken by Cochrane as "administrative chairman" at the head of an elected committee. The "fraction", which was said to contain "some incredibly bad Party comrades", was formally dissolved, although Cochrane later noted that the Communists still "insisted on keeping me under strict control".[30] Sinclair-Loutit later played down the significance of the ructions at Grañen, blaming inactivity resulting in "useless bitching . . . discipline was weak".[31] Cochrane went along with this to some degree, as he recalled that "we were divided by age, sex, class, intelligence, political allegiance, and mental stability – and had not enough to do". He felt that "for a considerable period of time we did quite a useful job at Grañen though I look back with horror to that period".[32] However, inactivity, even when compounded by personal and sexual tensions, was not the whole story. While Sinclair-Loutit described Grañen as merely a "dotty debating society", others at the time saw more sinister forces at work. For instance, a political report sent to London at the end of December complained of obstruction by three "proletarian members of the Transport staff" who were imbued with the Catalan "philosophy of Anarchism".[33] A subsequent report claimed that a group of personnel were advocating that the unit should be run by a "Soviet" committee – a style of administration "borrowed partly from the anarchists and partly from the P.O.U.M". Their intention was to make "the London Committee understand what we want".[34] While there is no evidence that the volunteers were actually converting to Anarchism, the outbreak of "democracy" at the Hospital was deeply unwelcome both to the Communists and to the more staid members of the SMAC[35] in

London. In political terms, at least, Grañen had been a disaster. The lesson was clear: never again would a large group of British medical volunteers be placed in an isolated location under weak and inexperienced political leadership.

The SMAC received a further set-back in late November 1936 when the Spanish authorities decided not to allow a second British medical unit to proceed to Spain. This was particularly demoralising as personnel had already been recruited, vehicles purchased, and an advance party (under Quartermaster Captain James White) was active in Barcelona. A number of reasons were given for this capricious decision at the time. The SMAC blamed the allegations of looting that had been made against the Scottish ambulance unit for temporarily souring its own relations with the Spanish government.[36] However, Captain White returned home convinced that Sinclair-Loutit had sabotaged his unit because he had been on friendly terms with the Anarchists in Barcelona. In White's opinion the second unit was cancelled because it would not have been as "slavishly and destructively under party-control" as the first had been. White's criticisms were rejected by the SMAC, but deserved to be taken seriously. Not only had he recently been entrusted with a responsible position by the committee, but he was also a member of the Communist Party; he was, he claimed, threatened with expulsion if he made his criticisms public.[37] Indeed, a confidential report by Sinclair-Loutit confirms that the second unit's cancellation was "requested and obtained" by Communist party members in Spain precisely due to concerns over White's reliability.[38]

Meanwhile, the SMAC itself was facing an internal crisis. The TUC had decided on 25 November 1936 no longer to support the committee until Communists had been excluded from its ranks, and this placed Dr Morgan in an invidious position. He would have been happy to resign from what he described as the "terrible job being Chairman of this rather difficult Committee", as he regularly found himself carrying out policies which he had "borne the brunt of opposing in committee".[39] Morgan saw the committee as sharply divided on political lines, but felt that the moderate Labour members did not always support him. For instance, when Dr Brook resigned as secretary in December, only Morgan opposed the appointment of Leah Manning as his successor.[40] (George Jeger, a Labour LCC Councillor, was at the same time appointed as a salaried Organising Secretary.) Morgan's decision to remain in office and not to split the committee on Labour/Communist lines was essential for the success of the SMAC, as his continuing presence ensured that the committee's cross-party image was maintained. Morgan was in many respects an ideal chairman as he was at the same time acutely sensitive to the political balance within the committee and committed to the view that "with good will and anxiety to help democratic humanity, good work could result". While he remained "on the qui vive to meet stratagems from one side", he was also patient and constructive.[41] Although Isabel Brown has been described as the SMAC's "motive force" and "master tactician",[42] the committee could not have retained its broad political and professional support if led by a Communist.

By the end of 1936 the problems at Grañen pointed towards a simple solution: the British hospital should be handed over to the Spanish authorities and many of the remaining personnel assigned to work with the International Brigades. A small number of nurses would remain at Grañen supporting the highly-regarded Spanish surgeon Dr Aguilo. On his return to Britain Sinclair-Loutit persuaded the committee of the necessity of this step, and later regarded this as his "major contribution".[43] Both Communists and non-Communists on the SMAC were satisfied with an outcome which not only offered an end to the damaging political indiscipline within the unit but also promised it a more high-profile role. Cochrane was asked to travel to the International Brigade headquarters at Albacete and offer the unit's services. He was aware, but unperturbed, that he was part of a "prearranged scenario" in which the Communists had appointed a non-Communist to "hand over" the medical unit to the Communist-controlled Brigades.[44] However, Sinclair-Loutit later denied that the move was a political ploy: "logistics, security and military tactical considerations IMPOSED on the unit the absolute necessity to abandon total independence . . . ".[45] It also represented a fresh start as, by the time that the transfer had been completed, only four of the original volunteers remained. They were joined in Albacete by a number of new personnel. The most notable was the Communist surgeon Alexander Tudor Hart who considered himself to be "considerably senior" to Sinclair-Loutit, and better qualified both politically and medically.[46] After a brief but wounding struggle with the younger man, Tudor Hart emerged as the new leader of the British medical personnel in Spain.

The decision to attach the British volunteers to the 14th International Brigade in January 1937 marks the beginning of the end of the central narrative of the British medical unit. In the course of 1937 "it became impossible to speak of 'British' hospitals etc. . . . . ",[47] although a number of medical facilities continued to be referred to as such. Throughout the war, many British medical staff felt deeply disappointed that they were not allowed to form a unit that would specifically serve the needs of the

British Battalion of the 15th International Brigade, although two British doctors were eventually assigned to it.[48] A hospital was established at Huete as a base for British medical operations in Spain, but this does not appear to have been strongly supported by the SMAC. Instead, during 1937 the British medical personnel were dispersed into smaller groups, increasingly scattered across the Republican zone both on the front-line and in rear hospitals. British staff served at all of the major battles from the Jarama (February 1937) onwards. Most of the SMAC personnel in Spain served in a hospital at the Escorial during the battle of Brunete, in July 1937. Five of them were killed there, including the American doctor Randall Sollenberger and the ambulance drivers Julian Bell and Anthony Carritt. During the battle of the Ebro in the autumn of 1938 a number of British staff served just behind the front line in the remarkable cave-hospital at La Bisbal de Falset. Others worked in evacuation and convalescent hospitals, as well as in laboratories and other medical facilities, in some cases until the very end of the civil war in March 1939. The last to leave was nurse Madge Addy who worked at a hospital that had been established by the SMAC at Uclés, deep in Republican territory. In late February 1939, she wrote that "we seem just cut off from the world, no electricity and no wireless . . . it is a real struggle to remember what day it is, and the date".[49] She eventually returned to Britain at the end of June.

The decision that the medical volunteers should be formally incorporated into the Spanish Republican armed forces with military ranks and discipline was not universally welcomed. In the spring of 1937 the members of the British unit voted against a resolution put by the American Doctor Murray Fuhrman that the unit should be autonomous of the Spanish army. Behind the scenes, the Communist Party fraction had "organised opinion among the weaker non-party elements" against Furhman's resolution "and the danger was averted".[50] Subsequently, on 10 April 1937, the British volunteers "passed a formal resolution reaffirming their submission to the discipline of the Spanish Army", while Fuhrman absented himself.[51] In a separate development, Tudor Hart reported in April 1937 that the drivers sent out by the SMAC were

> *now nearly all refusing to work in the sanitary service of the Army and insist on remaining in Spain as civilians: there are several at present in the employ of Churchill in Valencia who conduct vigorous anti-military propaganda on new recruits as they arrive. I am trying to get that liquidated at this end. But will you please see to it that the CP members on the medical committee [i.e. the SMAC] are made to take the trouble to see that there is a proper control of the type of driver selected.*[52]

Viscount Churchill's exact role in this affair is difficult to establish. It is clear that he shared some of Fuhrman's criticisms, and also that he attempted to keep some of the British personnel out of military jurisdiction. However, he had no sympathy for those drivers who, in his view, used their objections to militarisation as an excuse for driving around Spain "at their own sweet will".[53] Jim Fyrth has written that "one can only wonder that in the middle of a fierce war there should be those who thought that the army medical services should be independent of the army they served".[54] However, quite apart from the personal sentiments of some personnel who may not have understood that they were volunteering for military service, the decision to join the Spanish Republican army potentially placed the whole future of the unit in jeopardy. Under the Non-Intervention agreement the British government would now have been within its rights to ban the work of the SMAC just as it had banned volunteering for the International Brigades.

The establishment of a joint British-Spanish hospital at Uclés in the autumn of 1937 appears to have been one consequence of the decision to militarise the British unit. Nan Green who served there rather unhappily for a few weeks was dismissive of the initiative which she described as "one more effort from the London committee to establish a new and totally [politically] *uninvolved* charity venture", involving British nurses "hand-picked for their non-Left character . . . " In her view the hospital was intended to appeal to wealthy donors not otherwise willing to support the Spanish Republic.[55] The real motivation appears, however, to have been somewhat different. Dr Morgan visited Spain in August 1937 and was deeply impressed by the Belgian-run hospital established by the International Federation of Trade Unions at Onteniente. He concluded that the provision of a new hospital would provide more effective aid than "the glamour of any work, however well and meritoriously performed with risk of danger, nearer the front line".[56] On his return the SMAC agreed to set up a hospital under Spanish control with a joint British and Spanish staff. In Morgan's view such an arrangement would provide a model of "how foreign medical aid can be incorporated into the Spanish Government Medical Services", as well as offering training for Spanish nurses.[57] Indeed, Louise Jones, the first British nurse to work at Uclés, wrote that "the idea of the London Committee to use the new hospital as a training school for Spanish nurses was excellent".[58] Even so, there was much resentment amongst other British medical personnel in Spain that Uclés was receiving undue prominence, while other British projects such as the base hospital at Huete were starved of funds.[59]

At a conference on 18 September 1937 the SMAC confirmed a decision, originally taken by the committee in July, to place all of its work in Spain under the control of the Spanish government. This was designed to end the rather chaotic situation whereby the scattered British personnel made requests (via Lord Churchill in Valencia) for equipment and supplies direct to the committee in London. George Jeger, for instance, complained that he was receiving "frantic telegrams" containing long lists of demands from Tudor Hart, and yet it was "doubtful how far our jurisdiction now extends over him and our personnel in the hospital".[60] Under the new dispensation, it would be up to the Spanish health authorities to submit requests to the committee in London, working through a single SMAC representative in Barcelona. By July 1938 the SMAC was describing itself as merely a "forwarding agent for supplies and personnel", and enjoying "most harmonious" relations with the Spanish "Sanidad de Guerra".[61] The delicate and important post of representative was awarded to the young British administrator Rose ("Rosita") Davson. The centralisation of the SMAC's activities under government control, combined with the establishment of the Uclés hospital and a thorough review of the committee's organisation in London,[62] all pointed towards a more professional and efficient (if less politically glamorous) pattern of work during the final eighteen months of the civil war. Tellingly, on 27 September 1937 Morgan wrote to Lord Addison that "we have had a terrible struggle on the S.M.A.C, but I think I've now won".[63]

■ ■ ■ ■ ■ ■ ■

Who were the British medical volunteers, and what motivated them to serve in Spain? Although no complete personnel records have survived, it appears that the SMAC sent at least 150 staff to Spain. Gender divisions within the unit reflected those within the medical profession in Britain. All of the nurses were female, while the only non-male doctor was Dr Ruth Prothero, who was German-born but had trained in Edinburgh. Portia Holman, who was at an advanced stage in her medical studies, served as a nurse. In the recruitment of both doctors and nurses, it was necessary to balance professional considerations against political concerns. The committee soon learnt that there was no point in sending out sub-standard staff (or those with severe personal problems) as their colleagues were quick to demand their recall. The more conservative members of the committee would have preferred to recruit senior and experienced (and probably non-political) doctors, remunerated with pay and decora-tions. However, such men were not forthcoming. Instead, the SMAC doctors were young, energetic and politically committed. Most were in their twenties: Reggie Saxton, who served throughout the civil war, was born in 1911, the waspish Cochrane in 1909, Len Crome in 1909, and Harry Bury in 1913. Politics aside, the doctors were also professionally ambitious. The civil war offered a rare opportunity for gaining battlefield experience and experimenting with new procedures, and some went on to publish medical treatises on their work. Wogan Philipps, an ambulance driver and son of a wealthy businessman, did not warm to them. He found them "terribly bourgeois", the product of an "expensive training which makes it a monopoly of a class . . . They are superior in their manner, these English doctors & fight & squabble . . . They quarrel amongst themselves, are jealous of each other . . . "[64]

Most of the nurses were also in their twenties, although Molly Murphy, a former Suffragette, was in her mid-forties. They were well-trained and in many cases well-travelled (a significant minority came from Australia and New Zealand). Although Spain did not offer them as many professional opportunities as were presented to the doctors, there were other compensations. British nurses were highly valued compared to their less skilled (and often less resourceful) Spanish colleagues, and were given considerable authority. For instance, Penny Phelps was put in charge of controlling an outbreak of scarlet fever amongst Italian volunteers and briefly held the rank of Lieutenant.[65] One former volunteer later commented that for all of the foreign women Spain "was their finest hour . . . Many had lived narrow, hum-drum lives and here in Spain, despite the misery and fatigue, the pain and destruction, they found a romantic cause . . . "[66] For the front-line nurses in particular, although the work was hard and demanding, the atmosphere was relaxed and democratic. One journalist encountered a "happy, heroic little colony" on the Jarama front, where the nurses were dressed "in khaki, with their medical kit slung over their shoulders".[67] At Grañen the quartermaster requested khaki shorts and overalls, with small sizes for the women as "they do as much manual work as the men".[68]

Professional considerations applied less to the drivers, stretcher bearers and administrators who, in consequence were a far more varied group than the medical staff. A number of the drivers and mechanics were "typical working class lads",[69] but they were joined by others from privileged backgrounds for whom serving with the medical unit offered a means to participate in the civil war without fighting in the International Brigades. This category included Sir Richard Rees, former editor of the *Adelphi* journal, Julian Bell, who had been dissuaded from joining the Brigades by family pressure, and Wogan Philipps, husband of the novelist

Rosamond Lehmann. Rees's observation that he was using Spain to escape from an "impasse in England"[70] applied, in different ways, to all three men. Lehmann wrote of her husband that: "Wogan is obviously fired to the depths . . . It is what he likes best: to live at full pressure in a perpetual state of crisis."[71] All three found a new fulfilment in Spain, although in Rees's case only when he had left the service of the SMAC and joined the Quaker relief work in Barcelona. Collectively, the drivers formed a self-consciously masculine – and in some cases hard-drinking – society, driving long hours in difficult conditions. As Julian Bell reported, "most of our drivers are wreckers, neglect all sorts of precautions like oiling and greasing, over speed, etc".[72]

A number of volunteers, male and female, were sent out as administrative staff. One, Nan Green, proved herself to be particularly tough, hardworking and adaptable. Her husband George had already volunteered as a driver for the British unit and later died fighting with the International Brigades in September 1938. Wogan Philipps paid for the Greens' two children to be educated at Summerhill school during their parents' absence in Spain. Other appointments were less successful. Monica Milward was sent out in June 1938 primarily because, having grown up in Chile, she spoke excellent Spanish. However, she was only eighteen, and found that there was no real job awaiting her in Barcelona. She eventually went to work for the Propaganda Ministry where another former SMAC recruit, Alex Wainman, was already employed.[73] Frank Ayres, a veteran Communist who was given oversight of the Uclés hospital, was sacked by the SMAC for failing to discharge his duties. He was later reported to be working in a munitions factory in Valencia.[74]

The SMAC's policy was to recruit staff principally on the basis of professional capability, with "character, personal record and political sympathies" as lesser criteria.[75] In reality, however, this final consideration was taken extremely seriously, and volunteers were expected at least to be anti-fascists. This presented no problem in the case of the doctors, as almost all of them were either members of the Communist party (in Tudor Hart's case, since 1929) or very close to it politically. There were two doctors whose politics fitted more awkwardly. Archie Cochrane had gained a strong appreciation of the danger of fascism while travelling in Europe, but was independent-minded and outspoken. Even so, archival sources indicate that Cochrane was far closer to the Communist Party in Spain than he later admitted. According to a confidential report by Sinclair-Loutit, "he was not a member of the party, and had no immediate intention of becoming one, but he had recently been attending all meetings of the fraction, and was guided by the party line".[76] He acted as an adviser to the SMAC on his return to Britain, but soon resigned complaining of its inefficiency and "lack of humanity".[77] Ruth Prothero was forced out of the unit at Grañen for alleged professional shortcomings, but also because she plotted to establish a "private Committee, or fraction", and "avoided the censorship to correspond with political undesirables in Barcelona". Many years later she wrote that "unfortunately politics soon entered the unit mirroring the problems arising in Spain", while Sinclair-Loutit admitted that she tended to what "we then called a Trotskiite position".[78]

The political status of the nurses gave rise to more comment and concern. Phyllis Hibbert wrote on her return to Britain that 60 per cent of her fellow nurses had no definite political views and were "merely democrats with a desire to succour the suffering".[79] Similarly, Winifred Bates, who worked as an SMAC liaison officer for the nursing staff, later wrote that "about half" of them were "quite unaware of the historical importance of the war and its international implications".[80] Ann Murray's initial reaction to the party that she travelled out with was that "we are a very mixed company, some of the members have . . . undecided ideas and others are sound, others again are uninterested and just out for adventure, most of the nurses are so".[81] Nan Green, who had joined the Communist Party alongside her husband, recalled that SMAC volunteers were "[m]ostly middle class. Quite capable people but I wouldn't say as political as we were."[82] Nurse Lilian Urmston reflected that she had volunteered for "humanitarian and practical reasons" and because, having recently joined the Territorial Army nursing reserve, she "needed experience". She had even described herself as "politically disinterested" on her application form: "True – Party politics as such were not in my line."[83]

Such comments lend some support to Angela Jackson's view that many British women in Spain were not interested in left-wing factional politics, but were motivated by broader humanitarian considerations. However, whether they liked it or not, from the moment of recruitment onwards the nurses were enmeshed in the highly politicised culture of the British unit. Political considerations affected how nurses were selected, where they worked in Spain and whom they worked with. For instance, when the Australian nurse Dorothy Low was selected in June 1937, her views were described as "very unsound" and it was agreed that she "should only go to Spain if accompanied by a person of sound political views". (In the event, however, she was accompanied by Urmston who some felt "had no political views at all".)[84] A careful eye was kept on nurses' political views while they were in Spain, notably by their "*responsable*" Winifred Bates. In September 1938 Bates submitted a lengthy report describing the nurses' political development, future potential and value "to Spain and the Revolutionary movement". She commented, for instance, that "for political reasons" two New Zealand nurses "should be given every kind of experience possible including front work". She considered that Mavis King, a radiologist and CPGB member, "needs more political instruction [but] could be used and trusted if necessary. Bourgeois in origin but does not lack courage." Nurse Barbara Briscoe was described as quiet and disciplined with "no political ideas at all . . . Comrades must help her when she awakens mentally." [85] The duration of the volunteers' stay in Spain, as well as the prospects of being allowed to return for further service, often rested on such reports. The volunteers were also being evaluated in casual private correspondence. Ann Murray's letters home described nurse Jean Woodifield as "not a P.M. [party member] but is absolutely 'Left'", Susan Sutor as "brought up in bourgeois circles but now . . . very much improved politically", and Mary Slater as "very political" but not a good mixer. She dismissed one Australian nurse as "more or less non-political".[86] The Communist Party might even interfere prudishly in the women's private lives. For instance, at Grañen the party fraction determined that two British nurses should return to Britain. One had been involved in a "passionate Lesbian love-affair" with an interpreter, and the other had displayed a "sexual promiscuity [which] seemed to shock the Spaniards".[87]

Some of the non-Communist nurses undoubtedly suffered discrimination. Lilian Urmston, for instance, recalled that as a non-Communist she always felt "slightly outside the magic circle".[88] Portia Holman claimed that there was a "schism" between the Communist members of the unit, on the one hand, and "apolitical" and moderate members on the other. She included herself and Molly Murphy in this latter group, which she described as a small and unpopular minority. She claimed that the two of them were eventually forced to return home. This is supported by the diary of the unit secretary Aileen Palmer, who noted on 11 July 1937 that the two women had "had a brush with [Tudor] Hart and gone back. There was a fairly unanimous feeling against them, and even the nurses met and passed a resolution of some kind."[89] While it seems likely that Murphy's problems were principally due to mental and physical exhaustion, there is no question that Holman's were political. She had already been branded as a "Trotskyist" on an earlier visit to Spain, and Sinclair-Loutit later described her as an active campaigner against the British unit's integration into the Republican army.[90] The case of Winifred Wilson, who volunteered in December 1936 and spent seven months nursing in Spain, is also instructive. According to her account, she had told the SMAC that "my sympathy was with the Government, but that I wished to leave all politics out and work with only humanitarian views. This was readily accepted." Once in Spain, however, she was dismayed by the political frictions that she encountered there. She felt that her refusal to present herself "as a strong Communist" was held against her, and she fell further "out of favour" when news leaked out that she was a former missionary. She was subsequently employed more as a sanitary inspector than as a nurse. She volunteered again in the spring of 1938, but was told that the SMAC was not sending out any new personnel. Wilson had no doubt that she had been excluded on political grounds.[91]

One particularly poignant case is that of the hospital administrator Nan Green, whose commitment both to the Republican cause and to the Communist Party ran very deep. She was denounced by a doctor that she worked with at the Valdeganga convalescent hospital and classed as unfit to "undertake any party work" by Bill Rust, a leading Communist party official in Spain. The allegations caught her at a difficult personal moment as she was wracked with guilt over a brief affair that she had had with a wounded volunteer. She was rescued by Winifred Bates who determined that she was a good Communist and denounced the "irresponsible gossips . . . actuated by jealousy" who claimed that she was in Spain "for her own delectation". Even so, the taint of political unreliability continued to haunt her into the 1940s.[92]

The British medical unit found it difficult to dispel an aura of intrigue. Bill Alexander conceded as much when he explained to Jim Fyrth that the medical services were an obvious route for penetration by intelligence agents due to the incessant travel that such services were engaged in and the relative safety of their work. Moreover, the "differing political, emotional and moral attitudes of those who enrolled" in them and "the weaknesses in political leadership all made more likely gossip and tittle-tattle which can be a first step to suspicion and accusation".[93] There is, indeed, some evidence that medical aid was being used as cover for a range of clandestine operations. For instance, Alexander Foote, a former volunteer for the International Brigades who worked for Russian intelligence during the Second World War, was asked to drive medical supplies to Spain. He later claimed that his real mission would have been to act as a courier between the Communist Party in London and the leadership of the British Battalion.[94] It also seems likely, perhaps because of such practices, that SMAC activity in Britain was closely monitored by

MI5.[95] Due to a lack of archival sources the truth of many of these allegations cannot be tested. It is possible, however, to look in more detail at two individuals who attracted particular suspicion: Viscount Churchill and Rosita Davson.

Viscount Churchill, who was generally known in Spain as Peter Spencer, was the cousin of Sir Winston Churchill. His *Times* obituary described him as "something of an original" who worked at various times as a newspaper reporter, garage manager, film actor and dialogue writer. He had also served as an officer during the First World War.[96] Leah Manning described him as "agreeable, but incalculable", but Sinclair Loutit's judgement was blunter: "he was wildly homosexual, financially dishonest, *most* charming".[97] Churchill's memoirs offer little insight into how he came to work with the SMAC. He claimed to have been both "horrified and fascinated" by the rise of fascism, and increasingly drawn towards left-wing politics in the mid-1930s. With the outbreak of the Spanish Civil War he "no longer felt like standing on the sidelines".[98] The committee, for its part, was grateful for the social cachet and connections that Churchill could provide, and promptly appointed him as its representative in Spain.

Given that Churchill's relations with the SMAC eventually broke down, it should be acknowledged that the committee appears, at first, to have been happy with his performance. In addition to providing leadership and an organisational focus within Spain, he was also a prominent speaker at pro-Republican rallies in Britain. Indeed, as late as September 1937 Dr Morgan was strongly defending him within the committee: "Lord Churchill's excellent work is unjustifiably submitted to criticism."[99] He was also politically acceptable to the Communists. For instance, the Political Commissar Wally Tapsell described both Churchill and Viscountess Hastings as standing "pretty close to us" in April 1937.[100] Richard Rees noted that Churchill "talked like" a Communist in Spain.[101] However, there were already signs that all was not well. Sinclair-Loutit claimed that after setting up the Grañen hospital, Churchill was distracted by a relationship with the interpreter and poet Stanley Richardson.[102] In May 1937 Churchill wrote that he had been out of Spain for several months and returned to find SMAC affairs in "a real good mess".[103] According to a confidential report written in the autumn of 1937, Communist Party members had refrained from making full criticism of Churchill "because of the knowledge that he is engaged on other work more important than any he might be doing in connection with the unit".[104] By October 1937, Leah Manning concluded that Churchill's assistant Rosita Davson was doing the "real work of Spanish Medical

Aid".[105] Soon afterwards Churchill disappeared and had no contact with the committee until June 1938. Accordingly, on 15 June the SMAC agreed to terminate his services – with thanks – "in view of his prolonged absence and non-communication".[106]

What had gone wrong? Churchill later claimed that he had been asked by the Spanish Defence Minister Indalecio Prieto to assist with the clandestine work of breaking the Non-Intervention arms embargo. It appears that he was involved in a scheme to purchase military aircraft from Turkey which went badly wrong as, on 12 April 1938, the Spanish Ambassador to Britain informed his government that Churchill had "absconded with money and was henceforth a person of no confidence".[107] His behaviour caused considerable embarrassment to the SMAC, especially as the British press was rife with rumours about his activities.[108] Subsequently Leah Manning made a point of visiting Prieto to assure the Spanish government that "Peter Spencer was in no way connected with us and we were in no way responsible for his actions".[109] Churchill later implied that the real reason for his departure was his growing realisation of the extent of Soviet influence on the Republican side, and claimed to have helped International Brigade volunteers who had fallen foul of the Communists to escape from Spain.[110] However, while he was unhappy with the decision to militarise the British medical personnel, there is little evidence that he was an active opponent of the Communist presence within the unit. One can only conclude that, in the enthusiasm of August 1936, the SMAC had acted irresponsibly in giving such a sensitive job to a man with so little political experience. The folly of Isabel Brown's comment that "titled names always count"[111] was self-evident. Churchill, whose personal motto was "I advance masked" (Descartes), entitled the chapter of his memoirs dealing with Spain "the mask is off". However, his claim that Spain was a country in which "there were fewer disguises and more frequent moments of truth"[112] hardly does justice to his own role in the civil war.

Rosita Davson not only took over Churchill's role as representative but also some of the opprobrium that had begun to attach to him. She had accompanied the first unit to Spain, working initially as an interpreter and assistant nurse, and joined the "rebellion" at Grañen. The key to her subsequent success was that she spoke excellent Spanish (as a result of having lived in Spain) and was an efficient administrator – two virtues which the likes of O'Donnell did not possess. Leah Manning, who was her champion within the SMAC, described her as a "tiny, vivacious brunette" who was tough, resilient, "never depressed" and could work round the clock. Ann Murray found her to be "thoroughly conscientious" and willing to put "her hand to anything that is to be done", and Bill Alexander recalled her as "capable, hard" and efficient.[113] However, although she was considerably more competent than her predecessor, Alexander also commented that she was "universally" regarded with suspicion within medical aid circles. Jim Fyrth, who spoke to many former volunteers while researching his book, wrote that "there were many criticisms" about the way in which she forwarded supplies from Barcelona to the front-line hospitals. He added that many of her supporters in the London committee turned against her when they learnt that she had been employed by the British Embassy in Moscow during the Second World War and had later joined the Diplomatic Corps. As a consequence Davson − who was arguably the British woman in Spain who carried the greatest weight of responsibility for the longest period of time − has largely been written out of the history of the British medical volunteers.[114]

Criticism of Davson came to a head following a peculiar incident in May 1938 when two former medical aid volunteers were denounced to the Spanish authorities as undesirables by the SMAC and put in jail. Bill Rust, the CPGB agent in Barcelona, was incensed and claimed that this was "obviously the work of Rosita Davson" (who was currently in London). One of the men, driver Charlie Hunt, was a Communist party member, and "leading people in the B.M.U. are down on him accordingly". The other, David Johnstone, had been sent out as a technician but had transferred to the Republican army. Rust saw this incident as "patent provocation and sabotage" by reactionary elements in the SMAC, and demanded an enquiry into Davson's role: "You know our opinion of her." He added that he had met with the "leading Party comrades in the Unit, Winifred Bates and Roy Pool[e] . . . All comrades are extremely alarmed to hear that Rosita Davson is returning [to Spain]."[115] Rust also gave a "rather depressing view of Rosita" to his successor, Peter Kerrigan, and was possibly responsible for a rumour circulating in Spanish government circles that Davson was "politically unreliable" and might be in touch with foreign embassies. When pressed, however, on his return to Britain, Rust conceded that "nothing was known against her".[116]

Davson was also the subject of a highly critical and devastatingly personal report by Winifred Bates in September 1938. This remarkable piece of character assassination was intended to show that Davson was an obstructive, manipulative colleague, who sowed dissent and ill-feeling amongst the medical volunteers. In one graphic phrase, Bates claimed that Davson "has the power of the snake and the bird. She can make people say more than they want to say." She was also accused of bourgeois tendencies, such as a proclivity for taking weekends at Tossa de Mar and enjoying sunbathing. Most damningly, Bates argued that Davson was not, in fact, a good administrator, and that her post both could and should be eliminated. She concluded that "she is not a fascist, but is what we in popular language might call a 'mental case'".[117]

Leah Manning carried out a detailed investigation into various allegations levelled against Davson and, not having seen Bates' poisonous memorandum, found nothing to "confirm any criticism" of her. She concluded that the adverse comments came mainly from nurses who had never accepted the centralisation of the SMAC's work, and were unhappy with some of Davson's decisions concerning the deployment of medical aid. (Manning's comment was that "it appears to be impossible to take responsibility without incurring someone's displeasure".) Moreover, Davson had carried out the necessary but unpopular task of clearing out the unit's flat in Barcelona: "the rendezvous of all sorts of undesirable characters and where a large number of people who had no connection with Spanish Medical Aid spent a great deal of their time . . . " Manning noted that Davson had worked hard for two years "without receiving a penny piece in payment".[118] It should be added that Davson's post was not abolished and that, until the very end of the war, her work was highly praised within the SMAC.[119]

Why, then, was Davson treated with such suspicion? In part this must have been due to her personal manner as, apart from Manning, she won few friends in Spain. The teenager Monica Milward, who worked under Davson, felt that she was cold, unfriendly and rather frightening. However, there were also political factors at work. As we have seen, Davson, whose own political views are unclear,[120] had poor relations with Communists resident in Barcelona such as Winifred Bates and Bill Rust. Although the term should not be used lightly, both clearly displayed a Stalinist mentality in their work. Bates, despite the maternal care that she showed to nurses under her care, was an ardent anti-Trotskyist, while Rust readily denounced volunteers such as Nan Green on flimsy evidence.[121] Davson, as a non-Communist agent of the SMAC, was in an exposed position as she was doubtless perceived as an obstacle to Communist influence over the unit and its resources. Jim Fyrth has described Davson as being "in favour of independence" for the unit,[122] but her behaviour in Barcelona was, in fact, quite the opposite. One anonymous nurse told Leah Manning that Rosita "gives everything the committee sends out to the Sanidad"[123] (which was, of course, SMAC policy). Rust appears to have used the incident in May 1938 to mount an unsuccessful attempt to get rid of her. After the end of the civil war, Davson, unlike many other volunteers, presented no written or oral justification for her actions in Spain. Her subsequent career appears to have been less exalted than Fyrth and others have claimed, and does not give retrospective weight to any of the allegations made against her.[124]

■ ■ ■ ■ ■ ■ ■

Angela Jackson has written that in order to understand the politics of the British women in Spain, the definition of "political" must be broadened beyond "traditional hierarchical, largely male-dominated, political structures".[125] The case of Spanish Medical Aid, however, demonstrates the continuing power and influence of such structures over every aspect of the British volunteers' work. To tease out their impact by studying a succession of political conflicts and crises is hardly "cherry-picking". It would, however, be far too simplistic to claim, as Archie Cochrane subsequently did, that the SMAC was "Communist controlled".[126] Instead, both in the field and in London, it represented an arena in which different models of aid for the Spanish Republic were debated and tested. Indeed, from the perspective of the Communist Party the SMAC could be seen as something of a failure, as the need for broad political and professional support necessarily denied the Communists the level of close and direct control that they exerted over the British Battalion of the International Brigades. The distinction was plain to see in a personal report to the Central Committee of the CPGB by Bill Rust in the summer of 1938: "[The British Battalion] is a battalion to be proud of. We have comrades in other parts, the medical corps, artillery, anti-aircraft sections, chauffeurs, ambulance drivers, etc."[127] This may explain why the British medical unit received so little coverage, compared to that of the British Battalion, in the *Daily Worker*, as there was certainly no shortage of Communist journalists in Spain. There is no doubt that many prominent British Communists in Spain felt increasingly unhappy about the direction taken by the SMAC in 1937–8, from the centralisation of relief work to the establishment of the Uclés hospital and the continued failure to attach a designated unit to the British Battalion.[128] All of these developments told against the militarisation, the high propaganda value and the flexibility that the Communists valued in their solidarity work. Ultimately, both during the civil war and since, many Communists felt a marked ambivalence towards the SMAC, and even a sense that the committee in London was "hostile to the Communist Party as such".[129]

Chapter 4
The lost art of Felicia Browne

You say I am escaping and evading things by not painting or making sculpture. If there is no painting or sculpture to be made, I can not make it. I can only make out of what is valid and urgent to me. If painting and sculpture were more valid and more urgent to me than the earthquake which is happening in the revolution, or if these two were reconciled so that the demands of one didn't conflict (in time, even, and concentration) with the demands of the other, I should paint and make sculpture.

(Felicia Browne to Elizabeth Watson, spring 1936)

Towards the end of August 1936, soon after the start of the Spanish Civil War, a brief skirmish took place in Aragon between a Republican raiding party and a rebel patrol. Amongst the Republican dead was an English artist and Communist, Felicia Browne. Although her death is mentioned in many histories of the civil war, surprisingly little is known about her life, and even the exact date of her death is open to dispute. Indeed, she is now remembered principally for three reasons. First, she was the only British woman to play a combatant role and the first of the more than 500 British volunteers to die in battle. Secondly, there is the collection of sketches that she left, many recording her impressions of the Spanish militias, which were exhibited in London in October 1936. A selection of these drawings was published at the time by Lawrence and Wishart, and they have frequently been reproduced to illustrate books on the civil war. Finally, there is the passage quoted in the epigraph, first published in the programme for the London exhibition. It has been cited innumerable times since,[1] generally as evidence of Felicia Browne's significance as an artist who, when faced with the choice between art and anti-fascism, came down sharply on the side of taking direct political action. Accordingly, this otherwise elusive woman has become emblematic of the choices confronting all socially and politically conscious artists in the mid-1930s.[2] Given the paucity of knowledge about her life and politics,[3] this would seem to provide a perfectly legitimate interpretation of an unambiguous statement. However, this chapter, drawing on a small but very illuminating collection of previously unknown private letters,[4] will show that Felicia Browne's journey to her death in Aragon was far more tortuous than has previously been imagined. In particular, it will be argued that it is impossible to discern in the latter part of Felicia Browne's career any simple choice between art and political action.

■ ■ ■ ■ ■ ■ ■

Felicia Mary Browne was born on 18 February 1904 to a "comfortably off" London family with "progressive views", but she had to experience considerable adversity as a child. Her parents separated when she was young, and she was brought up by her father. According to one source she suffered from a crippling illness and spent many months in bed.[5] Like many intellectuals (and perhaps, above all, artists) of her generation she grew up with a deeply ambivalent attitude towards the family wealth which allowed her to live an independent life. Shortly before her death she wrote to her friend Elizabeth Watson that "I know well what it is to drown in the well-upholstered family household as I endured such a condition for some years, unwillingly".[6] However, her father must have supported her in her ambition to become an artist as she attended courses, intermittently, at the prestigious Slade School of Fine Art in London between the sessions of 1920–21 and 1927–28. The most remarkable aspect of her time at the Slade was that she arrived at an unusually early age, and that her studies in drawing and painting were unusually protracted. In 1925–26 she was awarded the Certificate in Drawing, but did not enter for the Fine Art Diploma.[7] A male contemporary has left a pen portrait of her as a student: "A rather plain dumpy young woman in horn-rimmed spectacles and a black hat. She was a showy but competent draughtsman and a great talker – bit of a gas – but with a saving sense of humour."[8] According to another source she had a studio in Euston Square which was the centre for a "circle" that included the young W. H. Auden and William Coldstream.[9] There was nothing in this period of her life to suggest any strong political commitment.

The turning point in Felicia Browne's life was her decision to go to

Berlin in 1928. Although intending to study sculpture, she appears to have spent more time learning metal-working and stone masonry (especially the carving of lettering and animals). She relished the communal life with her fellow craftsmen, many of whom she helped to support financially. While in Berlin she witnessed the rise of Nazism, and according to one account took part in anti-fascist street-fighting.[10] She returned to Britain in the early 1930s, leaving her sculptures and tools behind. In 1933 she joined the Communist Party of Great Britain (CPGB), and around the same time incurred the interest of Special Branch and MI5, which continued to monitor her activities until her departure for Spain in 1936.[11] These German experiences clearly made a lasting impression on her. She spent much of her money on helping German friends fleeing Nazi terror, and gained a precocious awareness of the threat of fascist violence. In the words of fellow artist Nan Youngman:

> Felicia was much more aware of the political situation than any of us, she knew what was happening and she was preparing herself for it; she used to go to self-defence classes. I can remember seeing this rather fat young woman being flung down by a tiny little Chinese gent.[12]

She also became involved in the influential Artists International Association (AIA), founded in 1933 by a group of young artists of whom a number had recently visited the Soviet Union. By the mid-1930s the AIA was becoming a significant force in left-wing cultural politics, notably with the November 1935 "Artists Against Fascism and War" exhibition in Soho Square. However, whereas her friend Elizabeth Watson became a leading figure in the association, there is little record of Felicia Browne's personal role in it.[13]

On returning to London from Berlin, she continued to study at Goldsmiths College and the Central School of Arts and Crafts (CSAC). The Goldsmiths' Corporation was so impressed with her designs for cutlery that it paid her fees at the CSAC.[14] In 1934 she entered a competition organised by the Trades Union Congress (TUC) for a commemorative medallion as part of its centenary celebrations for the Tolpuddle martyrs. In all, 237 designs were submitted by 119 competitors, and Felicia Browne alone submitted eight. One of her designs made the final shortlist of three and was submitted as a plaster model, for which she received £5. Although this design eventually came third, it certainly represented a success.[15] However, this was a solitary success, and it seems unlikely that she could have made a living from her art alone. One obituarist hinted that she was too much of a perfectionist to turn her craft to "practical use", and also alluded to her "difficulties in creation".[16] Felicia Browne referred to this herself in a letter to Elizabeth Watson of 31 March 1935:

> *I am no longer striving to get work but am learning something about design; having come here [her Billericay studio] for that purpose. The stuff being abstract, I cannot and will not make it into popular illustrations, this unavoidable decision is interpreted as a sort of rude, beastly indifference and is deplored by my decent friends. Whether the stuff being done now is worth anything or not, I don't know but the other was worth nothing; if there were any valid reason for further hacking for £ (sic) I would probably go on with it . . .*

It is not clear what work she was referring to here, and certainly there is no trace of abstract experimentation in her surviving art. The hallmark of her sketching was its confidence and attention to anatomy, betraying the enduring influence of Henry Tonks at the Slade. There was also consistency in her subject matter as, from her student days in the 1920s until her death, she was continuously drawn to sketch working people and, above all, animals (figure 1).

FIGURE 1   *Deer. From* Drawings by Felicia Browne, *London, 1936.*

The drawings published posthumously give a clear, but narrow, indication of her burgeoning talent. However, a painted self-portrait (figure

2) provides new evidence of the range of her skills, and a letter-head sketch (figure 3) reveals something of her ability as a vivid and humorous cartoonist. Indeed, one obituarist commented that she would have been an excellent illustrator for Dante and Kafka, "by whose strange and elaborate cosmogenies she became fascinated in the last year [of her life]".[17] A townscape (figure 4), possibly sketched in France or Spain, further demonstrates her distinctive style. Her letters to Elizabeth Watson give some insight into her eclectic interest in modernist art. While in Paris *en route* to Spain she was disappointed to find all of the main galleries, especially the Orangerie with its Cézannes, closed due to the 14th of July celebrations. She was clearly familiar with the memoir writings of the *fauvist* painter Vlaminck and declared at one point that "you can see Vlaminck country all round here". There is also evidence of her grappling with surrealism which, by 1935–6, had belatedly become an important issue for artists of her generation.[18] Although she ultimately dismissed surrealism as a product of the "extraordinary atmosphere of abnormal [bourgeois] leisure",[19] it is notable that one of her final acts before joining the militia in Barcelona was to visit the Spanish surrealist artist José Lanolla in Lérida.

In the early 1930s, in addition to developing her craft, Felicia Browne also travelled widely, helped by an ability to speak a number of Slavonic languages. It is not clear at what point she gained this facility, but it clearly existed as in 1935 she mentioned having "translated many Soviet posters, pamphlets and modern fairy stories".[20] During these years she visited the Soviet Union, as well as Hungary and Czechoslovakia. In one frightening incident, while camping in the Tatras mountains, she narrowly escaped being lynched by a "wild procession" of peasants who thought that she was a witch.[21] She enjoyed sketching workers and peasants on these expeditions, and, indeed, at least one motivation for her doomed Spanish journey appears to have been to make a similar sketching expedition to the Sierra Guarra in Aragon.[22] Her obituarists paid compliment to her sense of adventure and zest for travel. The reality, however, as her final letters show, was that she also experienced the vulnerability that many who travel on their own sometimes have to confront. In July 1936, she wrote from Paris that: "I am hideously bored, I am a rotten tourist, and these days revive too many memories of solitary explorations of strange cities, nothing is more deeply depressing; but it is a lovely city. In fact, this is rather like being in Moscow four years ago (only there was a lot to do) or Prague last year; but we shall leave tomorrow."[23] She also wrote: "Never go to an entirely foreign city entirely alone . . . I did this in Berlin, Budapest, Amsterdam, Prague, Moscow, and now in Paris, it is like no

FIGURE 2 *Felicia Browne, Self Portrait, undated.*

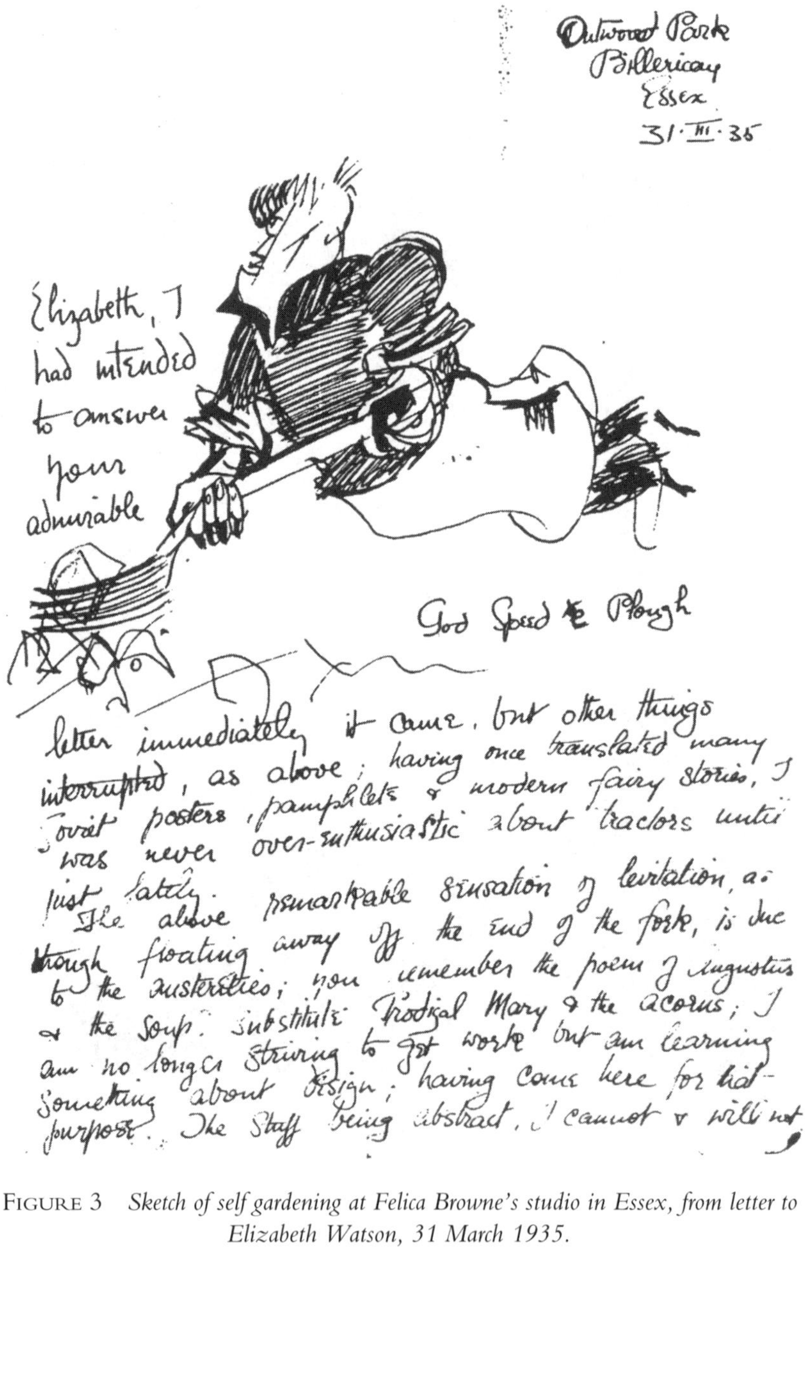

FIGURE 3   *Sketch of self gardening at Felica Browne's studio in Essex, from letter to Elizabeth Watson, 31 March 1935.*

FIGURE 4   *Townscape. From* Drawings by Felicia Browne, *London, 1936.*

other way of seeing a strange place and knowing it with a sort of horrible intimacy."

She was by now increasingly active in the Communist Party, and not averse to carrying out routine political work such as selling newspapers on street corners.[24] Shortly before departing for Spain she also found work as a scullion in a tea-shop working 10 or 11-hour shifts, although sources differ as to whether this was due to her temporary lack of money or for political purposes. She certainly saw this as a field for political activity. In a letter to Elizabeth Watson she wrote that the job was "hell", but that she "would not be in any other job in the world because so much is to be done getting the girls to fight (and will it be a fight?) to change unspeakable conditions". In a subsequent note she wrote that she was going to see a trade union official at Transport House as she was desperate to get the workers into a union before she was sacked.[25] She apparently wrote a draft of a novel based on these experiences, but no trace of it has survived. When considering whether her penury was a possible motivation for working in the tea-shop, it should be remembered that at this point, in 1936, she both owned a studio in Billericay and was renting one in Bloomsbury, as well as being able to go for a touring holiday in her car over the summer. One surviving letter records life in her Billericay studio, which she had helped to build and which was named "Yggdrasil" (the world-tree of Norse mythology). She clearly took great pleasure in her garden and in observation of the natural world. She delighted in the "incense" of her oak-burning stove ("like the smell of ancient country houses"). Here, as on her travels, she appears to have found it easy to relate to people from a different social background. She enjoyed working alongside two local labourers: "we drank coffee and talked about the armaments race . . . "[26]

Felicia Browne's attempt to immerse herself in a working-class environment at the tea-shop appears to have put a slight strain on her friendship with Elizabeth Watson. In one note, addressed to "young sluggard", she wrote that "while I am scrubbing monstrously around the floors, you are asleep". This tension is the context for the famous passage quoted in the epigraph, which, in fact, occurs on the eighth page of a rambling nine-page letter to Elizabeth Watson. In this letter, which clearly continued an earlier conversation, Felicia Browne gave her idiosyncratic interpretation of the Marxist theory of capitalist exploitation and the nature of leisure under capitalism, while also touching on the work of the surrealists. One of the most interesting passages, which may also be seen as a comment on her own situation, refers to a book that she had been reading by Gertrude Stein:[27]

The Gertrude Stein book is an amazing chronicle of this very thing . . . some of them WERE poor, some of them were playing at being poor, they thought they were poor but they sent their washing home every month and hardly ever paid for anything except now and again . . . They could choose to be poor if they happened to spend all the available money in time, like I can. I maintain there is a fundamental difference between this kind of poverty which isn't poverty until the ultimate reserves are exhausted . . . and the worker's kind of poverty which is more active and less avoidable . . .

The letter concludes with a long paragraph, the first part of which is the section abstracted for publication in the memorial programme after Felicia Browne's death. However, it is important to note the full context in which the passage occurs.

Am I talking beside the point, is nothing in this of any value? You may see it utterly differently, or be talking about something else. So often we are talking about completely different things that I think: my God, it is better not to say anything. <u>You say I am escaping and evading things by not painting or making sculpture. If there is no painting or sculpture to be made, I can not make it. I can only make out of what is valid and urgent to me. If painting and sculpture were more valid and more urgent to me than the earthquake which is happening in the revolution, or if these two were reconciled so that the demands of one didn't conflict (in time, even, and concentration) with the demands of the other, I should paint and make sculpture.</u> *Do you honestly think that any sort of Party job is an escape, for me? Perhaps you do. I have let you think that, cursing myself for not being able to paint, for being a paralysed fool. "Ah" you say "but you only think you're paralysed. That's an escape too. Stop thinking it." According to this, it is a convenient way of escaping responsibility. An equally good, if not better thing to say would be ["]if it is to any extent true find out why[?"]. I think the first and true reason is actual conditions in the world today which stop one from painting when there are other things to be done like this trade union stuff and the AI. Other reasons personal not possible to discuss obscure. [Emphasis added]*[28]

Thus, the passage was edited for publication in such a way that it emphasised the universal dilemmas of the clash between art and political commitment, rather than mentioning the mundane specifics of Communist Party and trade-union work. However, when reading the passage it should be remembered that it was not written for publication, and that one is eavesdropping on a private exchange of views between friends. Thus, it deserves also to be seen as a personal comment on the pressures that friends and peer groups place upon each other.

Why did Felicia Browne go to Spain in 1936? Numerous reasons have been given: that she went to study the works of El Greco; that she went to sketch in the Sierra Guarra, and that she went to observe or sketch the People's Olympiad in Barcelona (the left-wing alternative to the Olympic games in Hitler's Berlin that was disrupted by the outbreak of civil war). The only light shed on this subject by her letters is that Barcelona is identified as her destination, suggesting that she possibly intended to carry out the other projects when, and if, she reached the Catalan capital. What has not previously been sufficiently emphasised is the fact that, unlike on previous journeys, she was now travelling in the company of a friend, identified in the letters simply as a left-wing photographer called "Ed". From other sources it is clear that this was Dr Edith Bone, a Communist resident in Britain of Hungarian background, some fifteen years older than Felicia Browne.[29] This was an intense and troubled relationship and the letters are full of comments about its complexities. Felicia Browne clearly found Edith Bone's powerful combination of dynamism, social ease, technical skill and political sophistication attractive and undermining at the same time. She confessed that she felt unable to drive for more than a few miles on their journey to Paris because "Ed.'s immediate proximity destroys any vestige of nerve that I may yet possess".[30] On 14 July she wrote that :

> I am often deeply concerned about Ed. She is real and not real, human and devastating, _apparently_ logical, the logic suddenly disappears and there is not even a ghost left, she is enormously busy, her existence is vivid and real. We argue. Attacked by an almost complete inertia, the logical result of furious striving to belong to an alien existence (I do not mean Communism) I must be a devilish boring companion, she is the opposite, a very good person to travel with as everybody likes her even traffic policemen.

Thus, the relationship was fraught from the outset. Once the civil war started, and Edith Bone had effectively abandoned Felicia Browne, the friendship, as we will see, contributed to the fatal choices that the younger woman would make.

The couple arrived in Paris on 12 July,[31] having driven via Abbeville and argued over the relative merits of Montreuil and Beauvais. It was an exhilarating time for left-wing travellers to visit the French capital, still in a state of turbulence after the election victory of the Popular Front alliance in May and the subsequent wave of strikes and factory occupations. That year's 14 July national fête was particularly memorable, as the victorious Popular Front draped itself in the imagery of the French Revolution. Felicia Browne watched part of the demonstration in the

Place de la Bastille and was deeply impressed by a procession of women representing anti-fascist, anti-war women's groups. She commented that: "People here are sincerely alive, why the devil have we not got the same thing in England which seems to be in a sort of dream." She predicted that something "terrific is going to happen here" if the fascists tried to "get back". However, such political observations constituted only a small part of the lengthy letter that she sent to Elizabeth Watson from Paris. The problem was that Edith Bone was attending the Amsterdam–Pleyel anti-fascist conference and staying with friends, leaving Felicia alone in a hotel near the Gare Montparnasse. This left her drifting around Paris in precisely the listless, lonely fashion that she had come to dread: "knowing no-one [I] have nothing to do but wander savagely about the place . . . there is nothing to do here except to walk madly about the streets, or sleep or go to meetings". Her eye was drawn not so much to the capital's revolutionary tableaux, but to a fair in the Place d'Enfant Rochereau, with an infant's roundabout and a freakshow of "Le Vistral: Animal Monstre; Rongeur des Cadavres". It was probably with relief that she departed with Edith Bone for Spain. She was excited by the prospect, although aware that "the worst is knowing almost nothing of [Spain's] previous history or local history or anything".

In fact, Spain was now rapidly descending into political violence and civil war, and Barcelona, her destination, was to be one of the storm centres. Military garrisons on the mainland joined the *coup* over the following days, and the violence reached Barcelona on 19 July. Bereft of military authority, the Republican government was forced to turn to popular militias to crush the revolt, which in Barcelona primarily meant the Anarchists and the anarcho-syndicalist trade unionists (the CNT). After much bloodshed the rebellion was crushed in the city, and militia columns (including some women militia fighters) began to fan out into the surrounding region to confront the danger posed by the success of the rebels in the two major cities of Aragon, Huesca and Saragossa.

Felicia Browne had arrived shortly before the conflict erupted. She was extremely nervous about her own driving, and was convinced that she would cause a "bad accident". It was ironic, therefore, that it was Edith Bone who was driving when she, in Felicia's words, "murdered" the car towards the end of their journey by crashing into a lorry coming round a corner. By the time that she reported the accident to the British Consul in Barcelona, the rebellion had started and he had other things on his mind. He warned her not to go out of doors, and if she did "'and you meet any of *those fellows* with guns just do this' (he clenched his fist delicately) 'and smile nicely'".[32] His advice fell on deaf ears, as Felicia had already thrown herself into the thick of the action, although at this stage with no clear role in mind. In a letter of 31 July she described the frenetic activity of the early days of the civil war, during which time Edith Bone had immediately joined forces with the *Daily Worker* correspondent Claud Cockburn (who wrote at the time under the pseudonym Frank Pitcairn).[33]

> *Sunday and Monday [19th/20th July] were terrific days, spent in searching Barcelona for Ed. and later for her photographic apparatus which she needed badly (extra films etc) dodging guns and firing all over the place. I landed (unexpectedly, not knowing my way about) on the edge of the battlefield Plaza Cataluna at 11.A.M. on Sunday, terrific firing going on. There was no-one in that place except one cop (Guardi[a] Civil) who whistled frantically from the other side of the boulevard, and then disappeared in a doorway, shouting to me not to move. Between the firing, you could hear the wind going through the trees, peaceful as hell. You had to go miles round side streets to get anywhere. It seems rum now to see shops open and cars going around without guns sticking out of them and streets without barricades. Monday and Tuesday there were terrific queues outside all the pawn-shops, where a decree had been issued for compulsory restoration of all goods below a certain value. Order is amazing, also general organization and control. In the country as well as here.*

While Felicia Browne wished to do her best to help her friend, it appears that she was now something of an encumbrance, and Bone and Cockburn went on a visit to Lérida on Saturday 26 July without her. During this period Felicia seems to have become prone to dangerous indecision, contemplating a range of options including escape into the countryside, dabbling in journalism, joining the militia, and relief work.

When her friends did not return from Lérida, Felicia set out to look for them, helped by a pass that they had procured for her as a journalistic assistant. While waiting for official permission she had "another shot" at joining the militia, but was turned down as there were more recruits than rifles. The travel permission came through on Monday 28 July, and she left by train for Lérida on the Tuesday. She actually met Edith Bone on the way to the station, who advised her not to proceed, but she decided to go in any case as the prospect of "infinite esperando [waiting] in this city provoked savage melancholy". Once in Lérida she realised that further progress towards Saragossa was now impossible, and decided to make for the Pyrenees "which had been my original intention in coming here".[34] However, north of Lérida she was picked up by a car full of anarchists and held in the Casa del Pueblo in Lérida, where she sketched members of the militia (see jacket/cover illustration). A pencil note in diary form takes up the story:

Tuesday Continuation of the supreme nightmare of being a bogus journalist, single remaining chance of getting to the mountains from Lérida but that I saw Ed. in the Peninsular, she and C[laud]. had come back last night, in spite of which I got the Lérida train for a final shot at liberty. Turned back just outside the town by a beserk peasant who yielded to two intelligent cyclists. Stopped later by a car full of C.N.T. [the anarcho-syndicalist trade union federation] who consulted all their committees and searched me, not believing anything particularly my lack of Spanish, after which we went to the Casa del Pueblo I got cross-questioned and exonerated esp. after draft of telegram was seen and passed. Got a room here with (illeg.), food voucher etc etc. Bathroom. All exceedingly courteous and efficient.

Another note from this time is also relevant:

Lérida 29 [July] Waiting in the Casa del Pueblo
a peasant bribed by 30 Fascists to transport them in coffins
Eight Fascists recognized in L[érida]. carrying a.F[ascist]. flag etc. All shot
At Saragossa, civilians and peasants are being driven forward by F[ascists].
Death rate very high.

From Lérida she was able eventually to obtain a pass to the Republican headquarters on the Aragon front, where she hoped to acquire some information that she could present to Cockburn. However, on the way she encountered a "very beserk" Edith Bone, who told her to "get the hell out of here", which she did. Her brief journalistic career was at an end.

Having returned to Barcelona, these set-backs left Felicia Browne deeply frustrated. The confusion that she must have felt was captured in a letter written by Vanessa Bell to her son Julian on 10 October 1936, in which she described a visit from Elizabeth Watson after Felicia Browne's death. The course of events that Elizabeth Watson recounted was presumably derived from Felicia's letters to her. Vanessa Bell reported that Felicia went to Spain: "before the war began. Simply to work. but when it began she got drawn in and joined the government forces. Then she wanted to leave, but too late. All the boats that took people off went and there was some muddle about the friend she was with. So she was killed, which has been a terrible waste of someone gifted as she evidently was."[35]

In fact, Bell had got the wrong end of the stick. Felicia Browne's letter of 31 July clearly shows that she did not want to leave Spain where, as she put it, "grand things are happening", but she recognised that without any fluency in Spanish or Catalan her chances of getting a useful job were nil. Similarly, she wrote, "there seems no prospect of exploring, painting, or getting anywhere beyond this monstrous city, where for a foreigner existence is suspended for the time being". She therefore applied for work at the *Socorro Rojo* (Red Aid) but was told that there were 60 applicants for 10 places. In the interim she was doing a great deal of drawing, and conscious of the need to "do it up with black ink" in case the *Daily Worker* might take it.[36]

Suddenly, on 3 August, the ranks of the militia opened to her. According to the *Daily Express* correspondent Sidney Smith, she entered the Communist militia office and demanded to be enlisted to fight on the Saragossa front. She proclaimed that "I am a member of the London Communists and can fight as well as any man", a statement that raised eyebrows in her adopted town of Billericay.[37] Smith claimed to have accompanied her to the garrison gates, where she said that; "I am not at all afraid. I am fighting for a different country, but the same cause." Her final letter to Elizabeth Watson (7 August) records this strange new life, which involved "nothing to do but hang around until we get sent somewhere; no uniforms or rifles so everybody looks like pirates". The volunteers were cooked food by "enormous cubic women" in the "filthy" barracks. She found the mysteries of sentry duty baffling, and prevented her commandant from entering his own office. She wished to join aviation school, but was failed on account of her poor eyesight. She reported the arrival in town by bicycle of three Jewish tailors[38] from Stepney, all Communists, led by Nathan Cohen. All four were initially transferred to the "machine gun department"[39] as Cohen wished, thus missing the chance of being sent to Minorca. They went to look for boiler suits, the standard militia uniform, but found the supply exhausted.[40]

After this letter there is no further news of Felicia Browne until her death, for which three different dates have been given; August 22, 25 and 29.[41] This confusion is hardly surprising given the remoteness of the location, the difficulty in communications, and the lack of any formal investigation by the British authorities. However, 22 August seems the most likely date as it is given by Georges Brinkman in the only known eye-witness account; 29 August is probably the date on which the story was first widely reported, and Consul-General King in Barcelona reported on 31 August that she had been killed "about a week ago".[42]

According to Brinkman, Felicia Browne had been in the town of Tardienta for three days when she learnt of the proposed raid under the command of a Captain Lanti; this suggests that she had arrived there from Barcelona on or around 19 August. The chaotic but exhilarating atmosphere that she would have found on this section of the front was described in a series of articles published in the *Manchester Guardian* shortly after her death. Tardienta was reported to be the headquarters of the

Trueba–Estivill column, composed of members of the PSUC (the joint Socialist/Communist Catalan party), two battalions of regulars, some syndicalists, and some shock police (the pro-Republican Assault Guards). There were also many internationalists, including Germans, Italians, French, Belgians, a half-Czech/half-English girl and "one lone Englishman from Stepney". Tardienta was five miles from the rebel front line at Almudevar, which it overlooked, and was well protected. The place felt like a "big holiday camp" with abundant food and water and the militias billeted in the houses. The correspondent was, however, scathing about the quality of the armaments available – "this civil war is being fought with the weapons of the Boer war".[43] Another report made a number of comments about the front around Huesca that shed light on Felicia Browne's fatal mission. First, the front was relatively thinly held: there was no regular frontline and there was a large no-man's land, conducive to commando-style raids. This was a war of few major offensives, likened to the war fought by the partisans of Southern Russia in 1918. Secondly, the prime Republican target was no longer Saragossa but Huesca, as it still would be when George Orwell arrived on this same front in early 1937. The strategy for taking the town included cutting the railway links to Saragossa.[44] Finally, it was reported that small bodies of militia were being used as "special service detachments".[45]

It was presumably one such detachment of self-styled "Storm Troops" that Felicia Browne volunteered to join, intending to blow up a rebel munitions train. The party of ten set off at 2.00 p. m. on 22 August, driving to the farthest point of the front (possibly only a few miles away) prior to an 11 or 12 km hike to the railway. Felicia and two others were left as look-outs while the rest of the patrol set the explosives and waited for half a minute for the train to pass. On the way back the party passed the body of a crashed Republican airman, and soon afterwards saw a dog close by. Brinkman was sent to investigate; spotting a party of thirty-five to forty Fascists only some 15 metres away, he retreated under heavy rifle fire. An Italian comrade was hit in the foot, and Brinkman was able to drag him to cover behind a slight rise. "Felicia wanted to bring First Aid to the wounded comrade. When she reached him, the Fascists directed their united fire against the two of them. With several wounds in the breast and one in the back, Felicia, our brave fighter in the cause of Freedom, sank dead to the ground. The other comrade also lost his life." The militia had no choice but to leave their comrades' bodies, taking only their "personal things", and escaping into what presumably, by then, was the evening gloom.[46] These possessions soon found their way back to Tom Wintringham in Barcelona, who pointed out to Harry Pollitt that

Felicia Browne's sketch book, full of first-rate studies of the militia, should be sold by the AIA to raise money for Spain.[47]

■ ■ ■ ■ ■ ■ ■

Felicia Browne's death was both shocking and inspiring to her friends. For Nan Youngman it was "the thing that brought me into the AIA". She recalled sitting on a beach in Cornwall and reading the announcement of Felicia's death in a newspaper. "I did not want to believe it. I was horrified, and from that moment I began to be aware of living in history . . . I was 30, but I was a child."[48] Not all newspapers, however, reported her death, one notable lacuna being in the Labour movement's *Daily Herald*. The *Daily Telegraph* gave some coverage, but also took the opportunity to report that certain unnamed "friends" felt that "it is wrong to stress the political side of her activities . . . [she] never mentioned politics at the art school".[49] Another politically ambivalent comment came in *Everybody's Weekly*, where J. O'Donnell wrote that "this gallant woman . . . fought for what she thought was right, and – whatever her politics – she remains a sad monument to the futility and barbarism of war . . . "[50] For many her death, and the retrospective exhibition in October 1936, provided an opportunity to assess her work for the first time. The *Daily Worker's* cartoonist "Gabriel" reported that the sketches deserved to be seen not for "sentimental" reasons, but because she was revealed as a "fine and disciplined craftsman" whose drawings of the militia captured an impression of "tremendous latent energy".[51] The *New Statesman's* reviewer also felt that there was no need for any "indulgence" in appraising drawings that showed an "unusual standard of excellence".[52] According to Duncan Grant she had been "gradually extracting from her drawing a wonderfully flexible and personal language".[53] The AIA's newsletter commented:

> *Altogether, what a lesson in the use of a sketch-book! Here was an artist who escaped from the studio and the posed model and got nearer to the heart of life – especially the life of the common people. It is also impossible not to believe that these studies were a preparation for the more sustained work as a sculptor which a more settled period of existence or a different social order might have permitted. Alas, it was not to be!* [54]

At least one reviewer felt uncomfortable in the presence of the final sketches:

> *These heavy unshaven men with the jutting chins and the thin, disdainful little men looking at nothing are terribly authentic. Death seems to brood over that part of the show, but how much is evoked through her art and how much through the*

waste of this young, talented life and of what we feel about the horrors to-day in Spain one cannot say.[55]

What none remarked on openly was that it was only due to this tragic death that Felicia Browne's considerable talents were brought to public attention at all.

By far the fullest and most challenging appreciation of Felicia Browne's life and work came in the introduction to the published selection of her drawings. The anonymous author, who clearly had access to private knowledge and information, tried to marry a Marxist analysis with psychological insights in explaining her peculiar career. The author's initial reluctance to be satisfied with political slogans is striking. Thus, the comment that "it is a triumph for the idea of Communism that it fosters such women [as Felicia Browne]" was immediately subverted: "Subjectively [her death] remains a tragedy. She died fighting her real enemy, but to some extent her enemy was inside her." No attempt was made to glamourise the nature of her death: "her fighting was the expression of her deeply conscientious but less happy side." Felicia Browne was portrayed as "painfully truthful and honest", humane, generous and "socially much too gracious to belong credibly to the twentieth century". But her life was depicted as ultimately incomplete:

> *She had it in her to represent the very best type of the new woman, but the kind of upbringing to which she was automatically subjected and the forces with which she had to compete in a society where commercial values are pre-eminent, seriously and unnecessarily delayed her in harmonising all the remarkable powers within her.*

The conclusion was, however, trite. According to this author, the real "tragedy" of Felicia Browne was that "she was unable to realise her use to Communism as an artist". The implication was that had she realised her "practical revolutionary use" by learning to put her art at the service of Communism, she would have been a more fulfilled person – and probably still alive. This was precisely the political reductionism that so many left-leaning artists and intellectuals rebelled against after the 1930s. It was also warned against at the time when one reviewer noted that the absence of

> *all sentimentality, all propaganda, all effort to be 'proletarian' [in Felicia Browne's drawings] deserves the consideration of those who fancy that it is an artist's business to use his art for the expression of his political beliefs. Miss Felicia Browne was under no such delusion. When she drew she was content to draw as well as in her lay. And as for her convictions – she showed these by dying for them.*[56]

In conclusion, it is important to emphasise the limitations that still restrict any full understanding of Felicia Browne's life. The newly-discovered letters discussed above are illuminating, but amount to little more than shafts of light onto a life lived, until its final month, out of the public eye. Even so, a number of points should be made on the basis of this new information. First, Felicia Browne was sadly out of her depth in the exciting, frenetic and desperate days at the start of the Spanish Civil War. She lacked the survival instinct of a Claud Cockburn, whose own politically and journalistically valuable service in the militia was swiftly curtailed. She seemed to lack any appreciation of the danger that she might be facing, and was reckless with her own life long before she volunteered to join a raiding party without the benefit of any worthwhile military training. Edith Bone's failure to offer a steadying hand once the civil war had started surely magnified the effects of this recklessness. Secondly, contrary to the published contemporary accounts, Felicia Browne did not join the militia as soon as the conflict started, and it was by no means certain that she would do so. Instead, as we have seen, joining the militia was one of a range of options. She might have joined sooner than she did, if she had been accepted, or she might not have joined at all if other options had become feasible (such as work with the *Socorro Rojo* or journalism). Finally, the idea that Felicia Browne had made some definitive and irrevocable choice between art and politics, either before coming to Spain or even in joining the militia, is no longer tenable.[57] In Spain she not only continued to sketch, producing some of her best work, but also to see the world through an artist's eye. She wrote to Elizabeth Watson on 31 July that:

> *It is definitely a country for painting. Even Montserrat (not far from here) would be a good place if it were at all possible to get there. Country beyond that is superb, from Lérida to Bujarelos mainly desert, spotted hills (spotted with bushes and whatnot) and earth coloured towns only distinguishable from the hills by shadows, very thin colour, delicate; hard country. By Bujarelos is a salt lake. This country is like your painting, only less dark, it's your colour except for the gardens in the valleys.*

On 7 August she wrote to her again, this time from barracks: "You must come out here and paint (not Tossa, the country inland), good country". Some two weeks later she would die in this "good country".[58]

Chapter 5
Mobilising art
British artists and the Spanish Civil War

In the autumn of 1938 a group of Republican supporters brought Pablo Picasso's painting "Guernica", already both famous and controversial, to Britain.[1] It was displayed for three weeks in the New Burlington Galleries in London (4–29 October), alongside many of Picasso's preparatory sketches, as a fundraiser for Spanish relief. However, attendance was somewhat disappointing (there were some 3,000 paying visitors[2]) and reviews were mixed. After being exhibited in Leeds and Oxford, the painting was displayed for a further two weeks at the Whitechapel Art Gallery in January 1939. As a mark of its significance, the exhibition was opened by the Labour Party leader Clement Attlee. For Roland Penrose, the surrealist artist and friend of Picasso who had organised the tour, this final stage of the journey was something of a triumph. There were 12,000 visitors, and £100 was raised for an East End food ship on the first day alone. For Penrose the enthusiasm of these working-class audiences stood in stark contrast to the "semi-indifference" of the West End intellectuals, and he commented that "the misgivings of those who imagined that Picasso's work would mean nothing to the working classes have proved false".[3] His principal target was the Marxist critic Anthony Blunt, who had argued precisely this point and displayed consistent hostility to Picasso's work at the time.[4] For Penrose and other radical artists, however, "Guernica" represented all that they had been seeking to achieve in the later 1930s: the perfect combination of powerful creativity, political impact, a connection to a working-class audience, and the potential to raise significant funds for the Republican cause.

The fame of "Guernica" has, of course, only grown since 1939. Even Blunt abandoned his criticism and was, by 1957, describing it as "the last great painting in the European tradition".[5] Indeed, its reputation is such that the response of British artists to the Spanish Civil War has been almost wholly eclipsed. The activities of Penrose and other left-wing artists at this time are, for instance, often only remembered by their association with Picasso and his masterpiece. To compound matters, the role of British artists in the civil war has also suffered by comparison with the scholarly attention that has been lavished on British poets and writers.[6] It could be argued that this neglect is justified. After all, British artists produced no great or seminal work in response to the conflict akin to Auden's "Spain" or Orwell's *Homage to Catalonia*, nor did they generate a statement of solidarity to match *Authors take sides on the Spanish war*. It would be a mistake, however, to dismiss the role played by the British artists. They were as well, if not better, organised politically than their literary counterparts in the later 1930s, and many made significant sacrifices to assist the Spanish Republic. This is not to suggest that all artists were active supporters of the Republic,[7] or that those who were were committed to an equal degree. There was, of course, a spectrum of political engagement, ranging from a general identification with the Republican cause (which might be expressed in, say, the donation of a painting to raise money) to a willingness to devote freely of time, energy and creativity. A handful, of whom Felicia Browne is the best-known example, went as far as volunteering to fight for the Republic.

What is undeniable, however, is that, even within a decade marked by rising political awareness and activism on the part of many British artists, the three years of the civil war stand out clearly. In the words of the Surrealist Julian Trevelyan: "Until the Spanish War started in 1936, there was an air of gentle frivolity about our life in London . . . for the next three years our thoughts and consciences were turned to Spain."[8] The uniqueness of the era of the civil war was underlined by the political confusion and disillusionment that immediately followed it, with the Nazi–Soviet Pact and the "Phoney War". The artist William Townsend wrote to a friend in March 1940 apropos the war with Germany that "the issues seem so complicated, and the world line up so unsatisfactory, that I don't feel involved in the same way as over the Spanish War when what was at stake was unescapably defined".[9]

■ ■ ■ ■ ■ ■

The decade of the 1930s was a difficult time for most British artists, as the private art market dried up and the 1931 devaluation of the pound pushed up the cost of living in traditional havens such as France. According to one contemporary commentator 1937 was the "best year since the trouble at Invergordon [in 1931]" for sales, but auction prices were not yet back to 1927 levels. He described artists as the "most depressed profession in the country".[10] Those who could not rely on private incomes were either forced to take jobs as schoolteachers, to join the rapidly-developing commercial sector (in advertising, illustration and design), or to seek company sponsorship. William Coldstream found a niche with the GPO documentary film unit where he encountered talented young writers and composers such as Wystan Auden and Benjamin Britten. Some even abandoned art for politics: Coldstream commented in 1938 that "two very talented painters who had been at the Slade with me gave up painting altogether, one to work for the ILP, the other for the Communist Party. It was no longer the thing to be an artist delighting in isolation."[11] For the generation of younger artists, born in the first decade of the twentieth century and trained in the 1920s, the 1930s were a time of vulnerability, apprehension and anger. While not all of them joined political parties as a result, many moved sharply to the left. A stereotypical set of views began to emerge: disgust at the damage that capitalism could inflict on the working class through mass unemployment; a fear of German and Italian fascism as a threat not only to democracy, but also to artistic freedom and creativity; and a belief that the basis of a superior civilisation already existed in the Soviet Union. Many young artists visited the USSR in the early 1930s, and were deeply impressed by what they found. A postcard sent home by Ron Horton, for instance, describes the swimming enclosure on the Moscow River in glowing terms: "A vast place full of thousands of magnificent young people – bronzed athletes all. I have never seen such beautiful and healthy young people . . . Already I have seen enough to confirm and strengthen the belief – Communism is the hope of humanity."[12]

The Communist painter and illustrator Clifford Rowe spent 18 months in the Soviet Union in 1932–3, and returned to Britain determined to create a political organisation of artists on Soviet lines. The outcome was the formation of the Artists International – from 1935 known as the Artists International Association (AIA) – which became the principal political organ of British artists in the 1930s.[13] By the time of the Spanish Civil War it had about 600 members, with particularly rapid growth in 1938/9. Among the founders were the designer Misha Black (who became secretary), the illustrator Pearl Binder, and a trio of talented cartoonists and lithographers, all called James, whose work would become well known in *Left Review* – Fitton, Boswell and Holland. The core of the AIA was young, Communist and working in the commercial sector. The Association also offered an arena within which young women artists such as Elizabeth Watson, Nan Youngman and Betty Rea could play an unusually free and significant political role.[14] As initially conceived the association was intended to be a propagandistic, Marxist body committed to the "unity of artists against Imperialist War, War on the Soviet Union, Fascism and Colonial Oppression". From 1935, however, in line with the Comintern's policy of the Popular Front, the AIA was reformulated as a broad-based, anti-fascist organisation. One symptomatic change was the creation of an Advisory Council representing established and far less political artists, such as Augustus John, Vanessa Bell and Paul Nash. The AIA prided itself on being the only organisation that could "include the humblest commercial studio worker on the same terms as the most mature painter of easel pictures".[15] In artistic terms the AIA was highly eclectic, and there was no set style. However, a Soviet-inspired Realism did become increasingly influential, especially once Coldstream, Claude Rogers, Graham Bell and Victor Pasmore had established their "School of Drawing and Painting" (better known as the "Euston Road School") in October 1937.

One significant stylistic rift did, however, open almost at the moment of the outbreak of the Spanish Civil War. Only a month previously, on 11 June 1936, the first International Surrealist exhibition had opened in London. A principal figure within the movement in Britain was Roland Penrose, who had recently returned after living in Paris for thirteen years. The Surrealists' impact within the AIA was generally discordant, and there were a number of heated polemics between the Surrealists and their realist critics. The anarchist Herbert Read commented that "our English Realists are not the tough guys they ought to be, but the effete and bastard offspring of the Bloomsbury school of needlework".[16] For their part, the Surrealists were shocked when the AIA newsletter carried an article about the Second American Artists' Congress which stated that "the bad influences of expressionism, surrealism, futurism and abstractionism are still too much in evidence". The AIA committee felt compelled to issue a statement to the effect that the theory upon which an artist "may base his work, does not affect his status as a member [of the association]".[17] When the two groups clashed in a set piece debate in March 1938 even the realists' supporters had to confess, privately, that their work, "honest to goodness enough and intelligent, looked pretty dull" when compared to the work of the Surrealists.[18] However, this was essentially a debate within the Left, and did not greatly impact on levels of solidarity with Spain. The Surrealists were vocal in their opposition to Franco, and issued a manifesto in 1937 attacking the British government's policy of Non-Intervention.[19]

■ ■ ■ ■ ■ ■ ■

In gauging British artists' initial reactions to the Spanish Civil War, it should be noted that Spain was hardly *terra incognita* for many of them. Indeed, during the inter-war years the quality of the light and landscapes, as well as the low cost of living, had made the Costa Brava, Majorca and Andalusia highly attractive for artists' "colonies". Another attraction was the current vogue for the work of El Greco – regarded as "a sort of honorary godfather of the modern movement"[20] – which drew many British artists to visit Toledo. Henry Moore had travelled extensively in Spain in 1934, and stopped at Toledo en route between the Altamira caves and the museum of Episcopal art in Vic. In 1936 he wrote to friends that: "Of course one would be moved . . . by the happenings in the Spanish revolution, but our trip there makes the picture of it twenty times as vivid."[21] Artists who had recently spent time in Spain included Tristram Hillier and David Bomberg, who had returned to Britain from southern Spain in late 1935 precisely due to the mounting unrest.[22] Edward Burra was deeply affected by his experiences during a third visit to Spain, prior to the outbreak of war, in 1936. He recalled sitting in a restaurant in Madrid:

> Smoke kept blowing by the . . . window. I asked where it came from. 'Oh, its nothing', someone answered with a gesture of impatience, 'its only a church being burnt'. That made me feel sick. It was terrifying: constant strikes, churches on fire, and pent-up hatred everywhere. Everybody knew that something appalling was about to happen.[23]

One artist, George Bergen, who mistimed his departure from Spain, encountered "corpses in the streets" in Barcelona, and found that all of his paintings for an autumn exhibition were now "hopelessly stranded".[24]

Even so, some awoke to the importance of what was happening in Spain more rapidly than others. The Canterbury-based artist William Townsend, whose journal records his tireless efforts on behalf of the Spanish Republic, makes no mention of the civil war until September 1936. By this time Vanessa Bell was commenting that the war was "agitating everyone" and – by November – that many artists seemed "to feel it difficult to attend to their own affairs" as a consequence. But she was also appalled by the barbarity and massacres on both sides that accompanied the conflict. On 22 September she wrote to her son Julian in China that: "Now I feel that the only thing that much matters is that it should not spread – one can't go on being sorry for the wretched

Spaniards themselves – the horrors are far too great and quite as bad on one side as the other." Her only consolation was that "I don't have to reconcile myself to your rushing off to Spain."[25] (Of course, Julian would soon return to Britain, volunteer as an ambulance driver and die at the battle of Brunete in July 1937). Percy Horton, shut away in August 1936 on a farm with the newspapers spread before him, fell into depression that the recent fascist victory in Abyssinia was about to be repeated in Spain. He was far from convinced that the Popular Front could prevail against "the organisation of professional soldiers, legionnaires and help from Germany and Italy". As he wrote to his brother Ron, the Republicans seemed to face quite literally superhuman odds:

> *The Daily Express – the other day – had a poignant photograph of the rebels entering Badajoz. Women were pleading with out-stretched arms. But what struck me most was the enormous height of the rebel soldiers compared with the workers who were being rounded up – and the magnificence of their equipment – steel-trench helmets etc: etc: while the workers had just their ordinary clothes to fight in.*[26]

By the autumn of 1936, therefore, many British artists were broadly sympathetic to the Republican side, and the death of Felicia Browne, who was known to many, personalised and magnified the political impact of the war.[27] The AIA defended the right of artists to take a view on the Civil War, as many of them were "beginning to realise that they cannot shut themselves up in little self-contained worlds of their own".[28] From this perspective, the Republic was worth defending both as a democratic government subjected to fascist assault and as a bastion of culture against fascist philistinism. Much was made of the efforts by the Republicans to save Spain's art treasures in the Prado and elsewhere from aerial attack,[29] as well as the Republic's promotion of education and the arts. As William Hayter, who visited Spain in late 1937, commented: "The Spanish Government is undertaking schemes of modern education far in advance of any popular education in England." The Spanish people were "busy and bustling with a hundred and one cultural activities they were not able to indulge in the old days".[30] An AIA pamphlet of 1938 neatly elided the political and the cultural when it posed the question: "Why does the Spanish Government attract Spain's greatest artists to the cause of the people? Because democracy is not afraid of the truth."[31] The events of the latter years of the conflict simply served to reinforce these sympathies. Above all, the ability of Franco's side – with German and Italian support – to rain down destruction on the cities and civilian populations of the Republic seemed to form part of a horrifying and ugly turn in world events. As William Townsend reported bitterly in his journal for

September 1937: "Yesterday 8000 people were killed in a quarter of an hour by air raids near Canton. The destruction of Guernica, the bombardment of the refugees from Malaga . . . , the massacre at Addis Ababa – the great events of 1937."[32]

Amidst this enthusiasm for the Republic, little concern was expressed in artistic circles about the loss of a substantial amount of religious art during the church-burnings that occurred on the Republican side in the early months of the Civil War. Even the museum in Vic, which Moore had recently visited, only narrowly escaped destruction. In part, this was because British artists had already sided politically with the Republic. However, one can also detect an underlying awkwardness as to how they should relate to Spanish religious art (especially of the Baroque) and to modern Catalan architecture. (Gaudi's Sagrada Familia was frequently described by British intellectuals as the one Catalan religious building that *should* have been destroyed![33]) The British artist who engaged most directly with this question was Roland Penrose, who spent more than seven weeks in Spain in late 1936 investigating, amongst other things, the fate of Catalan religious art. He subsequently published a report with the French art expert Christian Zervos which concluded that less than 2 per cent of the artistic patrimony of Catalonia had been lost, while a substantially greater amount of art was now in public hands and open to view. That which was lost was often the "gilded shame" of the Baroque. Catalonia had, therefore, provided a successful experiment: "At last an opportunity had occurred of determining the direct reactions of the masses to works of art after the restraint of authority had been removed."[34] Penrose later recalled, however, that one episode did "challenge my hope that all was well", when he visited Picasso's mother, along with the Spanish artist's two brothers and sister:

> the old lady took us to a window at the back saying: 'Its only today that I have been able to open this after so many days when the smoke and stench, from the convent over there that had been set on fire, nearly asphyxiated us all'. This proof of violence and confusion so close at hand was disquieting, but in spite of it the flamenco music from the guitars of the two young painters renewed the heartbeat of Spain, passionate and steadfast.[35]

Although, Penrose had actually formed his own judgment, unlike so many who pontificated on this question, he clearly had had to suppress some doubts along the way.

As artists pondered how to respond to the shocking events of the Civil War a wider issue loomed: what should the political role of the artist be, both in general and in these specific circumstances? On 12

August 1936 Eric Ravilious wrote to his lover Helen Binyon that: "We can pledge ourselves to fight in the event of a class war here like the one in Spain . . . More to the point, we can assist by design and drawings for the rather bad leaflets and such that are produced and this I mean to do if I can later."[36] An interesting correspondence in the papers of William Coldstream also discusses this question. Coldstream had witnessed the departure of Auden for Spain —ostensibly to drive an ambulance – in January 1937 looking "most sinister in a Teddy Bear coat, cloth cap and glasses".[37] He had come to know Auden well in recent months. The poet had stayed with Coldstream's family, and was said to have horrified his younger sister by delivering a harangue to the trees in the back garden on the subject of Spain. Coldstream subsequently engaged in an exchange of letters with his friend Dr John Rake who disapproved of Auden contemplating "throw[ing] away his life in Spain". Coldstream's response was that: "You must not be depressed by people like him [Auden] going to Spain. I talked for hours with him over it . . . Thank God he will never be a fanatic anyway . . . Poets are all such good characters and so responsible. Painters are mostly bad characters and without principles so perhaps I have a chance."[38] Quite separately, William Townsend shared Rake's view that Auden was mistaken in going to Spain: "As man power he is only one unit, but as a voice for the cause he is thousands (sic) and it would be a fearful loss if he were killed."[39]

Apart from Felicia Browne, who was already in Spain when the conflict erupted, there was no sign of well-known artists flocking to Spain, either as volunteers, non-combatants or observers, in the fashion of many writers. There were a few prominent cases of artists joining the International Brigades. For instance, the cartoonist W. D. Rowney ("Maro"), who had trained at Sandhurst and served in the Indian army, died in action in early 1937.[40] Clive Branson, who had trained at the Slade in the 1920s, was captured and imprisoned in a Nationalist jail in 1938 (where he continued to sketch assiduously).[41] Wogan Philipps volunteered as a driver for Spanish Medical Aid and featured anonymously in one newspaper report as a "Welsh landscape painter . . . helping with the anaesthetic".[42] However, although he confided that "sometimes I long & long to paint", such creative energies as he could spare were confined to writing rather than art.[43] Philipps, who was promoted to the rank of sergeant at the Jarama, was wounded at Brunete in July 1937. The career of the young sculptor Jason Gurney was prematurely ended when he was shot in the hand by an explosive bullet.[44] Others were spared by their youth. Paul Hogarth left art school to volunteer, aged only 17, on deciding that "Spain's future seemed much more important than my own". However, although he was allowed to join the International Brigades, he was soon repatriated.[45] Likewise, the 15 year old Michael Ayrton appears to have got as far as Spain in a bid to volunteer before being recalled by his redoubtable mother, the Labour politician Barbara Ayrton Gould.[46] The sculptor Kanty Cooper, a former pupil of Henry Moore, spoke some Spanish and briefly worked with Basque refugee children in Britain. She later served for a year in a relief mission in Barcelona, 1938–9, after acute neuritis ended her sculpting career.[47]

Given that the option of joining the International Brigades was attractive to only a few British artists, in what ways did they seek to mobilise art on behalf of the Republican cause? One obvious possibility was to raise funds through the sale of donated paintings. Indeed, the AIA had raised enough money by this means to send a lorry full of medical supplies to the British Battalion on 15 January 1937.[48] A diverse group of artists contributed to an exhibition organised by the Chelsea Branch of Spanish Medical Aid at Whistler's House in June 1937. Contributors included Sir Muirhead Bone – who had strong Spanish connections – Sir John Lavery, Moholy Nagy and Ben Nicholson. The event was also supported by three generations of the Pissarro family. However, a cynical *Times* correspondent pointed out that the works displayed lacked any engagement with the cause that they were supporting, and that the exhibition might as well have been for "distressed Ruritanian agriculturists".[49]

In 1938 an ambitious "Portraits for Spain" scheme was established under which well-known artists would accept commissions and give the funds to the purchase of an "Artists Ambulance". Over one hundred commissions were offered, ranging from oil paintings to lithographs, and even the concrete sculptures of Peter Peri. The most expensive was Augustus John (who offered a "head and shoulders" portrait for 500 guineas), while Eric Gill and Henry Moore both offered far more modestly priced drawings. The Cambridge studio of Helen Muspratt, who had taken the iconic photograph of John Cornford shortly before his departure for Spain, offered a portrait for 25 shillings.[50] The Augustus John commission was discreetly purchased by the Cadbury family. George W. Cadbury wrote in January 1939 – even before his father had sat for John – that: "As the need for Spanish relief is so urgent I enclose a cheque for £500 now and will take steps at a later date to recover it from the Board of Directors."[51] Likewise, Ravilious accepted a commission from Lord Faringdon to paint a watercolour of his home at Buscot Park for ten guineas.[52]

The second sphere in which artists had a distinctive contribution to make was that of protest and demonstration. The AIA had its own "Peace Propaganda Bureau" which worked to enliven placards and decorate meeting halls. For this reason many felt that the Spanish demonstrations were both innovative and markedly superior in their design and execution.[53] At a Trafalgar Square demonstration to mark the second anniversary of the Civil War, for instance, AIA artists sketched the rally. The posters were later sold or sent on tour.[54] Some contributions were perhaps overly distinctive, such as the Surrealist contingent at the 1938 May Day rally in London. As Julian Trevelyan describes it a loudspeaker van blared out Spanish Republican records while inside there was a cage in which hung a skeleton. "Next came an ice-cream tricycle on to which we had rigged a superstructure of wire-netting culminating in a great white horse's head. Inside the wire-netting were coloured balloons." Trevelyan, Penrose and two others equipped with Neville Chamberlain masks designed by F. E. McWilliam, top hats and umbrellas then marched along shouting "Chamberlain must go."[55]

The AIA organised a number of more formal rallies and demonstrations during the civil war, as well as a cabaret in March 1938 involving Auden and Britten. The high point was undoubtedly the "Spain and Culture" rally at the Albert Hall in June 1937. Picasso gave his personal backing after a visit from the young Quentin Bell, but in the event he did not attend as he was by now working flat-out to finish "Guernica". There is a vivid account of the meeting in the journals of William Townsend,[56] who commented that, in the absence of Picasso, the singer "Paul Robeson was the great man of the evening". Robeson had told the audience that "the battle front is everywhere . . . and every artist must take his stand on one side or the other". There was also a typically productive appeal by Isabel Brown, the leading Republican fundraiser, which generated £1500.[57] But interestingly Townsend noted that even she could not sell the drawing that Picasso had contributed – "a recondite little piece of metaphysical abstraction, for which the highest bid was £80".[58] Even so, Townsend was electrified by the speeches and the enthusiasm of the audience: "I felt happy to have had the chance of being for once where I could feel in the centre of the conflict instead of hovering coldly at the circumference, with so much less hope." This final comment is poignant, as Townsend had been a student at the Slade in the 1920s but had failed to establish himself as an independent artist. By the late 1930s he was working in his father's dental practice in Canterbury and seeking work as an illustrator – a period which he saw as his melancholic "exile".

There were a number of AIA protests during the final months of the Civil War. The first was the idea of the young South African Graham Bell, who was emerging as one of the most politically aware and militant artists of his generation. For instance, his "Red, White and Blue" was deemed shocking for its depiction of police violence during a demonstration – one of the policemen had a Hitler-like face.[59] In January 1939 Bell enlisted his friends to paint a series of 7 feet × 4.6 banners based on Goya's "Disasters of War", which could then be taken on demonstrations. The banners were punctuated with slogans such as "Spanish Agony", "Chamberlain, Hitler, Mussolini and Franco are doing this to Spain" and "Is there nothing we can do?" Bell reported the power of these banners in a letter to his mother: "we had them hanging on the wall in the art school and a model posing had to look more or less at one of them. After half an hour she burst into tears and was inconsolable."[60] But at least one of the artists who took part, Geoffrey Tibble, did so with little prospect of success: "its fun working on that scale. I may be a pessimist but it seems a bit late in the day now to hope to alter things in Spain now. What a tragedy."[61] The banners were deployed at an "Arms for Spain" rally in Trafalgar Square on 12 February 1939, and "punctuated" the AIA's Whitechapel Art Gallery exhibition "as a broken frieze".[62] Sadly, if somewhat comically, the banners were seized from the home of the artist Rodrigo Moynihan by the Home Guard during the war as subversive material, and subsequently lost.[63] In February 1939 the London County Council made 22 bill board sites available to the AIA to produce posters appealing for food for Spain. These giant hoardings were worked on by teams of artists – as many as 90 took part – who were watched by interested crowds. A number of the posters were subsequently vandalised by British fascists.[64]

While the more radical artists deepened their activism as the war progressed, signs of frustration and war-weariness were also evident. Myfanwy Evans published a collection of essays by leading artists in 1937, in which she offered a telling list of the various battle lines that were distracting artists from their true calling:

> *Left, right, black, red . . . Hampstead, Bloomsbury, surrealist, abstract, social realist, Spain, Germany, Heaven, Hell, Paradise, Chaos, light, dark, round, square.*[65]

Even Graham Bell, that most "intensely partisan" and committed of the young artists, complained to his mother while working on the Goyas that he was "getting involved in bypaths and sidelines organising, talking writing letters doing propaganda and so on".[66] Another interesting response comes from an April 1938 letter from William Coldstream, indicating the sheer cumulative horror of the conflicts of the 1930s:

> *I wonder how long one must live with this nightmare of war and whether we shall even be able to cultivate our gardens – I feel sure the Marxist analysis is the nearest to the truth . . . but even so all politics are abominable – everyone is to be asked to kill in order to save . . . Someone from Madrid told me that all through the war people there had gone on planting seeds in their window boxes, some of them to flower a long time ahead – I don't think it sentimental to admire that – it is a very good thing and makes one believe that life will always have the possibility of being worth living.*[67]

It seemed a slender straw to grasp at.

While there is considerable evidence that the Spanish Civil War inspired the political and humanitarian passions of many British artists, to what extent did it inspire their creativity? At first sight, it appears that the body of work produced was so small that there is little to analyse. To some extent, however, this is because no systematic attempt has been made to catalogue it. There is, for instance, no equivalent to Valentine Cunningham's collections of Civil War verse and prose which have done so much – especially with regard to poetry – to create a canon of accessible texts.[68] Much that was produced has not survived, such as Bell's Goyas, or was essentially ephemeral, such as Felicity Ashbee's posters for the NJCSR.[69] Some survives quite literally in the margins, such as Ewan Phillips's doodled caricatures of the Duchess of Atholl and other participants at a Spanish aid rally.[70] One piece that has endured, the fairly indestructible 1939 concrete relief "Save Spain" by the refugee artist Peter Peri, is now in a museum in Bochum. Any complete record of the British artistic response to the civil war would have to include not only paintings, sketches, murals[71] and photographs but also cartoons, banners, posters, and even the puppet plays of the Binyon sisters, performed in July 1938 to the music of Benjamin Britten.[72] All this suggests that artists' work on behalf of the Republic was often both public and collaborative. Hence, the banner presented to the British Battalion by AIA members was designed by James Lucas, embroidered by Phyllis Landyman, and its pole carved by Betty Rea.[73] Other responses were intensely personal, such as Roland Penrose's poem written, in pencil, on the fall of Barcelona in January 1939. "Mentiras" ("Lies"), which does not appear to have been written for publication and has not been anthologised, celebrates

Penrose's memory of "a city strong in hope/that defied the world/slew its pious gaolers".[74]

Even if this scattered and diverse body of work were ever to be fully catalogued, it would probably still appear somewhat slight. This partly reflects the fact that serious art requires the right conditions. Many of these artists, struggling to make a living from portraits and illustrations, lacked the time and resources to respond more expansively to the civil war. Meanwhile, more senior artists were busily exploring new styles and materials which did not necessarily lend themselves to political expression. For others, the creative inspiration of the Civil War might take indirect forms, or take years to come to fruition – if at all. Henry Moore is an interesting case in point. He clearly felt passionately about the Republican cause. Indeed, he was poised to join a delegation of cultural luminaries on a visit to Republican Spain in early 1938, but the party was denied visas by the British government.[75] In general, he appears to have been happy to sign manifestos and letters to the press, although he did provide a 1939 charcoal entitled "Spanish Prisoner". This was a sketch for a lithograph intended to raise funds for Republican soldiers interned in France at the end of the war.[76] However, as Moore explained to Penrose in October 1939:

I'm sorry there are no good proofs of the lithograph I started for Spain. I only got as far as making 4 or 5 very rough trial prints, with the idea of me working on them to know what differences to make on each of the stones, when we all got back to London at the end of the summer. The rough prints are stuck up in a row on the wall here at the cottage, and there's plenty I now think I could do, if ever the work on the stones could be finished. They're at Camberwell School of Art, which is closed – and anyhow as you say, there are no longer any funds to pay the printer, so there's nothing to be done about it at present. But if there's a chance sometime I may go on with it just for my own fun and instruction.[77]

It is noteworthy that Moore's most committed piece of work in response to the Civil War was also highly innovative: this was his first lithograph, and the theme of the enclosed figure was one which he would return to and develop in the future.[78] Edward Burra provides another interesting case. He told John Rothenstein that he was "haunted by the Spanish Civil War, and obsessed by Spanish civilisation", and this is clearly reflected in his painting both during and after the late 1930s. However, his feelings about the conflict were far too complex to allow him to take a political position on it. Above all, his respect for order and horror of church-burning clashed with his distaste for Franco's arrogance.[79]

The most interesting body of work by a British artist in response to the Civil War – that of the engraver William Hayter – has been largely ignored, possibly because he was based in Paris and not closely involved with the AIA. Hayter had established Atelier 17 in 1927, soon after his arrival in the French capital. He was associated with the Surrealists during the 1930s and was a close friend of the poet Paul Eluard. Hayter was committed to the Republican cause, and organised two "portfolios" of work by prominent artists and poets (including Miró, Picasso and Spender) to raise funds. Moreover, he visited Spain at the invitation of the Spanish director-general of fine arts, and spent four months there from September 1937 sketching and painting prisons, trenches, batteries and schools. On his return he exhibited his work at the Mayor Gallery in London in February 1938. The exhibition received somewhat grudging praise from the *Daily Worker* which noted that, while Hayter's Surrealist style "may not appeal to everyone", this work was "vigorous and disciplined and grows on one". [80] Hayter also appears to have facilitated visits to Spain for other artists. [81] The Civil War found expression in his more substantial work. For instance, "Combat", his largest plate of the 1930s, expresses his horror of war. He made the first sketches in April 1936, but the plate itself was not completed until December: as he told a friend in 1941, "it was sort of prophetic, as the Spanish war started in July that year". [82] His pro-Republican sympathies surely lay behind his decision in 1937 to accept a major commission of five plates to illustrate Cervantes' play *Numancia*, although in the event only four had been completed when the patron died in 1939. [83] Hayter was also drawn into the bitter political divisions within French Surrealism. In November 1938 he wrote that he had fallen out with André Breton and his friends as "since his interview with Trotsky Breton is anti-Stalin to the exclusion of any other activity".

> *Their attitude about Spain provoked the las[t] row I had with them. One of the bastards tried to put a crimp in my collection for the Spanish children by suggesting to the perso[n] that the money would not go to the kids but to the people who were persecuting their friends the POUM.* [84]

In any case, it is trite to expect artists to make instant artistic responses to political events. "Guernica" has endured precisely because Picasso refused to make it a work of propaganda. (Indeed, many on the Republican side were annoyed that the responsibility of the German bombers was not specifically identified.) Picasso's later, more overtly political, work during the Cold War lacked "Guernica's" emotional power. Penrose made this point at the AIA Congress in April 1937, when he warned that the *"weapon of propaganda"* could be disastrous for the artist, as would a *"dictatorship of taste"*. *"Liberty of thought and expression"*, he continued, *"are essential*. For these things [the artist] will fight when they are menaced, even, as in Spain today, by offering his *life*."[85]

■ ■ ■ ■ ■ ■ ■

Penrose's comment was prophetic. Within a few years of the end of the Civil War a number of the artists discussed in this chapter were dead: Graham Bell and Clive Branson fell on active service in the British armed forces, and Ravilious while working as a war artist. Others were denied the opportunity to fight: for instance, Paul Hogarth claimed that he was discharged from the army precisely because he knew how to strip and assemble a Lewis gun, thus betraying his International Brigade training.[86] Like many other artists he then gravitated towards working in camouflage.

It would be wrong, however, to see the events of 1936–39 merely as a prelude to this larger conflict. A swathe of British artists responded generously to the plight of the Spanish Republic and believed in its ultimate victory. During almost three years of civil war they worked, above all through the AIA, to raise funds and to put pressure on the British government to change its policy. They used their creativity in innovative but frustratingly ephemeral ways. They felt the defeat of the Republic very deeply – David Bomberg, for instance, was "mortified" by the infighting that overtook the defenders of Madrid in the closing days of the Civil War.[87] The last word should go to William Townsend, who encapsulated this tenacious support for the Republic during his "exile" in Kent. He cajoled his friends not to support Non-Intervention, he briefed himself by reading the constant stream of books on the Civil War, he wrote tirelessly to the local newspapers, and he organised countless local meetings. On 6 April 1939, just after the end of the war, he had been asked to speak to the local Labour Party about the cultural achievements of the Republic. But he confided to his journal that: "it is something unspeakably sad to think about – the wonderful attempt to advance on all fronts, to teach people not just to read, but to read and love the best, to make it possible by printing those cheap editions of Lorca and others for them; the exhibitions, the libraries, the new schools in the stress of war and starvation and poverty and betrayal. Salud!"

Chapter 6

The death of Bob Smillie, the Spanish Civil War, and the eclipse of the Independent Labour Party

Smillie's death is not a thing I can easily forgive. Here was this brave and gifted boy, who had thrown up his career at Glasgow University in order to come and fight against Fascism, and who, as I saw for myself, had done his job at the front with faultless courage and willingness; and all they could find to do with him was to fling him into jail and let him die like a neglected animal. I know that in the middle of a huge and bloody war it is no use making too much fuss over an individual death . . . But what angers one about a death like this is its utter pointlessness.

(George Orwell, *Homage to Catalonia*)[1]

Like George Orwell, Bob Smillie was a volunteer for the Independent Labour Party (ILP) military contingent in the Spanish Civil War, who died while held in detention by the Spanish Republican authorities in June 1937. Orwell's oft quoted remarks on Smillie's death leave no doubt that this was an event with significant political overtones, as well as a personal tragedy for Smillie's family and friends. Indeed, the tone of bewilderment in Orwell's account has been echoed by his biographers, all of whom treat the death as an unresolved mystery. For Peter Stansky and William Abrahams, Smillie was "possibly murdered by the Communists and certainly ill-treated by them" while in captivity.[2] For Bernard Crick, whether Bob Smillie died "from acute appendicitis or [was] murdered by the Communists has never been cleared up".[3] For Michael Shelden, Smillie died "supposedly of appendicitis".[4]

Inaccuracies and contradictions abound in all published accounts of the episode.[5]

In fact, this degree of uncertainty ought to have been unnecessary. The ILP had a representative in Valencia, David Murray, for most of the duration of Smillie's imprisonment, and he was able to carry out a thorough investigation into the events surrounding the young volunteer's detention and death. Murray's extensive file on the case provided the core of the subsequent official ILP report, and helped to form the party's political and emotional response more broadly. These papers, now deposited in the National Library of Scotland, constitute a most valuable collection of documentary evidence on the death of Bob Smillie and, indeed, are the only primary source that views these events from the perspective of the ILP. Accordingly, this chapter, the first to draw on Murray's papers, has two distinct aims. First, it reconstructs the events surrounding Smillie's death as established by David Murray. Although it does not attempt a comprehensive re-investigation of the case, it does offer a corrective to the many erroneous accounts that have been published. Secondly, perhaps the real significance of the Murray archive is that it allows unique insight into the ILP's reaction to Smillie's death and offers powerful evidence of the party's desire to minimize the political impact of the case in Britain. The Murray papers give clear evidence that, despite inconsistencies in the official account, the ILP leaders allowed themselves to believe that Smillie's death was a tragic accident rather than risking the uncertainties of turning his death into a political *cause célèbre*.

An analysis of the events surrounding the death of Bob Smillie is not only of importance in its own right, but also offers valuable insights into the political position of the ILP in the later 1930s. Although at this time it was a party in decline, with a collapsing membership and organisational structure, the ILP did not feel itself to be a marginal force in British politics. Cushioned by a well-respected parliamentary presence, by a strong geographical basis of support (especially in Scotland) and by a deep sense of tradition, the ILP was still at the outbreak of the Spanish Civil War a self-confident and avowedly independent political agent. The events associated with the Civil War, of which Smillie's death was the most personally painful for the ILP leadership, did much to undermine that independence. Although the case of Bob Smillie cannot be construed as marking a turning point in ILP politics, the nature of the ILP's response to the death of one so full of youthful promise, bearing a name so redolent of ILP tradition, and in such circumstances, can be seen as symbolic of the political *cul-de-sac* which it had entered in the late 1930s, and of its eclipse as a significant force in British politics.

Twenty-year old Bob Smillie set off for Spain in October 1936, to work in a Barcelona armaments factory, some three months after the outbreak of the Civil War. He came from a staunchly political family. His grandfather, Robert Smillie, was born in Belfast in 1857 and moved to Glasgow at the age of fifteen to work in engineering factories. He later went in search of work to the mining village of Larkhall, south of Glasgow in Lanarkshire, and rose to become a famous coal miners' leader and Labour party MP.[6] The family continued to live in Larkhall where Bob Smillie's father Alex, who became a farmer, was a leading local member of the ILP. Thus, despite his youth, Bob Smillie was steeped in the politics of the ILP, and, already at his death, was chairman of the party's Guild of Youth. An ILP memorial pamphlet stressed his revolutionary socialist politics and complete involvement in the great political issues of the day, such as the 1935 "Great Scottish Hunger March" against the new unemployment benefit regulations. Although from a semi-rural background, he had already seen enough poverty in Glasgow and the Scottish coalfields to be well-known as a confirmed socialist "rebel against Capitalist Society" who, in the words of Dan McArthur, knew "the utter vileness of modern society".[7] Apart from being an exemplary young socialist, other tributes recall an exceedingly impressive and likeable young man, who forged strong personal friendships with his older colleagues both in Barcelona and on the front-line.[8]

Once in Spain, the plan to establish a factory for gun cotton fell through.[9] Smillie, however, stayed on to represent the International Revolutionary Youth Bureau (IRYB) and to work as an assistant to John McNair, who was running the ILP office in Barcelona. In January 1937 the ILP's military contingent arrived in Barcelona and Smillie joined as it set off for the front line outside Huesca in Aragon.[10] The 25-man unit was assigned to the 3rd Regiment of the Lenin Division, under the political control of the POUM (*Partido Obrero de Unificación Marxista*/Workers' Party of Marxist Unity), the Spanish "brother-party"[11] of the ILP. Smillie distinguished himself at the front. A letter from the commanding officer George Kopp paid tribute to the "splendid action of Eric Blair [George Orwell], Bob Smillie and Paddy Donovan" during an "audacious raid" on enemy lines on 13 April.[12] On 25 April the contingent went on leave to Barcelona. At the request of the ILP, Smillie obtained the consent of his superiors to travel on to Paris for a meeting of the IRYB, and then to tour Britain giving a series of lectures on Spain for the Guild of Youth.[13] However, he was picked up at Figueres on the French frontier by the Spanish police, and imprisoned in Valencia. Although he was arrested for not possessing papers – and, thus, as a possible deserter – Smillie's arrest and detention was also due to the shifting political balance within Republican Spain, and the increasing marginalization of the POUM (and, accordingly, of the ILP itself) within Spanish politics. It is, therefore, important to establish these contexts before looking at the details of the case.

The POUM was one of the political groups that had benefited from the revolutionary situation created by the military rebellion against the Popular Front government in July 1936.[14] The military rebels in Barcelona were defeated by the Anarchist-led working class, supported by the POUM. In the aftermath of the coup's collapse Luis Companys, the leader of the mainstream party of Catalan nationalism (the Esquerra), was allowed to remain in charge of the government, but real power was exercised on the streets by the Anarchists and their allies. Initially the POUM was represented on the Anarchist-dominated Anti-Fascist Militia Committee, and in October Andres Nin, one of the POUM's leaders, entered the Catalan government as Minister of Justice. The POUM rapidly grew in size in these months, from some 6,000 members in July 1936 to an estimated 30–40,000 by the end of the year.[15]

By the time of Bob Smillie's arrival in Catalonia strong tensions were, however, evident concerning the question of how far the social revolution should be allowed to proceed. The Communists, who lacked a strong political base in the Catalan working class, called for a halt to the revolution, at least until the war against the rebels had been won. In the meantime, they argued, the Spanish Republic should consolidate its position as a reforming, but visibly democratic and parliamentary, regime. In practice, the Communists became the leaders of the discontented Catalan middle classes, who feared revolutionary expropriations and arbitrary Anarchist justice. In a rapidly developing campaign against the revolutionary forces, Nin was sacked from the Catalan government in December 1936. In reply to the Communists and their allies, the Anarchists and POUM argued for a revolutionary war against the rebels, and stated that the war and the revolution were inseparable. Smillie strongly endorsed this outlook, seeing the war not as a conflict between "Capitalist-Democracy" and fascism, but as one that pitted the Spanish working class against the twin enemies of fascism and international capitalism. In a letter of 22 December 1936 he made clear his rejection of the Communist party line, writing that the POUM's youth section stood for "Social Revolution and *not* for the Democratic Revolution".[16] However, he also believed, perhaps optimistically, that political differences on the left would disappear in the struggle against fascism, and that there was "unity in the trenches".[17]

Parallel to this debate on the future of the revolution was the question of Catalan autonomy, an important consideration to the overwhelmingly Scottish leadership of the ILP who felt a particular affinity for the Catalans.[18] The initial success of the revolutionary forces had made Catalonia virtually independent of the central government located in Madrid (until October, when it moved to Valencia). However, as the war turned into a prolonged conflict in the autumn of 1936, the scope for autonomy shrank. In particular, the decision of the Soviet Union to send substantial military aid to the Republic in October 1936 placed considerable power in the hands of the Spanish Communist party which favoured a centralised state under its own influence. A widespread suspicion developed in Catalonia that military aid was being deliberately withheld or channelled to reliable Communist units and sectors of the front. The authority of the central government was deliberately flouted in Barcelona, increasing the pressure for an assertion of Valencia's will.

These tensions came to a head on 3 May 1937, when symbolic action by the police to retake control of the Barcelona telephone exchange resulted in four days of street-fighting between the authorities and the Anarchist and POUM militias. The international volunteers, as Orwell's *Homage to Catalonia* grimly recalls, were bemused onlookers to this fratricidal conflict. Like Orwell, Bob Smillie found himself in the POUM headquarters, and his role in defending the building was (perhaps ill-advisedly) made public in an article by John McNair published in Britain on 21 May.[19] By the time that the young man set off for France the Anarchist leaders had capitulated and reined in their more extreme followers. Catalonia's autonomy was virtually at an end, and significantly for Smillie, the central government had taken control of guarding the frontier.

The POUM was a recently established party – created in September 1935 as an amalgam of two anti-Stalinist and predominantly Catalan-based groups, the *Izquierda Comunista Española* (Spanish Communist Left) and the *Bloc Obrer I Camperol* (Workers' and Peasants' Bloc). It was frequently, and incorrectly, identified as a "Trotskyist" party. Admittedly, Andres Nin had previously acted as Trotsky's secretary, but by the time of the Civil War Trotsky was, in fact, intensely critical of the POUM's political stance. He had bitterly attacked the POUM's decision to join the anti-fascist Popular Front.[20] The POUM was attractive to the ILP not so much on grounds of political tactics (the POUM was genuinely revolutionary whereas the ILP was only rhetorically so), but rather due to its political position, as a party which rejected both the dictatorial and bureaucratic tendencies of Stalinism and the parliamentarism of mainstream socialism. In this sense the two parties had much in common – in 1936 both were small and marginal to left-wing politics.

This had not always been the case for the ILP. The party had been founded in 1893 and had formed the socialist kernel of the future Labour party when the Labour Representation Committee was established in 1900. Initially, membership of the ILP was the main route for socialists into the Labour party. The position of the ILP was, however, transformed by two developments. First, the new Labour party constitution of 1918 opened the way for individual party membership, and, thus, took away much of the ILP's *raison d'être*. Secondly, the formation of two minority Labour governments in the 1920s placed new strains on relations between the Labour party and what was increasingly a left-wing "party within a party", as the ILP advanced policies far more radical than Labour was able to implement when in office. The 1931 political crisis, when the second Labour government collapsed and Prime Minister Ramsay MacDonald formed a "National Government" with the Conservatives and Liberals, merely confirmed the view of left-wing ILP members that Labour party reformism would end in disaster. In July 1932 a Special Conference voted for disaffiliation and the resumption of the ILP's political independence.

Following disaffiliation, the ILP presented itself as a revolutionary socialist party. A July 1933 policy document committed it to agitation in order to "stimulate the mind of the workers for their revolutionary task", and to the establishment of Workers' Councils to "act for the workers in a revolutionary crisis".[21] However, while placing itself firmly within the Leninist revolutionary tradition, the ILP refused to adopt the Leninist party discipline of democratic centralism. Moreover, the real effects of disaffiliation were fatal for its ambitions to offer a revolutionary alternative to the Labour party. Membership plummeted from 16,773 in 1932 to 4,392 in 1935, as many members remained with the Labour party, joined the Communists, or established their own political groupings. The number of branches fell from 353 in 1934 to 284 in 1935[22], with the party retreating into its traditional strongholds, above all Scotland. At the 1935 election the ILP stood 17 candidates and won four seats, all in Glasgow.[23]

The survival of an ILP parliamentary presence, led by the widely respected James Maxton, gave the party a national visibility, but the most important consideration for a "revolutionary" party remained its relations with other parties on the left. Here, the attitude of the Communist Party of Great Britain (CPGB) was deeply ambivalent. It saw the ILP as a source of potential recruits, and hoped that the two parties would eventually merge. From 1933 they worked uneasily together for a United Front of socialist parties against fascism. However, as the ILP was moving to the left, the CPGB from 1935 began to look to a Popular Front of all anti-fascist bodies, including non-socialists, embarking on an expansion of membership that would leave it far larger than the ILP by the end of the decade. Wide divisions of policy and ideology continued to separate the two parties. For instance, the ILP completely opposed government rear-mament policies, and, although no longer dominated by pacifists, it remained committed to all-out resistance to war. While highly respectful towards the Soviet Union as the first "Workers' State", the ILP was often critical of Soviet foreign policy, and made no secret of its concern at the Moscow show trials which began in June 1936. These differences under-mined the "Unity Campaign" of the ILP, the CPGB and the Socialist League (a Labour party faction containing many former ILP members) which was launched in January 1937, even before the Labour party dealt the fatal blow by disaffiliating the Socialist League. In practice, the ILP and the CPGB had been able to agree only on short-term tactics, but not on broader strategy. When Bob Smillie was still in the trenches above Huesca, the ILP conference, while remaining loyal to the idea of "unity" rejected the Communist strategy of the Popular Front in favour of a federally-organized "Workers' Front of Socialist Parties".[24]

By this point the Spanish Civil War had already further complicated relations between the ILP and the CPGB. Like the Communist party, though for different reasons, the Civil War presented the ILP with polit-ical opportunities. The ILP saw in the successful revolutionary resistance to Spanish "fascism" the key to similar action in Britain, and praised the POUM for organising workers' "soviets".[25] For the Communists, however, the lesson of the Civil War was the success of the Popular Front against fascism, and the need for ever-wider circles of alliance with anti-fascist forces on the centre – and, indeed, right – of the political spectrum. Thus, the Civil War was bound to cause disruption to the close (but strained) relations between the two parties. ILP criticism of the Moscow trials had already resulted in a warning from the leading Communist Robin Page Arnot that "the ILP is in grave danger of falling into the hands of Trotskyists, and becoming a wing of fascism".[26] The May 1937 fighting in Barcelona had resulted in a spate of vitriolic attacks by the CPGB on the POUM, as well as on the ILP.

Significantly, the Communist attack on the ILP did not immediately follow the Barcelona fighting, but rather was triggered by the dissolution of the Socialist League on 17 May, which spelt the effective end of the Unity Campaign. On 22 May the Communist party's *Daily Worker* contained two inflammatory attacks on the ILP. An article by J. R. Campbell, starkly headlined "Is the ILP for winning the war or for aiding

Franco?", argued that the POUM and the ILP had "eternally disgraced themselves" by backing the "anarchist uncontrollables" in Barcelona against a sincere attempt to make the Catalan war effort more efficient. Rajani Palme Dutt, in the same issue, wrote that Trotskyism was the "armed ally of Franco", and stressed the "shame" of ILP volunteers being deployed against the legitimate government – "i.e. on the same side as Franco". A week later, at the 14th Congress of the CPGB, an emergency resolution condemned ILP support for the POUM. General Secretary Harry Pollitt appealed to the ILP rank and file over the heads of their leaders, whose support for the POUM and opposition to the Popular Front was "a big stumbling block to the more effective development of the Unity Campaign".[27]

At a local level, a particularly ingenious leaflet issued by the Glasgow Committee of the CPGB attacked the "criminal acts" of "groups of people armed to the teeth" in Spain, adding that "to this category belongs the POUM . . . supported, aided and defended by leading members of the ILP". A parallel was then drawn:

> *Suppose the Mosley Blackshirts were in control of the South-side of Glasgow . . .*
> *and the North-side was occupied by a Popular Municipal Council with the support*
> *of the great mass of the people, resolutely determined not only to prevent the*
> *Blackshirts from crossing the Clyde, but to advance and drive them out of the city.*

What would happen if the ILP, having "failed to play its part in the fight and retained their weapons in their homes and premises", then rebelled against the Popular Council in Bridgeton and Shettleston (ILP strongholds)? "Would it matter what the slogans of the revolt were?"[28] Although the ILP was not attacked directly, leading figures such as John McNair were clearly identified as aiding and abetting the POUM.

Bob Smillie's death occurred, therefore, at a moment of particular tension in the disaffiliated history of the ILP, and of its relations with Communism. The Barcelona fighting marked a turning point in the internal politics of the Spanish Republic, with the tide now running heavily against the Anarchists and the POUM. This had important consequences in Britain where the Communist party, no longer encumbered by the failed Unity campaign, felt free to deal much more aggressively with its critics in the ILP. The ILP, which throughout the 1930s remained true to its anti-war and anti-capitalist beliefs, found itself running out of potential allies. Ineluctably, it was being squeezed between a recuperating (but increasingly, in its view, right-wing) Labour party and an opportunistic and assertive Communist party.

David Murray, a Scottish freelance journalist and businessman from Motherwell, arrived in Barcelona on 14 May 1937 on a private business venture.[29] Immediately upon his arrival he became caught up in the case of Bob Smillie, who had been able to send a note to John McNair on 12 May to notify him of his imprisonment in Valencia's Modelo prison. It was decided that Murray should go to Valencia instead of McNair for three good reasons – first, he was a family friend of the Smillies; secondly, although an ILP member, his presence would be less "political" than McNair's; and thirdly, he spoke excellent Spanish. Murray was in many ways a remarkable man. Although a self-proclaimed "revolutionary", he had an immense capacity for establishing good relations with people from all backgrounds, ranging from Scottish socialists to Spanish businessmen. He was also a genuine internationalist, who regularly travelled abroad, spoke French and Spanish, and (as his archive files attest) had a peculiar capacity to make long-standing friendships in many different countries. Although he was also subject to bigotries (for instance, like many contemporaries on the left, he was blindly anti-Catholic), Murray was clearly well-equipped to act on Smillie's behalf. While he failed to procure Smillie's release, Murray certainly determined the manner in which the case was handled politically both before and after his death. Although the ILP General Secretary Archibald Fenner Brockway visited Spain and made inquiries soon after Smillie's death, Murray was the only ILP member who had both spoken to Smillie in jail and was able to carry out an immediate and thorough investigation. Moreover, from a surprisingly early stage in Smillie's detention he adopted the view that the actions of the Spanish authorities were not politically motivated, and even Smillie's death did not make him change his mind. Murrray thus became the leading exponent of the straightforward view that Smillie's detention and death was an unfortunate accident. It is, therefore, important to begin with an exposition of Murray's thinking about the case before going on to examine the flaws in it, and its political ramifications.

Despite Bob Smillie's own belief that the police were "waiting for him"[30] at the border, Murray believed that he had simply been held without premeditation as a possible deserter. He had been taken to Valencia as a military prisoner, and held there in the charge of the Military Fiscal. Indeed, Murray said that Smillie was "largely responsible for his own detention" because he had attempted to cross the border without written permission, at a time when frontier supervision had passed into the hands of the central government.[31] Murray visited the prisoner on 20 and 24 May, and, convinced that he would soon be released, departed for Barcelona on 26 May. In the interim, the ILP National Administrative Council (NAC) had begun to apply political pressure on the Spanish government for a swift conclusion to Smillie's case, and James Maxton was assured by the Spanish ambassador that the matter would be investigated.[32] Murray was called back to Valencia by the lawyer hired to represent Smillie on 9 June because his client was now being investigated for "rebellion against the authorities" for his part in the Barcelona fighting.[33] Upon returning on Thursday 10 June, Murray also learnt that Smillie had been taken ill. Attempts to see him over the weekend were unsuccessful, and on Monday 14 June Murray finally learnt that Smillie had been taken to the Provincial hospital on the night of Friday 11 June, and had died at midnight of peritonitis. Due to the heat and advanced nature of the illness the body had been buried immediately, and Murray did not see it. Although Orwell found the fact that Murray was "refused permission to see the body" particularly suspicious, Murray himself was not perturbed by this. After all, the prison itself had not been notified until the Monday evening, and a quick burial was "customary" in Spain.[34]

Why had Smilie been transferred to the secret police, and why had he died? Murray was convinced that the blame for his transfer lay primarily with Smillie's friends in Britain who had published garbled accounts of the story. These had, in turn, filtered back to Spain and convinced the police that they had "caught someone of importance".[35] He was particularly critical of a report that had appeared in the ILP's *New Leader*, which alleged that Smillie had been bringing with him reports by McNair on the Barcelona fighting, which the Spanish government did not want to reach Britain.[36] This story had then surfaced in Barcelona newspapers. Ironically, Smillie had indeed been taking a report with him from McNair, but its importance was not recognized and it was returned to him in his cell, where he was able to destroy it.[37] The only other papers in his possession were personal letters from family and friends, letters from ILP colleagues, and an unpublished article by Orwell.

Murray also believed that British consular officials were partly to blame for Smillie's prolonged detention, claiming that they had leaked the fact that he was carrying two discharged bombs (as mementoes),[38] and that this had been turned by the British press into wild stories that Smillie was on his way to destroy churches.[39] Murray was deeply hostile to the British consular authorities, on the grounds that their staff were "definitely pro-Fascist, and would rather help Franco supporters to get out of

THE DEATH OF BOB SMILLIE

Spain than lend a hand with a real Government supporter".[40] If his account is to be trusted, the British authorities were certainly unsympathetic to Smillie. When Murray pointed out with regret that it had not been possible to bury Smillie in the English cemetery, one official told him that: "so [he] was buried among the other stiffs, no use being sentimental about it, its all the same to him, that is the worst of people coming here and getting mixed up in other people's business."[41] However, as will be argued below, Murray's rejection of official help may well have closed off a useful avenue of assistance.

One further factor in Smillie's continued detention was, according to Murray, that he had put up little resistance to questioning. He freely signed a statement concerning "documents" and "materials of war" (the discharged bombs) that he had been carrying, and admitted that he had been in Barcelona during the fighting. Murray concluded that Smillie was held as an *"easy mark for interrogation"* (sic) and was seen by the police as a valuable source of evidence against others who had been with him during the troubles.[42] Murray chided Smillie about this in a letter written on 12 June – by which time, tragically, Smillie was already dead:

> There is nothing serious apart from your sickness, but you seem to have been bent on giving all the wrong answers to the questions put to you. You would have been out long ago but for your own actions and those of your well-meaning friends [in publicising the case] . . . You should have explained – as was the absolute truth – that you were merely there [in the POUM building in Barcelona] by chance and that you knew nothing about the events leading up to the riots and that you took no part in the affair. You have been accused out of your own mouth – due, of course, to your faulty knowledge of Spanish, and to your misunderstanding of the question put to you . . . The whole business is an unfortunate mistake, but you cannot blame the authorities for being very careful.[43]

Central to Murray's account, therefore, was the belief that Smillie had stumbled through bad luck into an increasingly serious situation. His prolonged detention was "typically Spanish"[44] (meaning inefficient and incompetent). This was compounded by the fact that the authorities were nervous because a number of International Brigade deserters had been allowed to leave Spain and had sold their stories, suitably embellished, to the British press.[45] The Military Fiscal, with whom Murray established a good understanding, encouraged him to think that release was imminent.[46] Unfortunately, Smillie had then caught the eye of the secret police. However, their interest was completely legitimate given the very real danger of espionage behind Republican lines. As Murray wrote in a different context in August 1937: "I know that there are many wrong things going on in Spain, but there are actually innumerable spies and the police have to be careful."[47]

Unlike Murray, George Orwell found Bob Smillie's death hard to explain. He concluded that "perhaps the appendicitis story was true", but was still mystified that a young man of Smillie's strength should die of such an illness — "People so tough as that do not usually die of appendicitis if they are properly looked after." He surmised that the cause must have been the appalling "eighteenth century" conditions of the Spanish dungeons where political prisoners were kept in crowded conditions with very poor diet, and where medical attention would be completely inadequate.[48] Murray would have agreed with Orwell's view of Smillie's toughness, but not with his description of prison conditions. Food was certainly poor in the Valencia prison following a hunger strike by "anti-fascist" prisoners, and the conditions were very basic — for instance, the International Brigade prisoners' only items of clothing were trousers and a jacket. Anti-fascist prisoners were housed alongside suspected rebel supporters and, indeed, the most immediate medical attention came from pro-Franco doctors who were fellow inmates. The prison hospital was not popular with the prisoners — one International Brigader had suffered in his cell for two weeks to avoid going there. However, Murray stressed that "considerable freedom of movement was allowed to the anti-Fascist prisoners and they were in the habit of visiting one another in the cells". Smillie was accompanied in prison by six fellow-Britons (alleged deserters from the International Brigades) and a number of Spanish POUM prisoners, including his two cell-mates.[49] They were free to exercise and play hand ball (*pelota*), and Smillie had had the POUM newspaper *La Batalla* delivered regularly.[50] When Murray interviewed fellow prisoners after his death no guards were present. Thus the regime was relatively relaxed, and hardly the appalling conditions envisaged by Orwell.

Murray carried out a full investigation into Smillie's death, talking to fellow prisoners, prison authorities, and doctors at the Provincial Hospital where he died. In addition, Smillie's lawyer, Vincente Martinez Uberos, made his own inquiries. On the basis of this evidence Murray maintained that there were no suspicious circumstances. Smillie had fallen ill, had eventually been transferred to a prison hospital for two days, and on the fatal night of 11 June was rushed to the Provincial hospital in such a hurry that the proper papers were not signed. Murray interpreted this as neglect due to overwork,[51] ignorance and administrative confusion, and dismissed the thought that Smillie had fallen victim to the Communist-dominated secret police, who had either deliberately withheld treatment or killed the young man in some other way. Although when pressed he went as far as to say that the various officials may have been "criminally culpable"[52] through neglect, the core of his argument was that, as he told Smillie's father on 6 December 1937, "in spite of every curious and mysterious circumstance, I am completely convinced that Bob was never ill-treated nor was he done to death".[53]

Although ILP documents for the period are scant, and on the subject of Smillie's death almost non-existent, it is possible to demonstrate the degree to which Murray had persuaded the ILP leadership to accept his interpretation of the case. The best evidence arises from the ILP NAC minutes for a meeting of 11–12 December 1937. A resolution was received from Dewsbury ILP "expressing dissatisfaction at the 'mystery' surrounding the death of Comrade Bob Smillie" and asking the Secretary for a copy of the report that he had received. Brockway read a reply, endorsed by the NAC, stating that:

> careful investigations had been made by David Murray, [Julián] Gorkin on behalf of the POUM Executive, and [Brockway] himself, and that all these reports agreed that Bob Smillie was ill in prison and that he did not receive the medical attention that he should have received, but that there was no evidence that his death was due to any other circumstances than this.

Given the limitations on the ability of Gorkin and Brockway to carry out independent investigations,[54] it is clear that Murray was the dominant force in shaping the ILP's response.

■ ■ ■ ■ ■ ■ ■

A close reading of Murray's papers, however, suggests that he may have disregarded significant evidence in accounting for Bob Smillie's death. According to his initial report for the ILP, written in early July, Murray had spoken to a prisoner (John Mudie) who told him that Smillie had been ill for ten days with a "sore side". A (pro-Franco) inmate doctor had stated that "he had appendicitis and was as good as done for".[55] According to other prisoners, whom Murray spoke to before telling them that their comrade was dead, Smillie had first fallen ill on Friday 4 June, had requested a doctor on the Saturday, but had not been seen until the Monday. Murray's report of the interview notes:

> Given powder, very sick vomiting, always asking for doctor. Left two days completely unattended . . . Prison official doctor apparently did not want to do anything. Went to hospital Wednesday, had to walk with shoes on and blanket,

prison inmate doctor stated that would never come back again. Comrades not allowed to see him Thursday . . . Impression that Smillie badly treated by neglect. Smillie's face on Thursday terrible 'red' . . . [56]

This information did not appear in full in the final ILP report, published in the *New Leader* and circulated to all party branches.

Other doubts about the official ILP story arise from two further documents. On 8 July Dr A. Ferrer Peris, the doctor on duty at the Provincial hospital, wrote to Alex Smillie (in a latter translated by Murray) that his son had died of a very advanced case of peritonitis which made medical intervention impossible when he arrived at the hospital. The doctor concluded that "there are misfortunes which we would never wish to happen, but which fatally do". He said that he had talked with the official prison doctor who had assured him that there had been no opportunity at any point for medical intervention, and that Bob Smillie had been "very satisfied" with his treatment. When leaving for the Provincial hospital the young man had shaken the prison doctor's hand and left "smiling".[57] This happy scene hardly squares with the ILP's conclusion that Smillie arrived at the hospital in a "state of coma".[58] Nor is it fully consistent with Murray's own investigations, having established from the doctor at the Provincial hospital that it was "rare" that appendicitis could advance so far without being observed.[59] This confirmed a report from investigating POUM officials that the doctor was "surprised" that a case of appendicitis could go long so long without an operation.[60] Murray candidly observed that Dr Ferrer Peris was "obviously trying to protect [his] colleague at [the] prison".[61] Further doubt is shed on the reliability of the prison doctor's evidence by the fact that Murray was told at the prison that Smillie's first complaint had been on 9 June – much later than the other prisoners had indicated.[62]

A document sent to Murray on 27 July by the lawyer, Uberos, is also of interest. This comprised an account of his own investigation which was to be translated by Murray for the ILP and Alex Smillie. According to Murray's translation, Bob Smillie had vomited twice on 8 June as his stomach pains persisted. However, the original Spanish states "dos vómitos fecales" (or faecal vomiting, a sure sign that Smillie was suffering from a very advanced stage of obstruction). Even so, he was not taken to the prison hospital until the next day, and medical intervention was not attempted because of "congestion in the affected area".[63] The only treatment that Smillie received at any point was "hot fomentations and ice".[64]

Having decided what he believed to have happened, to the exclusion of these areas of doubt, David Murray then sought to explain these events to his own satisfaction, and criticised any other possible interpretation. He believed that Bob Smillie had refused to seek treatment because of his physical resilience. In an article for a Scottish local paper he wrote that "adequate medical attention was admittedly remiss. To this the singular modesty and uncomplaining nature of the young Scotsman may have contributed." [65] In a letter to Eileen Blair (George Orwell's wife), who had been working in the ILP office in Barcelona, he wrote that : "There was certainly neglect, but it is hard to apportion blame. There were 1,500 prisoners and must have been many malingerers. Smillie was singularly uncomplaining and the family tradition is to doctor oneself." [66] When the first draft of the ILP's report into Smillie's death was circulated in February 1938, Murray took exception to the emphasis that was placed on the fact that Smillie had had to walk to the prison hospital. This, he argued, could simply be a reflection of his fitness. [67] John McNair, however, countered that "it is hard to assume that he was fit to do this twenty four hours before he died if he was absolutely unfit to be operated on and must have, therefore, been in a highly feverish and congested state". In a rare case of disagreement in the ILP ranks he added that:

> *The more I think about this the more I realise that there was gross carelessness or callousness on the part of the authorities which amounted to criminal negligence. Bob Smillie would probably be alive today if this callous treatment had not been inflicted on him. I know that this is your opinion [sic], and it seems to me that it is necessary it should be specified in the report.* [68]

Although Murray continued to argue that it was possible to maintain some "bodily vigour" while being unfit for an operation, the final draft of the report did contain this, more loaded, statement: "We also have reason to believe that Bob was not *taken* or *carried* to the hospital but was compelled to stagger there himself." [69]

A potentially more significant challenge to Murray's version of the case came from POUM officials who, facing the virtual extinction of their party after the May fighting in Barcelona, were naturally keen for political mileage to be made out of Smillie's death. [70] The local POUM leader, Luis Portela, had helped Murray right from his arrival in Valencia, making sure that Smillie's papers were belatedly presented to the authorities. At the time of Smillie's death Portela was accompanied by a national leader, Julián Gorkin, who was already facing charges in Valencia for his part in allegedly fomenting the Barcelona riots. Portela and Gorkin had visited the Provincial hospital immediately after Smillie's death and, indeed, had collected his death certificate. Gorkin had departed for Barcelona that afternoon, and was soon afterwards arrested in the political crack-down on the POUM leadership. In mid-July Brockway, on his return from Spain, told Murray that some POUM comrades had seen Gorkin's report. This, apparently, included a signed letter from the prison governor and medical officer to the effect that their first request for Smillie to be transferred to the hospital had been resisted by the secret police. Unfortunately, the report had fallen into police hands on Gorkin's arrest, and the prison governor had allegedly been sacked for signing the statement. Brockway freely admitted that:

> The POUM people want us to make clear that the secret service police under communist control were responsible for stopping Bob Smillie going to hospital, and therefore, in fact, for his death. I don't want to over-emphasise this, though they would like to see it stressed, but I think the point should be made.[71]

Brockway had publicised these allegations through the Press Association on his return.[72] Murray, however, was scornful of this new twist. Gorkin and Portela had, he claimed, been unable to carry out an investigation, other than questioning the doctor at the hospital. Indeed, when Murray had met them on Monday 14 June he had informed them for the first time that Smillie had been held by the secret police – "It was I who got the Secret Police connection."[73] A full statement was drawn up by the three men, and this was presumably the document which had fallen into the hands of the police on Gorkin's arrest.[74] There was no evidence that steps had been taken against the prison authorities on political grounds, although there would probably be an investigation into their possible neglect of a prisoner. In the light of these comments, the POUM's allegations were treated as politically motivated and did not appear in the ILP's official report.

A further challenge came from an anarchist political group that was based in the Glasgow region, and was a local rival to the ILP. The United Socialist Movement (USM) had been formed in 1934, partly as a splinter group from the ILP, and was led by the long-standing "anti-parliamentary communist" and gifted polemicist Guy Aldred. Aldred proudly claimed that the USM was "the first organisation in Great Britain to rally to the cause of the Spanish workers, and to insist on the Anarchist character of the Spanish struggle".[75] In October 1936 Ethel MacDonald, a young Scottish associate of Aldred's, had gone to Spain where she worked in the foreign language information centre of the Anarchist headquarters in Bracelona. Her critical account of Republican politics proved influential in Anarchist circles in Britain, and she had gone underground following the May fighting. Subsequently, she would make outspoken claims about Smillie's death. Guy Aldred staunchly supported the Spanish

Anarchists and, unlike Murray and the ILP, was very willing to make political capital out of Smillie's death in order both to help them and to score points against the ILP. Accordingly, even while MacDonald was still in Spain, he set about sensationalizing the Smillie case. Already, in a prescient letter of 5 June, MacDonald had written to him from Barcelona:

> *Poor Smillie! He looks as if he were jailed for life. I think, personally, it will be for life – or death. For they will never let him back to Britain alive with the facts he has collected against the Communist Party, it's activities and alliances in Spain. At least, it will be a very long time until he gets back. I am in touch with many comrades and I know.*[76]

On her return to Scotland in November 1937, MacDonald published a series of articles which heavily criticised the ILP (and especially Murray) for their handling of the case, and tugged tenaciously at the loose ends that remained. On 5 December she promised in the right-wing *Sunday Mail* that: "Next week I shall describe how [Smillie] was done to death in a hospital because he was carrying information out of the country, and how he was buried under a different – a Belgian – name." Her article for 12 December did not deliver any evidence for these claims, but did pose more questions: "No compatriot saw him die or saw him buried. Did he die as stated? Or was he murdered? I and many others suspect the latter because we believe he was a danger to the government . . . What was the charge against Bob? Did he ever appear in court? Where is he buried? These questions must be answered." In a letter to the socialist journal *Forward* she added that "the ILP hushed up the death of Bob Smillie. I refuse to do so." She blamed Stalinist infiltration of the ILP for its restraint over the case, and claimed to share the views of "Smillie's fighting companions" on this issue.[77]

Many of MacDonald's points were quite clearly mischievous, in the sense that the truth could be quite clearly established. For instance, after his death Smillie had been formally charged before a tribunal in Barcelona with "complicity" in the fighting there.[78] Moreover, Murray pointed out that her claim to be the person "who knows as much about [Smillie's death] as anyone in this country"[79] was clearly erroneous. By early June she was underground in Barcelona, and in no position to glean any information other than the highly charged gossip of passing internationalists.[80] Murray's sane observations, however, could do nothing to still the local speculation that already existed in Scotland, and which MacDonald was happy to feed, about the episode.

Her allegations were particularly disturbing to the young man's parents and close friends. They had received news of their son's death with remarkable dignity and restraint.[81] However, the continuing rumours in the local press, especially following Ethel MacDonald's return, led them to believe that the ILP had not been fully frank with them. This was partly Murray's fault, as he had not told them the full story in order to spare their feelings. For instance, he had initially told them that Bob Smillie had inadvertently left his papers behind in Barcelona instead of not possessing any.[82] Subsequently, Murray let them see his file on the case, but this only deepened their suspicions that there had been some kind of cover-up. As has already been noted, Murray's papers contain much more ambiguity than the final, rather bland, report. In December Murray had a heated discussion with Alex Smillie, and afterwards sent him a written statement to try to set the record straight. He apologized for having withheld information from the family, but said that this was certainly not due to a "conspiracy" by the ILP leaders. Brockway and McNair, who had come in for particular criticism, were "ashamed of their mistakes rather than trying to cover the situation". Murray thought that the family was reacting to "wild and unfounded statements" emanating from MacDonald and others "which are gaining currency", which needed to be rebutted.[83]

Murray was increasingly haunted by his part in the case. At the Glasgow conference of the ILP in February 1938 he was allowed to make a brief statement about the plight of Gorkin and Kopp, still languishing in Spanish jails. He was then publicly attacked by Alex Smillie for "suppression" of his son's case.[84] At the conference dance another ILP member and former volunteer had spread the false rumour that Murray had been in Spain as a correspondent for the *Daily Express*, adding that: "You were well paid for your work."[85] In mid-February 1938 Alex Smillie wrote to Murray to say that "the truth" must be made known to ILP members. Most of the facts "are in your file. They have never appeared in your reports." He added that "according to your first statement in Barcelona [Bob] was 'murdered' by the people in charge at Valencia. I am quite agreeable to put the same construction on that word *now* as you did *then*."[86] In fact, although Alex Smillie remained unconvinced,[87] he chose not to take the case further. He helped to amend the ILP draft report, which was published with his consent in March 1938. He had also met Ethel MacDonald and realised the shallowness of her claims.[88]

For all of the questions concerning Bob Smillie's death, David Murray had convinced himself and the ILP leadership that the tragedy was the result of unlucky circumstance, exacerbated by ignorance and inefficiency. Whereas in July 1937 Murray had written that whether Smillie's fatal neglect was due to "ignorance, indifference, callousness or *intent* is yet not very clear",[89] by February 1938 his judgment was simply that "ignorance, carelessness or negligence on the part of the responsible authorities may have contributed to his death".[90] The final ILP report, published in March 1938, clearly reflected these conclusions. The report was something of an amalgam of views. It contained hints of misdeeds by the authorities. For instance, it gave some evidence of "grave neglect" of the prisoner's health, and said that his death was due to "carelessness on the part of the medical and prison authorities which borders on criminal negligence". However, the main thrust of the report was to establish that Bob Smillie was "absolutely innocent" of any charge and remained an "utterly fearless, honest and intelligent socialist".[91] It was apparent that the case was closed.

■ ■ ■ ■ ■ ■ ■

The question must remain as to why Murray and the ILP leadership dropped the suspicion of "intent" on the part of the authorities which they had harboured in the immediate aftermath of Smillie's death. After all, in the succeeding months political events in Spain suggested the need for more, not less, suspicion. Soon after Smillie's death the POUM was, effectively, suppressed. Andres Nin was arrested on 16 June, and most other POUM leaders a day later.[92] Orwell and other volunteers fled Spain, hunted as "Trotskyists" and persecuted by the Communists on their return to Britain.[93] For POUM sympathizers the suspicious death of Smillie clearly heralded a similar fate for the jailed party leaders.[94] Indeed, Nin was soon done to death in captivity in mysterious circumstances, and for the rest of the Civil War the ILP was as preoccupied with saving the lives of POUM comrades facing death sentences on trumped-up charges as it was with working for a Republican victory. In August the Spanish Communist press attacked the ILP as a "gang of bandits, engaged in sabotage",[95] and at its 1938 conference the ILP charged the Spanish Communists with "introducing, under the instruction of the Communist International, the methods of the 'Cheka' in Spain".[96] It may be that the ILP leadership, lacking the evidence to sustain an allegation that Bob Smillie had been murdered on political grounds, chose not to see his death as part of a wider pattern of Communist-inspired terror in Spain. Even so, what is so strikingly lacking from the public response of the ILP is some kind of cry of outrage, such as that uttered by Orwell in *Homage to Catalonia*, that a brave young man, who had gone to Spain to fight fascism, should have been allowed to perish in such circumstances.

The answer to this peculiarity must lie in a series of personal and political considerations. Murray summed up the two most important aspects in a letter of August 1937: "The Smillie case was deliberately kept out of the papers to spare his people's feelings and to prevent the Fascists [in Britain] from making use of the story for anti-Spanish purposes."[97] On a personal level, it is apparent that Murray and the ILP leaders did not wish in any way to compound the grief of the Smillie family by revealing potentially disturbing aspects of the case, either to the public or to the family. This policy backfired – public interest was such, and speculation so rife, that the facts had to be made clear, and the family presumed that there must, accordingly, have previously been a cover-up. Moreover, ILP leaders such as McNair may well have felt personal guilt and responsibility about Smillie's death which would have inhibited their political response. At a political level, there were three other distinct factors to consider – the protection of Republican Spain from criticism; the maintenance of ILP relations with the Communists; and the possibility of helping other prisoners in Spain.

The ILP was unwilling to do anything which might damage the interests of the Spanish Republic. Despite their loyalty to the POUM and to the volunteers in Spain, the ILP believed that the survival of the Republic transcended simple party interest. As Murray put it very starkly in December 1937, "the welfare of a nation was more important than even the life of a young man who was in every way admirable".[98] Although the pendulum had clearly swung very sharply against the Anarchists and the POUM, the Republic, for all of its faults, remained preferable to a Franco victory.[99] Yet, what grounds were there for believing that the Smillie case, badly handled, could damage the Republican cause?

The political context within which the case was received in Britain is paramount. The Civil War had aroused immense public interest, nowhere more intensely than in central Scotland. Here the Civil War had proved divisive on religious grounds, as many working-class Catholics (otherwise potential Labour or ILP supporters) were appalled by the anti-catholic outrages which accompanied the outbreak of the conflict. In the catholic press, and from many pulpits, the Republic was freely depicted as a bastion of anti-religious Communism.[100] ILP leaders believed that any suspicion that Smillie had been murdered, especially at the hands of the Communist-controlled secret police, would be quickly picked up by right-wing newspapers as proof of more widespread Communist control over Republican Spain. This would make continued ILP support for the Republic much more difficult and exacerbate the religious objections to Republican Spain. The relish with which the

Sunday Mail had taken up Ethel MacDonald's stories lends credence to this belief, and explains Murray's comments to Smillie in his letter of 12 June: "when you get out you must forget all about your experiences as the Tory papers would dearly love to make a song about your arrest."[101] At the same time, the argument that Smillie's detention "may react seriously against the good name of Republican Spain abroad" (amongst its own supporters)[102] gave the ILP a bargaining tool against the Spanish authorities, although one that, sadly, became effective only after Smillie's death.

Similarly, concern for the good name of Republican Spain also conditioned the ILP's cool relations with the British consular authorities. Murray did not believe that the authorities had any genuine interest in Smillie's case, and that even if they were to take action, they would do so only to embarrass the Republican government. His suspicions were apparently confirmed on his arrival in Valencia, when a Spanish assistant at the consulate told him a false story that Smillie had been beaten into signing a confession.[103] Murray later confided dismissively to the staunchly anti-Catholic Labour MP Josiah Wedgwood that "the whole bunch of [the consular staff] are Roman Catholics".[104] Accordingly, he decided to make as little use of the consulate as possible. This may have been unwise. After Smillie's death Murray noted that "both the Ministry of Justice and the Direction of *Seguridad* [Security] stated that a word from the Ambassador would be effective" in procuring his release. Murray had, however, already decided that the embassy was not likely to be interested and he "in any case did no (sic) wish to implicate the cause of justice and to damage Spain".[105] Thus, Murray's conclusion that the British authorities were "not disposed to help"[106] has to be taken in the context of his prejudice against seeking their help in the first place.

The second major political consideration was that any ILP allegation of a Communist role in Smillie's death would severely strain relations with the Communist party in Britain, and, moreover, that these relations were worth preserving. It was far from clear that these feelings were reciprocated. Despite the ILP's genuine restraint in the matter, the Glasgow Communist Harry McShane still castigated it for using Smillie's death to discredit "those who are fighting to defend democracy". In a sinister twist, he added that Smillie's presence in Barcelona in early May was "not calculated to assist him".[107] Indeed, the ILP's continuing adherence to the Unity Campaign, and to the CPGB more generally, is difficult to explain, especially in the light of the condemnation of the ILP at the 14th Congress of the CPGB. By the autumn, the Communist party was freely stating that it was impossible to co-operate with the "Trotskyist" ILP.

However, the ILP by this stage had, in political terms, nowhere else to go. Re-affiliation to the Labour party would only be on the terms of the larger party, and at a time when Labour was moving to support rearmament for a possible European war, a policy unacceptable to the ILP. Moreover, ILP distaste for current Communist tactics was consistently tempered by respect for a party that appeared to have behind it the authority of Lenin and the Bolshevik revolution. Beyond working with insignificant political groupings such as the Anarchists, ILP leaders were increasingly aware of their party's dangerous isolation. Brockway, for instance, was openly critical of the political stance of the POUM when speaking at the ILP Summer School in 1937. He argued that the case of the POUM demonstrated that correct revolutionary socialist principles were not enough, and that "if they are maintained in isolation the Social Revolution will not come about. It is our duty to have not only the correct theoretical line, but the inner contact with the mass working-class movement which will allow it to become effective."[108] This talk of "inner contact" heralded a tentative return to Labour party affiliation in 1939, which was derailed by the outbreak of war in September of that year. Although the ILP had finally turned its back on the Communist party, describing it at its 1938 conference as a party set on betraying the workers, this process was reluctant, painful and hesitant.[109]

Concern for preserving relations with the Communists certainly played a part in the handling of the Smillie case. The ILP, in Brockway's terms, "deliberately refrained" from publicity during Smillie's imprisonment[110] and played down the most politically sensitive aspects of the story. In particular, any evidence compromising to the Communists was discarded. For instance, Murray admitted to Brockway that "the CP connection [i.e. the fact that the secret police which held Smillie was under Communist control] is, of course, not official – but in any case, I thought it best to suppress references to the CP connection [in his report]". He went on to affirm that the secret police was "unofficially under CP influence".[111] Similarly, evidence suggesting that Smillie was being held on political grounds as a "Trotskyist" was not made public. Murray was able to collect Smillie's personal correspondence on leaving Valencia, having struck a deal with the Military Fiscal that he would do all he could to limit newspaper interest in the story. However, he was unable to take away any letters with political content. As Murray noted with reference to these remaining letters, the mere mention of a "semi-bourgeois" name was enough for them to be retained. "Obviously [the secret police] thought Bob 'Trotskyist'".[112] The letters, he believed, were being kept as possible evidence against other victims of the arrests after the May fighting.

A final reason for restraint in handling the case was the belief that Smillie's tragic death could, at least, be used to secure the freedom of the remaining British and POUM prisoners, most notably the unit commander George Kopp.[113] There is some evidence to suggest that this pressure was effective. When Brockway visited Spain in July 1937 he was able to arrange the release of two prisoners, and the discharge from the army of eight of the surviving members of the ILP contingent who now wished to come home. He told Murray with some satisfaction that the British authorities were now only too keen to help, and arranged an interview with the Foreign Minister.[114] However, there was a clear limit to the leverage that a small political party could obtain, and the consular officials were only willing to intercede in the case of British nationals.[115] Kopp remained in jail for a further eighteen months and many POUM leaders were only released as the rebel forces marched on Barcelona in early 1939.

■ ■ ■ ■ ■ ■ ■

Amidst the many thousands of deaths in the Spanish Civil War, those of a few individuals have attracted unique interest and speculation. Understandably, the death of Bob Smillie has not received the same attention paid to that of the poet Federico García Lorca or the monarchist politician José Calvo Sotelo, and interest has, of course, been much greater in Britain than in Spain.[116] Even so, it remains an event of some political significance, and one which has long been shrouded in mystery. This mystery was deepened by two factors. First, *prima facie*, it was very hard for contemporary commentators not to see some evidence of politically motivated foul play in the young man's death. As the exiled former Bolshevik Victor Serge wrote from Paris in late June 1937, Smillie had been taken to Valencia where "il muert presque aussitôt en prison d'une bien inexplicable appendicite. Pauvre vaillant camarade! On sent dans sa fin *je ne sais quoi de Russe*."[117] Secondly, the unconscionable delay in issuing a formal ILP report on Smillie's death was guaranteed to encourage speculation of this nature. To take the most obvious example, the manuscript of *Homage to Catalonia*, the source of much subsequent confusion, was completed in mid-January 1938 and the book was published in April. Thus, although Orwell would possibly have been aware of the views of individuals discussed in this article, his book was not written in the light of the formal ILP report, which was not published until March.

The full facts of Bob Smillie's death may never be established.[118] Although Murray was well-placed to establish the truth, even his findings were essentially based on conjecture from circumstantial evidence. For instance, his favoured response to the claim that Smillie had been murdered was that the Valencia authorities would, in fact, want to keep him alive as a witness to the Barcelona fighting. This, however, they signally failed to do. David Murray may have been correct to emphasise the sheer bad luck and incompetence which led to Smillie's detention and death. However, the reinterpretation of the evidence on which he based his own judgments, and those of the ILP, suggests that he arrived at this verdict in the face of significant evidence to the contrary. Indeed, it is important to emphasize in conclusion that during his captivity Bob Smillie changed from being a military prisoner into a political prisoner, and that the events surrounding his death suggest a degree of neglect for which the official ILP formula of "criminal negligence" barely appears adequate.[119] The fact that the ILP leaders handled the tragedy with such restraint is witness to the web of political constraints within which they found themselves trapped. Committed to the victory of Republican Spain, the ILP would do nothing to harm Republican interests, even though the Republic had palpably rejected the revolution, and the revolutionary forces, which it espoused. Trapped in a tense, unproductive relationship with the Communist party, the ILP appeared powerless to fight back against the verbal contempt (in Britain) and physical violence (in Spain) to which it and its allies were subjected by international Communism. Thus, in part, the response to the death of Bob Smillie was formed by events beyond the ILP's control.

David Murray was never able fully to put behind him his role in these events. In 1955 an innocuous letter was written to a local Scottish newspaper by a Mr Moffat of Clydebank stating that "no wonder the author of *Animal Farm* hated totalitarianism". Orwell himself, it went on, had been persecuted by Stalinist terror, and Bob Smillie had been "captured and thrown into prison, where he died from appendicitis". Murray, now a Liberal and an unsuccessful parliamentary candidate in a number of Scottish seats in the 1950s, felt compelled to reply that "I am no totalitarian, indeed, I have come to believe that an unplanned, all out competitive system is the best one." In a closing comment on the fate of Bob Smillie that aptly sums up his role in the entire tragic case he wrote that: "It was all very sad, but it might have happened to anyone."[120]

Chapter 7

Loss, memory
and the British
"Volunteers for Liberty"

When the Fascist hordes by Franco led
Are overthrown in Spain
Our gallant lads who fought and bled
Have not sacrificed in vain.

'They Shall Not Pass!' is the battle-cry
Where the Flag of Freedom waves.
Thus did our comrades nobly die
That we might not be slaves.

The rest fight on; but not for gold.
When they win, they seek no prize.
Europe's destiny they mould
And a new, Free Spain shall arise.

('Inspired by Victory at Teruel'. "Composed in an idle
moment by the mother of one of our wounded comrades",
Daily Worker, 2 February 1938)

Volunteering for the International Brigades generated intense and mixed
emotions. The Spanish Civil War impinged with often devastating force
on the lives, careers and personal relationships of the approximately 2400
British volunteers. More than 500 died in Spain, where they were
frequently deployed as shock-troops, and most of those who returned
alive had been wounded at least once. Hundreds more experienced
sometimes lengthy imprisonment in Franco's prisons. For many volunteers, Spain was a transforming, even a redemptive, experience that set
them on course for a lifetime's political engagement. Strong friendships

forged in the Brigades evolved into lasting attachments in the decades after the Civil War. Others, however, returned disillusioned by alleged military incompetence and political manipulation, or embittered at a perceived lack of concern for their welfare. For the families and friends of the volunteers, meanwhile, pride and admiration might well jostle with private fears, frustrations and resentments. Even the stirring poem that opens this chapter derived, in part, from a personal story of maternal anxiety.[1] Throughout the Civil War and its aftermath, therefore, it was apparent that a heroic rhetoric of "breathless bravery, wonderful comradeship and mighty achievements"[2] could never conceal the ubiquity of loss in all of its forms. The Communist Party could not ignore this welter of emotions, but rather sought to embrace and channel them. Complex feelings would ultimately deliver an affirmation that the members of the British Battalion had, indeed, not "sacrificed in vain".

Historians of the British Battalion such as Bill Alexander and Richard Baxell[3] have steered clear of such personal and emotive territory, concentrating on the volunteers themselves and the details of their service in Spain. By contrast, the contemporary reporting of the British Battalion in the *Daily Worker* was drenched in emotion, as the Communist Party commemorated its fallen comrades and sought to justify their loss. At the height of the British involvement in the Civil War few days went by without the publication of black-rimmed lists of casualties in the *Daily Worker*, heartfelt testimonials from the family and friends of dead volunteers, and exhortations from Harry Pollitt for readers not to forget "the grief in the hearts of our comrades' relatives".[4] Pollitt even drafted such sentiments into the Communist Party's struggle with the hierarchy of the Labour movement when he posed the question of whether "Transport House leaders will ever be able to understand the kind of feeling" contained in relative's letters.[5] The first official history of the British Battalion (*Britons in Spain*, published in January 1939) contained an entire chapter of "Human documents" in which extracts of letters from British volunteers to their families and friends were reproduced as evidence of a "beautiful story of human hope, sacrifice and endeavour". The editor Bill Rust, a leading Communist closely associated with the British Battalion, also included some letters written by bereaved relatives. These were simple and moving, but their "brave stoicism" was surely intended to be instructive.[6] To investigate questions of loss and memory is not, therefore, to impose the susceptibilities of the modern era upon the past, but rather to re-engage with issues that were first raised – however partially – at the time.

This subject was opened up for historians by Hywel Francis, the author of a pioneering history of the Welsh volunteers,[7] in a thought-provoking article published in 1991. Francis warned against ignoring "the personal and family traumas, emotions and sacrifices" associated with any war – even one that was perceived as 'just'. He confessed that while carrying out his research "I was always reluctant to visit widows or close female relatives of volunteers who had been killed in action, often, I should say in my own defence, being warned against some visits by well-meaning Party comrades." For instance, the veteran Pat Murphy had told him in 1970 that "it's a bit touchy visiting these relatives as one often gets some nasty remarks instead of compliments". Francis appealed for historians not to neglect the "darker side" of volunteering in the Spanish Civil War: the "torment" of separation endured by the volunteers and the despair of many wives and mothers.[8] Indeed, in recent years, a new awareness of the personal costs associated with volunteering has, in different ways, informed the work of historians such as Angela Jackson, Robert Stradling and Natalie Suart.[9] This chapter falls into two principal parts. First, the personal impact of volunteering, and the question of loss in particular, is discussed from the perspective both of the volunteers and of their families, friends and communities; the second part looks at how the memory of the British volunteers was shaped, both during the Civil War itself and during the first decade after its conclusion. Initially, however, some contextual points must be established.

I

British volunteering in the Spanish Civil War was, with the minor exception of the ILP's military contingent, under the control of the Communist Party of Great Britain.[10] Recruitment in Britain was organised by R. W. Robson, a member of the CPGB's Control Commission who later claimed to have interviewed personally "more than four thousand men".[11] Within the British Battalion itself the "Political Commissars" were not only concerned with the volunteers' welfare and morale but also reported on their political reliability and discipline. The Communist Party's role was widely, albeit tacitly, understood at the time, and no secret was made of it subsequently. For instance, in 1951 Harry Pollitt wrote that: "I had the responsibility of organising the British Battalion of the International Brigades. I had more intimate knowledge of what went on in Spain during the time the British Battalion was there than perhaps any other person in this country."[12] Pollitt, in particular, took this responsibility extremely seriously: he made regular visits to the volunteers and maintained a genuine and personal interest in their well-being.[13] Nevertheless, there is no question that the British Battalion generated immense political capital, and that the Communist Party was the prime beneficiary. As John Mahon, a Civil War veteran and a leading Communist, reflected in 1965, the existence of the British Battalion provided the Communist-led "Aid for Spain" campaign with "a direct link and an emotional content which otherwise would have hardly been possible".[14] There were, however, those who felt that while the Communist Party was happy to accept the credit for the British Battalion it was rather less eager to accept responsibility for the hardships and misfortunes suffered by individual volunteers.

The terms and duration of service were initially unclear for the British volunteers, and even the toughest could become disenchanted with the lack of home leave. Record keeping in the multi-lingual brigades was also somewhat haphazard, and headquarters experienced genuine difficulties in establishing reliable information about casualties.[15] This meant that death notices were often delayed, and in some cases wrongly posted. For instance the mother of George Drever, who had in fact been captured, was sent a death certificate signed by the Divisional commander and even received £10 in life insurance.[16] Moreover, between 250 and 298 British volunteers are thought to have "deserted" during the war.[17] The term "desertion" is used advisedly, as it could relate to a wide range of issues such as cowardice, psychological trauma, political disillusionment, or a simple desire to take leave.[18] Indeed, a number of apparent deserters later returned to Spain. Even so, deserters had placed themselves outside of the protection that could be offered by the International Brigades in Spain. Many found themselves in Republican jails, pending either a return to the front line or, if they were fortunate, repatriation.

British volunteering took place within a largely hostile domestic environment. Service in the International Brigades was declared illegal by the British government in January 1937 and, while no successful prosecutions were brought, recruitment was driven underground.[19] In addition, the central institutions of the British Labour movement gave at best rhetorical support to the battalion, although some individual leaders, as well as many trade union branches and working-class communities, proved far more forthcoming.[20] Above all, the British volunteers faced an onslaught from right-wing newspapers such as the *Daily Mail* which were always ready to publish lurid, anti-communist stories emanating from disaffected Britons returning from Spain. For instance, the *Sunday Dispatch* reported that the mother of Victor J. Betts of Hendon had been falsely notified that her son was dead. Betts, who eventually deserted, complained that "they treated [his mother] most callously at Communist Party headquarters", and added that "the Reds got me to Spain on false pretences".[21] The *Daily Worker* devoted much space to rebutting allegations that the volunteers were well-paid mercenaries, or were the "dupes of Moscow". However, the prevalence of such stories was demoralising and contributed to the local rumour and gossip that the wives of volunteers, in particular, had to contend with. The leading Communist J. R. Campbell warned the party's Central Committee about the wives who were left feeling "isolated, with all the neighbours talking about 'the Communists who have taken your husband away' and 'why did he leave you?'"[22] One Glasgow volunteer claimed that a deserter (a "yellow renegade") had returned to spread alarm amongst his comrades' wives. He would encourage them to "plead that they have divers diseases and invent all the excuses they can to get their husbands home".[23] Families, friends and local political supporters were, therefore, consistently placed on the defensive, and this inevitably made the response of the Communist Party more obdurate in protecting the reputation of the British Battalion both during and after the Civil War.

There is no question that, amidst the rush to establish the British Battalion in late 1936, the care of the volunteers and their dependants was an afterthought for the Communist Party. Vincent Tewson of the TUC was quite correct to write in November 1937 that "certain people boosted the question of recruitment without looking sufficiently far ahead to see what they are going to do in the inevitable result of casualties".[24] Even so, a viable structure for fundraising did gradually emerge with the formal establishment of the International Brigade Dependants and Wounded Aid Committee (IBD&WAC) in June 1937 under the energetic leadership of Charlotte Haldane.[25] Although the committee's ability to meet its commitments was sometimes described as "touch and go",[26] a basic level of assistance was provided for the neediest dependants as well as, increasingly, for the wounded in need of medical care on their return to Britain. Over £63,000 had been raised by the end of 1938, principally from small voluntary contributions. Less obviously, the committee also played a political role during the Civil War. On 31 March 1938 David Springhall – a former Political Commissar in Spain – led an IBD&WAC delegation of eleven wounded volunteers and six bereaved women to meet leaders of the labour movement at Transport House. Although their demands – essentially for a programme of action to change British government policy towards Spain – were not met, it was evidence of the standing of the volunteers and their families that Labour leaders felt compelled to meet them at all.[27] Following the withdrawal of the

British Battalion in the autumn of 1938 the Communist Party was determined that this "esteem and high standing" among the "freedom-loving
men and women of this country"[28] should allow the volunteers to exercise a continuing political influence within Britain.

II

Bill Rust's *Britons in Spain* presented the decision to volunteer for the
International Brigades as an occasion that brought families together in
solidarity. For instance, in Fred Longden's account: "I never realised
before how selfless and devoted my mother is. She has not the political
understanding of a great many people to make her strong", but did not
seek to hinder him. She "felt that it was her duty as well as mine to make
some sacrifice that freedom should not die". For Rust, this was evidence
of a "deep mother-love", although there is almost a complete lack of
independent evidence to record such moments from the family's perspective.[29] For some volunteers, however, the very moment of departure
caused deep and lasting damage to relations with their families. Some
were aware that their wives would not approve of their decision – or
even try to prevent them from leaving – and took appropriate precautions. Hywel Francis cites the case of those who slipped away to Spain
"in the middle of the night", giving no word of their intentions to wives
and children.[30] Clearly, therefore, there was a wide range of possible
scenarios, and this is borne out by the interviews with surviving volunteers conducted in the 1970s and 1980s. Tommy Bloomfield from Fife
recalled that a friend was prevented from accompanying him to Spain
when his wife complained. Bloomfield added that: "If I had been married
I would never have gone, because I would have had obligations to a
wife."[31] George Leeson noted that his wife "didn't share my ideas at all,
but I was determined to go. 'You have a good job and why give this up?'
she said."[32] However, there are also many examples of wives wholeheartedly supporting the decision to volunteer even when, as in the case
of George Watters, the couple had three children.[33] Sometimes family
and friends were deliberately kept in the dark, but others were given clear
hints. Gerry McCartney, for instance, wrote to his mother that he was
going climbing in the Pyrenees with a friend.[34] In the more sensitive cases
the approval of close relatives might be sought. A Communist Party
organiser came to visit the widowed mother of prospective volunteer
Steve Fullarton, who was only eighteen. She replied that: "Well, if that's
what Steve wants to do there's no way I can stop him."[35]

Once the volunteers had departed for Spain, communication with their homes was often erratic. Some volunteers wrote frequently, and as fully as the Brigade censors would permit[36], while others made little effort to maintain contact. John Londragan of Aberdeen recalled that: "All I ever sent [home] was one Christmas card in the winter of 1937. You were sort of living from day to day . . . Home seemed far away, you know, you didn't think about it at all."[37] Bill Cranston's wife wrote to him throughout his 18 months in Spain: "But I wasnae a letter writer myself!"[38] Conversely, the Nottingham volunteer Walter Gregory wrote regularly to his sister, but during his first three months in Spain received only one of her many letters in return.[39] Amidst the confusion of war, it might well be fellow volunteers who were the first to convey important news. George Wheeler of Battersea spent many months as a prisoner of war after going missing at the battle of the Ebro. He later wrote to thank the Edinburgh volunteer John Dunlop for comforting his parents with the correct "surmise" that he had been captured and not killed. "Your letter came at a time when they were beginning to despair . . . [It] was the mainspring of hope in their hearts . . . "[40] However, such informal channels might also breed resentment and suspicion. For example, the family and friends of Frank Whitehead of Manchester told Harry Pollitt that they were appalled to hear of his death from a source other than the Communist Party.[41]

Married volunteers may well have constituted a fifth of the British contingent[42] and, while some were leaving troubled marriages behind them, the majority undoubtedly felt the pain of separation acutely. One wrote to tell Pollitt that his wife wanted him home: "You know what it is Harry, only three years married and still madly in love with each other."[43] Some concern was expressed that the willingness to accept married men was irresponsible. Eleanor Rathbone, an Independent MP and strong supporter of the British volunteers, was "rather perturbed" in March 1937 "to find that there are so many with dependants", and noted that the financial liability "seems to me excessive in proportion to the value of one man's service".[44] However, volunteers might also behave irresponsibly. For instance, some chose to conceal the fact that they had a dependent wife, fearing, as one put it, that this would have been a "deterrent to my coming to Spain".[45] Those with families, in particular, were perceived as a potentially weak link within the Battalion. In May 1937 Political Commissar Will Paynter asked whether it was necessary for so many volunteers with large families to be recruited: "Apart from the fact that they ultimately present a problem in the event of the worst happening, it is with these that the main problem of repatriation is raised."[46] There is a great deal of evidence in the commissars' reports dealing with repatriation requests to support this point. For instance, Leo Clarke of Salford produced a letter from his wife who had "notice to quit under a slum clearance scheme. His little girl is also reported 'poorly' and his mother likely to go daft if anything happens to him."[47] Others learnt of their wives pregnancies while in Spain, or were concerned about elderly parents. However, family ties might also strengthen the volunteers' resolve. Albert Parker, for example, wrote to his nine year-old daughter that "I am fighting to protect you and all children in England . . . "[48]

The inadequacy of the news from Spain greatly exacerbated the often debilitating anxiety felt by all family members. Janet Murray, whose husband Tom had recently volunteered, wrote to him in June 1938 that:

> *I saw Mrs Edwards (a poor creature) who has had no word at all from her husband and has written to Harry Pollitt about it. I had also a letter last week from Mrs McLeod of Aberdeen saying that she had not heard of her son for five weeks. I tried to comfort her as best I could, but I know how worried she must be. This lack of news is worse than anything else . . .* [49]

The refrain of one mother, that she wanted her son home because "he has broken my health",[50] was hardly uncommon. The British consular officials in Valencia and Alicante took an interest in the many British volunteers that passed through – some of them on the run from the authorities – and received many such heartfelt appeals from their families.[51] The wife of Frank Rush wrote that: "well sir as my health has broken down since my husband went away I should be in hospital only for the sake of my children as I have no one to look after them . . . "[52] William Bogle, who had been unofficially notified of the death of his son, said that: "I am broken hearted every night worrying over my son . . . I think it is a shame the way those lads were led away."[53] The mother of Michael Patton told British officials that he had lied about his age when joining the International Brigades (he was only seventeen but claimed to be two years older) and that she wanted him back: "he is my only child and I am quite alone".[54] The Foreign Office even carried word that the mother of volunteer Harry Daniels was dying and that "only Daniels' return can save her life".[55]

The lack of news and the peculiar circumstances of the Civil War left many families feeling powerless. An obvious first response was to contact local Communists, or even to write directly to Harry Pollitt, although the families of those volunteers accused of desertion were understandably reluctant to do so. Mrs Donald of Methil, who had learnt that her son James was in jail in Spain (having been initially reported killed) asked

David Murray of the ILP not to give any news to the local Communist agent, J. MacArthur: "he wants it to send to Harry Pollitt in London".[56] If an approach to the Communist Party proved unsuccessful families could pursue other avenues, such as contacting the British authorities in Spain. One woman wrote to Consul Sullivan in Valencia that, as a favour, "I want you to try and get him [her husband] home as soon as you possibly can. His son has got T.B. and I am ordered into hospital."[57] Such letters were, as we have seen, often candid and emotionally unguarded, and very different in tone from those published in the *Daily Worker*.

In fact, the Communist Party *was* susceptible to pressure when there was a danger of adverse publicity, as was the case when the volunteers under the age of eighteen were withdrawn in the spring of 1937. Families and friends might also exercise pressure through lobbying and local campaigns. In June 1937 Bill Rust (at this point representing the Lancashire District Committee of the Communist Party) wrote to Pollitt *apropos* "that charming couple, Mr and Mrs Pressman. It seems to me absolutely essential that you get this boy back as they are causing terrible bother here."[58] In South Wales a committee was formed in August 1938 to campaign for the return of two Welsh volunteers (W. J. Thomas of Aberavon and Griffith Jones of Dowlais) and a Scotsman (James Kempton of East Lothian) who had fallen foul of the Republican authorities. Thomas had been seriously ill and had suffered from "shattered nerves" after the battle of Brunete. Mrs Kempton had received no news of her husband since November 1937. All were currently in the Republican jail at Puig near Valencia, and news of their plight had been brought by Will Hopkins who had escaped from the prison in July 1938. The secretary of the committee circulated a letter to "influential people", such as Sir Walter Citrine of the TUC, in which he held the Communist Party responsible for the men's plight and accused it of

> *callous indifference to many appeals by the relatives . . . The tragedy is that leaders of the Communist Party are making brave speeches in this country whilst lads who they are responsible for sending to Spain are lying ill in hospital or suffering behind prison bars although not guilty of any crime.*

Both Thomas and Jones, he continued, had "aged parents" who were "naturally passing through a period of anguish and anxiety" due to lack of news.[59] The case was brought to the attention of the Spanish Ambassador, and was taken up by the Welsh miners' leader Arthur Horner. The two Welsh volunteers eventually returned home in early 1939.[60]

In the eyes of the Communist Party all of the dead volunteers were

"British heroes, glorious fighters for the cause of freedom and democracy".[61] As John Dunlop pointed out, even when one man was executed for desertion at Teruel and another sent to a labour battalion where he eventually perished, they were reported as killed in action in the *Daily Worker* "which would save their families the shame of knowing what these lads had been doing".[62] For their part, the grieving families were presented as bravely accepting of their loss and proud of the sacrifices made by their relatives. There were many published examples of how, in Pollitt's words, "grief and tears have mingled with pride and sorrow".[63] The widow of Ken Stalker was described as "big-hearted, courageous, loyal to the principles for which her man gave his life . . . ",[64] while the twelve year-old son of volunteer Fred Newbury stated that "I will always remember my father as a hero".[65] *Britons in Spain* recorded many other dignified and sombre reflections. Mrs McKie of Sunderland wrote of her husband, who died at Brunete, that: "it was his duty and I was in favour of it . . . I had hoped for the best, we were devoted to one another. He never lived to see his first little son born. He is very like his dad." Mrs Bradbury of Oldham wrote of the death of her son at Teruel that "he acted nobly . . . the blow has been a very heavy one as he was so good at home . . . I hope I shall be another mother added to the long list of mothers who have borne up bravely under the stress of this anxious time."[66]

Similar responses to personal loss can be found in other, less public, sources. Harold Fry of Edinburgh was imprisoned by the Nationalists after the battle of the Jarama and subsequently repatriated to Britain, but returned to die in action on the Aragon front. His wife wrote that Fry had left for Spain with his wounds barely healed and "without even seeing his baby which was born the day after he left. I would not have stopped him even if I could, because I believe he was right . . . " He had joined the International Brigades "because he believed it was the job he could do best".[67] The father of Bruce Boswell told Citrine that "as a socialist and as an old campaigner in the working class movement I do not regret my boy making the supreme sacrifice for the ideal which means so much to us", although he was also pursuing a claim for financial compensation.[68] The relatives of Charlie McLeod of Aberdeen, who had received a censored notification of his death at the Ebro, appealed to his comrade Tom Murray for information, as they knew nothing of the circumstances of his death. "We are proud of our son & brother," they concluded, "he gave his life for what he believed in. We only hope his sacrifice was not in vain." Murray replied in comforting terms that would be familiar to soldiers in both world wars: McLeod was one of the "bravest and most resolute comrades . . . well liked, honoured and appreciated". He and two others had been killed instantly by a shell and "did not suffer". Murray had personally supervised their burials "near the top of Hill 666, beside the town of Gandesa".[69]

Understandably, the public discourse of both the grieving families and the Communist Party emphasised the nobility of the cause for which so many men would eventually give their lives: there was no scope for questioning the rightness of the decision to volunteer, or the validity of the sacrifice made. However, not all families accepted their loss so unflinchingly. One particularly poignant case is that of Gilbert Taylor, a young Cardiff man from an educated, middle-class background, who died during the British Battalion's retreat following the collapse of the Aragon front in March 1938.[70] In December 1938 Taylor's mother-in-law, Mrs J. Shaxby, wrote to the left-wing scientist J. B. S. Haldane, whom she held partly responsible for Taylor's decision to volunteer. She complained that Taylor was physically unsuited for front-line service, and would have been far more effectively deployed in propaganda work. Despite consistent ill-health he was sent into the line on 12 March, the date that he had sent his final card home. Subsequently the Communist Party had been highly evasive about Taylor's fate, and his death was eventually confirmed by three Welsh comrades during the summer. Another, Harry Dobson, wrote to tell her that Taylor had "fought for four days in [the] retreat to Caspe where they had 'left him behind wounded' – and so the chapter ends". Amidst the anxiety as to Taylor's fate, his wife (also a Communist Party member) had failed her medical exams and was now sailing to India to recuperate. Mrs Shaxby's anger was intense and focused: "I at least curse Harry Pollitt and all of you who worked on that poor delicate lad's sensibilities – how I watched his face when *you* [i.e. Haldane] spoke last in Cathays Park." Above all, she resented the fact that Taylor's life had been "wasted" (he "fought at most for 4 days & all the years to come are gone") when he had much to contribute to the Republican cause in South Wales. "[H]e ought never to have been allowed to go." Her parting shot was that "I do not want or expect any answer – I only want you to *think*."[71]

Vanessa Bell also found it impossible to accept the death of her eldest son, Julian, who was killed while serving with an ambulance unit at the battle of Brunete. She suffered a breakdown on receiving the news on 20 July 1937, and drew little comfort from the thought – expressed by many who wrote to her[72] – that his death had been in some sense a worthwhile sacrifice. As she confided to one of his former girl-friends a month after his death: "I think there is one thing I want desperately to say to any one who will listen – if only I could – and that is simply that I am quite sure, reasonably and definitely sure, that the loss of people like Julian *is* a waste."[73] Her pain was sharpened by her close and intense friendship with Julian, by his failure to fulfil his talent as a writer, and by her own failure to dissuade him from joining the British Medical Unit. (This was itself a compromise decision as Julian had originally intended to join the International Brigades.) Vanessa drew some solace from discussing Julian's death with his former medical aid colleagues, such as Portia Holman and Richard Rees. However, Archie Cochrane, who had been the triage officer at Brunete when Bell was brought in, felt that the family blamed him for the young man's death.[74] Vanessa Bell was never reconciled to Julian's death and she refused to assume the role that so many grieving mothers accepted: "there was no willing sacrifice on my part".[75] It was a small consolation for the family to know that Julian had a grave (he had been buried at Fuencarral, north of Madrid) whereas many volunteers – in so far as their resting place was known – may only have had a small, unmarked cairn of stones.[76]

The surviving volunteers had also, of course, experienced profound loss during and after the Civil War. All had lost close comrades as well as witnessing close-quarter combat or the bloody aftermath of battle in dressing stations and front-line hospitals. Such harrowing personal experiences were bitterly compounded by the eventual defeat of the Republican cause in which all of the volunteers had come to believe. Even the resilient nurse Ann Murray wrote that her experiences following the fall of Barcelona and the subsequent flight to the French border in 1939 had "left a black mark in my memory which I shall *never* be able to throw off".[77] Some presented symptoms of mental trauma. Scottish volunteer Hugh Sloan recalled that "[w]hen I returned I found that I couldn't bear to talk about Spain and the sense of loss that I felt about it", and he did not talk "or even think" about it for many years.[78] Tony Hyndman, a Communist and former Guardsman who was jailed in Spain for desertion, wrote an agonised poem about his experiences at the battle of the Jarama but found that "the emotion lives on. I don't think I want to lose it". Many years later he reflected that he had been "living with ghosts" since the Civil War and described Spain as his "scar".[79]

Many volunteers undoubtedly benefited from a continuing sense of comradeship and, even in peacetime, still thought of themselves as "the Battalion". However, others felt diminished and undervalued by their return to civilian life, and even excluded from the community of veterans. Although the IBD&WAC was publicly portrayed as offering a high level of support for those "home from the battlefield",[80] not enough was done to reintegrate those former volunteers who felt bewildered and marginalised. Some came back to broken marriages, lost homes and unemployment, as well as facing persistent ill-health due to their wounds. One, Frank Bailey, complained of a forthcoming memorial meeting that it would be better if the "heros (sic) of the international brigade got a square deal". He later wrote that "we were as the soldier of the Imperialist on the scrap heap".[81] John Patterson, an Edinburgh volunteer who returned from Spain with a bullet lodged in his lung in May 1938, was quick to claim that he was the victim of "Stalinist" political discrimination when his allowance was cut. Tom Murray warned him against cutting "himself off from the general body of the Ex-Brigaders".[82] A wounded former adjutant, William McDade of Dundee, publicly complained about the "very lean time" that many returning volunteers faced: "left to starve, with no allowance . . . and an open wound". He was particularly critical of the "political heroes" created by the *Daily Worker*. The men of the British Battalion, in his view, were "real men, real democrats and heroes, but they were not all leading C.P. members and couldn't all be political heroes".[83] Even some senior figures never recovered their equilibrium after returning from Spain. Jock Cunningham, a former commander of the Battalion who was removed from his post after the battle of Brunete, was reported in 1952 to be "tramping the roads up and down the country. He had a sort of mental break-down, and . . . has been a patient in some mental institution."[84]

Given that a sense of loss could be expressed in such diverse ways, some of which were highly critical of the role of the Communist Party, why was its political impact so muted? One explanation is that such critical voices were essentially personal and isolated, lacking a political focus. Admittedly, an "International Brigaders Anti-Communist League" claimed 100 members in February 1939,[85] but it appears to have been short-lived. Even those volunteers who spoke out against alleged incompetence or political manipulation often tended to add the qualification that they had no regrets about their decision to volunteer.[86] In any case, horrific stories about the conditions under which the volunteers fought merely enhanced a sense of their heroism. In January 1939, for instance, the artist William Townsend attended a talk given by Ted Edwards, former battalion secretary. Although Townsend was astonished to hear of the "ridiculous staff inefficiency", and the resulting privations and lack of basic equipment, he merely took this as further proof of the ordinary volunteers' "incredible determination and bravery . . . every man of the brigade is accounted a hero".[87] Above all, the Communist Party proved extremely successful at providing meaning for the tragic loss of life in Spain and the suffering of the volunteers' relatives. Discordant individual voices could not be silenced. However, as the final part of this chapter will argue, a process of commemoration during the Civil War, followed by the rapid creation of a community of volunteers and their supporters in its aftermath, forged a powerful consensus of opinion that these lives had certainly not been wasted.

III

Even during the Civil War itself the Communist Party took great care to tend the memory of the British volunteers. A powerful political impulse was at work in fashioning the British Battalion not only as a military unit in Spain but also as a factor within domestic politics, and this meant that both the nature of the memory and the pattern of commemoration had to be established very swiftly. From the beginning the members of the British Battalion were presented as the heroic defenders of democracy, upholding the honour of the British labour movement, rather than – as their critics contended – dupes and mercenaries who had no place in a foreign conflict. Meanwhile, every effort was made to isolate disaffected elements from the rest of the volunteers.

The writer Ralph Fox, who died at the battle of Lopera in early January 1937, was the first leading British Communist to perish fighting with the International Brigades, and his death was immediately and extensively commemorated. For many days, whole pages of the *Daily Worker* were given over to appreciations by those who had known and worked with him, a memorial meeting was held, and a fund was started in his honour. Letters were also published from Fox's widow and his parents, who wrote that "we may at least feel proud and comforted that he was not backward in risking himself for an ideal to which he passionately devoted his whole life".[88] At Fox's memorial meeting the mood was described as one of "sorrow relieved by burning indignation against all the forces of reaction".[89] As Valentine Cunningham has noted, the tributes to Fox overshadowed the death – in the same action – of the young Cambridge academic John Cornford. This reflected the fact that Fox had already achieved a position of some eminence within Communist politics, whereas Cornford's fame (both as a poet and as an iconic figure for his generation) developed posthumously. By October 1938 Cornford, too, was being hailed as a "modern hero", typical of the "new kind of intellectual fighter for liberty . . . "[90]

Fox and Cornford joined a "Roll of Honour" that grew alarmingly when the British Battalion went into action in the Jarama valley in February 1937. Although the extent of the losses was slow to emerge, Pollitt eventually had to convey the horrifying news a month later that "our British Battalion of over 600 strong is now no more than 200. The rest of the comrades are either killed or wounded."[91] The appalling losses on the Jarama and at subsequent pitched battles inevitably changed the nature of commemoration as the individualised, *ad hoc* arrangements of the early months gave way to collective acts of remembrance, both locally and nationally. Such events were increasingly planned and choreographed to create the maximum emotional impact, especially as the British participation in the Civil War drew to its close. A "Memorial Service" at the Communist Party's Congress in September 1938, for instance, was praised for its "extreme simplicity", but the combination of low lighting, sombre music and pregnant silences ("save for an occasional repressed sob") made an indelible impression on all those present. Fred Copeman, a rough-hewn proletarian who had led the British Battalion, broke down while reading a message that would be sent to the remaining volunteers in Spain. He got no further than the phrase: "We remember Bill and Charlie, Harry, George and Jim and all those hundreds more . . . " The ceremony concluded with the mass singing of "Far from their homeland", a new song dedicated to the International Brigades.[92] There were similar scenes in late November 1938 when some two thousand people attended a rally to commemorate the five Aberdeen men who had died in Spain. They stood for a silence "broken only by the sobbing of women who were overcome by their emotions". A huge placard, spot-lit by a single light in the darkened hall, carried the men's names and slogans such as "They died for us" and "Long live democracy".[93]

This phase of commemoration reached a peak with the complete withdrawal of the International Brigades and the return of the remainder of the British Battalion in December 1938. A large crowd, joined by the Labour Party leader Clement Attlee, welcomed some 300 volunteers at Victoria Station. The men marched from the station as "soldiers of the real Britain, still mobilised in the cause of democracy and peace".[94] A month later, on 8 January 1939, nine thousand people took part in a national rally to honour the International Brigades at the Empress Hall, London. This event was also carefully planned, down to the opening "fanfare of silver trumpets accompanied by drums". The "thrills and emotional highlights" included a march past by more than 400 veterans, with gaps left in their ranks to indicate the fallen. At the end of the evening a group of former volunteers set off to tour Britain in an International

Brigade "convoy".[95] There was a final burst of activity in July 1939 when separate "Debt of Honour" weeks were held in Scotland and England. The principal purpose was to raise funds for the disabled volunteers, but the survivors of the British battalion marched again behind their banners at a large Communist rally in London, and they were eulogised in the *Daily Worker*. A poem by David Martin showed how the British volunteers would be woven into the party's future struggles:

> *When we fight in England the last campaign*
> *We will sing of the lads we buried in Spain*
> *Of hearts that beat bravely and strong.*[96]

To what extent can the Communist Party be said to have hijacked the commemoration of the dead volunteers? One family that appears to have thought so was that of Sid Hamm, who attempted to have a Communist memorial service in his honour in Cardiff broken up by the police.[97] There were undoubtedly many family members who felt that their fallen relatives had been "appropriated" and allowed to become "public property".[98] For the majority of families and friends, however, and especially for those who broadly shared the volunteers' anti-fascist outlook, such memorials were doubtless to be welcomed. For the families – often denied a body, a grave, or even reliable information as to how their loved one had died – these meetings provided a focus for grief that was, in any case, unlikely to be provided from any other source.

In the short term, the British Battalion's principal official "memorial" was a fund for assisting the disabled veterans. In July 1938 Bill Rust had told the CPGB Central Committee that "we have got to see these boys that come home are properly treated . . . no feeling on their part that they are forgotten and it is all over". He warned that finding jobs for returning volunteers would be a "very acute problem".[99] Charlotte Haldane had promised that the Spanish government would take financial responsibility for the volunteers once the war was over,[100] but this, of course, assumed a Republican victory. Instead, a National Memorial Fund was established in September 1938, which aimed to raise £50,000 in order that former volunteers would not have to "'live from hand to mouth'".[101] However, even fund-raising for the volunteers' daily requirements declined sharply after the withdrawal of the International Brigades in the autumn of 1938, as many donors assumed that the need had now passed. It is likely that only about a fifth of the intended memorial fund was ever raised. By the end of July 1939 half of a scaled-down objective of £20,000 had been collected.[102]

A more significant long-term task was to create a community of

returned volunteers, their families and supporters, dedicated to perpetu-
ating the memory of the International Brigaders as British "volunteers for
liberty." With this end in mind the International Brigade Association
(IBA) was formed shortly before the end of the Civil War in February
1939. This took the place of a number of *ad hoc* organisations that had
sprung up, as well as seeing off the ephemeral challenge of the "anti-
communist" League. The IBA was, at the same time, a campaigning body
committed to carrying on the British Battalion's anti-fascist struggle and
a veterans' organisation. Full membership was restricted to the volunteers, although families were entitled to associate membership.[103]
However, the IBA was far from fully representative of the British volunteers. Although barely any membership figures are available, it can be
established that in 1946 there were only 376 full members and 159 asso-
ciates, overwhelmingly based in London and Glasgow. Bill Alexander has
written that by the end of 1948 "the Association was in touch with 550
members of whom 200 were involved in Spanish issues". It seems likely,
therefore, that a decade after the withdrawal of the British Battalion
barely a quarter of the surviving volunteers was actively involved with
the IBA.[104]

An important part of the IBA's work was to claim the legacy and
protect the reputation of the British Battalion. In this respect there was
considerable continuity with the earlier efforts of the IBD&WAC to
deter those who were thought to be trading on their status as volunteers
for personal gain. In December 1937 Charlotte Haldane issued a circular
to warn public figures that the recently-returned Joseph Jenkins was
"making a profession" from writing begging letters, even though his
family had continued to receive assistance after his return from Spain.[105]
Another warning was issued against a young volunteer, George Watts,
who was described as a "fairly plausible liar".[106] At the foundation of the
IBA in February 1939 concern was expressed about the "bad elements"
amongst the returned volunteers,[107] and this was merely the beginning of
a long, watchful campaign. In 1947 the IBA secretary Nan Green referred
to a "small core" of former volunteers who were unworthy of their association with the Brigades, while in 1949 she reported a "handful of
no-goods who drift round the country and try and get help from the I.B.
in every town where they land".[108] Not only did a distinction have to be
drawn between the deserving and the undeserving former volunteers, but
also the currency of the International Brigade was far too precious for it
to be devalued by "no-goods".

During its early years, the IBA concentrated principally on political
campaigns, especially on behalf of former comrades stranded in French

and Spanish prison camps. It is striking to note how little attention was paid in this period to the creation of fixed public memorials, the overwhelming majority of which were erected from the mid-1970s onwards.[109] Indeed, in 1949 it is instructive to record the scathing response of Nan Green to a proposed campaign for such a memorial in Glasgow: "if people can't be won to think about Franco's role as a war danger and the Spanish people's fight for peace, I don't think they will be won for a memorial plaque."[110] The purpose of commemoration was not to be for its own sake, but to advance the political goals for which the British Battalion had fought and for which the Communist Party continued to fight.

Such considerations clearly underpinned a memorial volume in honour of Jack Brent (1912–1951), a popular veteran who had defied crippling wounds to play a leading role in the IBA. Brent was a totemic figure not only because of his courage and good humour in the face of constant physical pain,[111] but also because his story was one of redemption through self-sacrifice and political commitment. The Canadian-born Scotsman had made little of his life prior to his decision to volunteer, and even a friend confided that "he went to Spain as a soldier of fortune . . . he had no real conception of the struggle there".[112] Yet, although a bullet through the spine ended his career as a soldier after only a few hours in action, Brent would later recall that his decision to volunteer "began the only period of my life which I like to think has been worth while".[113] Stanley Harrison, the Communist journalist and former volunteer who was invited to draft the book, was fully aware that it was this wider political context which gave value to the project. He commented in 1952 that the book's underlying purpose must be to relate Brent's life to "the two main tasks today: the fight for peace, and the fight to build a party of the calibre to win it". The first theme, therefore should be "Jack as a type of the 'new man' made by the Party and the movement. Thirst for knowledge, broad humanity, unfailing optimism, quickness of eye for the potentialities of people whom some might 'write off', and courage." Brent's role as "fighter for Spain, and a representative man of the movement that kept faith to the cause of the Spanish people" came second.[114]

IV

On 29 April 1950 a plaque commemorating Ralph Fox was unveiled in his home town of Halifax, soon after what would have been the writer's fiftieth birthday. The memorial, mounted on a seat in the city's Bull

Green area, was the work of a committee representing the local labour movement and presided over by the Marxist historian E. P. Thompson. The plaque was dedicated in the presence of many Civil War veterans and the banner of the British Battalion. The "Himno de Riego" (the anthem of the Spanish Republic) was sung, along with "Jerusalem", "The Internationale" and, appropriately, "Nameless Martyrs". The committee also raised enough money to fund a series of annual lectures – the first was given by G. D. H. Cole in 1951 – which lasted well into the 1950s and was revived in 1986.[115]

The unveiling of the Fox memorial represents a fitting point to conclude this chapter, for two reasons. First, although modest, this memorial seat was the first permanent, public monument dedicated to the memory of those Britons who had fallen in Spain.[116] In this respect, it marked a small but significant shift in the pattern of commemoration, in favour of fixed, physical memorials. This would accelerate in the 1970s, and culminate in the unveiling of the national memorial on London's South Bank in 1985. Secondly, while the Fox memorial publicly appeared to unite the local community in honouring his memory, it also revived old and painful memories for his close family. His widow, Madge Moxley, approved of the plaque, but found the decision to create the memorial the occasion for almost overwhelming sadness: "when I look on rare occasions at [Ralph's] pictures, a lump comes to my throat and I wonder why such a person should have been taken so young". Moreover, Fox's parents and other relatives stated that due to "political differences" they were unable to associate themselves with the memorial committee. In a public statement they noted that Fox had died before Communism became "the evil thing it is now", and questioned the decision of "a small group of people, with probably no personal knowledge or acquaintance with their son" to appropriate his memory. Fox's mother died soon afterwards, and in line with her final wishes Ralph's name was inscribed on her gravestone along with the following comment: "He lies near Lopera, Andalusia, where he died in battle bravely as he lived."[117] Fox's bravery was not in doubt: however, loss and memory continued to pose far more profound questions for all those associated with the British volunteers in Spain.

Chapter 8
My country right or left
John Langdon-Davies and Catalonia

The train reached Barcelona at nine o'clock. Many a time have I welcomed the brilliance of that city, the sign that a tedious journey was nearly over; but now it seemed that we were plunging still further into night. Not a light burned in the streets save through thick blue glass, not a shop or café or cinema or electric advertisement shone out. Everywhere a blackness, a negative welcome prepared for the aeroplanes of 'unknown nationality' likely to come any night from the direction of Mallorca. Every window pane covered with thick paper . . . .Even the tram cars and the buses groped in gloom. A sad state for what was once the starriest city in western Europe.

(John Langdon-Davies, 1937)[1]

John Langdon-Davies (1897–1971) achieved many things during his life. A man described somewhat inadequately in his *Times* obituary as a "sociologist and author",[2] should also be remembered as a political and social activist, as an accomplished war correspondent and student of unconventional warfare, and as a brilliant populariser of science and technology. He was also a charismatic public speaker and ever-engaging companion, who made a vivid impression on his contemporaries.[3] His interests were remarkable for their sheer scope, and many of them were ahead of their time – notably his writings on the history of women and on sexuality.[4] Understandably for such a polymath, at times his enthusiasms appeared contradictory. For instance, he was a positivist who was also drawn to investigate the paranormal and the "unknown", and he was both fascinated and disturbed by the American modernity that he encountered in the 1920s. (Indeed, few British intellectuals of his day can have been as familiar as Langdon-Davies with the United States, which he visited many times.) The very variety and intensity of his interests may explain why the author of more than forty books, and a significant figure in the British intellectual and political life of the period 1935–45, is not better known today. His books are currently out of print – at least in English – and this means that his work is often remembered through the selective quotation of his most famous opponents.[5] However, at least one of the projects which he initiated, the Spanish fostering scheme that became the charity "Plan International", continues to thrive today.

Amongst the many facets of Langdon-Davies's public life there is one, his relationship with Catalonia, which links almost every phase of his career. His direct engagement with Catalonia spanned three specific periods: the 1920s; the Spanish Civil War; and (intermittently) the period between his return to Spain in 1949 and his death in 1971. Each of these periods produced a distinctive piece of writing: *Dancing Catalans* (1929); *Behind the Spanish Barricades* (1936), and *Gatherings from Catalonia* (1953). There was no doubting his deep affection for Catalonia: hence, the third of these books was written out of love "of Spain, its peoples, and Catalans in particular".[6] He came to appreciate the very different qualities of the mountainous valleys running down from the Pyrenees, the rugged coast-line with its resorts and fishing villages, and the bustling capital, Barcelona, which he memorably described as his "well-beloved mistress".[7] Even so, his relationship with Catalanism – the political and cultural expression of Catalan identity – was surprisingly complex and ambivalent. It was sensitive to changes in Spanish politics, as Spain veered between peace, civil war, revolution and dictatorship, as well as to changes in Langdon-Davies' own political outlook. To chart John Langdon-Davies's relationship with Catalonia is, therefore, to chart his attitudes towards politics more generally.

The nature of the available source material imposes certain limitations on the historian. In particular, although Langdon-Davies was a professional writer who wrote copiously throughout his life, apart from an early, experimental memoir (*Then a Soldier* . . . [1934[8]]) only fragments remain of the more substantial autobiography that he intended to write. Moreover, he did not keep a regular diary. The most valuable surviving record of this nature is a "Journal of Escape" which he wrote between 1950 and 1955 and which contains numerous reflections on his career.[9] Langdon-Davies was primarily a man of action and he was far less interested than, say, George Orwell in shaping a narrative of his career for public consumption. A very significant collection of Langdon-Davies's letters and other papers remains in the possession of his family, but this by no means provides a complete record of his activities and relationships during the period of his greatest political activity. Likewise, few of the campaigns with which he was associated kept archives of any substance. Hence, only a fleeting documentary record survives of the children's home that he established in the foothills of the Pyrenees in 1937, even though this significant humanitarian measure must have absorbed much of his time during the Civil War.[10]

The 1920s

John Langdon-Davies initially visited Catalonia on holiday with his first wife Constance (they had married in 1918) in May 1920.[11] He returned there to live, in Ripoll, between May 1921 and late 1922 with his young family. The family came back again, this time to live on the coast at Sant Feliu de Guíxols, between 1926 and 1928. During these years Spain was under the dictatorship of General Primo de Rivera, the opening phase of which Langdon-Davies had briefly reported as a journalist in September 1923. This first set of encounters with Catalonia is perhaps the least complex and the least well documented of the three. Langdon-Davies was still a young man, already a published poet, with an incomplete Oxford education that had been shortened by his wartime conscientious objection. He was fascinated by his discovery of Catalonia and, as his biographer points out, would consistently look to it as a refuge when he wanted to escape the "mechanised civilisation".[12] His willingness to embrace Catalanism led to him being welcomed into the heart of contemporary Catalan culture. He forged strong friendships (notably, with the engineer Ramon Casanova) and met leading lights of Catalan poetry and literature such as Josep Pla, Marià Manent and Ventura Gassol. Many of them were members of the nationalist party Acció Catalana, which was founded in 1922. Indeed, Langdon-Davies attended the party's first meeting in Ripoll. One particular point of contact was his interest in the Irish question, a topic of great current interest to Catalan nationalists on which he was sometimes called to speak.

For Langdon-Davies Catalonia – above all, rural and small town Catalonia – was a special and timeless place. When he offered a European summer "party" to American tourists (at $2000 per head) in 1927, the itinerary not only took in Paris and London, but also, "to correct the impression" gained there, the Pyrenees and the north Spanish coast. Here, "lounging amid the cork trees of the Mediterranean villages of North Spain" the visitors would encounter "old world Europe in its least spoilt form".[13] The most profound expression of Langdon-Davies's feeling for Catalonia is to be found in *Dancing Catalans*, published after his return to Britain. He later acknowledged that, while the book had not sold particularly well, it was one that "I had put my soul into".[14] From its opening account of an idyllic picnic in the woods above Sant Feliu, this enchanting book offers a loving but not romanticised evocation of the countryside, the way of life and the social rituals of what was still a relatively remote corner of Europe. It draws the reader into an understanding of Catalonia by means of a prolonged meditation on the Sardana, the Catalan popular dance. In fact, for Langdon-Davies the Sardana's complex circular formations and rhythmic steps represented not so much a dance as "a communal ceremony, a social ritual" and above all a "symbol of national consciousness: the Sardana is Catalunya". It captured all that he most admired in the Catalan national identity; it was spontaneous, unthreatening, "altogether democratic" and inclusive for men and women of all ages. The effect was to create a rapture in which the dancers "recreated human happiness".[15]

Langdon-Davies sympathised deeply with Catalan grievances under "Castilian" domination in the 1920s, and especially when, under the repressive rule of Primo de Rivera, his Catalan friends wrote to tell him of their "pitiful condition".[16] Many intellectuals were in exile, and Langdon-Davies was aware that Catalan language and literature were being "persecuted, political rights denied, education and culture throttled". However, in a striking passage in *Dancing Catalans* that in some respects foreshadows the turmoil of the Civil War, he warned that any violent resistance to such depredations would trigger even worse reprisals. Moreover, he predicted that even if such a rebellion could succeed it would still prove fatal to Catalan customs and traditions. In the modern world, he reflected, "only oppressed nationalities can retain their personalities".[17] Langdon-Davies felt most comfortable, therefore, with a Catalan nationalism that was irenic (Catalonia had no army or colonies) and rural. There is little reference in *Dancing Catalans* to Barcelona or the social and political tensions generated by Catalonia's rapid industrialisation. He had no time for violent separatism, let alone for those who dreamed of recreating a Catalan empire that would include the linguistically and culturally compatible regions of southern France.

Catalonia did not, of course, absorb all of Langdon-Davies's energies during the 1920s. In 1923, for instance, he stood unsuccessfully as the Labour Party candidate for Epsom, and the Divisional Labour Party would have liked him to stand again.[18] Moreover, in addition to his burgeoning career as a writer he was also building a reputation as a lecturer in the United States, where he spent most of 1925 with his family. Even so, Catalonia, with its "rare species of solitude",[19] provided a valuable counterpoint to this frenetic trans-Atlantic lifestyle. Here Langdon-Davies found relaxation, inspiration and an environment in which he could write. Meanwhile, he was steadily – and not necessarily intentionally – emerging as that rarest of creatures in the 1920s, an English Catalanist. However, the Catalonia that he had encountered during the 1920s was about to face abrupt change. During that decade the threat to Catalan aspirations had emanated from the conservative, centralising regimes in Madrid. What was not clear was how Langdon-Davies would respond to a reconfiguration of the problem, such as took place after April 1931, when a reforming, democratic Republic took power in Madrid. Writing soon afterwards he hailed the advent of the Republic as a "well-nigh bloodless and good-tempered revolution" that seemed to mark a "real break with the past". "Catalonia, Spain's Ireland," he continued, not wholly accurately, "gained without a blow the freedom which centuries of violent rebellion had failed to recapture."[20]

The Spanish Civil War, 1936–39

If the tone of these early encounters with Catalonia was largely one of serenity and optimism, that of Langdon-Davies's second prolonged engagement with Spain – during the Civil War – was altogether darker. His first wartime visit began on 6 August 1936, barely two weeks after the outbreak of the conflict, when he arrived at the Spanish border as the special correspondent of the liberal *News Chronicle*. He was travelling by motorbike and was accompanied by his fifteen year-old son Robin, who was subsequently lodged with the Casanova family in Campdevanol.[21] The most lasting product of this visit was Langdon-Davies's *Behind the Spanish Barricades*, an eye-witness account of Spain in the throes of revolution and civil war that also strongly attacked the British government's policy of Non-Intervention. Published by Secker & Warburg in November 1936, it was a critical and popular success which even received favourable mention in the House of Lords.[22] It sold 2,300 copies in the first four months[23] and soon ran to three editions. Langdon-Davies returned to Spain, alone, in April 1937 on behalf of the National Joint Committee for Spanish Relief (NJCSR) and opened a home for refugee children at Puigcerda, close to the French border.[24] It was during this visit that he witnessed the fratricidal street fighting in Barcelona of May 1937 (see below), an experience which crystallised his own thinking about how the war should be conducted on the Republican side. Against this violent backdrop of civil war, terror and internecine strife, many of Langdon-Davies's friendships (such as that with Casanova) as well as his Catalanist sympathies were strained and undermined. Indeed, *Spanish Barricades* reads in part as a repudiation of Catalan nationalism, which now struck him as selfish, utopian and, ultimately, self-destructive. What, therefore, had changed during the intervening years?

World politics had, of course, changed beyond recognition between 1929 and 1936. Langdon-Davies had been absent in the United States between 1931 and 1934, having divorced in 1932 and married his second wife (the actress Betty Barr) in 1933. He returned to a Britain in the grip of the Depression and (at least in liberal and left-wing circles) concern at the rise of Fascism. Later, in 1950, he looked back with some bitterness to this return, as marking a personal encounter with a new generation versed in Marxism and looking to the Communist Party for leadership. These young intellectuals seemed obsessed with power and deemed all but the "true believers" to be "evil, dishonest, suborned".[25] However, these hindsight comments betray the impact of Langdon-Davies's pronounced hostility towards Communism at the time of their writing. Looked at in the perspective of the mid-1930s, however, he seems an almost quintessential figure of the intellectual left. Although he was not a Marxist, he was familiar with Marxist thought and shared many of the left-wing assumptions of the time. His *Short History of the Future* (Routledge, London, 1936), the best guide to his political thinking at this point, was predicated on the concept of a world crisis in the capitalist system and argued that liberal democracy was unlikely to survive beyond 1950. He saw the Popular Front and an Anglo-French alliance with the economic and military might of the Soviet Union as the best bulwark against fascist aggression. However, while acknowledging the achievements of the Soviet regime in these spheres, he was by no means an uncritical admirer. The Catalan poet Marià Manent recorded a conversation in February 1937 in which Langdon-Davies stated that "many Marxists regret that Communism, rather than being first implanted in Russia, was not established in Spain. In this case it would have had a less rigidly dictatorial, more libertarian character . . . ".[26]

Langdon-Davies did not only take a theoretical interest in the crisis of the 1930s. From 1936 onwards he played a very active and high profile role in anti-fascist politics: he was seemingly a member of every committee and involved in every campaign. On his return from Spain he felt "numb with misery" at the bigoted, ignorant views that were being expressed about the Civil War in Britain,[27] and he flung himself into campaigning on behalf of the Republic. He was in great demand as a platform speaker, and during the autumn of 1936 he frequently addressed public meetings throughout Britain.[28] In addition to his work with the NJCSR, he served as secretary of the committee unofficially investigating breaches of the Non-Intervention agreement in 1936, and at the end of the war chaired a committee dedicated to rescuing writers from refugee camps in France.[29] He contributed the comment that "art and anti-fascism are synonymous" to the famous 1937 pamphlet *Authors take sides on the Spanish War*, and there was a suggestion that he should write a Left Book Club volume on the Spanish Civil War.[30]

Inevitably, Langdon-Davies worked alongside Communists during these campaigns. He was never a member of the Communist Party, and he secured a retraction from Hugh Thomas when the first edition of his *The Spanish Civil War* (1961) claimed that he was.[31] However, he later described the relationship with the Communists – as did many others in his position – as one in which each side knowingly "used" the other.[32] He had some admiration for the Communists' powers of organisation, and wrote in 1940 that "those who have been associated with progressive movements during [the 1930s] know . . . that no other political party has come within miles of the Communists in the capture of the enthusiasm and idealism of the younger generation in Britain".[33] Ten years later he would note that:

> *what a temptation it was to those of us whose politics were three parts emotion and quixotism to throw in our lot with these hard-working, enthusiastic, determined people who seemed the only people in England not content to fight Hitler and Mussolini with paper resolutions and umbrellas. I very nearly slipped.*[34]

He certainly recognised the importance of winning the support of the Communist Party over those issues on which he held passionate views. For instance, in 1938 he crossed swords – not for the last time – with the leading Communist scientist J. B. S. Haldane over the question of air raid protection (ARP), as the two men had drawn quite differing conclusions from their experiences of aerial bombing in Spain. He wrote to the Communist intellectual Rajani Palme Dutt offering to brief the relevant Communist Party committee, but only if there was a prospect of exercising some influence. "Of course," he added, "if the party line on A.R.P. is to be regarded as fully determined and static, it is obvious that I cannot be of any great help."[35]

Spain had also changed greatly since the late 1920s. The declaration of the Second Republic in April 1931 had opened the door to moderate reform and the peaceful fulfilment of the dream of Catalan autonomy. A devolved Catalan government (the *Generalitat*) had been constituted in 1932, dominated by the non-separatist *Esquerra Republicana de Catalunya* of Lluis Companys. However, Langdon-Davies was aware that an attempted rebellion in October 1934 (which was intended to resist the rightward tendency within the elected Republican government in Madrid, and which was supported by the *Generalitat*) had collapsed very tamely in Catalonia. Many Catalan leaders, including his friend Ventura Gassol (the Catalan Minister of Culture) were subsequently jailed and Catalan autonomy suspended until the election victory of the Popular Front in February 1936. Langdon-Davies returned to Spain in the spring and early summer of 1936 as a journalist, following the election, and reported on the febrile atmosphere of strikes and intense political polarisation that he encountered in a country "plastered with revolutionary manifestoes".[36] Even so, he admired the Republic's political leaders and remained optimistic about its prospects. He argued that "Spain today [mid-May 1936] has perhaps the most constitutional and least corrupt government on the continent of Europe", and that tourists should not be deterred by occasional acts of violence. Even the Spanish Anarchist was a "gentleman" to foreign visitors.[37]

Following the outbreak of the Civil War, Langdon-Davies's passionate anti-fascism led him to adopt a straightforward interpretation of the conflict, which he saw as a criminal assault by Franco and his foreign backers on a democratically elected Spanish government supported by the overwhelming majority of the Spanish people. Accordingly, throughout the war his prime loyalty was to the anti-fascist Republican state. He saw little scope for Catalonia as an independent agent, and he hailed Companys, president of the *Generalitat*, as "the greatest man in Catalunya today" precisely because of his constructive, realistic policies.[38] Conversely, Langdon-Davies was dismayed by the obstructive attitude that many of his Catalan friends took towards the defence of the Republic. For instance, late in 1936 he described himself as one who had been "once a Catalanist, but since October 1934, when the Catalans let the Asturian miners down, I have been less so".[39] He noted that the Catalan separatists "refused to realise that when the bourgeois go fascist, liberals can only survive by putting their trust in the workers".[40] He became convinced of the "moral bankruptcy" of his Catalan friends, who refused to place their skills at the Republic's disposal.[41] Thus, although far better qualified than George Orwell to write a "homage" to wartime Catalonia, he chose not to do so. Catalonia is discussed at some length in *Behind the Spanish Barricades*, yet the book opens with May Day on the streets of Madrid and ends with the

Republican militias besieging the Alcazar in Toledo. One of the most sympathetic characters is an unnamed "Marquis" who, unlike the Catalan intellectuals, is capable of humanitarian feeling for his fellow Spaniards in the conflict. The book's heroes are definitely not the Catalan intellectuals, but rather the "humble folk of Spain".[42]

But could the Catalan middle classes be expected to trust the workers when, during the initial stages of the civil war, gunmen principally associated with the Anarchist movement were conducting a murderous reign of terror? Like many other Britons of his generation and political beliefs Langdon-Davies found Spanish Anarchism attractive and even heroic, but he had no illusions that Anarchism could organise an effective defence of the Republic during the civil war. Even so, he did not share the revulsion that many of his old Catalan friends felt for the Anarchists as "Murcian" interlopers intent on destroying Catalan culture.[43] In 1938 he described the Anarchists as "superb, lovable human beings" who "had to be mentally changed before the power of the people in Spain could be effectively used".[44] Writing some years after the civil war one still finds some trace of this sympathy for the Anarchists who – unlike the Communists – are described as still being "capable of love". In Barcelona, Langdon-Davies noted, the Anarchists tore down jails in 1936 while the Communists planned the "brightly lit prisons and interrogating rooms of their future world-paradise".[45] He had far less sympathy for the POUM, the other leading revolutionary group with a Catalan base. He regarded them as at best "yapping like a troublesome puppy at everybody's heels and spoiling for a dog fight". At worst they were a divisive, destabilising force with – wittingly or not – immense nuisance value for Franco.[46]

Langdon-Davies struggled to understand the leftist violence – directed against suspected "fascists", clerics and religious property – that was so disfiguring to the Republic's cause and so damaging to its international standing. His principal argument was that the blame should rest with those who had launched the rebellion, rather than with the Spanish people who were desperately clinging on to their recent social and political gains. There was, he noted, a "disintegration of human nature" which inevitably accompanied civil war.[47] Accordingly, he presented a massacre of thirteen fascist sympathisers (including priests) in Ripoll as: "Ugly? Yes, but how natural; thanks to those who let loose the supreme horror of civil war . . . ".[48] Similarly, he saw the Terror as not being the fault of the Anarchist political organisation (the FAI), but of "a few dozen psychopaths" hiding in its ranks.[49] He also believed that the extent of the political violence had been greatly exaggerated. In early September 1936 he visited the Foreign Office and explained that in normal times some ten murders took place each night in Barcelona, compared with a current figure of twenty. He calculated that there had been as few as 200 violent deaths in the city since the military rising. This was, without question, a serious underestimation of the nightly carnage in and around the Catalan capital, and one that did little for Langdon-Davies's credibility in diplomatic circles.[50]

At the same time, Langdon-Davies also believed that the breaking of the influence of the Catholic Church, and the fact that Spain had "rooted out the sacred symbols",[51] should be seen as a political act rather than as vandalism. The destruction of the churches – and more specifically of their contents – represented an attempt by the Anarchists to destroy the spiritual, even "magical" sources of clerical power, akin to the iconoclasm of Cromwell's Roundheads.[52] He welcomed the fact that a great deal of art previously owned privately by religious establishments was now in public hands – indeed, he told a meeting in September 1936 that, despite the church-burnings, "the gain is greater than the loss".[53] His choice of language on this issue – at one point he alluded to a mistaken belief that churches were being burnt "well greased with monks and nuns" – was misunderstood by his opponents in the Catholic press, to their cost. Following attacks on him in the *Tablet* and the *Catholic Herald*, Langdon-Davies brought a successful libel action against both newspapers, and forced them to acknowledge publicly that he was not an "inhuman or heartless" person who gloried in acts of anti-religious violence.[54] He used part of the resulting damages to publish a pamphlet which was intended to demonstrate to English Catholics that the Spanish Church "wishes to destroy . . . that very form of political liberalism to which he, as a Catholic, owes his social, political and religious freedom in England".[55]

By the time of Langdon-Davies's return to Spain in April 1937 with the NJCSR, the fundamental division in the Republican ranks between the supporters of the centralising Republican government and the revolutionaries – or as he later put it "between authoritarianism and libertarianism"[56] – could no longer be avoided. Indeed, like Orwell, Langdon-Davies was personally caught up in the street fighting in Barcelona in early May that finally broke the back of the revolutionary groups as a political force. He described how this tragic conflict moved to a bloody conclusion in an unpublished manuscript written some months after the May fighting.[57] Here he recorded the localised violence between the Anarchists and their opponents, both in Barcelona and the valleys to the north, which was in his view driving the Republican war effort to the brink of collapse. He referred to the murder of the socialist militant Roldan Cortada as "an example of the sort of action which shows brutally why [the] social revolution had to be liquidated". He added that "at least we can say that if order had not been brought to the rearguard . . . Franco would have been now amid the smoking ruins of Barcelona."[58]

Although he was officially engaged in relief work, the Barcelona fighting immediately brought out the journalist in Langdon-Davies. He spent most of 3 and 4 May on the streets, notebook and camera in hand, avoiding bullets and recording his impressions of the edgy but generally good-natured militias. His immediate thought was simply that "the whole thing seems more futile than anything", and that "enough armament to take Zaragoza" had been wasted.[59] On 10 May he reported in the *News Chronicle* that four hundred had been killed in the fighting, which he described as being the result of a "frustrated putsch by the 'Trotskyist' POUM, working through their controlled organisations, 'Friends of Durruti' and Libertarian Youth". He went on to predict that one consequence of the rising would be "the elimination of the POUM". This interpretation went largely uncontested in Britain at the time, given that the POUM and the Anarchists had few political friends.

However, George Orwell's criticism of Langdon-Davies's report in *Homage to Catalonia*, a book which has grown immensely in its impact since its initial publication in 1938[60], has – unfairly – placed an image in the public mind of Langdon-Davies as a defender of Stalinist tactics. Orwell accused Langdon-Davies of "very serious misrepresentation" of the situation, and of being incautious and uncritical in his handling of official information.[61] In reality, of course, neither man was in a position to reach a definitive judgment on the May events in Barcelona, events which remain hotly disputed by historians even after the opening of the Comintern archives in Moscow during the 1990s. Langdon-Davies was certainly mistaken to blame the fighting on a "putsch" by the POUM. Most historians would now agree that the POUM was, if anything, a hapless bystander to a conflict between elements of the Anarchist movement and the forces of the central and Catalan governments. The POUM was subsequently scapegoated by the Republican authorities and by the Communist Party as it was more politically vulnerable than the Anarchists. However, it should be noted that Langdon-Davies's broader argument, that the imposition of order was a political necessity for the building of a Republican state capable of winning the war, is one that has found favour amongst some recent historians.[62]

In the context of this chapter, it should be noted that Langdon-Davies arrived at his analysis of the "May days" as a result of his own expert appreciation of the political situation in the Republican zone and his exasperation with the violent nihilism which he perceived within elements of the Catalan revolutionary left. His dislike of the POUM, in particular, was visceral and did not toe a party line. Indeed, there was some evidence that the Communist Party did not deem Langdon-Davies wholly reliable on this issue when he took part in a public debate with ILP leader Fenner Brockway in October 1937. Langdon-Davies, just back from Barcelona, defended the resolution "that the suppression of the POUM was essential to the anti-fascist cause in Spain." The ILP, while not liking his "cheap sneers", was delighted that Langdon-Davies appeared to make two "important admissions" in the debate. First, he had abandoned the "Communist pretence" that the POUM and the Anarchists had been treated fairly in the distribution of weapons, and had argued that the supply of weapons to such groups would merely swell "their vast private armouries". Secondly, Langdon-Davies had stated that it was correct for the Spanish government to liquidate the social revolution in Spain because a Syndicalist revolution (as opposed to a socialist one) "was bound to fail, as a dozen similar Spanish revolutions had failed in the past". The *Daily Worker* was quick to point out that Langdon-Davies was not a member of the Communist Party, and neither was he representing it in the debate.[63]

The Barcelona fighting marked a watershed in Republican politics and, indeed, in Langdon-Davies's own involvement in the Spanish Civil War. Although he made further visits for the NJCSR in the course of 1937 and 1938, he largely ceased to write on political matters. Indeed, in the latter part of the war his attention was increasingly focused on the implications of aerial bombardment – which he had witnessed in Barcelona – for Britain's own security. Following the imposition of internal order in May 1937, Langdon-Davies welcomed the formation of a new Republican government under the socialist Juan Negrin (although Negrin was, in fact, no friend of Catalanism.[64]) He acknowledged that this government was formed "thanks to the initiative and close co-operation of the Spanish Communist Party", and was optimistic that it would at last create a disciplined war economy.[65] And yet, with the resurgent power of the central Republican state, the unavoidable conclusion was that Catalan nationalism was – at least in the context of the civil war – a political dead end. The only way forward was for the Catalans to ally with the emerging Republican regime in order to retain order in the rearguard and defeat Franco's Nationalists. It was Langdon-Davies's adherence to this logic which caused so much damage to his Catalan friendships, although it hardly helped that he had made his criticisms of his friends so publicly, so harshly and in so thinly-veiled a manner in *Behind the Spanish Barricades*.

One final point should be made about Langdon-Davies's wartime experiences in Catalonia. The writer was reassured to find that the popular culture of Barcelona, in areas such as the proletarian Fifth District, was able to survive the war and the revolutionary puritanism of the Anarchists. This had not been apparent in August 1936, when the cabarets and bars of the Paralelo had largely been closed. However, by April 1937 he found the city's night life reviving and only marginally constrained by Anarchist decrees. The female cabaret performers were as he remembered in his youth – "their songs, their smiles, their lips, their dances, always the same". There was no sign of the emergence of a "revolutionary Spanish drama" or of "a dramatic revival in Spain such as came so quickly to liberated Russia". The only significant change that he noticed in the music halls was an "increased use of the theme of homosexuality". Despite the Anarchist notices that read: "Verguenza – no. Art – si. Shame, no! Art, yes!", Langdon-Davies concluded that "Verguenza like Art ha[ve] not yet been appreciably altered by the revolution."[66] This faith, and pleasure, in the resilience of popular culture under a hostile political regime would have implications in the longer-term for his understanding of Catalonia under Franco's dictatorship.

Interlude, 1939–1949

Catalonia impinged little on John Langdon-Davies during the decade following the end of the Civil War, when he was principally absorbed with the Second World War and its aftermath. His dismay at the defeat of the Republic was only compounded by the bewildering changes in Communist international policy soon afterwards. Like many of his generation who had worked alongside the Communist Party during the anti-fascist campaigns of the 1930s, he felt bitterly let down by the Nazi–Soviet Pact and the Soviet invasion of Finland (which he covered for the *Evening Standard*). For Langdon-Davies, both developments showed the true face of Communist power politics, and "ruined the small beginning of solidarity that we saw over Spain".[67] He confessed to a sense of "loneliness" when those who had "worked along with me, spoken on the same platform" over Spain could now condone Russian aggression.[68] Nowhere was this disgust more forcefully expressed than in his letter of 10 April 1940 to his son Robin, who had joined the Young Communist

League on his return from Spain in 1936.[69] John Langdon-Davies later wrote that after the Communist "buffoonery" during the Second World War, Communists induced in him the same "acute discomfort" as "any other psychotic".[70]

For many on the Left, such as Orwell and Victor Gollancz, fierce disagreement with the Communist Party merely sharpened their anti-fascism and their quest for some useful role in the war with Nazi Germany. In the case of Langdon-Davies – as in the better-known case of Tom Wintringham[71] – this resulted in a significant involvement with the Home Guard. In the summer of 1940 Langdon-Davies wrote extensively on the danger of the "Fifth Column", which he now saw as the principal reason for the defeat of the Spanish Republic,[72] and embarked on a series of lecture tours designed to communicate the military lessons that he had learnt in Spain and Finland. He subsequently established a fieldcraft school for the Home Guard at his farm in Burwash, Sussex, over which he presided with the rank of captain and which, by early 1943 had trained more than 3000 students.[73] However, unlike many military commentators he was pleasantly self-deprecating: at one point he confided that "it is amusing to think how much anybody who writes on military matters can get away with".[74]

Nearly a decade of conflict, 1936–45, left Langdon-Davies exhausted and ill at ease in the post-war world. He described himself in 1949 as a "good social democrat" who also believed that Russian Communism was the "chief danger in the world today" and a danger to the non-Marxist British brand of socialism.[75] He was appalled by the Lysenko affair, which he saw as a final triumph of politics over objective science in the Soviet Union, and published the hard-hitting *Russia puts the clock back* (1949) in response.[76] He also told Julian Huxley, the head of UNESCO, that: "it is most important that the realities of the Cold War or Cold Peace whichever it is, should be reiterated publicly, not in the political sphere but in the cultural sphere . . . unless you are a Communist you simply cannot excuse the Lysenko affair."[77] At the same time he was uncomfortable with the drabness of post-war Britain under the new Labour government. While accepting that the Welfare State was "right and inevitable" he resented the heavy rates of taxation that sustained it and, even more, the threat that it posed to individual freedoms. Above all, he felt that it had destroyed "writing as a profession, that is free writing".[78]

1949 – 1971

Again, Catalonia offered Langdon-Davies the opportunity of "escape", with his third wife Patricia whom he had recently married. In 1949 they departed for Spain, living for two years in the house of the writer Marià Manent at Premià de Dalt. In 1952 the couple opened Casa Rovira in Sant Feliu de Guíxols as a hotel offering friends accommodation and "simple Catalan cuisine" at modest cost. Langdon-Davies joked at the time that he had "retired to become a *hotelier*".[79] The return to Spain was an escape from the grim realities of post-war Britain. As Patricia Langdon-Davies has written, the decision to establish a hotel on the Mediterranean had obvious attractions: "A long November had settled on England with everything in short supply, and the light of battle no longer shone in our eyes. John could write anywhere, and I longed for a warm climate."[80] There was also a chance to renew old friendships and – perhaps – heal wounds from the Civil War. Langdon-Davies had reopened correspondence with Ramon Casanova in 1947, when the Catalan fondly recalled the early "childish" days of their friendship. In 1953 he publicly expressed the hope that Casanova had "forgiven me by now the many things about which we disagree".[81] Shortly before his death in 1968 Casanova would comment that "time buried thick walls between all friends since 1936".[82]

Even so, this third engagement with Catalonia was not without its complexities. Spain in 1950 was languishing under Franco's corrupt and inefficient dictatorship, and had barely begun to emerge from the shadow of the Civil War. Patricia Langdon-Davies has commented on the "ever-present rather forbidding atmosphere of the need for caution" that enveloped Catalonia in the early 1950s, and recalls her husband's fury at being "fiercely hushed" when he tried to talk to a waiter in Catalan. "He had to put up with things, and so did I and so did everybody else."[83] Although Langdon-Davies had lived previously under the dictatorship of Primo de Rivera, unlike Primo's regime, Franco's was one that he had detested and struggled against. In 1961, for instance, he noted that in order to gain the right to reside and run a business he had "had to satisfy the Falange that I was not a member of the Communist party, it being accepted that I was in sympathy with the Republicans".[84] Therefore, like a number of other Britons who had also returned to live in Spain at this time (such as Gerald Brenan, David Bomberg, and Robert Graves), he had to make some form of mental accommodation with Spain as it now existed in the Franco era (although this by no means implies that he offered any formal support or endorsement to the regime). This accommodation was doubtless eased in Langdon-Davies's case by his strong opposition to Communism, and by the knowledge that the centre of world conflict was no longer in Spain. Indeed, on reading of the outbreak of the Korean War in June 1950 he commented: "is it 1938–9 all over again?"[85] The move to Catalonia did not signify an end to his interest in politics, and in May 1950 he was at work on an "Anti-Communist Manifesto", which sought to define a path between Communism and reactionary anti-Communism.

This was the somewhat constrained environment within which Langdon-Davies wrote *Gatherings from Catalonia*, a title that knowingly echoed Richard Ford's renowned *Gatherings from Spain* (1846). His third book on Catalonia makes an informative companion to *Dancing Catalans*, but lacks the exuberance of that first book or the political passion of *Behind the Spanish Barricades*. The book's mood is somewhat sombre: Langdon-Davies acknowledged, for instance, that the brilliance of the public intellectual life of 1920s Barcelona had been destroyed, and that the Catalan bourgeoisie was "frankly not altogether attractive". Even the dubious attractions of the Paralelo were somewhat dimmed, although there is a new awareness in this book of the lasting importance and "simple joys" of popular religion.[86] The intended readership had also changed. This was not a book written for anti-fascists, but for the post-war tourists contemplating a holiday in Catalonia: as Langdon-Davies put it, he was now writing for "prospective, returned and arm-chair travellers alike".[87] It is also a book which – of necessity – was largely silent on many salient themes of the 1950s, not least the legacy of the Civil War and the Franco regime. Instead, it presents Catalonia as a country in many ways unchanged by war and dictatorship, presided over by a repressive state, but one which had little purchase on ordinary citizens. For instance, he commented that Spain was an unusual "police state" as it had so few police[88]. While this may have been the case in Sant Feliu, it hardly did justice to the regime's repressive machinery in cities such as Barcelona, as well as its particular hostility to Catalan language and culture. As for the civil war, Langdon-Davies expressed in his private journal the comment that was only made obliquely in print: namely that "Spain to-day is a fascinating example of mass-repression of uncomfortable thoughts."[89]

Although *Gatherings from Catalonia* is an avowedly non-political book, it still reveals much about the way in which Langdon-Davies coped with the remarkable changes that he had witnessed since the 1920s. In that sense it can be said to mark the end of his Catalan journey: afterwards, he turned far more explicitly away from politics. From the mid-1950s onwards he led an Anglo-Catalan life, raising a young family with Patricia between homes in Sant Feliu and Sevenoaks, Kent. Although his later books lacked the impact of some of his earlier work, he remained a successful and prolific writer both of popular history (sometimes under a pseudonym) and on science and the paranormal. He was also a pioneering educationalist, whose "Jackdaw" series offered school children unprecedented access to facsimiles of historical primary source material. He seems to have had little left to say either about politics or about Catalonia despite the rebirth of radical Catalan politics in the 1960s.[90]

Perhaps this declining interest in politics can be explained as a reaction against the turbulence of the previous three decades. John Langdon-Davies had immersed himself in Europe's wars and its ideological and political crises during the 1930s and 40s as much as any of his contemporaries in British intellectual life. In 1950 he reflected that, during these years of struggle, he had allowed himself to become a "stunted personality". He commented, rather ruefully, that it had taken him three wars to realise that the true quality of life lay in the very "escapism" which he had rejected in the mid-1930s.[91] Now, the return to Catalonia allowed him at last the freedom to do "the work I really wanted to do".[92] By the 1950s he had seen Catalonia in the heyday of intellectual nationalism, in the hands of the revolutionary Left and, finally, under a dictatorship of the Right. It is hardly surprising, then, that eventually in *Gatherings from Catalonia* we see a retreat into a form of essentialism: a belief that the essence of cultures will live on – and may even flourish – irrespective of the political regime. In other words, to paraphrase George Orwell, Catalonia had become his country – right or left.

Chapter 9

Spain rediscovered

*British perceptions of Franco's Spain and
the advent of mass tourism, 1945–1975*

In March 1949 the British writer Giles Romilly visited the village of
Morata de Tajuña, south of Madrid, and attended High Mass on the
Feast of St Joseph. He was no ordinary tourist. What he did not reveal
in his subsequent conversations with the villagers was that "twelve years
ago, when I last saw this church, there were no congregation, no Mass,
no sacred images. It was scrawled with the hammer and sickle, with the
initials and slogans of Republican parties and unions, and stored with
ammunition and provisions for the Republican Army."[1] Indeed, in the
spring of 1937 Morata had been a base for Spanish Republican forces
during the battle of the Jarama, which Romilly had taken part in as a
volunteer with the British battalion of the International Brigades. Now,
after a "timeless hour" in the village tavern, he could not resist returning to the battlefield where so many of his comrades had fallen.
Walking up the hill he found the British trenches, still 4 to 5 feet deep,
and the "sunken road", a well-known feature in which the volunteers
had "crouched [during] one night of the battle". Reflecting on his visit,
however, Romilly was struck, above all, by the dour tranquillity of village life. How "could one believe . . . that Morata had ever been a
powder-box of international emotions, or had ever known clashes more
brutal than those of a donkey-cart and a van?" The local people, he
concluded, had developed a "defensive blankness . . . hard all over, like
the back of a turtle" that had enabled them to survive the upheavals and
disappointments of the Civil War and its aftermath. This was "the speck
of character in Spain which outlasts its droughts and wars", and which
Romilly felt compelled to admire whether it was personified in the village priest, walking amongst "parishioners of proved blood thirstiness",

or in Franco himself, driving through the sullen Madrid crowds in an open-top car.

Romilly's case was a somewhat unusual one, in the sense that few British veterans of the Civil War had either the opportunity or the inclination to return to Spain while Franco was still in power. In late 1946, for instance, one former member of the British Battalion went to stay in the south of France and wrote to friends that "if Franco left while he was there, we should next hear from him on the other side of the border".[2] It would prove a long wait, and many of the volunteers did not return to Spain until after Franco's death in 1975.[3] However, Romilly's visit, and the series of articles that it gave rise to, are not wholly without context. Many of those British writers and intellectuals who had been most familiar with Spain at the time of the Civil War were, by the later 1940s, making a serious attempt to come to terms with the conflict itself, with the dictatorship that it gave rise to, and with the social and cultural changes that had taken place in Spain since 1939. Between 1949 and 1954 Gerald Brenan (whose first visit to Spain for thirteen years exactly coincided with Romilly's), V. S. Pritchett, Rose Macaulay, John Langdon-Davies and Sacheverell Sitwell all wrote significant books on Spain. Each one combined an appreciation of Spain's artistic and cultural heritage with asides on its more recent history. This spate of writing by such well-qualified commentators was the harbinger not only of a tide of less politically reflective travel writing from the mid-1950s onwards, but also of the advent of mass British tourism in Spain. Despite much hand-wringing on the part of the left, by the 1960s millions of British workers were seeking cheap, sunny holidays on the beaches of Spain irrespective of the history – and, indeed, the continuing spasmodic brutality – of the Franco regime.

From the later 1940s onwards, Franco's Spain made steady progress towards gaining international acceptance and respectability. Although the ultimate prizes of NATO and EEC membership were to be denied until after Franco's death, Spain was admitted to the United Nations and many other international organisations, and signed bi-lateral treaties with the United States and the Vatican. Relations with Britain also greatly improved during this period, although certain obstacles – notably the British possession of Gibraltar – remained.[4] This chapter will examine the process of cultural "normalisation" between Britain and Spain that accompanied this strengthening of diplomatic and economic relations: a process by which Spain passed from being widely perceived as a pariah state, governed by a bloodstained dictatorship, to a country which many Britons, of all social groups and political backgrounds, felt comfortable about visiting. This shift in British public opinion was captured in the Gallup polls. In February 1946, 60 per cent of those consulted favoured a complete break in relations with Spain and only 16 per cent disapproved, while in March 48 per cent supported a complete severing of trade relations. Fifteen years later, however, British attitudes to Spain were far more complex. A poll of June 1961 revealed that 14 per cent favoured having "little to do" with Spain at the present, 29 per cent said that it should be treated as "any other country", 29 per cent supported closer relations, and 28 cent offered no opinion.[5] Polls taken towards the end of Franco's dictatorship suggested that there was still some discrimination against Spain on specific issues – for instance, in 1973 53 per cent said that Britain should not sell arms to the Spanish government. However, on a range of issues Spain was regarded with no more or less hostility than many other European states with which Britain had far closer relations.[6]

The chapter begins with an analysis of the most significant writing on Spain of the late 1940s and early 1950s, which emphasised the unchanging, timeless nature of Spanish life. It will pay particular attention to Macaulay's *Fabled Shore* (1949), Brenan's *The Face of Spain* (1950), Sitwell's *Spain* (1950), Langdon-Davies's *Gatherings from Catalonia* (1953) and Pritchett's *The Spanish Temper* (1954). Reference will also be made to the experiences of other writers, such as Robert Graves and Norman Lewis, who, likewise, rediscovered Spain during this period. The second part of the chapter examines the advent of mass tourism in Spain, the political debates which it engendered within Britain, and the longer-term impact on British perceptions of Franco's Spain.

■ ■ ■ ■ ■ ■ ■ ■

The Republican defeat in the Civil War, followed so swiftly by the Second World War and then by post-war austerity, imposed a caesura in Britain's non-governmental contacts with Spain that lasted for the best part of a decade. For those lacking official business in Spain it had almost become the stuff of daydreams. Rose Macaulay, for instance, confided to a friend in 1943 that "when the war is over I shall try and visit Spain. It would be fun. And one of the only countries left to visit; the others will mostly be smashed to bits. I shall get the ancient Morris that is mouldering in a garage, and fling it across the Channel."[7] She was eventually able to embark on this journey in May 1947. During these years Spain, seen from a British perspective, had reverted to being the unknown, remote and somewhat alien land that it had been in the years before the

Second Republic (see chapter 1), an effect magnified by the sheer unpopularity of the Franco regime within Britain. Gerald Brenan was aware of this when he commented in 1950 that: "We have been calling [Franco Spain] names in Parliament and in the press for many years, but few English people have any idea what it feels like to live in it."[8] Indeed, all of the writers discussed here were, in their own way, seeking to challenge the idea, encapsulated in the widely-used term "Franco Spain", that the country and the regime were one and the same.

These writers' credentials as authorities on Spain were considerable. Gerald Brenan had established his reputation as an expert on modern Spanish history with *The Spanish Labyrinth* (1943), a seminal work that set the Civil War within longer-term patterns of Spanish social and political change. However, his connection with Spain went back to the three and a half years that he had spent in the Andalusian village of Yegen in the early 1920s, followed by periods of residence in the house that he purchased in Churriuana, outside of Malaga. Having bravely refused to leave during the first chaotic months of the Civil War, Brenan and his wife, the writer Gamel Woolsey, were eventually evacuated by the Royal Navy in September 1936.[9] V. S. Pritchett had spent two years as a journalist in Spain between 1923 and 1925, as well as reporting for the BBC on the problems afflicting the Second Republic in 1935. His *Marching Spain* (1928) revealed him to be a highly perceptive and original commentator on Spanish customs, landscape and daily life. John Langdon-Davies had lived in Catalonia in the 1920s and published *Dancing Catalans* (1929), as well as extensively covering the Civil War as a journalist (see chapter 8). Sacheverell Sitwell, aesthete and poet, had first visited Spain in 1919 and published numerous books on Spanish Baroque art.[10] The novelist Rose Macaulay was less well-travelled in Spain, but her novel set there during the aftermath of the Civil War (*And no man's wit* [1940]) showed what a powerful grip the country and its troubled history already exercised on her imagination.

In political terms, Sitwell stood out as the only member of this group who was openly sympathetic to the Franco regime. Indeed, he had returned to Spain in 1947–8 at the invitation of his old friend Luis Bolín, the Director-General of Tourism, who had been the much-feared head of press censorship for Franco's forces during the Civil War. As Sitwell's biographer points out, the list of acknowledgments for his *Spain* "reeled with the names of Spanish grandees who had helped him",[11] including the Duke of Alba, Franco's erstwhile Ambassador to London. All of the others had, to varying degrees, been identified with the Republican cause, most explicitly in the case of Langdon-Davies, most reluctantly in the case of Pritchett who disliked the "conformist attitudinising" of many writers during the Civil War.[12] Even so, both he and Rose Macaulay had made their pro-Republican sympathies clear in their responses to the famous questionnaire circulated by Nancy Cunard and subsequently published as *Authors take sides on the Spanish War* (1937). Macaulay's stark reply had been "AGAINST FRANCO".[13] Although Brenan did take part in pro-Republican campaigning, he largely channelled his energies into the historical research which eventually produced *The Spanish Labyrinth*. He told Leonard Woolf that he had written the book "full of the violent rages of the Civil War and had to make a great effort to be impartial".[14] In fact, he came to see that a book which had initially been intended as his contribution to the Republican cause was "an indictment of the follies and illusions of the Left, with whose general aims I sympathised".[15] Brenan had also, during the latter stages of the Second World War, broadcast to Spain for the BBC, and he was particularly concerned that this activity might result in a hostile reception on his return.[16]

Even when these writers had actively supported the Republic, however, they were not necessarily prejudiced in what they wrote about contemporary Spain. Much had changed in the ten years since Franco's victory, not only in Spain but also internationally. Fear of fascism had given way to fear of Communism and the Cold War, allowing Franco Spain to be judged on its own terms rather than as part of a constellation of fascist states. Brenan, for one, wrote that he returned "full of questions" and keen to avoid politics (although, in the event, this was to prove impossible).[17] In trying to make sense of contemporary Spain, all of these writers were drawn towards comparisons with other dictatorships, either in Europe's recent past or under Communism. When Brenan, for instance, wrote of the "Belsen atmosphere" that he encountered in the Andalusian town of Lucena he was referring to the "miserable, starved appearance of its inhabitants" and, above all, its dirty, ill-clad and broken-spirited women.[18] Sitwell regarded the destruction of the Infantado Palace in Guadalajara by the "Reds" as "bad as anything which happened in the wars of Hitler".[19] Rose Macaulay found Victor Kravchenko's *I Chose Freedom* a helpful companion during her journey through Spain in 1947. The Soviet defector had, she noted, conjured up an "awful atmosphere of suspicion & espionage & intrigue" within Soviet-dominated Eastern Europe, by comparison with which Spain was "*much* less bad, but still rather bad".[20]

Meanwhile, the Second World War and its aftermath of austerity under a majority Labour government (as well, of course, as the climate) all conspired to make Britain seem less attractive than Spain. When

Sitwell set off for Spain at the end of the spectacularly harsh winter of 1946–7 there were still snow drifts on southern English roads in April. Brenan noticed how little trace of the Civil War was to be observed in Madrid compared with the "small progress" made in patching up the war damage in Britain.[21] His book was peppered with comments about the greyness and torpidity of British life, and the "pudding faces" that one encountered on the streets of London. Robert Graves was eager to return to his family home at Deya, Mallorca, from which he had been evacuated in August 1936, "since we are getting tired of this struggle against domestic shortages and of the wet winters and the tourist-traffic in the summers".[22] Norman Lewis, who had travelled within Spain in the mid-1930s, returned looking for reassurance: "After three war years in the Army overseas I looked for the familiar in England, but found change. Perhaps it was the search for vanished times that drew me back to Spain . . . "[23]

How, then, did these writers respond to their return to Spain? In assessing their published work it is important to note that different genres were involved, which, quite apart from any political predilections, may well have coloured their responses. Some, for instance, were writing to commission: in the case of Sitwell (for Batsford) and Macaulay (for Hamish Hamilton) they were contributing to new series aimed at a reviving tourist market. Sitwell, for instance, praised the Spanish government's Parador hotels for opening up "inaccessible parts of Spain to the tourist".[24] Even Brenan, who wrote most pointedly about Spanish poverty and corruption, did his best to encourage others to visit Spain, commenting that it was cheap and welcoming and that "the northerner in search of new sensations has every reason for going there".[25] Another constraint was that all of these writers – and especially those who wanted to settle in Spain – had to be judicious in their comments on contemporary politics and society. After all, censorship prevailed within Spain and the dictatorship was highly sensitive about its foreign image. Even so, there was considerable uniformity in the contents of these books. All took as their starting point an understanding that, long before the phrase was coined by Franco's Minister of Tourism Manuel Fraga in the 1960s, "Spain is different". Indeed, a central goal for all of these authors was to explain this Spanish "exceptionalism" to a North European audience, ironically, at the very moment that it was beginning to be eroded by the forces of economic and cultural change.[26] A second common thread was the attempt to measure the impact of the Civil War on Spain's society and its cultural heritage. In addition, some of this literature also dealt candidly with social change, modernisation and poverty. However, the question of the Franco regime (and especially how it might be replaced by a more benevolent government) was approached far more obliquely, if at all.

Underlying this emphasis on Spain's difference there was, in part, sheer relief that the essence of Spanish culture had survived the trauma of civil war and its bitter aftermath. Spain was still a country that these writers could recognise, feel at home in and enjoy. Moreover, it appeared that a long-standing debate about Spain's developmental path, and its relationship to Europe, had finally been resolved. Returning to Spain in 1951–2, V. S. Pritchett found a country that was "often greatly changed on the surface", but not "fundamentally changed". It was still possible when crossing the border to "feel the break with Europe", and to encounter a country largely untouched by modern industrial life. Outside of Catalonia, in his view, Spain did not possess a solid middle class, and the life of its cities ran "much closer to what life was like in England in the seventeenth century". Spaniards were still highly regional in their mentality, essentially anarchistic, fearless of death and "cruel or undisturbed by cruelty". [27] Brenan noted that the Mediterranean peoples had "not yet been conquered by the pattern of industrial life with its crushing discipline": there was in Spain a "kind of freedom and spontaneity that I missed at home".[28] In his later book *South from Granada* (1957) he would write that "it is still true that south of the Pyrenees one finds a society which puts the deeper needs of human nature before the technical organisation that is required to provide a higher standard of living".[29] Norman Lewis felt that the Spain that he returned to in the late 1940s was "still as nostalgically backward-looking as ever, still magnificent, still invested with all its ancient virtues and ancient defects".[30] Rose Macaulay's account of Spain's Mediterranean coast presented a landscape that was, unlike the corresponding regions of Italy and France, still peopled with the "ghosts" of its past. Its cultural heritage had been preserved because the Spanish lacked "that restless drive towards change that makes so many Europeans perpetually at odds with the life they know, perpetually impelled to grasp at and achieve the new . . ."[31]

This perception of Spanish "difference" was reinforced by these writers' treatment of the Spanish Civil War which, however marginal, consistently provides the most awkward and interesting aspect of this literature. They were not so much concerned with the conflict itself as with the atrocities that accompanied it and which – to an extent – defined it as uniquely "Spanish." Sitwell's account was the least nuanced, as he simply presented a stocktaking of the Communists' "disgraceful excesses"[32] in terms of the destruction of religious buildings and works of art, or the massacre of priests. Others took a less reverent view of the anti-clerical outrages. Pritchett, for instance, commented that the fires had burned out the "traditional gloom" of some Spanish churches, while Langdon-Davies noted that some priests may have deserved the "rough justice" of 1936.[33] Rose Macaulay shared Sitwell's revulsion at what she deemed a "holocaust" of life and art, but made more effort to explore the roots of the "mysterious madness" which periodically drove the Spanish into "these strange pyrrhic frenzies". In the market place in Figueres she speculated as to whether the market women had "tossed pictures and images on the bonfire in San Pedro as now they tossed oranges and apricots into straw bags, and with the same zest?"[34] Only Brenan dealt extensively with the rebel atrocities, partly because he travelled in a region of Spain which had fallen under their control at an early stage in the war, and he recorded the numbers of Republican supporters slaughtered in cities such as Granada and Cordova. He gave a gripping account of how he and his wife sought the unmarked burial place of the murdered playwright Federico García Lorca – fruitlessly, and possibly at some personal danger – in the gorges outside of Granada. For Brenan, these rebel "holocausts", like those described by Macaulay in the Republican zone, had deep roots within Spanish culture: "The Spaniards' innate love of destruction, their obsession with death, their tendency to fanaticism found full vent in these orgiastic scenes because there was no civil or religious authority, no moral force or inhibition, that could restrain them."[35]

While the legacy of the Civil War could not be ignored, these writers were by no means blind to the fact that Spain was changing. (The exception was, again, Sitwell, who saw Spain as firmly rooted in the "old and dwindling Europe"[36] and appears to have ignored all signs of modernity.) Pritchett, for instance, commented on how "skyscrapers and tall white blocks of flats like upended sugar tablets" gave Madrid "an American appearance from the distance", while Brenan noted that in Malaga the new social elite was easily recognisable by its American cars.[37] Both men felt, somewhat surprisingly, that the position of women had improved, although Rose Macaulay confided to Gilbert Murray that she would "hate to be a woman in Spain". She found that a lone woman driver was still greeted with wonderment and some hostility.[38] The steady draining of the rural population into the cities was another common theme. Langdon-Davies noted that some of the younger Catalan peasants had flourished as industrialists under Franco and were now building "stately pleasure domes" in their villages as weekend retreats.[39]

By far the most significant barometer of change was the growth of tourism, which was both encouraged and deplored. Rose Macaulay warned that if the Costa Brava should ever become "a continuous chain of luxury hotels and villas, I should not revisit it".[40] Indeed, in 1952 she wrote to John Langdon-Davies that, whereas in 1947 the Costa Brava had been "beautifully untourised", she had heard that it was now "impossible to find a quiet spot", and that Tossa de Mar was "quite spoilt".[41] Langdon-Davies shared this judgment on Tossa, and wrote in 1953 that the region might retain its charms "for as much as five years more; after that there will be less point in visiting it".[42] Macaulay and Brenan were able to visit future tourist resorts such as Marbella and Torremolinos when they were still largely undeveloped. Prophetically, however, it was in Torremolinos – a "pretty country place" – that Macaulay met the first British tourists that she had met in Spain, who were also the first drunks that she had encountered.[43] The steady erosion of the traditional ways of life was nowhere captured more elegaically than in the writing of Norman Lewis, who spent three seasons in the fishing villages of the Costa Brava in the late 1940s. His *Voices of the Old Sea* (1984) records how the villagers succumbed not only to natural disasters such as the death of the cork oaks and the decline of the fishing, but also to the allure of better and easier money to be made in the nascent tourist industry, promoted by a new social elite grown wealthy through the black market.[44]

A final theme that united these books was that they all, to some degree, testified to the defeat of ideology and political experimentation both within Spain itself and, indeed, internationally. Spain was still, in Brenan's words, a country in "shell-shock", or, as Pritchett put it, "exhausted and cynical and silenced by guilt about the Civil War".[45] Langdon-Davies alluded to the "shattering realism" of the last fifteen years that had "murdered" the dreams of the Catalan nationalists: the "icy wind" of the Cold War prevented their resurrection.[46] Robert Graves wrote with regard to Mallorca that "the Terror of the Civil War times is now ancient history . . . life is certainly very hard for the labouring classes, but no revolution is talked. They have had it."[47] For Brenan, the experience of the Civil War had demonstrated how "the moment the doors of an ideology are unlocked in Spain, the old Utopist (sic) spirit bursts out and miracles are just round the corner". In his view, what Spain desperately needed now was to realise that prosperity was based on the prosaic virtues of "work and intelligent organisation".[48] Such views found support in the pioneering anthropological work of Julian Pitt-Rivers, who published his study of the social structure of the Andalusian village of Grazalema in 1954. Pitt-Rivers presented a local society still scarred by memory of the

Civil War, in which matters of government were regarded as "the business of the state not of the pueblo [village], as something dangerous and immoral which sensible people have nothing to do with".[49] As one reviewer noted, Pitt-Rivers described a community in which, given the failure of democracy and religion "what is left is a sense of neighbourly solidarity . . . still the strongest cohesive force in modern Spain".[50]

This turn away from politics represented far more than a mere defeat for the Left, for just as the Second Republic of 1931–9 now appeared as a parenthesis in Spanish history, similarly the Franco regime seemed unable to do anything more than keep the lid on social discontents. A dictatorship that could do little but govern, however badly, and was largely ignored by its subjects, should hardly present a problem for foreign visitors. A special correspondent for *The Times* wrote in 1950 that a Spanish authoritarian regime was "unlike any other" as "none of its manifestations digs very far below the surface of daily life". The only Spanish governments which could survive – and Franco's was no exception – were those which "issue broad edicts but overlook their detailed application whenever it is convenient".[51] Rose Macaulay caught the drift of these sentiments when she wrote privately in 1951 that her 1940 novel had been an "indictment of the Franco regime, which was then very shocking and barbarous and unjust. It still is Fascist, of course, but time has toned it down, and it has improved".[52] With hindsight, her Spanish journey seemed "like a lovely dream of beauty and interest". However, we know from her private correspondence that, during it, she was aware of the continuing torture of political prisoners by the authorities in Barcelona.[53]

Just as Rose Macaulay omitted this significant detail from *Fabled Shore*, few of these books engaged in any sustained fashion either with the dictator or with the nature of his regime. Pritchett, for instance, presented Franco as an "amiable little fat man", allowed to win the Civil War due to the Western democracies' fear of Germany and Mussolini, and allowed to survive only because of their fear of the Soviet Union.[54] The main exception was Brenan's *Face of Spain*, although even here Franco himself was largely absent.[55] Brenan emphasised the cynicism and corruption that were rife in Spain, and the disillusionment in the ranks of the Falange (the fascistic movement that had been co-opted by Franco during the Civil War as the principal basis for the one-party state). For Brenan, the Spain of the late 1940s was dominated by poverty, inflation, the ubiquitous black market, and the still-powerful memory of the Civil War, far more than it was by politics. Brenan was also the only author to offer any kind of political prognosis. In a strikingly measured passage he argued that there was a strong moral case for extending financial assistance to Spain (such as the US Marshall Aid for reconstruction from which the democratic states of Western Europe were beginning to benefit). In his view, there was nothing to be gained from driving Spain deeper into poverty; nor was an overnight transition to democratic government a feasible objective. Instead, Spain "for some time to come needs to live under an authoritarian régime", backed by Britain and the USA, which could work to reduce political and social divisions.[56] Such views were, of course, anathema to many on the left. Basil Davidson, who visited Spain in 1950, argued that hard currency aid would merely reinforce the oligarchies which dominated Spain: accordingly, "even the humanitarian case for aid falls through".[57] Giles Romilly warned that Franco was "trailing a very dirty coat, and decent people outside Spain, who can't see the dirt, are urging for reasons commercial, chivalrous or strategic that we should go after it".[58]

For all of its limitations,[59] the literature discussed here played a significant role in the development of British perceptions of Spain during this period. A number of these books came to be regarded as classics and passed through numerous editions. Brenan's *Face of Spain* sold particularly well and the section dealing with Lorca was acquired by the *New Yorker* for $1000.[60] They not only introduced (or re-introduced) thousands of potential tourists to Spain, but more importantly presented a country that both could and should be visited. The intrinsic interest of its culture and heritage transcended the reservations which potential tourists might have about its political regime. In many respects, this group of authors could be seen as – whether advertently or not – preparing the ground for the British tourist invasion that was to follow. At the same time, these were serious books that engaged at many levels with the contemporary reality of Spain. In this sense they were superior to most of the travel books on Spain in the later 1950s and 1960s, which largely ignored the political context altogether.[61] For instance, the prolific output of the writer Anthony Carson focused almost exclusively on Spain's quirky charms. Carson, apart from reporting some mild harassment by the secret police, had nothing at all to say about the Franco regime.[62] H. V. Morton, a popular travel writer but hardly a Spanish specialist presented this view of Franco without any qualification in a book written in 1955: "He isn't a dictator in the European sense at all. He's just a soldier who has put down a rebellion and proclaimed military law and intends to see the law kept."[63]

Brenan's realistic approach to "the Spanish Question" in *The Face of Spain* contrasts strongly with the inflexible thinking of much of the British left during this period. At the same time, for instance, the Communist Party was still demanding the re-establishment of the Spanish Republic.[64] The left was initially slow to appreciate the durability of the Franco regime and could only see a "fascist" dictatorship which, with the demise of its German and Italian sponsors, must surely collapse sooner rather than later. The regime seemed moribund and incapable of renewal, and one visitor to Barcelona in 1948 compared Franco Spain to a "giant Meccano" which had "somehow managed to run on, regardless of the fact that it's motor inside had long since gone dead".[65] In 1952 Aneurin Bevan wrote of Spain and its authoritarian neighbour Portugal as "frozen societies" which "share many of the most repulsive features of the monolithic [i.e. Soviet] type without its active genius . . . They represent the future refusing to be born."[66]

This attitude began to change in the later 1950s when the Franco regime embarked on a policy of economic liberalisation accompanied by largely cosmetic political reforms. Although Spain experienced an economic boom during the 1960s, there was also a revival of opposition activity amongst groups such as workers and students which, in turn, was met with further repression. In particular, the execution of the Communist leader Julián Grimau in 1963, for crimes allegedly committed during the Civil War, attracted worldwide condemnation. The British left found a new focus for its anti-Franco campaigning by placing a heavy emphasis on human rights and political imprisonment. At a time when concerns over human rights were increasingly salient within Western Europe, the Franco regime became ever more vulnerable on this issue. Two significant British campaigning organisations were established in 1959 – Appeal for Amnesty in Spain and the Spanish Democrats' Defence Fund – while Amnesty International, which was founded in 1961, also had a strong early emphasis on Spain.[67] These organisations did not emphasise the "fascist" roots of Franco's regime so much as its sheer anachronistic viciousness. Appeal for Amnesty commented in 1964, for instance, that recent "political executions and torturing of arrested strikers [in Spain], have brutally recalled the methods of the Inquisition".[68]

The resurgence of anti-Franco campaigning in Britain from the late 1950s onwards re-established a public view of the Franco regime as a threat – if not to world peace, at least to its own citizens. The hope of many leading Conservative politicians in the early 1960s that Franco's Spain could be integrated into NATO remained unfulfilled.[69] And yet, at the same time ever-increasing numbers of Britons were experiencing the "new" Spain of the Mediterranean tourist resorts. Just as the image of the regime was being tarnished by its own abuses, therefore, Spain itself was consolidating a reputation as a place of pleasure and relaxation. As one visitor to Tossa in 1958 commented, "English resorts seemed very staid by comparison".[70] For the left this represented both a problem and an opportunity. Quite apart from posing the ethical question of whether to visit Spain at all, there was also a political issue at stake. Franco's regime had consistently promoted mass tourism, not only as a means of generating precious foreign currency and jobs, but also with the purpose of improving Spain's poor international image.[71] Accordingly, to challenge tourism in Spain would be to kick away a "crutch"[72] from under the Franco regime, and, during the 1960s, British tourism in Spain became the focus of quite novel political criticism.

The growth of British tourism in Spain since the early 1950s had been both remarkable and unprecedented. In 1951 150,000 Britons travelled to Spain (out of a total of 1.26 million foreign visitors); by 1960 this figure had risen to 624,000 (out of 6.1 million), and by the time of Franco's death in 1975 it stood at some 3.42 million out of a total of 30 million. During this period the proportion of British visitors remained remarkably consistent at between 10–13%.[73] The amount of money spent by Britons in Spain – principally on tourism – also rose. Indeed, in one year alone (1967–8) the amount increased from £39.5 million to £46.4 million.[74] This expansion was encouraged by the Spanish government, which from 1951 had a cabinet-level Minister of Information and Tourism. The state offered highly favourable credit terms for the construction of hotels and restaurants (essential when one considers that as late as 1956 there were only 3820 hotel rooms on the Costa Brava),[75] while price controls ensured that accommodation remained cheap by North European standards. The transport infrastructure was also improved, notably through the construction of new airports, while the scrapping of tourist entry visas in 1959 and periodic devaluations of the peseta offered further incentives. For much of this period British tourism to Spain grew in spite of the highly restrictive policy of successive British governments which – for economic and commercial rather than political reasons – imposed limits on charter flights and the amount of currency that tourists could take abroad.

The advent of cheap air travel during the 1950s played a crucial role in opening up the Spanish resorts – especially those in more distant or remote areas such as the Costa Blanca and the Balearic islands. Moreover, for working-class holidaymakers with limited time, less of their holiday was now spent on lengthy rail journeys. The first significant charter flight operator was Horizon Holidays which from 1950 onwards offered package holidays in Corsica, and in 1953 began to offer flights to Majorca. Other operators such as Skytours and the well-established Workers' Travel Association soon entered this rapidly growing market. These early charters possessed a certain adventurous charm, but were also tinged with danger: one holidaymaker recalled flying, disconcertingly, over the wreckage of a plane crash in the Pyrenees.[76] They also involved an element of speculation for the agents in terms of how many flights and hotels to book. As one commentator put it 1954, the "plane-charter agents merit good wishes as pioneers – and gamblers".[77]

The question of whether to visit Spain was not treated as a political issue during the first two decades after the Civil War. A member of the Westminster Labour Party who travelled to Spain in the late 1940s wrote that while "I am still no better disposed towards Franco . . . politics fortunately have nothing to do with a good holiday and reunion with friends".[78] Indeed, Franco's critics felt few inhibitions in this regard. For instance, Harold Nicolson cited his "extreme prejudice against Franco" as one reason for not taking a cruise to the Canary Islands in 1956. But his real reason appears to have been hypochondria, and he was happy to suggest a visit to Malaga instead. Later in the year Nicolson and his wife Vita Sackville-West visited Tossa de Mar during a motor tour of southern France and north-eastern Spain.[79] A spirit of inquiry sustained Eric Hobsbawm, the Marxist historian, on a visit to Teruel (the scene of a gruelling civil war battle) in 1954.[80] The *New Statesman*, consistently critical of the Franco regime in its editorial section, happily ran adverts for Spanish holidays, while its staff writers recommended holidays in Spain alongside many other Mediterranean destinations.[81] Visits to Spain were only frowned upon when they caused political embarrassment. For instance, in the late 1940s Ronald Chamberlain, a maverick Labour MP, and Halliday Sutherland, a former Labour candidate, both accepted official invitations to visit Spain, and spoke glowingly about the virtues of Franco's reforms.[82] For its part, the Franco regime was more concerned with combating contemporary subversion than with fighting the battles of the past. Gerald Brenan and John Langdon-Davies do not appear to have experienced official harassment on their return to live in Spain, despite their pro-Republican stance during the Civil War.[83] Indeed, it is striking to note that even such a vocal opponent of Franco as Nancy Cunard was, by 1958, able to write that "I like being in Spain very much indeed and have even thought that I would do well to spend a great deal of every year here."

She added that it was the "only country I feel well in (the food, wine, coffee, tobacco, no doubt all very pure)".[84]

Even so, there were growing signs of concern about the ethics of Spanish tourism as it began to burgeon from the later 1950s onwards. For instance, a columnist in the *New Statesman* wrote in 1957 that:

> *I want to see Andalusia, and especially Granada. But, twenty years after the civil war, I still have personal doubts about the propriety of spending a holiday in Spain. I wonder how many others feel the same now. Each year I hear that X has just been there, or that Y has some friends who know a small place . . . (sic) or that Z has been arguing against going in a way that suggests he wants to be persuaded.*[85]

He reserved his particular dislike for those who went to Spain to "'see the facts for oneself'". Another correspondent marvelled at the "mental somersaults" which allowed many on the left to ignore their anti-Franco opinions "for the benefit of a luxury holiday in Spain".[86] Such concerns were fuelled by the reality of increased working-class travel, as well as by the continuing brutality of the regime. In April 1960 Sam Russell, who had reported on the Civil War for the *Daily Worker*, wrote that: "lured by an almost unbelievable tourist exchange rate, fascinated by the gay travel posters, thousands will be leaving these shores this year for a holiday in Spain". While not wishing to be a kill-joy, he felt compelled to remind such tourists of the democrats "rotting" in jail and the millions living in "medieval squalor".[87] Three year's later, amidst the uproar following the execution of Grimau, he posed the question: "Who'll holiday on Grimau's grave?"[88] In the mid-1960s the British Workers Tourist Centre in Italy began to run increasingly hard-hitting adverts intended to play on the consciences of British socialists and trade unionists: "A holiday in the sun means finance for Franco: DON'T GO TO FASCIST SPAIN."[89] Alongside such political arguments, there was also a hint of snobbery. For instance, the Labour MP Tom Driberg commented that he had never been back to Spain since the Civil War, and had "watched with disgust the rush by British tourists, including many working-class Labour voters, to help Franco's economy by crowding his repulsive beaches. (Okay, the package-tours are cheap, but so they are to Yugoslavia and Malta, and other non-Fascist countries)."[90]

Despite such concerns, action against tourism was not initially deemed politically feasible. In1963, for instance, Spanish Communists advised their British comrades against a holiday boycott because "nowhere in Western Europe could this be made effective". In any case, only Communists and militant socialists would stay away, and "their presence in Spain, even on holiday, is regarded as helpful". Moreover, there was concern at the impact on local Spanish businesses.[91] However, the issue was not allowed to go away. In the late 1960s there was a revival of working-class militancy within Spain organised by the Communist-led (and still illegal) Workers' Commissions. This combined with unrest amongst students and some Catholics, and growing opposition in the Basque country and Catalonia. Trials such as those of sixteen Basque ETA militants in Burgos (1970) and the "Carabanchel Ten" trade unionists (1973) aroused considerable anger in Britain, and the left became increasingly direct in its criticism of the tourist industry. In the spring of 1970, for instance, Amnesty International placed hoardings near British airports which depicted imprisoned faces against a background of sand and blue skies. The slogan was: "Have a good time – but remember, Amnesty for Spain's political prisoners."[92] In July 1969 the National Union of Mineworkers appealed to its members not to holiday in Spain given that tourism was the "economic anchor" of the regime.[93] The Trades Union Congress, however, was reluctant to take action. The General Secretary Vic Feather replied to one request that British trade unionists should "refrain from going to Spain for a holiday on the cheap" by pointing out that "holiday arrangements are part of the private life of a person".[94]

Feather's comment was telling, for there was no contest in this battle between political principle and the power of the consumer. So long as Spain continued to deliver the tourist industry mantra of "sun, sights and savings" there was no reason why working-class holidaymakers should stay away. They were, after all, merely following in the footsteps of wealthier tourists – some of whom had far stronger political reservations about the regime – in the 1950s. Of course, had Spain's political unrest spilled onto the tourist beaches matters might have been different. Interestingly, the organisers of a campaign against tourism in Greece following the Colonels' coup of April 1967 felt that British tourists had been responsive in this instance even when they "felt able to tolerate holidaying in countries with long-standing fascist Governments [such as Spain and Portugal]".[95] The Turkish invasion of Cyprus in 1974 caused jitters in the British tourist industry as many feared that similar chaos would follow Franco's death.[96] Ultimately, however, there were two realities which were potentially far more damaging to British tourism in Spain than any appeal to conscience. One was the periodic worsening of Anglo-Spanish governmental relations. For instance, when Foreign Secretary Michael Stewart told MPs in 1969 that Britons should "think twice and many times" before going on holiday in Spain, he was responding to the Spanish government's recent closure of the Gibraltar frontier.[97] An even more lethal threat was the surplus of tourist agencies operating with ever-tighter margins following the oil shock of 1973. The collapse of the Court Line charter company in 1974 inflicted more damage on the Spanish package holiday industry than the moral suasion of the left.

■ ■ ■ ■ ■ ■ ■

In 1964 Sam Russell commented that the Jarama valley, where this chapter started, lay "far from the sun-baked beaches where British tourists enjoy themselves in their thousands to the greater glory of Franco and his fascist regime. Yet that valley is more British than ever those beaches will be, however many thousands bathe and besport themselves there."[98] Such reproachful sentiments were understandable in the bitter aftermath of Grimau's execution, and betokened a broader sense of exasperation. If the left had won the battle to brand the Franco regime as an oppressive police state during the 1960s, why did so many Britons still choose to holiday there? Had a struggle against Franco started at the battle of the Jarama valley suffered defeat on the beaches of Torremolinos? In fact, such connections were misleading. The voices of British holidaymakers are easy to overlook and have only recently been subject to academic study.[99] However, there is no doubt that they chose to visit Spain because it offered escape and excellent value. Profound changes were at work in patterns of leisure activity, especially amongst the British working class, and the left was mistaken in believing that action against tourism might offer a "magic bullet" against the Franco regime. In any case, the presence of millions of British tourists in Spain did not repudiate the left's campaigns against the regime's human rights abuses which had, in many respects, proved highly effective. Instead, it marked the final stage of a process that started with the "rediscovery" of Spain after 1945, whereby the country, its people and its heritage were decoupled from the excesses of its government.

Chapter 10

The Spanish Civil War in British politics since 1939

In 1967 the BBC investigated the possibility of broadcasting Leonard Woolf's 1939 play *The Hotel*, a tale of gun-running during the Spanish Civil War. Eventually, however, the idea was turned down. As Martin Esslin, head of sound drama at the BBC explained to Woolf: "Alas, I feel that this aspect of the play [i.e. the Civil War context] . . . would be very difficult to appreciate for present day listeners, most of whom will not have lived through those times."[1] Whatever the virtues of Woolf's play, this comment raises a wider question about the degree to which the Spanish Civil War continued to enjoy any resonance within British political culture during the years following the Republican defeat? This chapter will argue that, quite apart from the separate but closely related issue of the continuing political opposition to the Franco regime,[2] the Civil War did play a tangible, if diminishing, role within British politics, most notably in the three decades after 1939. This went beyond the mere adoption of phrases such as the "Fifth column", which gained a currency that lasted long after its origins in Spain were largely forgotten.[3] The Spanish Civil War continued to obtrude into British politics in many and complex ways: it helped to shape – not always helpfully – the way in which popular politics was imagined and enacted; it provided a gauge against which all subsequent idealistic causes measured themselves, but also could be used to criticise the apathy of the young; it boosted the careers of those who had had a "good war" in Spain, and blighted the careers of those who had not.

The Political Context

It must be noted at the outset that the memory of the Civil War within British politics was essentially the preserve of the left. Admittedly, Conservatives did develop an argument that sought to justify their record in government during the conflict. For instance, Quintin Hogg's 1945 polemic *The Left was Never Right* posed the question "was it desirable that we should shatter the peace of Europe in 1936 by our active and effective intervention in a cause which was not primarily ours?" Far better, he argued, to refuse to help either side, which was "the course we took".[4] R. A. Butler put it even more bluntly in 1964 when he told parliament that his task as a Foreign Office minister in 1938–40 had been one of "keeping us out of the Spanish Civil War".[5] Conservatives were also cynical about the much-vaunted idealism of those who went to fight in Spain, seeing behind them the organisational hand of the Communist Party and, ultimately, of Moscow. However, they were aware that, at least so long as Franco remained in power in Madrid, raking over their own record during the Civil War could only bring embarrassment. Certainly, there were few political points to be scored against their contemporary opponents.[6]

The memory of the Civil War was most cherished amongst Communists and on the left wing of the Labour movement. The fact that more than 500 Britons had died fighting for the Republic in Spain meant that the war could not be viewed in purely abstract terms. In the words of the art historian and Soviet spy Anthony Blunt: "the conflict was too near and involved too many of one's personal friends".[7] A former volunteer told the TUC Congress in 1949 that he had a "blood relationship" with Spain owing to the many friends that he had left there.[8] This sacrifice was felt particularly keenly by Communists. As Harry Pollitt wrote in 1951: "About 50 per cent of the volunteers were members of the Communist Party and just over half of the dead were ours. We lost the flower of our party . . . "[9] Even with the passage of many years the International Brigades continued to evoke very powerful feelings. Recalling the 1938 congress of the Communist Party thirty years after the event, a Communist activist wrote that: "Harry Pollitt stood up to read out the names of our lost comrades. When he became overcome, Fred [Copeman] carried on until it also became too much for him and Chopin's funeral march closed this grand and sad occasion . . . These things make good memories."[10] The anniversary of the Battle of the Jarama in February 1937, when the British Battalion of the International

Brigades first went into action and suffered heavy losses, became the occasion for annual rallies of veterans and their supporters. Moreover, with the formation of the International Brigade Association (IBA) in 1939, the left possessed the only organisation that was dedicated to keeping the memory of the Civil War fresh and pertinent within British politics. The IBA was an effective political campaigning organisation which, although clearly Communist-dominated, managed to retain broad support within the Labour movement.[11]

For the left, the heavy loss of life amongst the volunteers merely confirmed the political and moral rectitude of the cause for which they had fought, a cause which shone ever more brightly amidst later disappointments. For instance, Nan Green who had served in the British Medical Unit recalled that she was able to sublimate her doubts over Communist policy at the start of the Second World War by throwing herself into work with Spanish refugees. Those who had gone to Spain were, she wrote in her memoirs, fortunate to be involved with a "clear, uncomplicated cause that has remained untarnished to this day!" Elsewhere Green, who had lost her husband at the battle of the Ebro in 1938, described the Spanish Republican cause as "so flawless and so black and white and so good and so wholesome".[12] Another medical volunteer, Kenneth Sinclair-Loutit, later recalled that: "The devotion of many was indeed *later* betrayed but there was something very pure, pure gold in the aspiration, the work and the self-abnegation of those who gave themselves to the Spanish Republic."[13]

Unambiguous views about the Civil War were by no means restricted to those who had served in Spain. Kingsley Martin, former editor of the *New Statesman* wrote "with assurance" in 1962 that the left had been "on the side of liberty and progress and that Franco stood, and still stands, for greed, tyranny and black reaction".[14] The Labour politician Ernest Davies reflected in 1959 on how he had been caught up in the "emotional orgy" of the Civil War and saw the conflict only in "black and white".[15] For many years after the end of the Civil War, this emphasis on the unsullied nobility of the Spanish Republican cause drowned out a minority view on the left, epitomised by George Orwell's *Homage to Catalonia* (1938), which emphasised the sectarian and counter-revolutionary role of the international Communist movement in Spain. Above all, the Communists were held responsible for the suppression of the POUM, the Spanish revolutionary party, in 1937 and the death of a number of its foreign sympathisers. Orwell's interpretation of the Civil War, which was largely ignored during the writer's lifetime (1903–50), gained a new purchase during the Cold War in the 1950s, and was then seized upon by the burgeoning Trotskyist and Anarchist movements in the later 1960s.[16] The seal was set on this remarkable recovery by Ken Loach's 1995 movie *Land and Freedom* which, in effect, brought Orwell's version of the Civil War to the cinema screen.

While different groups on the left, and even the Conservatives, had well-defined and enduring positions on the Civil War, the same did not apply so easily to the mainstream Labour movement. Both the Labour Party and the TUC had supported the British government's policy of Non-Intervention well into 1937, and only latterly threw their institutional energies into campaigning on behalf of the Republic. It was, therefore, impossible for them to extract any single narrative of the Civil War, beyond a general distaste for the Franco regime. Matters were further complicated by the very different personal responses amongst Labour leaders. Clement Attlee, leader of the party between 1935 and 1955, had visited the British Battalion in Spain in 1937, and even had a company named after him. This visit, for which Attlee incurred considerable criticism from Conservative MPs on his return to Britain, was greatly appreciated by the British volunteers at the time. Conversely, the leading trade unionists Ernest Bevin (leader of the Transport & General Workers' Union) and Sir Walter Citrine (General Secretary of the TUC) were strongly identified with anti-communism, and perceived as reluctant supporters of the Republic. Citrine declined a number of invitations to visit Spain during the Civil War, while Bevin vigorously defended Non-Intervention before an international conference of trade unionists in March 1937.[17]

The Spanish Civil War, therefore, meant different things to different groups within British political and cultural life. For a broad swathe of liberal and left-wing opinion, however, the principal lesson of the Civil War concerned the dangers of Fascism and, above all, the need to resist international aggression. To take but one example, Peter Benenson, the founder of Amnesty International, recalled his reaction to the outbreak of the conflict as a fifteen year-old schoolboy at Eton: "I was more shocked by the illegitimacy of Franco's rebellion than by anything else. The failure of Britain and France to do more than stand and watch seemed shameful; even more so was their subsequent arms embargo on shipments to Spain."[18]

"Imperialist" War and Winter War, 1939–40

The memory of the Civil War was still fresh when, a bare five months after Franco's victory, Britain found itself at war with Nazi Germany.

The coming of war in September 1939 represented a release for many anti-fascists. For instance, Jennie Lee and Aneurin Bevan, pillars of the non-Communist left, celebrated the news by listening to Spanish Republican records that they had, until that point, been too ashamed to play.[19] For British Communists, however, Stalin's *rapprochement* with Hitler (under the Nazi–Soviet Pact of August 1939) committed them to almost two years of political frustration and isolation. The CPGB leadership had initially supported war with Germany in a manifesto issued on 2 September 1939, the day after German forces invaded Poland. Within weeks, however, this policy was dramatically reversed following instructions from the Comintern that this was an "imperialist and unjust" war. During heated debates between 25 September and 3 October 1939 the party's Central Committee was won over to the new "line", in the face of resistance from Harry Pollitt (who stood down as General Secretary), J. R. Campbell and William Gallacher MP. During the debates Rajani Palme Dutt, the leading advocate of the new policy, had to concede that the distinction that was being drawn between Poland (which was deemed unworthy of support against fascist aggression) and Republican Spain had "raised enormous feelings for comrades. It has not been easy for them to understand."[20] One Central Committee member put the situation very clearly: if Poland was "to be left to its own miserable fate . . . it does not put us in a favourable light, particularly after the stand we have taken on Spain, Czechoslovakia etc".[21] When Pollitt publicly recanted his opposition in mid-November, he argued that he had been blinded to the true nature of the war by his hatred of fascism. In particular, he cited "the strong personal feelings which had been aroused by what I had witnessed in Spain, and the responsibility I felt I had in regard to the sacrifice made by the British Battalion of the International Brigades".[22]

The new Communist policy was incomprehensible to many, and evinced strong feelings. Indeed, Aneurin Bevan wrote of the Communists in May 1940 that: "They shame their own dead in Spain."[23] Even so, the Communists continued to lay claim to the legacy of the Civil War, but could only utilise it with considerable ambiguity. For instance, when Harry Pollitt contested a by-election at Silvertown in February 1940 he presented himself as an anti-fascist candidate and prominently cited the party's role in organising the British Battalion. However, he went on to oppose the war with Germany as a "war run by the Tory ruling class which wants Fascism here".[24] The Communists' political isolation deepened when Soviet forces invaded Finland in November 1939, and suffered unexpected initial reverses. The "Winter War", which ended with Finland's defeat in March 1939, carried numerous echoes of the Spanish Civil War. For those many Britons sympathetic to Finland's plight, here was a small democratic state subjected to unprovoked aggression by a powerful, authoritarian neighbour. The parallels were particularly evident to the journalists who covered both conflicts, such as George Steer, John Langdon-Davies and William Forrest. Steer reported on the Soviet destruction of the town of Viborg in February 1940, and commented that "the only other place where I have seen such havoc was Guernica".[25] Forrest wrote that "those who wept for the Spanish children but had no tears for the Finnish children must be put in the same class of shallow hypocrites as those who lavished their sympathy on 'gallant little Finland' but refused to let Spain buy anti-aircraft guns for the defence of her civilians".[26] In a further twist, a "brigade" of British volunteers was assembled to fight on Finland's side, although only a handful had arrived by the time that the war ended.

Such parallels were, of course, deeply troubling to the Communist Party, and to many of the British veterans of the Spanish Civil War, for whom any comparisons between the Finns and the Spanish Republicans were spurious. From their perspective, the quasi-fascist Finnish government of Marshal Mannerheim was obstructing the legitimate security demands of the Soviet Union, and they deeply resented the fact that the British Labour movement had rallied so quickly to Finland's defence. On 1 March 1940 the secretary of the IBA circulated a letter to the organisation's District Secretaries urging former volunteers to speak out. "This matter of Finland," he wrote, "is being treated sufficiently often as a parallel to Spain (by Labour leaders in particular) that the influence of the Battalion should be particularly effective."[27] Moreover, the association sent a letter, signed by many of the surviving officers of the British Battalion, to Clement Attlee, condemning the Labour Party for supporting Neville Chamberlain's government during the war and, more specifically, for supporting "Butcher Mannerheim and the Banker's Government of Finland". Attlee's previous solidarity with the volunteers in Spain counted for nothing now that he was deemed to be "allied with the Fascists". The letter went on: "we wish your name to be no longer coupled with [the British Battalion]. You have dishonoured and insulted our comrades who fell in Spain, you have ceased to fight for the things they fell for."[28] It is not known how the Labour leader responded to this act of excommunication. However, the attempt to utilise the political capital accumulated during the Civil War proved to be a profound embarrassment for the IBA, which, thereafter, only rarely spoke collectively on any political issue apart from Spain.

In one sense, however, the Communists had a point: the moderate leaders of the Labour movement undoubtedly rallied to the cause of Finland more readily and wholeheartedly than they had to the Republic during the Spanish Civil War. Citrine, for instance, readily took part in a fact-finding delegation to Finland, alongside the Labour MP Philip Noel-Baker, having resisted opportunities to visit Republican Spain. The Winter War, it seemed, offered far less ambiguities than the Spanish Civil War. Finland presented a moderate, social democratic face, and possessed a strong co-operative movement. As Noel-Baker reported to the National Council of Labour on his return, "politically, the country was an excellent example of a successful Democracy – there was national union in its best sense".[29] Numerous correspondents wrote to Citrine to point out the apparent inconsistency between his positions on Finland and on Spain.[30] The point was also made at a public meeting held on his return to London when Citrine stated that the Labour movement had always been willing to "stand up to aggression from whatever quarter . . . (Interjection: What about Spain?)"[31] Sensitivity on this issue was reflected in the interim report of the Labour delegation, drafted after the cessation of hostilities. The document noted (not wholly accurately) that Finland should have been entitled to the same rights to arms and volunteers that the Labour movement *always demanded for the Spanish Government*. To have refused such help would have been to commit against Finland what the Labour Movement denounced as a crime when it was committed against the Spanish people."[32]

"A People's War", 1939–45

While the Communists painted themselves into a corner during the first two years of the war, it was left to maverick socialists such as George Orwell and, above all, Tom Wintringham to attempt to articulate lessons from the Spanish Civil War that were relevant to Britain's war with Nazi Germany. Wintringham had briefly been the commander of the British Battalion at the Jarama, where he was wounded, and had made something of a reputation during the 1930s as a left-wing expert on military affairs. He was a founder member of the CPGB but was expelled from the party in 1938 due to his relationship with the American journalist Kitty Bowler, whom he subsequently married. Spain, and the camaraderie of the International Brigades, became pivotal to Wintringham's career. Looking back in 1941 he wrote that "Spain woke me up. Politically I rediscovered democracy, realising the enormous potentialities in a real alliance of workers and other classes . . . [But] I was disgusted by sectarian intrigues . . . "[33] Wintringham's unorthodox Marxist ideas struck a chord when Britain faced the threat of invasion in the summer and autumn of 1940. At the height of the crisis the government created the Local Defence Volunteers (LDV), soon to be better known as the Home Guard. While many in official circles viewed the Home Guard with ill-concealed contempt, as useful only for boosting morale, Wintringham saw it as the embodiment of the same spirit which had animated the Spanish militias. As he wrote in *Picture Post*: "I could not help thinking how alike these two armies were", not only at the superficial level of their somewhat ragged appearance, but, more fundamentally, in terms of their resolve and "serious eagerness to learn."[34]

Wintringham seized the opportunity to train this eager new body of volunteer soldiers, not only to inculcate in them the methods of irregular warfare, but also the political values of an anti-fascist people's army. As he had written immediately after Dunkirk, the "answer to totalitarian war is a people's war",[35] and the Home Guard appeared to offer the perfect vehicle. With the help of Edward Hulton, proprietor of *Picture Post*, he established a private Home Guard training school at Osterley Park to the west of London. He was assisted by a number of Spanish Civil War veterans, such as Hugh Slater and "Yank" Levy, as well as by Roland Penrose, the surrealist artist, who taught camouflage. There was even a group of Spanish miners, skilled in the use of explosives. Understandably, one trainee recalled that "we saw ourselves as the heirs of Spain".[36] Even so, they were the heirs to a somewhat idealised legacy of the Civil War. There is no evidence that Wintingham had actually practised any of the guerrilla warfare that he preached at Osterley Park. Indeed, the military role of the International Brigades had been remarkably orthodox, and at the Jarama Wintringham had been wounded leading a bayonet charge that would not have been out of place on the Western Front. Therefore, the "lessons" of the Spanish Civil War had been learnt the hard way by Wintringham and his colleagues. Eventually the War Office, which disapproved of Wintringham's politics, paid him the compliment of taking over the school while progressively marginalizing its staff. He finally resigned in June 1941 and, from 1942, poured his energies into the leftist Common Wealth party. Osterley Park also incurred the disapproval of the IBA, which ruled that the Home Guard could not be a genuine people's militia, and instructed its members not to assist Wintringham in his work. In the summer of 1940 Victor Gollancz asked one former volunteer "whether he and his comrades would help to train certain L.D.V.s in the methods of the Spanish War. He replied, 'No: we don't support the war yet.'" [37]

The German invasion of the Soviet Union in June 1941, therefore, not only unleashed Communist Party support for the war effort, but also allowed the Communists to utilise the anti-fascist memory of the Spanish Civil War more wholeheartedly and constructively than had been possible since October 1939. The entry of the Soviet Union changed the war's political character, rendering it far more recognisable as the anti-fascist struggle envisaged in the 1930s. After this lengthy detour, it was now possible again for the Communists to argue that a Britain at war with Nazi Germany was not only avenging the defeat of the Spanish Republic, but was also completing the struggle that had been started on the battle-fields of Spain. Communists could now, without embarrassment, declaim: "Its all the same war, all the same war."[38] In such circumstances, the memory of the Spanish Republican struggle clearly had a role to play. For those who had fought in Spain, the present war seemed almost a re-enactment of that earlier struggle. Peter Kerrigan, a leading Communist, told British International Brigade veterans in January 1942 that Churchill should drive any remaining appeasers from his government just as "pro-fascists were eliminated from the [Spanish Republican] Government". Likewise, he alluded to the Ebro offensive of 1938, an attempt to relieve Valencia, as proof of the need for a Second Front in Europe to relieve pressure on the Soviet Union.[39]

For most British people, however, this greater conflict pushed the Spanish Civil War into the background. Images of the mass evacuations from Britain's cities superseded those of the 4000 Basque refugee children who had escaped to Britain in May 1937, just as those of the London Blitz overlay those of the bombing of Guernica. Indeed, those who had experienced air raids in Barcelona, such as Rosita Davson, knew that the Blitz was "far worse than Spain – at least there it was nerve racking for about half an hour, but once the all clear went . . . one knew that the rest of the night would be more or less peaceful".[40] In any case, the Republicans had suffered defeat – however heroic – whereas by 1941–45 there were new and successful anti-fascist struggles to support in China, in Yugoslavia and, above all, the Soviet Union itself. There was a further complication, as Spain's wartime neutrality meant that – much to the dismay of many former volunteers – the overthrow of the Franco regime was not campaigned for as a major war aim by the IBA.

Even so, the Spanish Civil War formed a valuable component within the broader political offensive which, during the latter stages of the war, the left launched against the record of the Conservatives in government during the 1930s. Hence, *The Trial of Mussolini* (1943) by the journalist Michael Foot, which described a fictional trial of the Italian dictator, in fact placed the British policy of appeasement in the dock. A representative "Spaniard" gave evidence to the effect that: "Spain was defeated in London and Paris . . . where cowardly men believed that the freedom of Europe could be salvaged even if Spain became a corpse." The "judge's" summing up contrasted the England of the Conservative Party, which "consorted with Fascism", with the England of Labour, which "denounced the policy which led to the massacre in Spain". The immodest conclusion was that "it was the resurrection of this other England which saved the world".[41] Although the leading "guilty men" (to cite one of Foot's earlier polemics) had already been marginalised within government during 1940–1, there is no question that the left conclusively won the battle to apportion blame for the foreign policy failures of the 1930s.

In this sense, the memory of the Spanish Civil War undoubtedly contributed (as one factor among many) to the historic victory of the Labour Party in the July 1945 election. Indeed, the Civil War was invoked, barely subliminally, during the election campaign. The *Daily Herald* ran the headline: "A vote for Churchill is a vote for Franco" and urged voters to question Conservative candidates as to Churchill's "friendly attitude" towards Franco's government. Meanwhile, a hastily-assembled "Emergency Committee in Aid of Democratic Spain" issued a six-point questionnaire for all candidates on future relations with Spain.[42] Of course, such interventions not only addressed an important issue for post-war diplomacy, but also revived memories of the Conservative record during the Civil War. Beyond this, however, generalisations are easy to make, but difficult to substantiate. Bill Alexander, a former commander of the British Battalion, expressed a view in 1956 that subsequently became commonplace amongst left-wing historians. He argued that the aid for Spain movement, "which brought new political ideas into many towns and villages where Toryism had been unchallenged, laid the basis for Labour's victory in 1945".[43] Likewise, Jim Fyrth has written that Spanish aid offered a "political apprenticeship" for the activist generation that carried Labour to victory in 1945, although he rightly points out that their sense of jubilation rapidly turned sour.[44]

The Cold War

Following the defeat of Nazi Germany and Fascist Italy, the Spanish Civil War lost its special salience within British politics. Although the

Communist Party continued, unsuccessfully, to argue that the Franco regime was a fascist threat to the peace of Europe, the greatest significance of the Civil War was now as a point of reference for judging Britain's response to other international conflicts. Moreover, with the coming of the Cold War in the later 1940s, the legacy of Spain became an increasingly contested one. The Communists laid claim to the memory of the Civil War through organisations such as the IBA, and attempted to utilise their authority in support of the Communist party's current policies.[45] Meanwhile, their opponents attempted to show that the lessons of Spain were generic and not the property of any particular party. At the Labour Party conference in 1950, for instance, the Chairman Sam Watson cited Spain in defence of the Labour government's controversial rearmament programme: "When the Fascists attacked Spain in 1936 was it because the Spanish Republic was engaged in an arms race with Hitler and Mussolini, or was it because the Spanish Government in its idealism had neglected to prepare itself against the counter-revolution [?]."[46]

One episode in particular encapsulates the way in which the legacy of the Spanish Civil War could become the object of dispute during the Cold War. The Labour government, led by Clement Attlee and Ernest Bevin, had responded to the outbreak of the Korean War in June 1950 by contributing British troops to the US-led United Nations force, on the grounds that there should be no appeasement of North Korean aggression. At the TUC Congress in September 1950, Sir Will Lawther, a former left-winger and now President of the National Union of Mineworkers, spoke out in favour of the intervention in Korea. He concluded by reminding delegates that he had previously spoken against aggression in Spain, where his brother Clifford had died fighting in the International Brigades. Lawther quoted from the last letter that he had received from his brother:

> *"Wherever you are, whatever you do, let it be known that you will stand with us in resisting aggression wherever it comes from . . . I am going up into the line, and if it needs be to give my life".* Look upon the roll of honour [Will Lawther continued] and at least you will find that many of those who shouted so much are not mentioned there. I would not betray that trust for all the money or all the position in this world.[47]

Some in the audience might have recalled that Sir Will had invoked his brother on previous occasions – in 1943, for instance, in support of the affiliation of the Communist Party at the Labour Party conference.[48] On this occasion, however, he did not escape controversy. Soon afterwards Cliff Lawther's nephew publicly stated that his uncle had died for the "workers of Spain and therefore for the workers all over the world". He could not believe that he would have stood beside his "beknighted brother in support of American intervention in Korea". In death, he went on, Cliff Lawther's ideals had been "stripped from him", and his words "twisted and shouted from platforms in support of policies that in life he could not have supported because he had a conscience".[49]

These comments highlighted a political problem that both the Communists and the left in general faced after 1945. The Soviet Union was increasingly seen as the most likely potential aggressor, all the more plausibly following the Prague "coup" in February 1948 and the outbreak of the Korean War. The left's argument that the true aggressor was US imperialism lacked broad-based support at a time when many saw an Atlantic alliance as essential for the defence of Western Europe. The question of Spain was a microcosm of this wider problem, as the Franco regime was an unpleasant dictatorship, and until the mid-1950s an international pariah, but hardly a threat to world peace. Communist attempts to argue otherwise, such as the claim that former Nazi scientists were building an atomic bomb in Spain, smacked of desperation.[50] The Civil War was only invoked with any real effect within British politics when a raw nerve was touched. This was notably the case in 1953, when the USA signed a military agreement with Franco's regime allowing it to establish nuclear bases in Spain, and again in 1960 when it was proposed that the recently-created West German army should have bases in Spain. In 1953 the *Daily Worker* noted apropos the US-Spanish pact that "it was not for this that the British labour and democratic movements fought in 1936–39",[51] while in 1960 strident protests were led within parliament by the Labour MP Bob Edwards, who had commanded the ILP contingent in the Civil War.

During the Cold War, as politics reached a pitch of intensity and negativity, the Communist Party was increasingly forced to defend its record during the Spanish Civil War. A spate of memoirs by those formerly involved with the British Battalion and now firmly in the anti-communist camp, such as Fred Copeman and Charlotte Haldane, were published in the late 1940s. While Copeman and Haldane pulled their punches about the International Brigades, the publication of *I Believed* by Douglas Hyde, the former CPGB organiser in North Wales during the Civil War and a recent convert to Catholicism, was particularly resented. Hyde's book, which was serialised in the Beaverbrook press, alleged, for instance, that a party organiser had the task of looking for able-bodied down and outs on the Thames Embankment whenever "cannon fodder" was needed in Spain. The *Daily Worker* responded that Hyde had "spat upon the memory of the glorious men who fought (and died) in Spain for liberty and the future of humanity against the tyranny and cruelty of Mr Hyde's new friends". Harry Pollitt gave a personal assurance that none of the volunteers had been motivated by drink.[52] Likewise, in 1952–3 Bob Darke, a longstanding member of the Communist party and a former Hackney councillor, launched a series of attacks on his former colleagues. Particularly painful was his claim that the party had been callous in its attitude to the British volunteers: "The Party didn't mind them dying in Spain. Some Communists had to go there and get shot, and it was best that they should be the expendable ones." He alleged that Peter Kerrigan – who, he claimed, was known as "The Butcher" for his disciplinary work in Spain – embodied the new "cold-blooded" attitude that had prevailed in the Party in the 1940s.[53]

The Communist Party was further put on the defensive when Harold Macmillan, explaining the defection of the Soviet spies Guy Burgess and Donald Maclean to parliament in November 1955, urged MPs to recall the circumstances in which the men had grown up. The Spanish Civil War had divided British opinion and "had a particularly disturbing effect upon young people, many of whom, we remember, thought it their duty to take part in these fierce revolutionary struggles".[54] Although the *Daily Worker* dismissed this as a "sneer" at those who had fought in Spain and a "witch-hunt", Macmillan's comments had established a putative connection between the idealism of the 1930s and treason.[55] (Rather gratuitously so, given that Kim Philby, the only one of the British spies to visit Spain during the Civil War, who did not defect until 1963, had reported for the *Times* from Franco's side and had even received a Nationalist decoration.) Nor was the discomfort purely that of the Communist Party. In May 1953 the Red-baiting US Senator Joseph McCarthy launched a scathing attack on Clement Attlee, now Leader of the Opposition, whom he identified with the "treasonable" policies of the former Secretary of State Dean Acheson. He then brandished a photograph of Attlee giving a clenched fist salute while reviewing "Communist" troops in Spain in 1937. In a rather pained statement the Labour leader emphasised his longstanding anti-Communism and noted that the International Brigades contained "liberals and people of all kinds of view who stood for liberty against fascism".[56]

The Last Great Cause?[57]
Spain and Popular Protest after 1945

Having felt for Spain, what further can we feel?

With these words written in 1940 Jack Lindsay, captured both the "dull prolonged anguish of spirit" that followed the defeat of the Spanish Republic and his belief that the idealism of the 1930s "held a goodness, a human wholeness, which could never be repeated".[58] Lindsay, a Communist poet who had written the stirring "On Guard for Spain" for "mass declamation" in 1937, was addressing a widely-held view that the Spanish Civil War was an unprecedented – and possibly unique – event. This belief rested above all on three principal factors: first, the "black and white" clarity of the issues at stake, which compelled many individuals to take sides; secondly, the unprecedented breadth of the international political mobilisation in support of the Spanish Republic; and thirdly, the intense emotive power of the Republic's doomed struggle. For many years after 1945, political commentators were engaged in a rather fatuous attempt to identify the next "Spain"; alternatively, they saw the absence of another "great cause" as proof not of the peculiar complexity of international politics during the Cold War, but rather as a failure of the young. It was perhaps not surprising that, in the words of one writer in 1958, "the young are bored with [the Civil War]",[59] although perhaps more accurately they were bored with the generational snobbery that memory of the Civil War fuelled (and that was later to be emulated by the generation that came of age in the 1960s).

After 1945 Spain itself did not become the next "Spain". The Franco regime proved surprisingly adept at navigating the difficult post-war years, its exiled opponents were deeply divided, and the British Labour government pursued a largely pragmatic policy. Moreover, although the anti-Franco cause was kept alive within Britain, it proved impossible to revive the spirit (or the mass protests) of the "old Spain days".[60] What was more surprising was that the Greek Civil War (1946–9) did not create a greater impact within British politics, especially given the intense unease within the Labour Party when British troops were used to suppress the Greek Communists in December 1944. The ensuing civil war bore many similarities with Spain, as a progressive left claiming to represent the Greek people confronted a Monarchist Right, allied with the remnants of the wartime collaborationist forces. Crucially, however, the right had won the elections of March 1946 (which the left had boycotted) and could claim a democratic mandate. Moreover, the Cold War spread a blanket of confusion over the conflict. For instance, the young Labour MP Francis Noel-Baker, a staunch opponent of the Franco regime, took a very different line on Greece. He told Parliament in January 1948 that Greece had been selected for the first major post-war experiment in Communist aggression, and invoked the parallels with the Spanish Civil War to argue that there should be no "Non-Intervention" or appeasement of Communism in Greece.[61] It should also be noted that the Greek Communists – who led a largely rural and somewhat internationally isolated rebellion – lacked the Spanish Republicans' facility in fashioning images or a compelling narrative that would appeal to foreign supporters. Thus, although solidarity campaigns did emerge in Britain, they remained small.

There was a far stronger link between Spain and the British support for the Chinese revolution. The left's solidarity with China dated back at least to the 1930s, and this interest was merely intensified by the triumph of the Communists in 1949. From the perspective of the left, there were striking similarities between the two cases. In particular, both China and the Spanish Republic had been victims of fascist aggression in the 1930s, suffering high levels of civilian casualties, and the image of a "new" China struggling to shake off the shackles of the old was almost identical to the left's interpretation of Spain in the 1930s. In the late 1930s there had been considerable overlap of personnel between the campaigns in solidarity with China and Spain: indeed, a China Medical Aid Committee was established specifically to help exiled German and Austrian doctors to travel from Spain to China at the end of the Civil War.[62] Moreover, following the establishment of the People's Republic in 1949 some of the Britons active in the Spanish Civil War became heavily involved with China. The medical volunteers Nan Green and Patience Darton, for instance, both worked in China during the 1950s, and the former International Brigader David Crook settled there permanently. Yet, while China was undoubtedly a "cause" of the post-war years, apart from at the height of the Korean War (in 1950–51) it lacked both the urgency and the salience of the Spanish Civil War.[63]

By the mid-1950s the memory of the Civil War was being held up as a somewhat unattainable measure of political engagement. This bred a sense of exasperation most famously expressed by John Osborne in his play *Look Back in Anger* (first staged in 1956). The central character Jimmy Porter, whose father had fought in Spain, complains that "people of our generation aren't able to die for good causes any longer. We had all that done for us, in the thirties and forties, when we were still kids . . . There aren't any good, brave causes left."[64] Similarly, in 1957 Kingsley Amis wrote a Fabian Society tract on "the present political apathy of the intelligentsia", in which he argued that intellectuals had run out of "interests and causes that are not one's own", or at least had lost the ability to become enthused by them as they had during the 1930s. Cyprus, where Britain was engaged in conflict with nationalist rebels, was the "one political issue of anything like the same proportions and of the same kind as the Abyssinias and the Spains of the Thirties", but had failed to galvanise any substantial action. Amis also predicted that the recent Hungarian and Suez crises (of November 1956) would fail to make any substantial impact. "What is needed," he concluded, "is a good, long, steadily-worsening crisis out in the open where everyone can see it."[65]

Despite Amis's cynicism, commentators at the time were impressed by the revival of activism over Hungary and Suez, and its parallels with the 1930s. Paul Johnson, who like Amis would subsequently move to the right, responded that: "Nobody who attended the great Suez demonstration in Trafalgar Square feels the need for another Spain." On this occasion, he argued, the intellectuals were not only militant and united, but successful: "After all, Messrs. Auden, Spender and Co. lost their battle [in Spain]; we won."[66] However, many would have shared the view of the writer Julian Symons that the true analogy with Spain was not Suez but Hungary. Indeed, there was no question that the Hungarian resistance to the Red Army, albeit fleetingly, triggered a very similar range of responses in Britain to those generated by the Spanish Republic. *The Times*, for instance, noted that "nothing in time of world peace since the Spanish Civil War has moved the universities of Britain so profoundly as the Hungarian rising",[67] and the *New Statesman* likewise claimed to witness a popular "revulsion of feeling . . . not seen since the Spanish War".[68] A Conservative MP even stated that he would have been willing to join an international brigade to fight on the Hungarians' side.[69] The great exception, of course, was the Communist Party in Britain, which found the idealism generated by the Hungarian revolt deeply embarrassing and sought to portray the rising as a fascist rather than a nationalist movement. Soon after the Red Army had re-entered Budapest, the *Daily Worker* cited the singer Paul Robeson's view that the forces at work in Hungary were "the same as those which overthrew the Spanish Republic".[70]

In one respect, however, Kingsley Amis was absolutely correct, as the Vietnam War would provide exactly the kind of long, deepening and highly public crisis that would create the context for another "Spain" (although, understandably, far more so in the United States than in

Britain). Rajani Palme Dutt could claim that like "Spain in the 30s, so Vietnam today represents the cause of all mankind".[71] Indeed, increasingly it was Spain that was viewed through the prism of Vietnam rather than vice versa. For instance, in his memoirs Edward Heath recalled the passions aroused by Spain as "every bit as fierce as those stirred up by the war in Vietnam thirty years later".[72] Of course, it is essential to emphasise at the outset not only the very substantial differences between the two conflicts, but also the considerable novelty of the agitation over Vietnam. Above all, the role of the university students was far more pivotal in the 1960s than in the 1930s, while that of the Labour movement was correspondingly smaller (not least because a Labour government was in power). Even so, it is striking that many on the left not only drew abstract parallels between Spain and Vietnam, but also saw the experience of the Spanish Civil War as a clear guideline for how to respond to what they perceived as US aggression in Indo-China.

Three specific cases illustrate this point. The first was the publication in 1967 of a book entitled *Authors take sides on Vietnam*, which quite explicitly drew its inspiration from the collection edited by Nancy Cunard thirty years earlier. The book was dedicated to Cunard's memory, and reproduced in full the "Question" that she had famously posed. Strikingly, twenty-five surviving authors of the 149 who had originally responded in 1937 also took part in this later survey. However, there were substantive differences, not least to the questions posed. Whereas the 1937 questionnaire had posed a sharp and clear choice, one of the 1967 questions was far more open and evaluative: "How, in your opinion, should the conflict in Vietnam be resolved?" In comparison with the few sentences that authors were invited to submit in 1937, many respondents wrote lengthy essays which doubtless reduced the political impact of the collection. In particular, the editors noted that, unlike their predecessors, they were "constantly confronted with the notion that writers have no business expressing themselves on matters of politics and world affairs". Indeed, W. H. Auden, who had expressed staunch antifascist views in 1937, now expressed bewilderment: "Why writers should be canvassed for their opinion on controversial political issues, I cannot imagine." Other respondents took the chance to take a swipe at the idealism generated by the Spanish Civil War. For instance, Anthony Powell replied that the 1937 pamphlet had shown writers "at their silliest and most pompous".[73]

If *Authors take sides on Vietnam* demonstrated how far attitudes had changed since the 1930s, at least with regard to the role of intellectuals in politics, there was also evidence of history repeating itself as farce. In

1965 John Mahon, a leading Communist and former political commissar in Spain, was asked to carry out a historical analysis of the Communist party's work during the Civil War, with a view to assessing the viability of the party sending volunteers to fight in Vietnam. He conceded that "no direct parallel" could be drawn between the two conflicts, and that the problems posed by communicating over distance, the quality of Vietnamese food, and the "highly technical level" of the fighting created immense problems. The cost of transporting the volunteers was likely to be prohibitive and "could only really be solved by us up to the socialist frontiers". "Whether anything we could send," he concluded, "would have any military significance in Vietnam is very doubtful. It could, on the other hand, have a tremendous political value."[74] At the Communist Party's Congress in November 1967, while moving an emergency resolution on behalf of the Executive Committee, Mahon offered to organise volunteers to fight in Vietnam "should the call be made".[75] His status as a Civil War veteran was seen as "adding force to the offer".

More productive, and a final concrete link between Spain and Vietnam, was the work of the British Medical Aid Committee for Vietnam, an organisation formed in June 1965. This committee was organised by Dr Joan McMichael, a member of the Communist Party since 1937. As she recalled in 1967: "Since I had previously been involved in Spanish Medical Aid, and had, for a brief period in 1938–39, been secretary of China Medical Aid, I had been actively considering a proposal to form a Medical Aid Committee for Vietnam, and had been consulting comrades and former colleagues and friends who had worked on these committees."[76] While the experience of Spanish Medical Aid contributed more to the committee's inspiration than to its actual practice, there is no doubt that for a radical section of the medical profession this bridge spanning thirty years seemed wholly appropriate.[77]

Political careers and the Spanish Civil War

For many young British soldiers a "good war" (implying bravery on the battlefield and rapid promotion) in 1939–45 formed the basis for a successful post-war political career. For the left, in particular, Spain offered a similar form of *kudos*, as to have fought in Spain was at once a badge of honour and a mark of political commitment. During the fraught Central Committee meetings of the CPGB in early October 1939 one participant noted that all present had been tested in some way: "I can look around at everybody, and in a minute's recollection discover that so-and-so has been in Spain or prison . . . "[78]Although there is no evidence to suggest that volunteers took part for careerist reasons, and given the casualty rate this would have been highly unwise, for a number of the survivors the Civil War undoubtedly moulded and defined their careers. At the same time, a "bad" war in Spain, especially for established politicians, often provided detractors with an enduring supply of political ammunition.

The political impact was most visible in the Communist Party. In the February 1950 general election, for instance, the *Daily Worker* proudly claimed that nine of its 100 candidates "fought against Franco".[79] The association with the Civil War was so powerful that at least one Communist candidate in local elections in 1947 falsely claimed that he had fought in Spain.[80] A number of Communists who had been prominent in the International Brigades, such as Peter Kerrigan, Bert Ramelson and John Mahon, went on to hold leading positions within the Communist Party well into the 1960s. Unlike in many East European Communist parties, the British volunteers did not become the object of suspicion or political victimisation during the early 1950s.[81] No career was shaped more profoundly than that of Bill Alexander, who had commanded the British Battalion in Spain, prior to serving as a Captain in the Reconnaissance Corps during the Second World War. In 1945 he stood for election in Coventry East with the endorsement of 153 NCOs and fellow soldiers.[82] He rose through the Communist Party bureaucracy to become Assistant Secretary from 1959 until 1967, when, feeling increasingly out of touch with contemporary politics on the left, he resigned to become a teacher. His later years were dominated by his involvement with the IBA, of which he was Secretary from 1970 until his death in 2000, which he ruled with a "rod of iron".[83] He became the principal defender of a highly dogmatic interpretation of the Civil War and the role of the International Brigades within it. In many respects, the trajectory of Alexander's public life, which worked backwards to the receding glories of the Spanish Civil War, largely to the exclusion of his later experiences during and after the Second World War, became symptomatic of the Communist Party's own relationship with the conflict.

In 1961 Richard Crossman wrote that the Spanish Civil War had "pervaded left-wing politics [in the 1930s] and conditioned the mental attitudes of many of those who lead the Labour movement today".[84] This certainly applied to a number of prominent trade unionists, notably Will Paynter (President of the National Union of Mineworkers (NUM), 1959–69) and Jack Jones (General Secretary of the Transport & General Workers' Union, 1969–78). Although their success could not be said to have been determined by their service with the British Battalion in Spain, the connection was often made in the press, and in both cases reinforced an image of resilience and toughness. When Paynter arrived at the helm of the NUM, for instance, he was hailed as "the fighting democrat".[85] Jones had the satisfaction of being able to play a role in facilitating Spain's transition to democracy in the mid-1970s.[86] Within the Labour Party, however, Crossman's point is more difficult to establish. Harold Wilson, who became leader in 1963 and who, like Crossman, had been an Oxford don in the later 1930s, appeared largely immune to the passions of the Civil War. Ironically, it was Wilson's great political rival, the Conservative politician Edward Heath, who joined a delegation to Republican Spain as an Oxford student in 1938 and, indeed, met Jack Jones while visiting the front. While this counted for little during the industrial confrontations that dogged his period as Prime Minister in 1970–4, this evidence of Heath's anti-fascist internationalism marked him out from fellow Tories and earned him a grudging respect on the left.

Conversely, a number of Conservative politicians were haunted by their record during the Civil War. This applied above all to those young enough to have held positions of responsibility during the National Government (1931–40) who had then gone on to serve in the Conservative administrations of 1951–64. R. A. Butler's role at the Foreign Office in 1938–9 was particularly resented, as it coincided with a series of attacks on British merchant ships in Republican ports by Nationalist aircraft. Butler's image as an appeaser was therefore compounded by his apparent weakness towards the Franco regime, and this tainted his entire political career. His failure to defend British shipping during the Civil War was regularly held against him in Parliament in the 1950s, and in 1964 he was asked directly by Michael Foot if he had no "guilt on his conscience" over Spain.[87] When Butler, on a private visit to Spain as Home Secretary in May 1961, made ill-judged comments that seemed to hint at Spain's admission to NATO, the subsequent political furore was doubtless magnified by his previous "form". In the left-wing press Butler was accused of returning to the "scene of the crime", or even returning "to his vomit", while the *New Statesman* detected an "instinctive sympathy for his hosts" on Butler's part.[88] A number of other senior Tories, such as Allan Lennox-Boyd ("Franco Boyd" during the Civil War) and Alec Douglas Home, were also vulnerable to attack on this score. When Home, as Prime Minister in 1964, hoped to sell arms to Spain, the *Daily Worker* responded that "A vote for Home is a vote for Franco", and claimed that he and Butler merely wanted to do now what they "dared not do" in the 1930s.[89]

A far away country

Any direct influence that the Spanish Civil War had exercised on British politics was palpably ebbing by the later 1960s. Not only were those politicians whose formative experiences lay in the 1930s now beginning to leave front-line politics, but also the Civil War was a far less obvious point of reference for a younger generation that came of age with the anti-nuclear and anti-Vietnam War protests. The death of Franco in 1975 and Spain's rapid transition to democracy in 1975–8 appeared to draw a further line under the Civil War. As Nan Green commented in 1971, the Civil War veterans were now "historical figures", increasingly consulted by students for help with their dissertations.[90] Even so, the memory of the Civil War continued to be invoked within British politics, whether in response to the Nicaraguan revolution in the 1980s or the Bosnian conflict of 1992–5.[91] As recently as 2005 the radical journalist John Pilger stretched this memory to breaking point in order to admonish those who had planned the invasion of Iraq. For Pilger the legacy of the International Brigade volunteers – men who understood and confronted fascism – endured as "a warning about sinister ambitions behind democratic façades: about Messianic politicians, apparently touched by God, and their denial of the consequences of their violence, and it is a warning about those who shout down the reasons why in the name of fake patriotism".[92]

Such parallels aside, however, the influence of the Civil War had largely mutated into an inspirational legend of bravery and political commitment mediated, above all, by the volunteers. This influence could operate on an individual level. For instance, the anarchist Stuart Christie grew up in the Scottish mining town of Blantyre amongst many International Brigade veterans. The memory of three local miners who had fallen at the Jarama was still revered, while the old tensions between Communists, Anarchists and Trotskyists could still cause punch-ups in the miners' welfare. Christie saw his ill-fated visit to Spain in 1964, attempting to assist the armed opposition to Franco's regime, as carrying on the work of the volunteers.[93] Ian Davison, who volunteered for the PLO in the 1980s, described how prior to his departure he had visited "an old hero of his, Joe Blair, a veteran of the Spanish Civil War: 'Keep your head down and get as many of them as you can' he advised."[94] This influence might also operate at the level of entire communities. The publication in 1984 of Hywel Francis's book on the Welsh volunteers helped to consolidate a particular vision of the class consciousness of the Welsh miners just as they were facing defeat – and the ultimate collapse of their industry – in a doomed struggle with the Thatcher government. More recently the central, enduring role of the volunteers was emphasised by *The Guardian*'s decision to devote an entire edition of its supplement to interviews – poignantly accompanied by portrait photographs – with "the last British survivors of the International Brigades". The elderly veterans spoke of a conflict now seemingly remote from modern Britain, but the interviews drew an ecstatic response from many readers.[95] The volunteers had not generally cultivated a heroic image. Even so, after seven decades their heroism had become the essential reference point for understanding the resonance of the Civil War – and, above all of the International Brigades – within modern British politics.

Notes

Chapter 1   *"A far away country of which we know nothing"?*

1   For fuller accounts of British responses to the Civil War see K. W. Watkins, *Britain Divided: The Effect of the Spanish Civil War on British Political Opinion* (Thomas Nelson, London, 1963); Jill Edwards, *The British Government and the Spanish Civil War, 1936–1939* (Macmillan, London, 1979); Jim Fyrth, *The Signal was Spain: The Aid Spain Movement in Britain, 1936–1939* (Lawrence & Wishart, London, 1986); Enrique Moradiellos, *Neutralidad Benévola: El Gobierno Británico y la Insurección Militar Espanola de 1936* (Pentalfa Ediciones, Oviedo, 1990) and *La Perfidia de Albión: el Gobierno Británico y la Guerra Civil Española* (Siglo Veintiuno Editores, Madrid, 1996); James Flint, "'Must God go Fascist?' English Catholic Opinion and the Spanish Civil War", *Church History*, 56 (1987), pp. 364–74; Tom Buchanan, *The Spanish Civil War and the British Labour Movement* (Cambridge University Press, Cambridge, 1991); Tom Buchanan, *Britain and the Spanish Civil War* (Cambridge University Press, Cambridge, 1997). There is as yet no comprehensive study of right-wing attitudes to the Civil War, although see Judith Keene, *Fighting for Franco: International Volunteers in Nationalist Spain during the Spanish Civil War, 1936–39* (Leicester University Press, London, 2001), chapter 2. There is a useful contemporary source in Simon Haxey, *Tory MP* (Gollancz, London, 1938), chapter 8.

2   Ralph Bates, *The Olive Field* (Jonathan Cape, London, 1936), p. 477 (emphasis added).

3   *Morning Post*, 21 July 1936.

4   Even this degree of knowledge cannot be assumed. Laurie Lee, who tramped through Spain in 1935–6, wrote that: "My small country school, always generous with its information as to the exports of Queensland and the fate of Jenkins's ear, had provided me with nothing more tangible or useful about Spain than that Seville had a barber, and Barcelona, nuts", *As I Walked out one Midsummer Morning* (1969; 1971 edition, Penguin, Harmondsworth), p. 48.

5 See Douglas Little, *Malevolent Neutrality: The United States, Britain and the Origins of Non-Intervention* (Cornell University Press, Ithaca, NY, 1985), and "Red Scare 1936: Anti-Bolshevism and the Origins of British Non-Intervention in the Spanish Civil War", *Journal of Contemporary History*, 23 (April 1988).

6 For an interesting account of the nexus of business, landowning and political interests supporting the Nationalists, see "Franco's followers in Britain", *Labour Research*, 27, 5 (May 1938). See also "Imperialist interests in Spain", *Labour Research*, September 1937. The left also had business interests in Spain – the co-operative movement owned a food depot near Almeria, and early coverage of the Civil War in *The Co-Operative News* was preoccupied with the fate of the two British staff members (25 July, 1 August 1936).

7 According to Edward Conze:"Ferrer has remained a hero of European progressives, and when the *Daily Herald* (on 7 May) referred to the 'notorious' Ferrer, a wholesome storm of protest arose among socialists." (*Spain Today: Revolution and Counter-Revolution* (Secker & Warburg, London, 1936), p. 31).

8 The People's Olympiad was widely covered in advance in the British left-wing press. The British team comprised 28 athletes, 5 cyclists, 4 swimmers, 5 tennis players, a boxer and a chess player (*Daily Herald*, 2 July 1936).

9 Gerald Brenan, *South from Granada* (1957; 1980 edition, Cambridge University Press, Cambridge, 1980), p. 1. Brenan went on to become a leading authority on Spain: see chapter 9.

10 Sir Peter Chalmers Mitchell's *My House in Malaga* (Faber & Faber, London, 1938) describes expatriate life as well as offering an eye-witness account of the first months of the Civil War. The *Daily Herald* of 5 February 1936 advertised a WTA cruise to "Sunny Spain" beginning on 18 July – just as the rising began. See also E. Francis Williams, *Journey into Adventure – The Story of the Workers' Travel Association* (Odhams Press, London, 1960), pp. 122–3.

11 Southern Railways, *Spain – Land of Colour and Romance* (London, 1933). See also Sydney A. Clark, *Spain on £10* (London, 1935) and Spanish Travel Bureau, *Spain for Holidays* (London, 1929).

12 *Forward*, 1 August 1936.

13 *Daily Herald*, 10 October 1936.

14 Mary Low and Juan Breá, *Red Spanish Notebook* (Secker & Warburg, London, 1937), p. 23.

15 *Daily Worker*, 22 July 1936. I am grateful to Edmund Weiner of the *Oxford English Dictionary* for his advice on the origin of this phrase.

16 TNA, FO 371 29584, W16047/62/41, 13 November 1936.

17 Sir Peter Chalmers Mitchell, 'Introductory Note' to Ramón J. Sender, *Seven Red Sundays* (Faber & Faber, London, 1936), p. 9.

18 Franz Borkenau, *The Spanish Cockpit* (Faber & Faber, London, 1937), p. 76.

19 *Labour*, May 1936.

20 In April 1937 Anthony Eden told Walter Citrine, General Secretary of the

TUC, that he felt "personally very sympathetic towards the Basques". Soon afterwards Sir Robert Vansittart, Permanent Under-Secretary at the Foreign Office, told Citrine that Franco had made a "profound mistake" in attacking the Basques as "this autonomous government had behaved in the most exemplary fashion, and all they wanted was to be left alone" (Buchanan, *The Spanish Civil War and the British Labour Movement*, pp. 101–2). This point will be discussed further in chapter 2.

21 *Parliamentary Debates (Parl.Debs.)*, vol. 340, col. 271, 2 November 1938, Captain Graham.
22 *Daily Herald*, 3 February 1938.
23 National Library of Scotland, David Murray Papers, Acc 7914, Box 3, no date. From an article intended for publication in the *New Leader*.
24 Leah Manning, *What I saw in Spain* (Gollancz, London, 1935), p. 20.
25 *Daily Worker*, 15 April 1931.
26 *Daily Herald*, 9 October 1934.
27 *Parl. Debs*, vol. 327, col. 117, 21 October 1937.
28 *Daily Herald*, 15 April 1931.
29 *Daily Herald*, 18 May 1936; 2 June 1936.
30 *Daily Herald*, 22 June, 18 July and 5 August 1936.
31 Buchanan, *The Spanish Civil War and the British Labour movement*, chapter 5, pp. 167–95, discusses Catholic working-class disquiet over the Civil War. My article "Divided loyalties: The impact of the Spanish Civil War on Britain's Civil Service trade unions, 1936–9", *Historical Research*, 65/165 (1992) offers a detailed account of the problems experienced by one section of the labour movement.
32 *Daily Herald*, 1 September 1936.
33 Manning, *What I saw*, pp. 40–1.
34 *Parl. Debs*, vol. 318, col. 2848, 18 December 1936.
35 *Daily Herald*, 10 August 1936.
36 Union of Democratic Control papers, Hull University Library, DDC, 5/373, September 1936.
37 *Daily Herald*, 17 October 1936. See Anthony Aldgate, *Cinema and History: British Newsreels and the Spanish Civil War* (London, 1979), pp. 105, 109.
38 *Daily Worker*, 1 and 6 June 1938.
39 *Daily Worker*, 14 September 1936.
40 Article by Alexander Thompson in *Labour*, September 1936.
41 María Rosa de Madariaga, 'The intervention of Moroccan troops in the Spanish Civil War: A reconsideration', *European History Quarterly*, 22/1 (1992), pp. 80, 87. See also Sebastian Balfour, *Deadly Embrace: Morocco and the Road to the Spanish Civil War* (Oxford University Press, Oxford, 2002).
42 Borkenau, *Spanish Cockpit*, p. 78.
43 *Railway Review*, 20 November 1936.
44 *The Draughtsman*, December 1936.
45 *The Bank Officer*, November 1936.
46 London Trades Council, Minutes, 16 August 1936.

47 *TUC Congress Report*, 1936, p. 368. Behind the scenes at Congress there was an interesting debate about whether a formal call for the withdrawal of Moroccan troops should be included in the Conference resolution. This was opposed by J. Clynes and Hugh Dalton, on the grounds that it would be impossible to implement, and that "they had no authority with the rebels". Bevin favoured its inclusion, arguing that the question of "the recruitment of native races" should be brought before the newly formed Non-Intervention Committee "on grounds of humanity"; TUC archives, Box 431, File 946/521, verbatim report of Labour Movement Conference, 9 September 1936.

48 *The Draughtsman*, December 1936.

49 Seamus MacKee, *I was a Franco Soldier* (United Editorial Ltd, London, 1938), p. 19.

50 *Daily Herald*, 30 July, 16 September, 27 November 1936.

51 *Daily Herald*, 24 November 1936.

52 'Londoner's Diary', *New Statesman and Nation*, 5 December 1936.

53 *The Bank Officer*, December 1936.

54 *Daily Herald*, 1 December 1936.

55 *Labour Party Conference Report*, 1936, p. 214.

56 See Buchanan, *The Spanish Civil War and the British labour movement*, p. 69. The Labour leaders were not the only ones to be embarrassed. The two Spaniards had received extensive interrogation at Croydon airport, and a Foreign Office official noted that: "I don't quite know why these people were so treated. Jimenez de Asua is a Professor of Law and a well known man and Sra de Palencia is well known too. Neither is in the 'Pasionar[i]a' class." In fact, such was de Palencia's impact that many in the audience, and many subsequent authors, were convinced that they had heard the famous Communist orator La Pasionaria herself.

57 *Daily Worker*, 11 August 1936.

58 The Duchess of Atholl, *Searchlight on Spain* (Penguin, Harmondsworth, London, 1938); see chapter 16, 'The Republic sets to work'.

59 Harry Gannes and Theodore Repard, *Spain in Revolt* (Gollancz, London, 1936), pp. 198 and 278.

60 Many historians have concluded that some form of revolution, which was subsequently liquidated, took place in Republican Spain in 1936. For a particularly polemical account see Noam Chomsky, 'Objectivity and Liberal Scholarship', in *American Power and the New Mandarins* (Pelican, London, 1969), pp. 23–130. The most recent and fullest exposition of the alleged communist manipulation of Republican politics is Burnett Bolloten's posthumous *The Spanish Civil War: Revolution and Counter-Revolution* (University of North Carolina Press, Chapel Hill, 1991).

61 Gannes and Repard, *Spain in revolt*, p. 165.

62 Conze, *Spain today*, p. 142.

63 George Orwell, 'Caesarean section in Spain', *The Highway*, March 1939 (emphasis added), pp. 146–7.

64 Neville Thompson, *The Anti-appeasers: Conservative Opposition to Appeasement in the 1930s* (Oxford University Press, Oxford, 1971), chapter 6, 'The Spanish Distraction'. See also N. J. Crowson, *Facing Fascism: The Conservative Party and the European Dictators, 1935–40* (Routledge, London, 1997).

65 L. S. Amery, *My Political Life, vol. 3, The Unforgiving Years, 1929–40* (Hutchinson, London, 1955), p. 193.

66 There is a good account of Churchill's changing stance on the Civil War in Robert Rhodes James, *Churchill: A Study in Failure, 1900–1939* (Penguin, Harmondsworth, 1973), pp. 406–9. Initially he was highly sympathetic to the Nationalist side, and saw their victory as the lesser of two evils. By mid-1938, however, he had changed this view, writing in December that year that "the British Empire would run far less risk from the victory of the Spanish Government than from that of General Franco".

67 On the Duchess's career, see S. J. Hetherington, *Katharine Atholl, 1876–1960, Against the Tide* (Aberdeen University Press, Aberdeen, 1989), and Stuart Ball, 'The Politics of Appeasement: the fall of the Duchess of Atholl and the Kinross and West Perth by-election, December 1938', *Scottish Historical Review*, 187 (April 1990).

68 Robert Benewick, *The Fascist Movement in Britain* (Allen Lane, London, 1972), p. 162. On BUF involvement in commandeering shipping see Buchanan, *Britain and the Spanish Civil War*, p. 91.

69 G. C. Webber, *The Ideology of the British Right, 1918–39* (Croom Helm, London, 1986), pp. 4, 47.

70 The leading Tory supporters of Franco in the Commons were Sir Henry Page Croft, Anthony Crossley, Harold Mitchell, Captain Cazalet, Captain Ramsay, Wing Commander James, Charles Emmott, Alfred Denville, Sir Nairne Stewart Sandeman, Patrick Donner, Sir Arnold Wilson, and Alan Lennox-Boyd. In addition, the following MPs are identified by Simon Haxey as Franco sympathizers: Henry Channon, George Balfour, Alfred Knox, and Patrick Hannon (*Tory MP*, pp. 217–19).

71 See 'Franco's followers in Britain', *Labour Research*, 27/5 (May 1938).

72 Douglas Jerrold, *Georgian Adventure* (Collins, London, 1937), p. 362.

73 Eleanora Tennant, *Spanish Journey – Personal Experiences of the Civil War* (Eyre & Spottiswoode, London, 1936), p. 112.

74 *The Tablet*, 9 January 1937.

75 Sir Henry Page Croft, *Spain: The Truth at Last* (Bournemouth, 1937), pp. 18–19.

76 *Parl. Debs*, vol.344, col. 1133, 28 February 1939.

77 *Parl. Debs*, vol. 321, col. 3144, 25 March 1937.

78 *Morning Post*, 16 September, 1936.

79 Bernard Wall, *Spain of the Spaniards* (Sheed & Ward, London, 1938), p. xxi.

80 *Parl. Debs*, vol. 340, col. 288, 2 November 1938.

81 *Parl. Debs*, vol. 326, col. 1829, 19 July 1937.

82 *Morning Post*, 9 December 1936.

83 *Morning Post*, 11 August 1936.
84 *Morning Post*, 24 August 1936.
85 Ibid.
86 *Morning Post*, 14 September 1936.
87 *Parl. Debs*, vol. 343, col. 142, 31 January 1939.
88 *Morning Post*, 3, 7 and 16 October 1936.
89 Florence Farmborough, *Life and People in Nationalist Spain* (Sheed & Ward, London, 1938), pp. 31, 54 and 143.
90 *Parl. Debs*, vol. 344, col. 1179, 28 February 1939.
91 This sympathy in certain Catholic circles far outlasted the Civil War. In December 1950 and January 1951 the *Christian Democrat* ran articles by 'Trade Unionist in Spain' F. Dutton, lauding Franco's social policies. "Class-war" he claimed "has been eliminated without depriving either side of the fullest liberty to negotiate . . . Thus, the State is the servant of the Spaniards."
92 *Parl. Debs*, vol. 342, col. 2577, 19 December 1938.
93 *Parl. Debs*, vol. 344, col. 1175, 28 February 1939, Patrick Donner MP.
94 Tennant, *Spanish journey*, pp. 116–17.
95 Croft, *Spain: The truth at last*, p. 18.
96 *The Tablet*, 9 January 1937.
97 Brigadier-General The Lord Croft, *My Life of Strife* (Hutchinson, London, 1949), p. 275.
98 Captain Cazalet, quoted in Haxey, *Tory MP*, p. 215.
99 *Parl. Debs*, vol. 344, col. 1189, 28 February 1939. The Tory MP Sir Nairne Stewart Sandeman had said that "Franco is an angel in comparison with what Negrin's Government would have been".
100 Arnold Lunn, *Spanish Rehearsal* (Hutchinson, London, 1937), p. 43.
101 Opinion polling was still in its infancy. Polls taken in 1938–9 by the British Institute of Public Opinion revealed the mass of British opinion to be increasingly sympathetic to the Republic, while support for Franco was below 10 per cent. The poll taken on 15 October 1938 showed the sympathies of those approached as 57 per cent for the elected government, 9 per cent for Franco, and 34 per cent with no opinion. A poll published in January 1939 showed that many of the 'don't knows' had by then swung to support the Republic, with figures of 72 per cent for the government, 9 per cent for Franco, and 19 per cent offering no opinion (*News Chronicle*, 25 January 1939). It would have been interesting to know the depth of government support in the summer and autumn of 1936, but unfortunately no polls were taken at this time.

Chapter 2 *Journalism at war*

I am very grateful to George B. Steer for his helpful comments on this chapter and to Nick Rankin and the late Professor Kenneth Kirkwood for their kind assistance.

1   Noel Monks, "I Hate War" in Frank C. Hanighen (ed.), *Nothing but Danger* (Harrap, London, 1940), p. 75.
2   Scott Watson can be identified here for the first time as the author of the *Star* dispatch (Churchill College Archive (CCA), Cambridge, Philip Noel-Baker papers, NBKR 4/660, Sir Walter Layton to Philip Noel-Baker, 1 June 1937). Scott Watson had briefly served in the International Brigades, before working for Sefton Delmer of the *Daily Express* in Madrid. He subsequently became a correspondent for the *Daily Herald* and worked in Spain until the end of the war. According to Layton of the *Star*, the story "came to us out of the blue long before any other news came through and we dare not print it without confirmation. As soon as the first flash came from Reuters we printed Watson's cable in full . . . It is still something of a mystery story."
3   Page Croft, *Spain: The truth at last*, p. 14.
4   Robert Sencourt, *Spain's Ordeal* (Longman's, London, 1938), p. 247.
5   "He no longer makes contributions to *The Times*: nor is he in Spain. It had been felt that, already in Ethiopia, he had been unduly partial to the Negus [i.e. the Emperor]" (Sencourt, *Spain's Ordeal*, p. 247).
6   Herbert R. Southworth, *Guernica! Guernica! A Study of Journalism, Diplomacy, Propaganda and History* (University of California Press, Berkeley, 1977).
7   Phillip Knightley, *The First Casualty: The War Correspondent as Hero, Propagandist and Myth Maker* (Quartet, London, revised edition, 1982), p. 193.
8   Monks, "I hate war", pp. 86–7.
9   Franklin Reid Gannon, *The British Press and Nazi Germany, 1936–1939* (Clarendon Press, Oxford, 1971), p. 115.
10 Nick Rankin, *Telegram from Guernica: the Extraordinary Life of George Steer, War Correspondent* (Faber and Faber, London, 2003).
11 Sidney Barton, Preface to G. L. Steer, *Sealed and Delivered: a Book on the Abyssinian campaign* (Hodder & Stoughton, London, 1942), p. 1.
12 Steer, *The Tree of Gernika: a Field Study of Modern War* (Hodder & Stoughton, London, 1938), p. 14; Rankin, *Telegram from Guernica*, p. 134.
13 There is an almost visionary passage in his book on North Africa in which he describes the beauty of the Wiltshire countryside during his "first English summer" in 1921. "You English, born with silver streams and golden wheat in your mouths, can never tell the controlled hysteria of a South African boy when he looked at so much natural beauty after so much wilderness" (G. L. Steer, *A Date in the Desert* (Hodder & Stoughton, London, 1939), pp. 121–2).
14 John Ryland's Library (JRL), Manchester, *Manchester Guardian* archive, A/594/3a, Steer's 1932 application.
15 Letter to the author from Professor Kenneth Kirkwood, 24 March 1997; Rhodes House, Oxford, Mss Afr. S. 1667, Saamwerk file.
16 Most notably Philip Noel-Baker (see the correspondence in CCA, NBKR, 9/55/3).

17 JRL, A/594/3a.

18 Ibid.

19 JRL, A/594/10, Olivier to Scott, 9 February 1932; A/594/11, Scott to Olivier, 10 February 1932. Sydney Haldane Olivier (1859–1943) was a Fabian socialist and Secretary of State for India in the first Labour government.

20 CCA, NBKR 9/55/3, Steer to Noel Baker, 1 August 1932; W. H. Hindle (ed.), *Foreign Correspondent* (Harrap, London, 1939) p. 214.

21 Times Newspapers Limited Archive (TNL Archive), Steer file, Ralph Deakin to Steer, 21 May 1935.

22 G. L. Steer, *Caesar in Abyssinia* (Hodder & Stoughton, London, 1936), pp. 19–20.

23 TNL Archive, Steer file, *Times* to Steer, 9 September and 13 October 1935; Deakin to Editor, 29 August 1935.

24 TNL Archive, Steer file, Steer to Deakin, 23 July 1935. One of Steer's colleagues later claimed that he had engineered this interview for Steer by means of a faked telegram from *The Times* (Knightley, *The First Casualty*, p. 159).

25 TNL Archive, Steer file, Steer to Deakin, 23/5 August 1935.

26 Ibid.

27 CCA, NBKR 4/663, letters by Noel-Baker to Foreign Office, 4 June and 18 June 1940.

28 Noel Monks, *Eyewitness* (Muller, London, 1955), p. 36.

29 Rankin, *Telegram from Guernica*, p. 51.

30 G. L. Steer, "Exit the Emperor", in Hindle, *Foreign correspondent*, pp. 214–38 (these references are to pp. 237 and 225).

31 University of Warwick, Modern Records Centre (MRC), Mss 292/946/530, 5 February 1937, memorandum from William Gillies to Walter Citrine; on 4 February Steer had given a very similar account of his expulsion to Lt-Col Arnold at the War Office, FO 371 21284 W2902/1/41. It should be noted that in 1939 he was allowed to travel and report with relative freedom on the Italian empire in North Africa.

32 Steer, *Tree of Gernika* p. 13 merely says that he was on the Franco-Spanish border in August–September 1936; Southworth states that neither the *Times* archivist nor his colleague Christopher Holme were aware of Steer's visit to Nationalist Spain (Southworth, *Guernica! Guernica!*, p. 402, fn. 4). Peter Kemp, a British volunteer for Franco, met Steer in Toledo in November (*Thorns of Memory*, Sinclair-Stevenson, London, 1990, p. 21), and William Stirling, a young temporary correspondent for the *Times*, was grateful for his assistance (Rankin, *Telegram from Guernica*, pp. 84–5).

33 Steer, *Tree of Gernika*, pp. 135, 138.

34 Steer, *Tree of Gernika*, p. 13. See above, chapter 1, p. 6

35 TNA, ADM 116/3512, M 01841/37, report of 5 February 1937. This detail is confirmed by the recollection of the British Pro-Consul in Bilbao, interviewed in 1970 (James Cable, *The Royal Navy and the Siege of Bilbao*,

Cambridge University Press, Cambridge, 1979, p. 75), and this suggests that Steer's activities were being closely monitored by the British government.

36 TNL Archive, Steer file, Steer to Lints Smith, 5 February 1937.

37 Rankin, *Telegram from Guernica*, p. 113.

38 For this episode, which is not recorded in the Times archive, see CCA NBKR 4/2, Steer to the editor, *The Times*, 20 March 1937 and subsequent correspondence, and CCA NBKR 4x/22, Noel-Baker to Steer, 30 March 1937.

39 TNL Archive, note from Managers' Department to Steer's solicitors, 1 May 1939.

40 Steer, *Tree of Gernika*, p. 198.

41 CCA, NBKR 4x/118, Steer to Noel-Baker, 19 April 1937.

42 Steer, *Tree of Gernika*, pp. 208–9.

43 Ibid.

44 Steer, *Tree of Gernika*, p. 229.

45 Steer, *Sealed and delivered*, p. 7.

46 Steer, *Tree of Gernika*, p. 230.

47 Steer, *Sealed and delivered*, Chapter 1, pp. 7–10. Monnier had died of fever while on a single-handed reconnoitre of the situation in Abyssinia.

48 CCA NBKR 4/660, Noel-Baker to Megan Lloyd George, 13 May 1937.

49 CCA NBKR 4/660, Noel-Baker to "Minister" 13 May 1937. The recipient was probably the Republican foreign minister Alvarez del Vayo.

50 CCA NBKR 4/660, Megan Lloyd George to Noel-Baker, 14 May 1937.

51 CCA, NBKR 4/2, Noel-Baker to Steer, 6 [May] 1937.

52 CCA NBKR, 4/660, Noel-Baker to Steer, 29 April 1937.

53 Aldgate, *Cinema and history*, pp. 158–60.

54 Page Coft, *Spain: The truth at last*, p. 13.

55 Kemp, *Thorns of memory*, p. 55.

56 CCA NBKR 4/660, Noel-Baker to Walter Layton, 31 May 1937.

57 Knightley, *The first casualty*, p. 191; Paul Preston, *The Spanish Civil War: A Concise History* (Fontana, London, 1996), p. 192.

58 *The Times*, 28 April 1937 (my emphasis).

59 Bodleian Library, Oxford, Ms Dawson 79, 11 May 1937, Dawson to H. G. Daniels and 23 May 1937, Dawson to Daniels.

60 *The Times*, 16 July 1986

61 CCA NBKR 4x/118, Steer to Noel-Baker, 29 April 1937.

62 TNA, FO 371, 21332, Nevile Henderson to Foreign Office, 5 May 1937. Henderson, the British Ambassador to Berlin, said that if *The Times* had been misled by its correspondent it should issue a "handsome retraction". Immediately after the bombing of Guernica the Catholic Bishop of Southwark wrote to John Walter, chairman of Directors at *The Times*, appealing to him to "use your influence with the Times on behalf of the Nationalists in Spain" (see Michael Clifton, *Amigo: Friend of the Poor* (Fowler Wright, Leominister, 1987) p. 148).

63 Steer met Dawson on his return from Bilbao on 24 June 1937, but there is

no record of their conversation (Bodleian Library, Ms Dawson 40, Dawson's diary). At this time Steer was engaged in a row with the *Times* over his expenses. *The Times* claimed that he was accredited to the Spanish frontier rather than to Bilbao, even if he did send "some very useful messages" (!) 1 July 1937, Burn to Manager (Times archive).

64 William Foss and Cecil Gerahty, *The Spanish Arena* (Right Book Club, London, 1938) p. 434.

65 CCA NBKR 4x/122, copy of Kingsley Martin to Attlee, 17 December 1937.

66 CCA NBKR, 9/64, Steer to Noel-Baker, 24 January 193[8]. Noel-Baker replied that *The Times* had given the book "an extremely good review considering everything . . . " (7 February 1938).

67 Steer, *Date in the desert*, p. 141.

68 CCA, Thurso papers, THRS II 33/3, typed copy of 8 May 1937, Steer to Noel-Baker. In the original letter, sent from the "Presidencia, Bilbao", Steer had first written that he would "lie", before prudently altering this to "deny" (CCA NBKR 4x/118). The reference to "I.S." men is intriguing, and presumably relates to members of MI6 or, as it is formally known, the "Secret Intelligence Service". For Steer's connections to military intelligence see above p. 38.

69 CCA NBKR 4/660, Noel-Baker to Steer, 25 May 1937.

70 *Foreign Relations of the United States, 1937*, volume 1 (1954), p. 306, 29 May 1937. Steer (named as "Pierce") apparently showed Consul Gilbert "a map annotated by directions in German for the aerial bombardment of Guernica and he asserted that the actual bombardment fulfilled these directions . . . He stated further that he had sent this data to his paper which had not published it." For the meeting with Roberts see TNA, FO 371 21293, report dated 31 May 1937.

71 CCA NBKR 4x/118, Steer to Noel-Baker, 31 May 1937.

72 CCA NBKR 4/660, Steer to Noel-Baker, 4 June 1937.

73 Steer, *Tree of Gernika*, p. 359.

74 CCA NBKR 4/2, Steer to Noel-Baker, undated [3 August 1937 (?)] and E. C. A. Steer to Noel-Baker [15 August, 1937].

75 Steer, *Tree of Gernika*, p. 385; see also the typescript in CCA NBKR 4x/121.

76 CCA, NBKR, 9/64, Steer to Noel-Baker, 24 January 193[8].

77 CCA, NBKR, 4/8, Steer to Noel-Baker, 12 October 1938.

78 CCA NBKR 4/2, Steer to Noel-Baker, undated [3 August 1937 (?)] and 10 August 1937, Noel-Baker to Henri Rollin.

79 CCA NBKR 9/64, Steer to Noel-Baker, 12 November 1937, and reply of 18 November 1937.

80 Probably the happiest part of this period for Steer was the week that he spent exploring Basutoland in January 1938 (see his letter to the Oxford academic Marjory Perham, 25 January 1938, Rhodes House, Oxford, Mss Perham, 382/4). He described Basutoland as "a lovely country – a little Abyssinia, and free, thank God" (CCA, NBKR 9/64, Steer to Noel-Baker, 24 January 193[8]).

81 CCA, NBKR 4/8, Steer to Noel-Baker, 18 October 1938.

82 CCA NBKR, 4/8, Steer to Noel-Baker, 12 October and 18 October 1938.

83 CCA NBKR 4/8, Steer to Noel-Baker, 26 November and 27 November 1938. Steer also advanced this argument in series of articles in the *Daily Telegraph*. In his letter of 27 November Steer referred to "the Jewish issue, on wh[ich] we seem to have struck gold . . . " Candidly, he admitted that he had proposed a number of 5000 Jewish emigrants in one of these articles when, in fact, 2000 would be a more appropriate figure: he had mentioned the larger number "really in order to make the scheme look more important and therefore more newsworthy".

84 Steer, *Sealed and delivered*, pp. 130–1 and 164.

85 Bolín, p. 280, and citing review of *Sealed and delivered*, *The Tablet* 26 September 1942).

86 Monks, *Eyewitness*, pp. 70–1. Of course, Steer's decision to report the civil war almost wholly from the Basque country meant that he was not placed in the position of having to explain away Republican political violence and atrocities. Indeed, the one exception, the massacre of prisoners in Bilbao in early January 1937, was heavily punished by the Basque authorities and was used by Steer to demonstrate their essential order and humanity.

87 Dorothy Legaretta *The Guernica Generation: Basque Refugee Children of the Spanish Civil War* (University of Nevada Press, Reno, 1984), p. 101; CCA, THRS II, 33/3, Steer to Noel-Baker, 8 May 1937.

88 Southworth, *Guernica! Guernica!*, p. 442, fn. 132, citing *The Observer*, 22 August 1937.

89 Southworth, *Guernica! Guernica!*, p. 110.

90 CCA, NBKR, 4/8, Steer to Noel-Baker, 18 October 1938,.

91 GL Steer, *Judgment on German Africa* (Hodder & Stoughton, London, 1939), p. 3.

92 Sussex University, Kingsley Martin papers, Box 25/5, typescript on "George Steer". This was the basis for Martin's obituary in the *New Statesman*.

93 See Tom Buchanan, "Anti-fascism and democracy in the 1930s", *European History Quarterly*, 32, 1, January 2002, 39–57.

94 Steer, *A date in the desert*, pp. 147–8 and 163–4.

95 Steer, *Caesar in Abyssinia*, p. 173.

96 Steer, *Judgment on German Africa*, p. 180.

97 CCA, NBKR 4/8, 27 November 1938, Steer to Noel-Baker.

98 Steer, *A date in the desert*, pp. 162 and 52.

99 CCA, NBKR, 9/64, Steer to Noel-Baker, 24 January 193[8].

100 Rankin, *Telegram from Guernica*, p. 5.

101 Peter Davison (ed.), *Orwell in Spain* (Penguin, Harmondsworth, 2001), p. 265 (the review was originally published in *Time and Tide*, 5 February 1938).

102 CCA NBKR 4x/122, Steer to Noel-Baker, 30 December 1937 (emphasis in original).

Chapter 3 *The masked advance*

I would like to express my gratitude to the following for their very generous assistance: Andy Buchanan and Mary Nell Bockman for consulting the Fredericka Martin papers at the Tamiment Library, New York, on my behalf; Professor Judy Simon for sending me copies of Wogan Philipps' letters from Spain; and Dr Richard Baxell and Professor Robert Stradling for allowing me to see copies of documents in their possession from the Moscow archives.

1 SMAC *Bulletin*, February 1938, p. 5.
2 This was Ruth Ormsby, a nurse who died as a result of a fire at the British unit's flat in Barcelona.
3 Rosamond Lehmann papers, owned by King's College, Cambridge, Wogan Philipps to Rosamond Lehmann, 28 February 1937.
4 Ralph Darlington, ed, *Molly Murphy: Suffragette and Socialist* (Institute of Social Research, Salford, 1998), p. 142; Richard Rees, *A Theory of my Time: An Essay in Didactic Reminiscence* (Secker & Warburg, London, 1963), p. 96.
5 *Daily Worker*, 14 April, 1937.
6 No formal archives of the committee appear to have survived. Fortunately, however, committee minutes from 25 May 1938 onwards have been preserved in the papers of the TUC.
7 MML, IBMA, Box B-8, Alexander to Fyrth, 21 October [1985].
8 Fyrth, *The signal*, chapter 12, p. 187.
9 Angela Jackson, *British Women and the Spanish Civil War* (Routledge, London, 2002), pp. 113–14.
10 Jackson, *British women*, p. 85. (See also pp. 209–10).
11 For a historical overview of the SMAC see Fyrth, *The signal*, pp. 43–157 and Buchanan, *Britain and the Spanish Civil War*, pp. 101–6. There is also a helpful summary in John Saville, "The Aid for Spain Movement in Britain, 1936–9", in *Dictionary of Labour Biography*, volume IX (Macmillan, Basingstoke, 1993), pp. 25–32.
12 Charles W. Brook, *Making Medical History* [1946], pp. 10–12.
13 Bodleian Library, Oxford, Ms Addison.dep.c.207, Report by a sub-committee appointed to consider matters of office organisation, 23 September 1937, p. 4, and a response from the Organising Secretary, 27 September 1937. Fyrth notes that the sub-committee (sic) "tended to be more left-wing than the Committee" (*The signal*, p. 47).
14 Fyrth, *The signal*, p. 47.
15 Leah Manning, *A Life for Education: An Autobiography* (Victor Gollancz, Letchworth, 1970), pp. 107–8.
16 SMAC *Bulletin*, November 1936.
17 For the tortuous history of the TUC's relations with the SMAC see Buchanan, *The Spanish Civil War and the British labour movement*, pp. 156–9.
18 K. Sinclair-Loutit and Aileen Palmer, "Survey of a year's work with the British Medical Unit in Spain", 1937, RGASPI, Moscow, 545/6/88, p. 1. This was an important fiction in Sinclair-Loutit's case as, in a related inci-

dent, Dr Morgan told Captain James White that he would not have approved his appointment to lead the abortive second unit if he had known that he was a Communist Party member (MRC, Mss 292C/946/2, Dr Morgan to White, 5 January 1937). This concealment of political loyalties should be borne in mind when evaluating Angela Jackson's comment that it is "overly simplistic to regard the members of [SMAC and similar committees] . . . as little more than devious political opportunists" (*British women*, p. 55).

19 MRC, Mss 292/946/41, Brook to Citrine, 5 September 1936.

20 Archibald L. Cochrane and Max Blythe, *One Man's Medicine: An Autobiography of Archie Cochrane* (Memoir Club, Cambridge, 1989), pp. 20–1.

21 Cited in Hugh Purcell, *The Last English Revolutionary: Tom Wintringham, 1898–1949* (Sutton, Stroud, 2004), p. 106.

22 MRC, Mss 292C/946/2, Miss F. I. Harris to Dr Morgan, 14 September 1936.

23 Fax message from K. Sinclair-Loutit , 24 June 1994, in the papers of John Langdon-Davies.

24 NLS, Acc 9083, Box 1/ 3, Murray to "everyone", 23 Oct. 1936.

25 Margot Bennett (née Miller), "Notes from the Spanish Civil War", in Michael Collins (ed.), *Hampstead in the Thirties: a Committed Decade* (Hampstead Arts Council, London, 1975), pp. 34–5. No mention is made in this later account of claims made at the time that Miller was shot going to the assistance of a wounded German militiaman. SMAC *Bulletin*, October 1936; *Daily Herald*, 30 November 1936.

26 MRC, Mss 292/946/41, resolution adopted by SMAC, 4 November 1936. "Marrack in Spain", *Hospital: The Journal of the Inter-Hospital Socialist Society*, 3, 1, April 1937, pp. 5–6. Communist members of the Unit had originally been instructed that the unit should "go to Madrid, and not elsewhere" (Sinclair-Loutit, "Survey", p. 1).

27 The "rebels" were particularly aggrieved about an incident in which Ralph Bates had come to Grañen to tell the volunteers that the medical unit was about to be thrown out of Spain by the health authorities in Barcelona (the "Sanidad"). Accordingly, he insisted that they must all immediately join the Del Barrio Column of the PSUC. Two nurses left in protest, yet nothing more was heard of this development. A later document confirms that the British Communists in Barcelona were on the point of transferring the unit to the Del Barrio Column of the Division Carlos Marx, but that the move was botched by O'Donnell. "This transference would have freed us from a sabotaging Sanidad, rendered us independent of the local anarchist 'incontrollable' PANCHOVILEA ["Pancho Villa", the mayor of Grañen], and provided us with that close military cooperation without which a front-line hospital cannot function efficiently" (Sinclair-Loutit, "Survey", p. 8). It is not clear whether the London committee was aware of these manoeuvres.

28 Cochrane, *One man's medicine*, p. 26.

29 The document is in MRC, Mss 292/946/41, "memorandum number 1", 30 November 1936. Four of the signatories were female. It was claimed that the memorandum was written by Arnold Kallen, an American medical student, and that many of the typewritten signatures were appended without permission (Sinclair-Loutit, "Survey", p. 8). For a parallel account of these events see the letter from the unit secretary Aileen Palmer to R. Robson in MML IBMA, Box C, 7/5, 30 November 1936.

30 MML IBMA, B-3, COC/1, Cochrane to Fredericka Martin, 15 July 1971.

31 MML IBMA, B-3, SIN/4, Sinclair-Loutit to Fyrth, 11 August 1985.

32 Cochrane, *One man's medicine*, p. 26. (This was possibly a gloss on Fyrth, *The signal*, p. 57: "the group was also divided by class, politics and sex, as well as by clashing personalities . . . ")

33 MML IBMA, B-3, SIN/4, 11 August 1985, Sinclair-Loutit to Fyrth, and COC/1, letter to SMAC from "Supervisor of transport", 27 December [?] 1936.

34 Sinclair-Loutit, "Survey", p. 8.

35 Sir Walter Citrine was shown some of the Grañen documents, and concluded that there was "open mutiny" in the unit (MRC, Mss 292/946/41, Citrine to D. M. Stevenson, 31 December 1936).

36 MRC, Mss 292/946/41, resolution by SMAC, 4 November 1936.

37 MRC, Mss 292C/946/2, White to Morgan, 21 December 1936, and subsequent correspondence.

38 Sinclair-Loutit, "Survey", p. 7.

39 MRC, Mss 292/946/2, Morgan to Tewson, 28 November 1936.

40 On 21 December 1936 Morgan wrote to Manning confirming her appointment: he added that "you will be interested to know that I was the only person dissenting" (MRC, Mss 292C/946/2).

41 MRC, Mss 292C/ 946/2, Morgan to Cochrane, 27 September 1937; MRC, Mss 292C/946/2, Morgan to Addison, 22 January 1937.

42 IWM, 13771/1, interview with Alexander Tudor Hart, reel 1; MML IBMA, B-3, SIN/3, Sinclair-Loutit to Fyrth, 17 July 1984.

43 MML, IBMA, B-3, SIN/5, Sinclair-Loutit to Fyrth, 2 November 1985.

44 Cochrane, *One man's medicine*, pp. 30–1.

45 MML IBMA, B-3, SIN/3, Sinclair-Loutit to Fyrth, 17 July 1984.

46 IWM, 13793/3, interview with Alexander Tudor Hart, Reel 1.

47 MML, IBMA, B-8, Alexander to Fyrth, 11 December 1984.

48 This was a legitimate grievance. As the Political Commissar Wally Tapsell reported in April 1937: "One of the main complaints of our chaps is the fact that when in Hospital they are often entirely on their own, no one speaks English and they consequently not only have a thoroughly bad time, but are unable to assist the doctors in their diagnosis, consequently there are often outstanding cases of quite innocent medical mismanagement. Wounds go undressed, men discharged without examination, and etc." ("Position in the BMU", MML IBMA, C:12/3).

49 MRC, Mss 292/946/43, SMAC minutes, 1 March 1939. Addy was involved in a relationship with Dr Holst at the hospital, and later married him (Jackson, *British women*, p. 106).

50 MML, IBMA, Box 29, File A/3, "Report of activities of Party Group" by Sinclair-Loutit for 23 March 1937; the activities of this fraction ran counter to the specific order of Political Commissar Jeanette Bloch that all party meetings must cease.

51 Ibid., 10 April 1937.

52 MML, IBMA, Box 29, File A/3, Tudor Hart to D. Springhall, 21 April 1937.

53 MRC Mss 292C/946/2, Churchill to Morgan, 1 July 1937; University College London archives (UCL), Richard Rees papers, Box 7, Rees to Churchill, 6 September 1937; Bodleian Library, Oxford, Ms Addison.dep.c.207, Churchill's letter of 5 July 1937.

54 Fyrth, *The signal*, p. 87.

55 Nan Green, *A Chronicle of Small Beer: The Memoirs of Nan Green* (Trent Editions, Nottingham, 2004), p. 84; for a fuller account see Fyrth, *The signal*, pp. 119–22.

56 MRC, Mss 292/946/42, Morgan to Citrine, 23 August 1937.

57 MRC, Mss 292C/946/2, Morgan to C. Holock, 19 October 1937.

58 Jim Fyrth and Sally Alexander (eds.), *Women's Voices from the Spanish Civil War* (Lawrence & Wishart, London, 1991), p. 93.

59 A. Tudor Hart, "Report of work of British Medical Aid Unit in Spain", [?1937], RGASPI, Moscow, 545/6/88. Some Communists working for the SMAC in Spain also believed that they were being deliberately denied access to Uclés (see Winifred Bates, "Summary and critical survey of my work in Spain since the outbreak of the war", September 1938, RGASPI, Moscow, 545/6/88, pp. 1–3).

60 Bodleian Library, Oxford, Ms Addison. dep. c. 207, statement by Organising Secretary, 27 September 1937.

61 SMAC *Bulletin*, July 1938.

62 The papers relating to this review are held in Bodleian Library, Oxford, Ms Addison. dep. c. 207.

63 Bodleian Library, Oxford, Ms Addison. dep. c. 207, Morgan to Addison, 27 September 1937.

64 Rosamond Lehmann papers, Wogan Philipps to Rosamond Lehmann, 20 May 1937.

65 Penelope Fyvel, *English Penny* (1992), pp. 32–44.

66 Tamiment Library, New York, Fredericka Martin papers, Box 2/36, Folder 22, Monica Milward, "Some notes on Spain", April 1970, p. 2.

67 *Daily Express*, 12 March 1937, article by Hilda Marchant.

68 MRC, Mss 292/946/41, L. Preger to C. Brook, 15 November 1936.

69 NLS, Acc 9083, Box 1/3, Murray to "Lily", 3 April 1937.

70 Rees, *A theory*, p. 95.

71 Lehmann papers, Rosamond Lehmann to John Lehmann, 30 April 1937.

72 Valentine Cunningham (ed.), *Spanish Front: Writers on the Civil War* (Oxford University Press, Oxford, 1986), p. 286. The only female driver appears to have been Cristina, Viscountess Hastings.

73 Monica Milward's experiences are described in a typescript diary, Fredericka Martin papers, Tamiment Library, New York, Box 2/36, Folder 22.

74 MRC, Mss 292/946/43, SMAC minutes, 17 August 1938 and 30 November 1938.

75 MRC, Mss 292/946/41, Report of meeting between TUC and SMAC officers, 19 August 1936.

76 Sinclair-Loutit, "Survey", p. 6. This fits with other sources, which show that Cochrane was entrusted with both political and administrative authority in the unit, and presents a different impression to that given by Cochrane in *One man's medicine*. However, at some point in Spain Cochrane appears to have distanced himself from the Communists. Julian Tudor Hart, whose father had worked with Cochrane in Spain and who, himself, worked with Cochrane in South Wales, described him as "always a dissident, protected from much of reality by exceptional inherited wealth". He recalled that Cochrane's commanding officer in Spain, Len Crome, had simply commented that "*Archie is hostile*" [to Communists]. (See F. Xavier Bosch (ed.), *Archie Cochrane: Back to the Front* (Cochrane Collaboration, Barcelona, 2003), p. 39). Many years later, Dr Reggie Saxton described Cochrane as one who sat "in judgement above other people" (IWMSA, interview with Dr Saxton, 00 8735/09, transcript, p. 89).

77 MRC, Mss 292C/946/2, Morgan to Cochrane, 27 September 1937; unfortunately, Cochrane's resignation letter is not in the file, so his exact grievances are unclear.

78 MRC, Mss 292/946/41, report on Dr Ruth Prothero by Sinclair-Loutit, 8 November 1936; MML IBMA, B-3, PRO, 1 July 1985, Prothero to Fyrth; MML, IBMA, B-3, SIN/4, Sinclair-Loutit to Fyrth, 11 August 1985. According to Fyrth, Prothero left the unit because she "did not like the political atmosphere" (Fyrth, *The signal*, p. 58).

79 SMAC *Bulletin*, June 1938.

80 Fyrth, *The signal*, p. 104.

81 NLS, Acc 9083, Box 1/3, Murray to "Dear all", from Paris, 27 September 1936.

82 David Corkill and Stuart J. Rawnsley, *The Road to Spain: Anti-fascists at War, 1936–1939* (Borderline Press, Dunfermline, 1981), p. 68.

83 MML, IBMA, Box D-1, File B, 5 November 1985, Lilian Buckoke to Fyrth.

84 Bodleian library, Oxford, Ms Addison. dep. c. 207, report of sub-committee, p. 8. This came to light as a result of a broader internal inquiry. In his defence the Organising Secretary George Jeger replied that Urmston was "without doubt an Anti-Fascist in whom confidence could be placed".

85 Bates, "Summary and critical survey", pp. 4–9.

86 NLS, Acc 9083, Box 1/3, Murray to "everybody", 3 March 1937; Murray to "Lily", 3 April 1937.

87 Sinclair-Loutit, "Survey", p. 6.

88 Corkill and Rawnsley, *The road to Spain*, p. 133.

89 MML, IBMA, B-3, HOL, Bill Alexander's taped interview with Portia Holman, 24 January 1983; MML IBMA, Box D-1, File G/9, Palmer's diary entry for 11 July 1937.

90 MML, IBMA, Box C, 9/1d, 1 January 1937, Richard Bennett to CPGB; MML, IBMA, Box B-3, SIN/5, Sinclair-Loutit to Fyrth, 2 November 1985.

91 CCA, NBKR 4x/122, Wilson to Philip Noel-Baker, 9 April 1938; Sinclair-Loutit later described Wilson as a "Freudian gold mine" (MML IBMA B-3, SIN/5, Sinclair-Loutit to Fyrth, 2 November 1985, while Thora Silverthorne recalled her as much older than the other staff and difficult to work with (MML, IBMA, B-3, F/5).

92 James K. Hopkins, *Into the Heart of the Fire: the British in the Spanish Civil War* (Stanford University Press, Stanford, 1998), pp. 283–6; Green, *Small beer*, pp. 78–81 and 87; Bates, "Summary and critical survey", p. 6. MML, IBMA, Box 37, File E. On 6 July 1943 Sam Wild wrote to Peter Kerrigan about a conversation that he had had with John Mahon concerning Nan Green's assignment to work for the International Brigade Association. All three men had played important roles in Spain. Mahon "expressed doubt as to the correctness of [Green's] political line. He inferred that she might be wobbly due to her acquaintanceship with Frank Ayres", who was alleged to have "left tendencies". Ayres had been political commissar at Valdeganga and a friend of Green's. She was subsequently given political clearance by Mahon. (In her memoirs she also admitted to briefly flirting at this time with the heretical "Browder line" within American Communism, *Small beer*, p. 143.)

93 MML, IBMA B-8, Alexander to Fyrth, 21 December 1985 (see also Fyrth, *The signal*, p. 190).

94 Alexander Foote, *Handbook for Spies* (1949; 1964 edition, Digit, London), pp. 8–9. In *Reynolds News*, 11 September 1938, it was alleged that an SMAC volunteer had been asked by an unnamed agent in Perpignan to take money to a Francoist spy in Barcelona.

95 Ritchie Calder claimed that an MI5 dossier was kept on him for his SMAC activities (*New Statesman*, 21 April 1956, pp. 418–19).

96 *The Times*, 24 December 1973.

97 Manning, *A life*, p. 121; MML, IBMA, B-3, SIN/1, Sinclair-Loutit to Fyrth, 3 March 1985. Archie Cochrane also commented on Churchill's "fairly obvious homosexuality or bisexuality" which, he feared, might endanger the unit (*One man's medicine*, p. 23).

98 Viscount Churchill, *All my Sins Remembered* (Heinemann, London, 1964), pp. 151 and 161.

99 MRC, Mss 292C/946/2, Morgan to Secretary, SMAC, 15 September 1937.

100 MML, IBMA, Box C, 12/3, Tapsell's report. Winifred Bates was even "given to understand" in 1937 that Churchill was a member of the CPGB ("Summary and critical survey", p. 1). He was listed as part of the unit's Communist "fraction" in August 1936.
101 Rees, *A theory*, p. 97.
102 MML, IBMA, B-3, SIN/1, Sinclair-Loutit to Bill Alexander, 3 March 1983.
103 UCL, Rees papers, Churchill to Rees, 27 May 1937.
104 Sinclair-Loutit, "Survey", p. 17.
105 MRC, Mss 292/946/43, Leah Manning's "Report on Personnel in Spain", September 1938.
106 MRC, Mss 292/946/43, SMAC minutes, 15 June 1938.
107 Gerald Howson, *Arms for Spain: The Untold Story of the Spanish Civil War* (John Murray, London, 1998), pp. 222–3.
108 Max Cohen, an SMAC mechanic, claimed that Churchill had taken £1 million of the Spanish Republic's gold (IWMSA, 00 8639/06, interview with Max Colin/Cohen, transcript, p. 64.
109 MRC, Mss 292/946/43, Manning, "Report on Personnel".
110 Churchill, *All my sins*, p. 170.
111 Fyrth and Alexander, *Women's voices*, p. 247. She was referring to the presence of Viscount Hastings on a delegation to Spain.
112 Churchill, *All my sins*, pp. 5, 158, and 159.
113 Manning, *A life*, p. 121; NLS, Acc 9083, Box 1/3, Murray to "Lily", 3 April 1937; MML, IBMA, B-8, Alexander to Fyrth, 21 December 1985.
114 Fyrth, *The signal*, pp. 50 and 189; Jackson, *British women*, p. 273, fn. 126. Davson is not mentioned in the index of Jackson's British women, although the allegations made against her are briefly mentioned in the footnotes (*British women*, p. 273, fn. 129).
115 See the documents sent to the CPGB by Rust, 26 and 30 May 1938, MML, IBMA, Box 39/A/44.
116 MRC, Mss 292/946/43, SMAC minutes 31 August 1937 and 14 September 1937; Leah Manning's "Report on Personnel"; Rust denied that he was the source (SMAC minute, 14 September 1937).
117 Bates, "Summary and critical survey", pp. 1–17.
118 MRC, Mss 292/946/43, Leah Manning, "Report on Personnel".
119 MRC, Mss 292/946/43, SMAC minutes, 2 November 1938 and 22 February 1939.
120 Bates claimed that Davson had joined the PSUC at the start of the war and had, subsequently, applied unsuccessfully to join the CPGB ("Summary and critical survey", p. 11).
121 See her article "Trotskyists in Spain help Franco", *Daily Worker*, 24 February 1937. In the 1970s she wrote that: "Years afterwards I am asking: Are we, who lived through those days, doing enough to warn the young people of today of the awful danger that the Trotskyite influence is to world Socialism?" (typescript in W Sandford [Bates] papers, IWM, 000816/06, p. 80).

122 Fyrth, *The signal*, p. 87.

123 MRC, Mss 292/946/43, Leah Manning, "Report on Personnel".

124 Fyrth indicates that Davson worked for the Russian-language newspaper *British Ally* in Moscow. I have found no evidence to support the claim that she subsequently joined the Diplomatic Corps. The only solid information on her career after leaving Spain comes from two letters. The first indicates that she was living in London in October 1940, where she was still in touch with Spanish refugees, working for Gillette, and contemplating teaching English for the British Council (MRC, Mss 292c/946/2, Davson to Manning, 2 October 1940). In 1946 she was living in London and offering to help with Nan Green's anti-Franco campaigns. She reported that she was doing "quite a lot of stray work at the Basque centre (39 Victoria Street) and am busy helping the postcard campaign" (MML, IBMA, Box 38, B/129, Davson to Nan Green, November 1946).

125 Jackson, *British women*, p. 210.

126 Tamiment Library, New York, Box 2/36, Folder 29, Cochrane to Fredericka Martin, 15 July 1971.

127 National Museum of Labour History (NMLH), Manchester, CPGB papers, CC minutes, July 1938 [?], Rust. p. 21.

128 See, for instance, the overt criticisms made by Harry Pollitt during his visit to the Valdeganga and Huete hospitals in January 1938: "I wish that every member of the Spanish Medical Aid Committee could see these two places . . . They would insist that everything possible should be done to retain them for British comrades, and that everything needed by these places should be given them from London." He added that with proper publicity the SMAC could "easily raise thousands of pounds for the extension of the whole work of medical aid in Spain" (*Daily Worker*, 14 January 1938).

129 MML, IBMA, Box B-8, F/13, Max Colin [Cohen] to Jim Fyrth, 21 December 1985.

Chapter 4   *The lost art of Felicia Browne*

I would like to thank Mrs Lin Lobb for allowing me to consult Felicia Browne's letters and to reproduce some of her work. I am also grateful to Stephen Chaplin and Richard Lowndes for their support and encouragement, to Jim Carmody for his advice, and to Martin Conway, Frances Lannon, Mary Vincent, Pat Wain and the editors of *History Workshop Journal* for their comments on the first draft of this article. Dominic Hughes provided valuable further information which I have incorporated into this revised version. I acknowledge that the sketches reproduced from *Drawings by Felicia Browne* were first published by Lawrence & Wishart.

1   See for example, James K. Hopkins, *Into the heart of the fire: The British in the Spanish Civil War* (Stanford University Press, Stanford, 1998), p. 40; Christine Colette, *The International Faith: Labour's attitudes to European Socialism, 1918–39* (Ashgate, Aldershot, Hants, 1998), p. 143; Lynda Morris

and Robert Radford, *The Story of the Artists International Association, 1933–1953* (Museum of Modern Art, Oxford, 1983), p. 31; Fyrth and Alexander, *Women's voices* p. 51; Colin Williams, Bill Alexander and John Gorman, *Memorials of the Spanish Civil War* (Sutton, Stroud, 1996), p. 21.

2   See, for instance, Robert Radford, *Art for a Purpose: The Artists International Association, 1933–1953* (Winchester School of Art, Winchester, 1987), p. 49.

3   There are only two significant biographical sources on Felicia Browne's life. The first is the "appreciation" which forms an introduction to the pamphlet *Drawings by Felicia Browne* (Lawrence & Wishart, London, 1936). This was presumably either written by, or with the close assistance of, her friend Elizabeth Watson. The second is the article entitled "The first volunteer" which appeared in *Spain Today*, September 1949. While drawing on the 1936 pamphlet, the article contains some different and original information. Unless otherwise specified, biographical details come from these two sources.

4   These letters are in the possession of Mrs Lin Lobb, daughter of Felicia Browne's friend Elizabeth Watson. Unless specified otherwise, all documentary references are to this collection.

5   J. O'Donnell in *Everybody's Weekly*, 31 October 1936. For more on the family see *Royal Leamington Spa Courier*, 6 November 1936.

6   Undated letter, 1935/1936.

7   Details from Felicia Browne's index card and student record, courtesy of University College London, Central Services Department. I am grateful to the Slade's archivist, Stephen Chaplin, for additional comments on Felicia Browne's period at the Slade.

8   Description by Michael Reynolds, cited in Catherine Naomi Deepwell, "Women artists in Britain between the two world wars" (PhD, London University, 1991), p. 359.

9   Bruce Laughton, *The Euston Road School* (Scolar, Aldershot, 1986), p. 28.

10   *Spain Today*, September 1949.

11   Felicia Browne's confidential file has recently been released at The National Archives (KV2/1560). She came to the attention of Special Branch when, as a patient at Guy's Hospital, she attempted to "convert some of the nurses in her ward to communism" (Superintendant Canning to Mr Harker, 15 July 1933). The subsequent spasmodic surveillance of her activities revealed little of interest for the British authorities, but does mean that a small number of Felicia Browne's intercepted letters have survived as Photostat copies. A letter of 23 June 1934 to "Kate" describes – uproariously – a holiday in southern France during which Felicia met up with old friends from Berlin. There is a particularly interesting passage which suggests her essential loneliness. Describing her friendship with "Priscilla" (otherwise unidentified), Felicia writes that she liked her "but there would never be any deep personal relationship between us . . . That a blasted wreck such as me should be amiably dealt with by good people is probably a mistake."

12 Cited in Morris and Radford, *The Artists International Association*, p. 31. According to *Everybody's Weekly*, 31 October 1936, she became an expert in ju-jitsu.

13 There are a number of good histories of the AIA, which is dealt with in more detail in chapter 5, below. See, in particular, Radford, *Art for a purpose*, Radford and Morris, *The Artists International Association*, and Tony Rickaby, "Artists' International", *History Workshop Journal*, 6, Autumn 1978, pp. 154–68. On Elizabeth Watson (1906–1955) see the biographical note by her daughter Felicia France in the 1994 edition of her 1941 collection *Don't Wait for it: or, impressions of war, 1939–41* (Imperial War Museum, London, 1994).

14 *Daily Telegraph*, 5 September 1936.

15 MRC, Mss 292/1.91/40. The often-repeated comment in *Drawings by Felicia Browne* that she received a "special prize" is somewhat misleading.

16 *Drawings by Felicia Browne*.

17 *Drawings by Felicia Browne*.

18 David Gascoyne's *A Short Survey of Surrealism* had been published in late 1935, and the International Surrealist Exhibition opened at the New Burlington Galleries on 11 June 1936 (see Charles Harrison, *English Art and Modernism, 1900–1939* second edition, Yale University Press, New Haven, 1994), pp. 302–3, 309.

19 Felicia Browne to Elizabeth Watson, undated [spring 1936].

20 Felicia Browne to Elizabeth Watson, 31 March 1935.

21 *Daily Worker*, 4 September 1936.

22 *Left Review*, October 1936.

23 Felicia Browne to Elizabeth Watson, 14 July 1936.

24 MRC, Mss PKTF/18/3, agenda for printing workers' rally, 11 September 1936.

25 An intercepted letter of 25 April 1936 to Edith Bone gives more detail about this trade union work, as well as describing Felicia Browne's relations with the other staff: "And sometime when I am scrubbing and flapping a wet floor cloth skilfully in the neighbourhood of the customers' legs, a waitress passes and bends down swiftly as though looking for a piece of soap which I may have lost, and says in a low voice ain't she an old sod, or another one comes and says open your mouth and I do and she fills it with chocolate which is amazing and very pleasant."

26 Felicia Browne to Elizabeth Watson, 31 March 1935. In a letter to Nan Youngman of 4 May 1935, Felicia invited Youngman for a weekend visit: "that is, if you can bear it, straw mattresses full of new straw, nightingales shouting on the roof and owls moaning about the place all night, otherwise peaceful and fairly comfortable" (TGA, Nan Youngman papers).

27 In Paris in July 1936 she wrote to Elizabeth Watson, "I wish I knew where Gertrude Stein lives".

28 In the letter the words "personal not possible to discuss" had been half-erased. The AI was the original name of the AIA. It is possible that her

thinking had been influenced by C. Day Lewis' *Revolution in Writing* (first ed., London, 1935), which contains this comment; "I believe a revolution in literature is now taking place. But I also believe that a revolution in society is incomparably more important, and without it the other would be futile and meaningless" (2nd ed., 1938, p. 17).

29 Edith Bone was identified as Felicia Browne's traveling companion by the journalist William Forrest in an interview recorded in 1992 (Imperial War Museum Sound Archive, 12416/4, Reel 1). Forrest adds that he was visiting Edith Bone in Barcelona when a letter arrived notifying her of Felicia Browne's death. Edith Bone was working at this time for the socialist-communist Catalan party (PSUC) in Barcelona (Fyrth, *The signal*, p. 59). There are numerous references to her role in Barcelona in letters sent to Harry Pollitt by the *Daily Worker* correspondent Tom Wintringham (see letters of 4 September 1936, 5 September 1936, 13 September 1936, in MML, IBMA, Box C, 5/1, 5/2, and 5/4). Bone wrote an autobiography that is mainly concerned with her seven-year imprisonment in Hungary, 1949–56, as an alleged spy (*Seven Years Solitary*, Hamish Hamilton, London, 1957). The first chapter reviews her early life and membership of the Communist Party, but does not mention the Spanish Civil War. Bone, who was born Edit Hajos in 1889, had lived in Berlin from 1923 to 1933 and may conceivably have met Felicia Browne there. On leaving Berlin she records taking her "Leica camera" (p. 30) with her. TNA KV2/1560 contains numerous items of correspondence between the two women between 1933 and 1936. It also reports that Felicia Browne was one of two witnesses at Bone's wedding to Gerald Martin in February 1934. In a bizarre mistake, *The Times* on 4 September 1936 reported the death of "Miss Edith Browne" in Spain. I am very grateful to Jim Carmody for identifying Edith Bone.

30 Felicia Browne to Elizabeth Watson, 12 July 1936.

31 The letter from Paris appears to be dated June ("vi") 1936, but the contextual information in the letter (such as references to the 14th of July celebrations) as well as other sources clearly indicate that the letter was written in July. Special Branch reported that the two women had left Dover for Calais on 11 July 1936, driving a blue Austin coupé.

32 This episode is also described by Claud Cockburn (writing as Frank Pitcairn) in *Reporter in Spain* (London, 1936) p. 40. The Consul was alleged to have described "with considerable glee" that a rebel column was advancing on Barcelona from Saragossa.

33 Cockburn has left numerous accounts of his Spanish experiences, but, while briefly mentioning Felicia Browne, none refer to Edith Bone. It is interesting that Bone mentions having worked with the Communist propagandist Otto Katz/Andre Simon in Paris, and may well have already known Cockburn through him (Bone, *Seven Years Solitary*, p. 30).

34 Presumably this refers to the planned sketching trip.

35 Tate Gallery Archives, London, TGA 9311, Julian Bell papers. There is no

mention in the Felicia Browne letters of her wanting to leave after joining the militia. In the letter of 31 July she reported that she thought that the "fat and shapeless" British cruiser was still in harbour, and gave no indication of wishing to be evacuated on it.

36 She added that the *Daily Worker* would have "innumerable photographs from Ed.", and this suggests that many of that newspaper's photographs of the early stages of the civil war, currently unattributed, were probably taken by Edith Bone. Therefore, Caroline Brothers' comment that "there is no evidence that [the *Daily Worker*] sent its own photographer to Spain" (*War and Photography: A Cultural History*, Routledge, London, 1997, p. 9) needs to be qualified.

37 *Daily Express* cutting in MML, IBMA, Box A-12, file Bro. According to *The Billericay Times*, 8 August 1936: "It is understood that this adventurous lady used to be a resident of Billericay and still has property in Outwood Common Lane. It seems a far cry from the peace of that vicinity to the horrors and noise of battle in Barcelona!"

38 With the casual racial stereotyping common in the 1930s, even amongst progressives, she referred to these new arrivals as "yiddish" and "yids".

39 This is probably the origin of Cockburn's belief that Felicia Browne died operating a machine gun (*Reporter in Spain*, p. 40).

40 On the female members of the militia see Mary Nash, *Defying Male Civilisation: Women in the Spanish Civil War* (Arden Press, Denver, 1995). Despite Nash's pioneering research there is still little reliable information on the exact numbers of *milicianas* and their role in the conflict.

41 Both *Drawings by Felicia Browne* and the AIA's *Drawings of Felicia Browne* give 29 August; *Spain Today*, September 1949, gives 25 August, and this is the date given in most secondary sources such as Bill Alexander, *British Volunteers for Liberty; Spain 1936–1939* (Lawrence & Wishart, London, 1982) and Buchanan *Britain and the Spanish Civil War*.

42 This communication is reprinted in *British Documents on Foreign Affairs*, Series F, volume 27, p. 28.

43 *Manchester Guardian*, 12 September 1936.

44 *Manchester Guardian*, 8 September 1936. See also F. L. Kerran's report on the same sector in the *New Statesman*, 12 September 1936: "There are zones of fighting and large tracts of no-man's land."

45 *Manchester Guardian*, 9 September 1936.

46 In the absence of any other accounts I am here following Brinkman's typescript, written in Barcelona on 30 August 1936 (MML, IBMA, Box 21/B/1a), which appeared, with a few passages omitted, in the *Daily Worker*, 10 September 1936. On 4 September 1936 Claud Cockburn in the *Daily Worker* had stated that the objective was to dynamite a railway station. It is worth noting that the account given in *Spain Today*, September 1949, differs slightly from Brinkman's story. First, the fatal patrol was said to be "in search of arms and ammunition"; and secondly, it is stated that Felicia Browne was "shot through the head" rather than the back and breast. The wounded

Italian has been identified as Paolo Comida (*International Solidarity with the Spanish Republic, 1936–1939*, Progress Publishers, Moscow, 1974, p. 64).

47   MML, IBMA, Box C, 5/3, 10 September 1936, Wintringham to Pollitt.

48   Morris and Radford, *The Artists' International Association*, p. 31.

49   *Daily Telegraph*, 5 September 1936.

50   *Everybody's Weekly*, 31 October 1936.

51   *Daily Worker*, 16 October 1936.

52   *New Statesman*, 31 October 1936.

53   Foreword to *Drawings of Felicia Browne*.

54   *Artists' News-Sheet*, 1, November 1936, p .2. According to this source 170 drawings were sold at the exhibition, raising £150 for Spanish Medical Aid.

55   *Manchester Guardian*, 17 October 1936.

56   *New Statesman*, 31 October 1936.

57   For a recent restatement of this view see Angela Jackson's comment that Felicia Browne is assured of her place amongst those perceived as "'warrior heroes'. Her story has all the ingredients essential to heroic legend, *the willing sacrifice of her artistic career to take up arms for a greater cause*, and the ultimate sacrifice of her life to save that of a comrade" (*British women*, p. 180) (my emphasis).

58   There is an astonishing final twist to the story. It is now known that Felicia Browne's younger brother William ("Billy") served in the International Brigades, where he was known as "Michael" or "Poonah" Browne. He had formerly served in the colonial police in Palestine, Rhodesia and Bermuda. He wrote home to his family on 5 March 1938, and was killed a week later. According to the former volunteer Tony Gilbert he was summarily executed by his own Company Commander, Tom Glynn Evans, for attempting to desert (Tony Gilbert interview, IWM SA). I am grateful to Dominic Hughes and Jim Carmody for this information.

Chapter 5   *Mobilising art*

1   The fullest account of this episode is in Gijs van Hensbergen, *Guernica: the Biography of a Twentieth-Century Icon* (Bloomsbury, London, 2004), pp. 82–97.

2   Incomplete attendance figures suggest that there was an average of 150 visitors per day, paying 1/3d each, with a peak of 244 and a low of 63 (Scottish National Gallery of Modern Art (SNGMA), Edinburgh, Roland Penrose papers, RPA, 0742).

3   *London Bulletin*, 8/9, January-February 1939, p. 59.

4   For the controversy see Cunningham, *Spanish front*, pp. 213–20.

5   Miranda Carter, *Anthony Blunt: his Lives* (Macmillan, Saffron Walden, 2001), p. 415.

6   See Radford, *Art for a purpose*, pp. 7–9; on the literature of the Spanish Civil War see *inter alia*: Stanley Weintraub, *The Last Great Cause: the Intellectuals and the Spanish Civil War* (W. H. Allen, London, 1968), Hugh D. Ford, *A Poets' War: British Poets and the Spanish Civil War* (University of Pennsylvania

Press, Philadelphia, 1965) and Katharine Hoskins, *Today the Struggle: Literature and Politics in England during the Spanish Civil War* (University of Texas, Austin, 1969).

7   Some artists took an anti-Republican stance, but they were very much in a minority. For instance, William Russell Flint's 1938 "In their own homes: Spain's agony of civil war 1936–38" depicted gypsy women shot by Republican riflemen (David Mellor, "British art in the 1930s" in Frank Gloversmith, ed., *Class, Culture and Social Change: a New View of the 1930s* (Harvester Press, Brighton, 1980), p. 202), and Wyndham Lewis, painted "The Siege of Barcelona" in 1936. It is not clear exactly when Lewis painted this historical work: perhaps more significant was his decision to rename it as "The Surrender of Barcelona" in 1939, the same year in which this Republican stronghold fell.

8   Julian Trevelyan, *Indigo Days* (MacGibbon and Kee, London, 1957), pp. 57 and 72.

9   Tate Gallery, Claude Rogers papers, TGA 8121.9.20, notebook, Rogers' copy of "Willy" Townsend's letter to him, 6 March 1940.

10 Francis Watson, *Art Lies Bleeding* (Chatto & Windus, London, 1939), pp. 15 and 214.

11 Cited in Morris and Radford, *The AIA*, p. 43. Coldstream later identified these artists as Clive Branson and Hugh Slater, who both fought in Spain.

12 East Sussex Record Office (ESRO), Acc 8112, Ronald Horton papers, 4/3, 15 August 1935, Ronald to Margaret Horton.

13 On the AIA see Radford, *Art for a purpose*, and Tony Rickaby, "Artists International", *History Workshop Journal*, 6, autumn 1978, pp. 154–68.

14 However, this point should not be pushed too far as, even amongst the younger artists, there was still a male-dominated hierarchy. For instance, although many trained at mixed schools such as the Slade, the male artists tended to define themselves in relation to their fellow male students.

15 Editorial in *Artists News Sheet*, 3, February 1937.

16 *London Bulletin*, 1, April 1938, p. 20.

17 SNGMA, Penrose papers, RPA 0019, 19 February 1938, James Holland to Roland Penrose. On 16 February 1938, 13 surrealists had written to the AIA complaining at Jack Chen's article in the AIA's *Artists News Sheet*, January 1938, pp. 4–5.

18 Andrew Forge, ed., *The Townsend Journals: an Artist's Record of his Times, 1928–51* (Tate Gallery, Wisbech, 1976), 16 March 1938, p. 43. The Surrealist "team" was Penrose, Trevelyan and Humphrey Jennings , while Graham Bell, William Coldstream and Peter Peri represented the realists.

19 Henry Moore Foundation archive, Perry Green, Hertfordshire. Henry Moore, a somewhat hesitant Surrealist, provided the trombone-player design for this poster entitled "We ask for your attention".

20 Roger Berthoud, *The Life of Henry Moore* (Giles de la Mare, London, 2003 edition), p. 142.

21 Berthoud, *Henry Moore*, p. 155.

22 William Lipke, *David Bomberg* (Evelyn, Adams and Mackay, London, 1967), pp. 77–80.

23 John Rothenstein, *Edward Burra* (Tate Gallery, London, 1973), p. 23.

24 Tate Gallery, Julian Bell papers, TGA 9311, Vanessa to Julian Bell, 5 September 1936.

25 Tate Gallery, Julian Bell papers, TGA 9311, Vanessa to Julian Bell, 26 July, 1936; 1 November 1936; 10 October 1936.

26 ESRO, Acc 8112, 4/4, n.d., Percy to Ron Horton.

27 See above p. 80.

28 Editorial in *Artists News Sheet*, 4, April 1937.

29 See, for instance, "Maria Theresa Leon, saviour of Spain's art treasures" in *Daily Worker*, 12 March 1937.

30 *Daily Herald*, 1 February 1938; *Daily Worker*, 2 February 1938

31 AIA, "Hitler attacks London Art Exhibition" (in TGA 8217, AIA box).

32 UCL, Townsend papers, journal, 24 September 1937.

33 For instance, Georges Duthuit in *The Listener*, 25 November 1936, p. 977 argued that the Sagrada Familia was a "positive insult to the intelligence of humanity, and might have been specially built to be destroyed at such a time as this".

34 Christian Zervos and Roland Penrose, "Art and the present crisis in Catalonia", in C. Zervos, et al., *Catalan Art from the Ninth to the Fifteenth Centuries* (Heinemann, London, 1937), pp. 28–9. Penrose's original notes are available in Penrose papers, RP 0630. These papers also carry a letter of introduction for Penrose and his wife from Fenner Brockway of the ILP, who stated that they were visiting Barcelona to assist in the making of a pro-Republican "news film" (7 October 1936).

35 Roland Penrose, *Scrap Book 1900–1981* (Painters and Sculptors, London, 1981), p. 84.

36 Alan Powers, *Eric Ravilious, Imagined Realities* (Imperial War Museum, London, 2003), p. 64.

37 Tate Gallery, Rake papers, TGA 787.19, n.d., Coldstream to J. Rake. Coldstream stated that Auden was "either going to drive an ambulance or work in the censor's office in Madrid or Valencia". Auden's time in Spain remains shrouded in mystery, and there is no evidence that he was ever attached to Spanish Medical Aid. Robert Stradling, *History and Legend: Writing the International Brigades* (University of Wales Press, Cardiff, 2003), chapter 4, pieces together the story.

38 Tate Gallery, Coldstream papers, TGA 8922.4.548, Rake to Coldstream, 21 April 1937; 8922.4.547, Rake to Coldstream, 17 January 1937; TGA 787.20, Coldstream to Rake, 18 January 1937.

39 UCL, Townsend papers, journal, 12 January 1937.

40 *Artists News Sheet*, 4, April 1937, p. 4.

41 MML IBMA, Box 50, File Bs, contains Branson's prison sketches. Coldstream joked that: "Yes, it was our Chris Branson (sic) whom Franco captured! I wonder if he is still wearing his school blazer with the brass

buttons . . . " (TGA 787.23, Coldstream to John Rake, 6 April 1938). For Branson in the 1930s see Morris and Radford, *The AIA*, p. 32.

42 *Daily Worker*, 14 April 1937.

43 Rosamond Lehmann papers, Philipps to Lehmann, 27 April 1937. This letter continued: "There are such objects out here – such groupings of men doing something – bending over a wounded man, cooking bathing. When I find somebody else interested in pictures and in some foreign tongue can just reel off some artists' names, I thrill."

44 Jason Gurney, *Crusade in Spain* (Faber and Faber, London, 1974), p. 174.

45 Paul Hogarth, *Drawing on Life; The Autobiography of Paul Hogarth* (David & Charles, Newton Abbot, 1997), pp. 15–16. (See also *The Guardian*, 31 December 2001 and *The Independent*, 7 December 2001).

46 Justine Hopkins, *Michael Ayrton: a Biography* (Deutsch, London, 1994), pp. 28–29 and 213. In the 1960s Ayrton was a staunch supporter of anti-Franco organisations such as the "Appeal for Amnesty in Spain".

47 Kanty Cooper, *The Uprooted: Agony and Triumph Among the Debris of War* (Quartet, London, 1979), pp. 1–15.

48 AIA, *Artists News Sheet*, 3, February 1937, p. 2. (This source confirms that a medical supply lorry was sent and not, as the January edition of the *News Sheet* stated, a field kitchen).

49 *The Times*, 18 June 1937; *Eastern Daily Press*, 8 June 1937. Sydney Causer offered a painting of "the Alcazar while it still stood" seemingly oblivious of the fact that this ruined fortress in Toledo had come to symbolise Nationalist resistance.

50 Copy of list in Tate Gallery, Ewan Phillips papers (uncatalogued).

51 Tate Gallery, Ewan Phillips papers (uncatalogued).

52 Helen Binyon, *Eric Ravilious: Memoir of an Artist* (Lutterworth, Guildford, 1983), pp. 109–10. This painting is still on display at Buscot, which was also a home for Basque refugee children at this time.

53 Jenny Pery, *The Affectionate Eye: the Life of Claude Rogers* (Sansom & Co, Bristol, 1995), p. 55.

54 AIA, *Artists News Sheet*, September 1938, p. 7.

55 Trevelyan, *Indigo days*, p. 79. This was, apparently, a response to Chamberlain's recent comment at a Royal Academy banquet that "I am sometimes accused of being in politics a realist – some might almost say a surrealist" (cutting in SNGMA, RPA, 973, Penrose's "Wartime scrapbook").

56 Forge, *Townsend journals*, pp. 40–1 (entry for 24 June 1937).

57 Rickaby, "Artists International", p. 159.

58 Roland Penrose later claimed that the Picasso drawing had been sold "for a good price": SNGMA, Penrose papers, RPA 640, 30 March 1976, Penrose to Caroline Odgers.

59 Laughton, *The Euston Road School*, p. 196. Bell was also at this time an art critic for the *New Statesman*.

60 Tate Gallery, Graham Bell papers, TGA 947.3, Bell to "Mamma", c13

March 1939. Goya's 82 prints (which date from 1810–20) recorded the violence of the war against Napoleon with unprecedented candour. They were a doubly appropriate source as the "realist" Left generally preferred Goya's work to the abstraction of Picasso (see *Spain Today*, July 1946, pp. 5–6).

61 UCL, Townsend papers, Letters 1926–46, 30 January 1939, Geoffrey Tibble to Townsend.

62 *The Times*, 15 February 1939.

63 John Moynihan, *Restless Lives: the Bohemian World of Rodrigo and Elinor Moynihan* (Sansom & Co, Bristol, 2002), pp. 65–6. The captain in charge apparently said to his sergeant: "Just look at this . . . executions, firing squads, pure Nazi propaganda . . . "

64 AIA *News sheet*, March 1939.

65 Myfanwy Evans, *The Painter's Object* (G. Howe, London, 1937), p. 5.

66 Tate Gallery, Graham Bell papers, TGA 947.3, Bell to "Mamma", c13 March 1939. The description of Bell is Claude Rogers' (Pery, *The affectionate eye*, p. 84).

67 Tate Gallery, Rake papers, 787.23, Coldstream to John Rake, 6 April 1938. In the original letter the more optimistic wording "life will always be worth living" had been deleted.

68 Valentine Cunningham, *The Penguin Book of Spanish Civil War Verse* (1982) and *Spanish front*. The most helpful listing of works of art is in Nigel Glendinning, "Art and the Spanish Civil War", in Stephen M. Hart, *'No Pasaran'; Art, Literature and the Spanish Civil War* (Tamesis Books, London, 1988).

69 Reprinted in Jackson, *British women*, p. 155.

70 Tate Gallery, Ewan Phillips papers, TGA 9610/1, notebooks (meeting of November 1938?)

71 See for instance the fresco "Spanish Government Militia" by Viscount Hastings, reproduced in *The Studio*, CXIII, February 1937, p. 107.

72 Binyon, *Eric Ravilious*, p. 14 and p. 19, fn. 8 records the July 1938 performance of "Old Spain". The lyrics survive in Montagu Slater, *Peter Grimes and Other Poems* (1946), pp. 171–5.

73 Colin Williams, Bill Alexander and John Gorman, *Memorials of the Spanish Civil War* (Sutton, Stroud, 1996), pp. 128–9; this banner was lost in action in 1938 and replaced.

74 SNGMA, Penrose papers, RPA 0630. The poem contains much imagery familiar from surrealist visual art: hence "the walls were painted with flesh/trees hung with liquid offerings from eyes/broken burnt twisted into the smile of the dead".

75 *Evening Standard*, 29 January 1938; *Daily Herald*, 31 January 1938. Jacob Epstein, another delegate, commented that "if the invitation had come from Franco we should probably have got our visas" (*Reynolds News*, 30 January 1938).

76 Susan Compton, *Henry Moore* (Royal Academy of Arts, London, 1988), p.

217. This design was a forerunner of Moore's later sculpture "Helmet".

77 SNGMA, Penrose papers, RPA 0707, 30 October 1939, Moore to Penrose.

78 *Henry Moore: War and Utility* (Henry Moore Foundation, 2001), p. 11.

79 Andrew Causey, *Edward Burra: A Complete Catalogue* (Phaidon, Oxford, 1985), pp. 58–60; Rothenstein, *Burra*, pp. 29 and 31.

80 *Daily Herald*, 1 February 1938; *Evening Standard*, 29 January 1938; *Daily Worker*, 2 February 1938.

81 Hayter's letter to Julian Trevelyan of 23 October 1936 carries this interesting comment: "PPS – I have just seen Zervos – he took your name and Reiser's with note of what you could do and will submit them to propaganda committee – you will receive instructions and safe conducts if accepted. There is no salary except 12 pesetas a day while in Spain which is the pay of a militiaman – if you give film (Roland [Penrose] did) or something it is always welcome" (Trevelyan papers, Trinity College Cambridge, 16/16). Trevelyan later wrote that "Bill [Hayter] wanted me to join a cinema unit run by Zervos on the Catalan front, but I decided against it, partly because I felt that I should be just another mouth to feed" (*Indigo days*, p. 79).

82 Letter to Robert Isaacson, cited in Peter Black and Desiree Moorhead, *The Prints of Stanley William Hayter* (Phaidon, London, 1992), p. 49.

83 P. M. S. Hacker (ed.), *The Renaissance of Gravure: the Art of S. W. Hayter* (Clarendon Press, Oxford, 1988), pp. 14 and 79. The theme of the undying fame of the defeated was, by 1939, appropriate.

84 Trinity College Cambridge, Julian Trevelyan papers, 16/24, Hayter to Trevelyan, 6 November 1938.

85 SNGMA, Penrose papers, RPA 0642/3/4, notes for speech. (Emphasis in original).

86 Hogarth, *Drawing on life*, pp. 18–19.

87 Tate Gallery, Bomberg papers, TGA 8811.1.1, David Bomberg to "Kit", 13 March 1939.

Chapter 6   *The death of Bob Smillie*

The principal archival source is the David Murray collection at the National Library of Scotland, Accs 7914 (hence "DMP"). Unless otherwise specified, reference is to Box 1, File 1.

1 George Orwell, *Homage to Catalonia* (1938; 1974 edition), p. 206.

2 Peter Stansky and William Abrahams, *Orwell: The Transformation* (1979; 1981 edition, Paladin, Aylesbury), p. 207.

3 Bernard Crick, *George Orwell: A Life* (Secker & Warburg, London, 1980), p. 337.

4 Michael Shelden, *Orwell: The Authorised Biography* (Heinemann, London, 1991), p. 295.

5 Jennie Lee, who met Smillie while visiting Spain for the ILP wrote in her memoirs that: "He became ill and had an appendix operation in circum-

stances that never became clear. Was there foul play, or was there neglect? Certainly, he would not have died if he had been operated on in a Scottish hospital" (*My Life with Nye*, 1980; 1981 edition, Penguin, Harmondsworth, p. 123). Part of the mystery, however, is why no operation was attempted. The brief account by R. Dan Richardson in *Comintern Army: The International Brigades in the Spanish Civil War* (University Press of Kentucky, Lexington, KY., 1982) is also misleading: "An even more pointed example of Cheka terror was that of the Englishman (sic) Robert Smillie . . . He was arrested, incarcerated, held incommunicado by the Communists, and eventually died in one of their secret prisons", p. 161.

Richardson's source may have been the Soviet defector Walter Krivitsky's ghost-written memoirs which record that "[t]here were countless such disappearances [during the Stalinist terror in Spain]. Some men were kidnapped and taken to Soviet Russia. Others were assassinated in Spain [such as the POUM leader Andres Nin] . . . Another outstanding case is that of young Smillie, son of the famous British Labour leader Robert Smillie, murdered in an Ogpu [NKVD] prison in Spain. Still another is that of Mark Rein . . . " (W. G. Krivitsky, *I was Stalin's Agent*, 1939; 1992 edition, Faulkner Publishing, Cambridge, pp. 116–17). This statement is not substantiated and should be discounted. Krivitsky, Chief of Soviet Military Intelligence in Western Europe in 1937, is not a reliable witness on NKVD operations in Spain which were under the command of Alexander Orlov, another defector. Even those who treat Krivitsky as a reliable source, such as Burnett Bolloten, have chosen not to repeat his allegation about Smillie's death. Frustratingly, Orlov did not mention his activities in Spain in his *Secret History of Stalin's Crimes* (Jerrold's, London, 1953). A recent book based on NKVD/KGB documents from the *Rezidentura* in Spain makes no mention of Smillie, although there is reference to the liquidation of the foreign "Trotskyist" Kurt Landau. (See John Costello and Oleg Tsarev, *Deadly Illusions* [Century, London, 1993], pp. 285–92).

6   For the family background see Robert Smillie, *My Life of Labour* (Mills and Boon, London, 1924), chapter 1. In *The Road to Wigan Pier* (1937) Orwell referred to the elder Robert Smillie's militant reputation in the years immediately after the First World War: "That was the period of the great coal strikes, when a miner was thought of as a fiend incarnate and old ladies looked under their beds every night lest Robert Smillie should be concealed there" (1974 edition), p. 123.

7   *We Carry On: Our Tribute to Bob Smillie*, Dan McArthur (Chairman of the Scottish I.L.P. Guild of Youth) (1937), pp. 3–7.

8   Orwell, *Homage to Catalonia*, p. 39; John McNair, "Memories of Bob Smillie", *New Leader*, 9 July 1937; tributes to Bob Smillie, *New Leader*, 25 June 1937.

9   DMP, Accs 7914, box 2, file 6, Guilermo Neuman to Murray. It is far from clear exactly why Smillie initially went to Spain. According to contempo-

rary press reports he had gone to work "as a chemist in the workers' armaments factory in Barcelona" (*New Leader*, 16 October 1936). However, there was no further mention of this in the press. The Murray papers indicate that he was involved in setting up an arms factory with a "Belgian engineer". This suggests that the scheme may have involved George Kopp, later Smillie's unit commander, who was an engineer from Belgium and who admitted manufacturing explosives for the Republic there (*New Leader*, 13 August 1937). For more on the life (and double-life) of Kopp see Shelden, *Orwell*, pp. 297–8.

10 Bob Smillie's decision to join the ILP contingent was very much his own. He was under no political pressure to do so. An article by Jennie Lee (*New Leader*, 15 January 1937), perhaps significantly, described Smillie accompanying her to the highly emotive funeral of a POUM youth leader killed in the fighting immediately prior to his decision to volunteer. For the context see Peter Thwaites, "The Independent Labour Party contingent in the Spanish Civil War", *Imperial War Museum Review*, 2, 1987, pp. 50–61

11 This was the ILP's favoured phrase to describe its relationship with the POUM. Both parties were affiliated to the International Bureau for Revolutionary Socialist Unity.

12 Quoted in McArthur, *We carry on*, p. 4.

13 It is unclear whether Smillie was intending to return to Spain after this tour – he had initially agreed to serve for three months. His family appear to have been expecting him not to return to Spain (DMP, Murray to Eileen Blair, 1 July 1937).

14 For a comprehensive, if partisan, history of the POUM see Victor Alba and Stephen Schwartz, *Spanish Marxism versus Soviet Communism; a History of the POUM* (Transaction Books, New Brunswick, NJ, 1988). There is much useful information and a critique of the POUM's politics in Ronald Fraser, *Blood of Spain; the Experience of Civil War in Spain* (1981 edition), pp. 340–45, 388–89. In *Marxism and the Failure of Organised Socialism in Spain, 1879–1936* (Cambridge University Press, Cambridge, 1990), p. 232, n. 89, Paul Heywood discusses the POUM in the context of Spanish Marxism, and argues that its significance has been overstated – "The brutal assassination of Andreu Nin by the NKVD, the subsequent liquidation of the POUM, and – it must be acknowledged – the continued popularity of George Orwell's *Homage to Catalonia*, have contributed to the construction of something of a myth around both Nin and the POUM."

15 Bolloten, *The Spanish Civil War*, p. 405, refers to an estimated membership of 6000 in July 1936 and 30,000 in December. According to Ronald Fraser, POUM membership grew "ten-fold to nearly 40,000" after the start of the Civil War (*Blood of Spain*, p. 340). According to the NKVD agent Orlov's report to Moscow, 22 February 1937, there were some 5000 POUM members in Barcelona, with an equal number of sympathisers. He also estimated about 6000 members in the rest of Catalonia, and a regiment of 2000 ("about 50% armed") in Barcelona (Costello and Tsarev, *Deadly illusions*, p. 468).

16 Quoted in MacArthur, *We carry on*, p. 7.

17 "Unity in the trenches", *New Leader*, 25 June 1937, by Smillie and Stafford Cottman. Cottman was at this time still a member of the Young Communist League. He was expelled on his return to Britain.

18 According to John McNair, Bob Smillie "thinks Barcelona is just like Glasgow!" (*New Leader*, 13 November 1936). The visiting ILP MP John McGovern gave a radio broadcast in the city, saying that "Catalonia reminds me in many ways of my native Scotland, but Barcelona is much more revolutionary than Glasgow" (*New Leader*, 27 November 1936). Even so, for many Scottish socialists, the comparison between Glasgow, the city of the post-First World War "Red Clydeside", and the Catalan capital, was a tempting one.

19 *New Leader*, 21 May 1937.

20 Paul Heywood, "The development of Marxist theory in Spain and the Popular Front", in Martin Alexander and Helen Graham (eds.), *The French and Spanish Popular Fronts: Comparative Perspectives* (Cambridge University Press, Cambridge, 1989), pp. 129–30.

21 Robert E. Dowse, *Left in the Centre: the Independent Labour Party, 1893–1940* (Longmans, London, 1966), p. 190.

22 Dowse, *Left in the centre*, p. 193.

23 Dowse, *Left in the centre*, p. 194. On Scottish left-wing electoral politics in this period see Ian Donnachie, "Scottish Labour in the Depression: The 1930s", in Ian Donnachie, Christopher Harvie and Ian S. Wood (eds.), *Forward! Labour Politics in Scotland, 1888–1988* (Polygon, Edinburgh, 1989), pp. 49–65.

24 Dowse, *Left in the centre*, p. 198.

25 *New Leader*, 14 August 1936.

26 Dowse, *Left in the centre*, p. 197. In fact, especially in London, Trotskyists had infiltrated the ILP in the course of the 1930s, although most had left the party in late 1936.

27 *Daily Worker*, 31 May 1937.

28 DMP, Accs 7914, box 1, file 3, undated leaflet entitled "Onward: Towards victory in Spain".

29 Murray was invited to Spain by Guilermo Neuman, a business associate and importer of potato seed, both for a holiday and to discuss possible post-war business ventures. In the light of allegations that Murray had been able to visit Spain because he was working for a right-wing British newspaper (see below) it is worth noting that he was granted a visa as the Scottish representative of his friend's business.

30 DMP, 11 February 1938, Murray to John McNair.

31 DMP, July 1937, Murray's 32-point summary of events to the end of May; point 26.

32 DMP, February 1938, first draft of ILP NAC report, p. 3.

33 DMP, 11 June 1937, Murray to Eileen Blair.

34 Orwell, *Homage to Catalonia*, p. 205; DMP, February 1938, first draft of NAC report, p. 4.

35 DMP, 11 June 1937, Murray to Eileen Blair.
36 *New Leader*, 21 and 28 May 1937. In an editorial comment on 28 May Fenner Brockway wrote that "the real reason [for Smillie's detention] was the possession of political documents".
37 DMP, July 1937, Murray's report for ILP NAC, pp. 1–2.
38 DMP, Accs 7914, Box 3, file 2, 23 December 1937, Murray to Josiah Wedgwood MP. According to one of his comrades, Albert Gross, Smillie had been planning to bring home two discharged bombs, "one an old Anarchist bomb, a crude thing containing nuts set off by lighting with a cigarette or match, and the other a Falangist bomb captured during a raid into the Falangist trenches" (*New Leader*, 28 May 1937).
39 DMP, undated memorandum from Murray to William Naesmith, editor of the *Hamilton Advertiser* (July 1937).
40 DMP, 5 July 1937, Murray to Brockway. Following the move of the Republican government to Valencia, Britain had established a temporary Embassy in the city, manned by a chargé d'affaires. The Smillie case was dealt with by the Consul, Mr Sullivan, and a Spanish assistant, Sr Hullier. Fenner Brockway was distinctly unimpressed by the British offices in Barcelona, describing them as "the most cock-eyed, ramshackle hole I've ever seen decorated by Government emblems: they might have been the offices of a disreputable stockbroker" (*Inside the Left*, G. Allen & Unwin, 1942, p. 312).
41 DMP, July 1937, Murray's report for ILP NAC, p. 6.
42 DMP, 16 July 1937, Murray to Brockway, point 8.
43 DMP, 12 June 1937, Murray to Bob Smillie.
44 DMP, 13 June 1937, Murray to Eileen Blair.
45 DMP, 15 February 1938, Murray to McNair.
46 The Military Fiscal, Jose Ballaster Gozvalo, was a Professor of the Normal School in Madrid, and an ex-member of the Cortes. He and Murray were in close agreement about the case. Their friendship continued after the Civil War, when Ballaster and his wife had fled to Paris. Murray arranged for them to come to Scotland, but the plans were abandoned because Ballaster's wife was too ill to travel. Murray and Ballaster shared a common anti-clericalism. Murray's papers contain a copy of Ballaster's book *La iglesia, nuestro mayor enemigo en la Guerra*, with the dedication "To my friend David Murray, 16 June 1937".
47 DMP, 5 August 1937, Murray to Mr and Mrs MacDonald (parents of Ethel MacDonald).
48 Orwell, *Homage to Catalonia*, p. 206.
49 DMP, 27 July 1937, Uberos to Neuman; DMP, 19 July 1937, Murray to "The Editor", and 3 February 1938, Murray to McNair.
50 DMP, 3 February 1938, Murray to McNair.
51 DMP, 30 June 1937, Murray to the editor, *Hamilton Advertiser*, published 3 July 1937.
52 DMP, 16 February 1938, Murray to Alex Smillie.

53 DMP, 6 December 1937, Murray to Alex Smillie.
54 Harvester Microfiche, Archives of the ILP, series II, card 25. On Gorkin and Brockway's investigations see above p. 113.
55 DMP, July 1937, Murray's report for the ILP NAC, p. 5.
56 DMP, July 1937, Murray's report for ILP NAC, p. 7. The prisoners interviewed were three members of the International Brigades accused of desertion, Sneddon, Mudie and Thomas, and a Moroccan called Raisumi (brother in law of Abd el Krim, the rebel Moroccan leader of the 1920s).
57 DMP, 8 July 1937, Dr A. Ferrer Peris to Alex Smillie (my translation).
58 DMP, February 1938, first draft of NAC report, p. 4.
59 DMP, July 1937, Murray's report for ILP NAC, p. 7.
60 DMP, July 1937, Murray's report for ILP NAC, p. 5.
61 DMP, July 1937, Murray's report for ILP NAC, p. 7.
62 DMP, July 1937, Murray's report for ILP NAC, p. 5.
63 DMP, 27 July 1937, Uberos to Neuman.
64 DMP, February 1938, first draft of NAC report, p. 4.
65 DMP, 30 June 1937, Murray to editor, *Hamilton Advertiser*.
66 DMP, 1 July 1937, Murray to Eileen Blair.
67 DMP, 11 February 1938, Murray to McNair.
68 DMP, 14 February 1938, McNair to Murray.
69 DMP, 15 February 1938, Murray to McNair; DMP, February 1938, redrafted ILP report, p. 4 (emphasis in original).
70 There was also genuine outrage in what was left of the POUM press after *La Batalla* had been suspended in the first week of June. The party's *Juventud Obrero* on 12 July described Smillie's death as "Un crimen horrendo del que debe responder el Gobierno Negrin" (Richardson, *Comintern army*, p. 161).
71 DMP, 15 July 1938, Brockway to Murray.
72 Press Association release, 13 July 1937.
73 DMP, 16 July 1937, Murray to Brockway, point 15.
74 DMP, 3 February 1938, Murray to McNair.
75 Mark Shipway, *Anti-Parliamentary Communism: The Movement for Workers' Councils in Britain, 1917–1945* (Macmillan, Basingstoke, 1988), p. 160.
76 Mitchell Library, Glasgow, Guy Aldred Collection, bundle 107, 5 June 1937, MacDonald to Aldred.
77 *Forward*, 25 December 1937; *Sunday Mail*, 26 December 1937.
78 See report in *El Noticiero Universal*, Barcelona newspaper of the Communist-dominated Catalan Socialist Party (PSUC), 19 and 22 June 1937 (DMP, Accs 7914, box 1, file 3).
79 *Sunday Mail*, 12 December 1937.
80 For instance, another internationalist sympathiser of the POUM wrote in her unpublished memoirs that "this was the week that we learned the Russians had arrested Bob Smillie" (Alba and Schwartz, *Spanish Marxism*, p. 293).
81 DMP, 28 July 1937, Alex Smillie to Dr Ferrer Peris; 28 July 1937, Alex Smillie to Uberos.

82 DMP, 16 July 1937, Murray to Brockway. According to this letter, Murray had withheld information on the prompting of ILP leaders Maxton, Carmichael and Aplin.

83 DMP, 6 December 1937, Murray to Alex Smillie.

84 DMP, 15 February 1938, Murray to McNair.

85 Ibid.

86 DMP, 15 February 1938, Alex Smillie to Murray.

87 In May 1938 Alex Smillie wrote to Eileen Blair, thanking her for a copy of *Homage to Catalonia*, and still unsure as to whether his son had been killed by the Communists or allowed to die in prison by neglect (Crick, *Orwell*, p. 346).

88 DMP, 27 December 1937, Murray to McNair.

89 DMP, Box 3, file 1, 16 July 1937, Murray to Brockway. My emphasis.

90 DMP, 3 February 1938, Murray to McNair.

91 11 March 1938, *New Leader*, "How Bob Smillie died".

92 DMP, undated manuscript by Murray, July 1937.

93 A security police report to the Tribunal for Espionage and High Treason in Valencia stated that Eric Blair and his wife were "known Trotskyists" and "linking agents of the ILP and the POUM". The report added that Orwell had taken part in the May fighting on the side of the anarchists. The document is reproduced in Victor Alba *et al*, *El Proceso del POUM: Documentos Judiciales et Politicales* (Lerna, Barcelona, 1989), p. 75.

94 Two French delegations visited the Spanish Ambassador in Paris on 21 and 22 June 1937 in order to express concern at the arrest of the POUM leaders, basing their fears on the mysterious death of Smillie. See Alba, *El proceso del POUM*, pp. 45–6.

95 *New Leader*, 27 August 1937.

96 *Socialist Policy for 1938*, resolutions from the ILP conference, 16–18 April 1938, p. 12. John McGovern denounced the work of the Cheka in his pamphlet *Terror in Spain* (1938), following his visit to Spain of that year. There were now, he wrote, two International Brigades in Spain – the fighting force and an "International Cheka – drawn from Comintern's paid gangsters, especially from Germany and Italy".

97 DMP, Accs 7914, box 1, file 2, 24 August 1937, Murray to Mrs J. Lacey.

98 DMP, Accs 7914, box 3, file 2, 23 December 1937, Murray to Josiah Wedgwood MP.

99 A similar stance is notable in the writings of George Orwell, who joined the ILP after his return from Spain. His passionate denunciations of Communist misdeeds in Republican Spain in *Homage to Catalonia* were later tempered by an awareness of the achievements of the Republic (see "Caesarean section in Spain", *The Highway*, March 1939).

100 See Buchanan, *The Spanish Civil War and the British labour movement*, chapter 5.

101 DMP, 12 June 1937, Murray to Bob Smillie.

102 DMP, 12 June 1937, Murray to Manuel Irujo, Minister for Justice.

103 DMP, July 1937, Murray's report for ILP NAC, p. 1.

104 DMP, Accs 7914, box 3, file 2, 23 December 1937, Murray to Wedgwood.

105 DMP, July 1937, Murray's report for ILP NAC, p. 4.

106 DMP, July 1937, Murray's 32-point summary of events since the end of May, point 14.

107 DMP, Accs 7914, box 1, file 3, undated cutting. McShane, who later broke with the Communist party, recalled that: "In Spain itself the communists looked upon everyone who was not supporting them as a deadly enemy. Bob Smillie . . . was actually imprisoned by the communists and died in prison. It was later argued that he died a natural death – but, of course, he shouldn't have been in prison in the first place" (Harry McShane and Joan Smith, *Harry McShane: No Mean Fighter* (Pluto, London, 1978), p. 223).

108 *New Leader*, 27 August 1937.

109 Dowse, *Left in the centre*, p. 198–99; *Socialist policy for 1938*, p. 8.

110 DMP, 15 July 1937, Brockway to Murray.

111 DMP, 16 July 1937, Murray to Brockway. Murray's reason for this suppression was that he "did not wish to endanger the life and liberty of my informant and I wished to retain some material for inside pressure in and out of Spain, on behalf of the remaining prisoners". Earlier he had proposed to "publicise certain facts that will be critical of the CP", but does not appear to have done so (DMP, 7 July 1937, Murray to Brockway).

112 DMP, July 1937, Murray's report to ILP NAC, p. 6.

113 DMP, 7 July 1937, Murray to Brockway.

114 DMP, 15 July 1937, Brockway to Murray. For a detailed account of his visit see Brockway, *Inside the left*, pp. 312–16.

115 Brockway, *Inside the left*, p. 312.

116 Perhaps the most startling omission, given his personal involvement in the case, is the lack of any reference to Smillie's death in Julián Gorkin's book *El Proceso de Moscú en Barcelona: el Sacrificio de Andres Nin* (Aymá, Barcelona, 1974). This account of the suppression of the POUM does, however, mention the death or disappearance of two other foreign sympathisers of the POUM, Guido Picelli and Marc Rein (pp. 54–5). This suggests that Gorkin did not, with hindsight, view Smillie's death as part of the unfolding pattern of Stalinist terror.

117 DMP, Accs 7914, box 1, file 3, Victor Serge, "Crimes à Barcelone" in *La Révolution Prolétarienne*, 25 June 1937. For Serge's account of the suppression of the POUM see his *Memoirs of a Revolutionary, 1901–1941* (Oxford University Press, Oxford, 1975 edition, pp. 334–40).

118 In 1998 the *The Historical Journal* published an article which claimed that a document written by George Kopp in 1939 might offer evidence that Smillie had been murdered in captivity (John Newsinger, "The death of Bob Smillie", *The Historical Journal*, 41, 2, 1998, pp. 575–8). I have since argued that this is not a reliable source, and that my original conclusions, therefore, stand (Tom Buchanan, "The death of Bob Smillie: a reply", *The Historical Journal*, 43, 2, 2000, pp. 1109–11).

119 In a brief memoir published after his death in 1968, John McNair remained convinced that this "inexplicable tragedy" was due to "criminal neglect" rather than a case of "political assassination" (*Spanish diary*, n.d., p. 21).

120 DMP, undated cutting from *Evening News*, 1955; 16 February 1955, Murray to the editor, *Evening News*. By the 1950s Murray had abandoned his political positions of the 1930s. He stood unsuccessfully for parliament in Western Isles (1950–51), Kelvingrove (1958) and Motherwell (1959) as an Independent Liberal, a Liberal and as an Independent Home Rule candidate.

Chapter 7   *Loss, memory and the British "Volunteers for Liberty"*

1   The poem was sent by a Mrs J. Lacey of Glasgow, whose son, George Keegan, was a twice-wounded volunteer with the British Battalion of the International Brigades. In April 1937 Mrs Lacey had written to Harry Pollitt that she was proud that her son had "done his bit like a true Communist", and this was published in the *Daily Worker* (6 April 1937). Subsequently, however, Keegan briefly deserted back to Britain while convalescing, and was "smuggled back to Spain with the assistance of a seafaring friend" against the advice of the Communist Party. In July 1937 Mrs Lacey wrote to David Murray of the ILP for advice as to her son's "foolish escapade", and expressed her disappointment at the Communist Party's "seeming indifference": the Communists promoted the International Brigades in the *Daily Worker*, "but don't seem to bother what becomes of [the volunteers] after." Keegan was briefly imprisoned on his return to the British Battalion, but returned to front line duty only to be wounded again at Quinto in August 1937. He was repatriated in September. (See NMLH, Pollitt papers, CP/IND/POLL/2/6, 1 April 1937, Lacey to Pollitt; NLS, David Murray papers, Accs 7914, Box 1, File 2, Lacey to Murray, 22 July, 2 August and 23 August 1937. I am grateful to Jim Carmody for information relating to Keegan's service in Spain).

2   William Rust, *Britons in Spain: The History of the British Battalion of the XV International Brigade* (Lawrence & Wishart, London, 1939), p. vi.

3   Alexander, *British volunteers for liberty*; Richard Baxell, *British Volunteers in the Spanish Civil War: The British Battalion in the International Brigades, 1936–1939* (Routledge, London, 2004).

4   *Daily Worker*, 25 March 1937.

5   *Daily Worker*, 19 April 1937.

6   Rust, *Britons in Spain*, chapter 10; these references are to pp. 129 and 136.

7   Hywel Francis, *Miners against Fascism: Wales and the Spanish Civil War* (Lawrence & Wishart, London, 1984).

8   Hywel Francis, "'Say nothing and leave in the middle of the night': the Spanish Civil War revisited", *History Workshop Journal*, 32, autumn 1991, 69–76. The article was based on a paper given in 1986. These references are to pp. 71–2 and 75.

9   Jackson, *British women*, pp. 72–82; Robert Stradling, *Wales and the Spanish Civil War: The Dragon's Dearest Cause?* (University of Wales Press, Cardiff, 2004), pp. 159–60; Natalie Suart, "The Memory of the Spanish Civil War and the Families of the British International Brigadiers", De Montfort University, PhD thesis, 2001, chapter 4.

10 For an overview of British volunteering see Buchanan, *Britain and the Spanish Civil War*, chapter 5. The current chapter deals primarily with the British volunteers in the International Brigades although some reference will also be made to medical volunteers, who were less directly under Communist Party control (see above, chapter 3).

11 MML, IBMA, Box 45, B/88, 7 November 1951, R. W. Robson to Chris Maxwell; Francis, *Miners against fascism*, pp. 156–9; Alexander, *British volunteers for liberty*, p. 44.

12 *Daily Worker*, 30 January 1951.

13 See Kevin Morgan, *Harry Pollitt* (Manchester University Press, Manchester, 1993), pp. 96–7.

14 NMLH, CPGB papers, CP/CENT/INT/29/01, John Mahon, "The forms of our Aid for Spain", May 1965. See also above, p. 192.

15 Baxell, *British volunteers*, p. 12

16 Ian MacDougall (ed.), *Voices from the Spanish Civil War: Personal Recollections of Scottish Volunteers in Republican Spain, 1936–39* (Polygon, Edinburgh, 1986), p. 287.

17 Alexander, *British volunteers for liberty*, p. 81, Baxell, *British volunteers*, p. 137 offers the lower figure.

18 For the best discussion of this topic see Hopkins, *Into the heart of the fire*, especially pp. 254–7.

19 See S. P. MacKenzie, "The Foreign Enlistment Act and the Spanish Civil War, 1936–1939", *Twentieth Century British History*, 10:1, 1999, 52–66.

20 See Buchanan, *The Spanish Civil War and the British labour movement*, pp. 159–61.

21 *Sunday Dispatch*, 13 June 1937 (in MML, IBMA, Box 39/A/42).

22 NMLH, Manchester, CPGB papers, CC minutes, January 1937, p. 16.

23 *Daily Worker*, 9 June 1937, citing a letter from volunteer Gilmour.

24 MRC, Mss 292/946/34, 2 November 1937, Tewson to W. Elger. In early February 1937 H. N. Brailsford, who ran the forerunner of the IBD&WAC, told the TUC that the question of provision for the families of the dead had "not been faced as yet" (MRC, Mss 292/946/34, Walter Citrine's memorandum of meeting, 4 February 1937). A few days later, immediately after the British Battalion had suffered grievous losses at the battle of the Jarama, Peter Kerrigan told Pollitt that it was essential for "political reasons" and for the morale of those in the front line that something should be done for the disabled volunteers (MML, IBMA. Box C: 10/9, Kerrigan to Pollitt, 18 February 1937).

25 For a contemporary account of the IBD&WAC see Rust, *Britons in Spain*, pp. 208–12. The most thorough academic study is in Suart, PhD thesis, pp.

164 *et seq*, which draws heavily on such papers that survive in the MML, IBMA. However, Suart underestimates the absolute centrality of the Communist party to the committee. This was made clear in comments by J. R. Campbell to the CPGB's Central Committee *apropos* the forerunner to Haldane's committee, which was chaired by the journalist H. N. Brailsford. Campbell stated that the intention was to form "a National Committee, with the idea of Brailsford becoming secretary, that is, nominally, as the actual secretary will be some Party comrade we will put in to assist Brailsford on this question" (NMLH, CPGB papers, CC minutes, 16 January 1937, p. 16). Brailsford was a member of the Socialist League and at this point the Communist Party appears to have regarded fundraising for the volunteers' dependants as part of its "united front" activities. In the event such subterfuge was not necessary as Charlotte Haldane was a member of the Communist Party.

26 *Daily Worker*, 20 September 1937. However, Bill Alexander referred to donations being made "from larger parties outside Britain" (*British volunteers for liberty*, p. 140), which suggests that Comintern or Soviet assistance underpinned the fund. This was also alluded to by Fred Copeman, who was briefly in charge of the IBD&WAC (*Reason in revolt*, Blandford Press, London, 1948, pp. 178–9).

27 MRC, Mss 292/946/34, report of meeting, 31 March 1938.

28 NLS, Tom Murray papers, Acc 9083, Box 4/1, letter of 17 February 1939 issued by the "Provisional Constituent Committee" of the International Brigade Association.

29 Rust, *Britons in Spain*, p. 130. The best account from the perspective of a volunteer's wife is that of Elsie Booth, discussed in Jackson, *British women*, p. 74. See also the story of Kath Gibbons, *Daily Worker*, 11 July 1939.

30 Francis, "Say Nothing", pp. 74–75; see, for instance, the cases of Welsh volunteers Jack Roberts and Leo Price, in Richard Felstead, *No Other Way; Jack Russia and the Spanish Civil War* (Alun Books, Port Talbot, 1981), pp. 35–6 and 42–3.

31 MacDougall, *Voices*, pp. 47 and 50.

32 Corkill and Rawnsley, *The road to Spain*, p. 78.

33 MacDougall, *Voices*, p. 34.

34 MacDougall, *Voices*, p. 242.

35 MacDougall, *Voices*, p. 289.

36 Censorship ranged from the blanking out of place names to the confiscation of entire letters, some of which turned up many years later in the Moscow archives (see Hopkins, *Into the heart of the fire*, pp. 213–14, 270–1, 363).

37 MacDougall, *Voices*, p. 180.

38 MacDougall, *Voices*, p. 192.

39 TNA, FO 889/2, 1 April 1937, Kathleen Gregory to Chargé d'Affaires.

40 NLS, John Dunlop papers, 12087/2, 18 May 1939, Wheeler to Dunlop.

41 NMLH, Pollitt papers, CP/IND/POLL/2/6, 19 April 1937, Marion

Teasdale to Pollitt, and Pollitt's reply of 20 April 1937. Whitehead's mother was said to be too ill to write.

42 No figure is currently available for the British contingent as a whole, but Francis reckoned that more than a fifth of the Welsh volunteers were married (*Miners against fascism*, p. 213).

43 MML IBMA, Box 39/A/8, Paul Lewis to Pollitt, 6 May 1937. Lewis was asking for his wife to be allowed to come to work in Spain.

44 University of Liverpool, Rathbone papers, RP xiv 2.12, 22 March 1937, Rathbone to Mrs Hamilton.

45 MML, IBMA, Box 39/A/1, D. R. Horradge to W. Paynter, undated (1937?).

46 MML IBMA, Box 39/A/11, "W. P" to Pollitt, 20 May 1937.

47 MML IBMA, Box 39/A/12, n.d., list of 18 repatriation requests.

48 *Daily Worker*, 24 March 1937.

49 NLS, Tom Murray papers, Acc 9083, Box 1, file 2, 26 June 1938, Janet to Tom Murray. The chaotic retreat from Aragon in March-April 1938, in which many British volunteers went missing, was a time of particular anxiety. For McLeod's death see above p. 131–2.

50 NLS, David Murray papers, Accs 7914, Box 1, File 2, Mrs D. Donald to David Murray, undated. She added that "he did not need to be there [in Spain] as he has a good home[,] his father works every day and he never wanted for anything".

51 For the role of British consular officials in Spain see Tom Buchanan, "Edge of Darkness: British 'Front-Line' Diplomacy in the Spanish Civil War, 1936–7", *Contemporary European History*, 12, 3, 2003, pp. 279–303.

52 TNA, FO 889/2, Mrs F. Rush to Consul Sullivan, 7 April 1937.

53 TNA, FO 889/2, George Bogle to Consul Sullivan, 30 May 1937.

54 TNA, FO 889/2, Mrs M. Weaving to H. C. Brooks, 17 May 1937.

55 TNA, FO 889/2, Foreign Office to Vice-Consul, Alicante, 14 April 1937.

56 NLS, David Murray papers, Accs 7914, Box 1, File 2, Mrs Donald to Murray [undated, but July 1937].

57 TNA, FO 889/2, Margaret Johnson to Sullivan, 28 April 1937.

58 MML, IBMA, Box 39/A/5, Rust to Pollitt, 14 June 1937.

59 MRC, Mss 292/946/34, undated letter from G. T. Owen, containing a statement of 20 August 1938 by Will Hopkins.

60 This episode is discussed in Stradling, *Wales and the Spanish Civil War*, pp. 155–7.

61 *Daily Worker*, 7 January 1937.

62 MacDougall, *Voices*, p. 151; *Daily Worker*, 8 February 1938 lists one of these men, P. Glacken. Richard Baxell discusses this episode in *British volunteers*, pp. 140–1.

63 *Daily Worker*, 20 March 1937 [?].

64 *Daily Worker*, 13 April 1937.

65 *Daily Worker*, 27 March 1937.

66 Rust, *Britons in Spain*, pp. 136 and 138.

67 NLS, Tom Murray papers, Acc 9083, Box 1, file 6, 15 November 1937, A. Fry to T. Murray. This last comment referred to the fact that Fry had previous military experience, having joined the British army in 1925 and served in India and China (*The Book of the XV Brigade*, ed. Frank Ryan, Newcastle-upon-Tyne, 1975 edition, p. 298).

68 MRC, Mss 292/946/34, A. E. Boswell to Citrine, 13 September 1938.

69 NLS, Tom Murray papers, Ms 9083, Box 1/1, Mr and Mrs McLeod to Murray, 20 October 1938, and his reply, 23 October 1938.

70 This case has been discussed in detail by Robert Stradling, who claimed that Taylor was "blackmailed" into volunteering and may have been executed by his own side for desertion (*Wales and the Spanish Civil War*, pp. 68 and 150–3).

71 In his defence, Haldane denied that his speech in Cardiff's Cathays Park could be described as a "recruiting speech", and pointed out that "the situation in March [1938] was so critical that every available man, however ill and however valuable, had to be used". UCL, Haldane papers, Box 15, Mrs Shaxby to Haldane, 8 December 1938, and Haldane's undated draft reply. Emphases as in the original.

72 Vanessa and Clive Bell received at least one hundred letters of condolence when Julian's death was reported in *The Times* .These letters are listed in King's College, Cambridge, Charleston papers catalogue, Appendix 3.

73 Vanessa Bell's letter to "Y" of 24 August 1937, cited in Frances Spalding, *Vanessa Bell* (Macmillan, London, 1984), p. 300.

74 Cochrane, *One man's medicine*, pp. 44–5.

75 Spalding, *Bell*, p. 300.

76 In this regard the Bells' official connections proved helpful after the Civil War had ended. Julian's friend Eddie Playfair, who worked for the Treasury, visited Spain in late 1939 and notified Vanessa Bell that the plot of Julian's grave was vulnerable and should be purchased in perpetuity. In addition, he enlisted the help of the British Consul. KCC, Charleston papers, 1/485, Eddie Playfair to Vanessa Bell, 14 and 26 December 1939, and 8 February 1940.

77 NLS, Tom Murray papers, Acc 9083, Box 1, file 3, Ann Murray to "Agnes", 7 February 1939 (emphasis in original).

78 MacDougall, *Voices*, pp. 236–7.

79 T. A. R. Hyndman in Philip Toynbee (ed.), *The Distant Drum; Reflections on the Spanish Civil War* (Sidgwick and Jackson, London, 1976), p. 129. For Hyndman see Stradling, *History and legend*, pp. 27–43.

80 For instance, Philip Bolsover's article in the *Daily Worker*, 22 October 1938, depicted returning volunteers progressing smoothly from a medical check-up to an employment bureau and, finally, "if he is willing to do a little public speaking he comes to the publicity department".

81 MML, IBMA, Box 39, 18 December 1939 and 30 December 1939, Bailey to Communist Party.

82 Patterson's case is documented in NLS, Tom Murray papers, Acc 9083, Box 4, file 4, and in MML, IBMA, Box 39/A/62. On 12 May 1939

Patterson wrote to Tom Murray that "the Stalinists cannot do without their trotskyite agents. Any natural rebel without much political aptitude who found his way to Spain was in great danger of being condemned as a trotskyist, fifth columnite etc if he persisted in his demands for an extra bean in his soup . . . " Murray's warning is reported in 10 May 1939, Murray to Fred Copeman.

83 *Forward*, 7 January 1939 and reply from Charles McLaughlin, 14 January 1939. McLaughlin revealed that McDade had received an allowance of 30s per week for over a year, but that this had been stopped following a medical report.

84 MML, IBMA, Box 45 B/44, Phil Gillan to Chris Maxwell, 11 February 1952. See also Judith Cook, *Apprentices of Freedom* (Quartet, London, 1979), pp. 97–8.

85 *Sunday Dispatch*, 19 February 1939; *Catholic Herald*, 31 March 1939. The actual level of support was probably far less. Bill Alexander claimed that it had a membership of only ten (*Volunteers for liberty*, p. 249). Bizarrely, the League's leader, the former volunteer Edwin Hall, had also been a member of the British Union of Fascists (Hopkins, *Into the heart of the fire*, p. 253).

86 See, for instance, Jason Gurney, *Crusade in Spain* (Readers Union, Newton Abbot, 1976 edition) p. 188; comments by Walter Greenhalgh in Cook, *Apprentices of freedom*, p. 148.

87 UCL, Townsend journal, 15 January 1939.

88 *Daily Worker*, 22 January 1937.

89 *Daily Worker*, 15 January 1937.

90 *Daily Worker*, 14 October 1938. See Cunningham, *Spanish Civil War verse*, p. 38. An independent fund was later started in honour of Cornford and other Cambridge volunteers

91 *Daily Worker*, 11 March 1937. (Kerrigan had already given a similar estimate in the *Daily Worker* for 6 March.) A list of those killed at Jarama was not published in the *Daily Worker* until 19 August, 1937, in order to make "absolutely certain" of its accuracy. Even then, it contained a number of errors. Confirmations of those killed on the Jarama continued to be published as late as the autumn of 1937 (see the announcement concerning William Coles, *Daily Worker*, 15 November 1937).

92 *Daily Worker*, 19 September 1938, and above p. 176.

93 *Aberdeen Press and Journal*, 28 November 1938.

94 Rust, *Britons in Spain*, p. 187.

95 *Daily Worker*, 3, 9 and 10 January 1939. For details of the convoy see NLS, Tom Murray papers, Box 4/2.

96 *Daily Worker*, 6 July 1939. (See also 18 July, 1939).

97 Robert Stradling, *Brother against Brother: Experiences of a British Volunteer in the Spanish Civil War* (Sutton, Stroud, 1998), p. 14.

98 Natalie Suart, "The British volunteers: the public and private legacy", paper given at OUDCE, Oxford, 17 March 2001.

99 NMLH, CPGB papers, report to CC, July 1938, p. 23.

100 MRC, Mss 292/946/34, memorandum of meeting, 26 May 1938.

101 Fred Copeman cited in *Daily Herald*, 31 January 1939. A few months later, however, it was stated that the fund would merely provide a few "small luxuries" for men who would be receiving state unemployment assistance (*Daily Worker*, 20 July 1939).

102 *Daily Worker*, 1 August 1939. In April 1939 Fred Copeman told the TUC that a "Memorial Trust Fund" had been established (with a number of prominent trade union leaders amongst the Trustees) with the intention of raising £20,000. By this stage, however, the fund had raised only £3,400 (MRC, Mss 292/946/34, 20 April 1939, Copeman to Citrine). A number of final settlements were made to disabled veterans and their families, usually worth between £80 and £100 (Alexander, *British volunteers for liberty*, pp. 243–4). The details of 51 of these grants are listed in Suart, PhD thesis, appendix 6.

103 For the IBA see Buchanan, "Holding the line".

104 Buchanan, "Holding the line", pp. 296 and 308.

105 CCA, Phillip Noel-Baker papers, 4x/122, letter from Charlotte Haldane, 29 December 1937.

106 MML, IBMA, Box 39/A/51; see also TNA, FO 889/2, correspondence concerning Watts.

107 MML, IBMA, Box 37, File A, London Area Conference, 5 March 1939, comments in discussion by B. Beauchamp, Jock Cunningham and Fred Copeman.

108 MML, IBMA, Box 40, File B, 26 February 1947, Green to Mrs Tomasik; Box 41, File C, 7 July 1949, Green to Dave Goodman.

109 Suart, PhD thesis, chapter 2 offers a detailed account of the proliferation of public memorials from the 1970s onwards. See also Williams, *Memorials*. Tellingly, one memorial that was envisaged during this early period was a ward in a Stalingrad hospital (Stradling, *Wales and the Spanish Civil War*, p. 162).

110 MML, IBMA, Box 40, File B, Green to R. Milton, 8 November 1949.

111 This had been acknowledged in a *Daily Worker* editorial entitled "The story of Jack Brent" as early as 24 April 1939.

112 MML, IBMA, Box 45, B/17, Sally Carson to Peter Kerrigan, 5 October 1951.

113 Stanley Harrison, *Good to be Alive: the Story of Jack Brent* (Lawrence & Wishart, London, 1954), p. 15.

114 Notes by Stanley Harrison in MML IBMA, Box 44, C/15, 1 September 1952.

115 Williams, *Memorials*, pp. 86–8; MML IBMA, Box A-12, Fx 9, minute book of the Halifax committee.

116 However, the *Daily Worker*, 21 November 1938, reported the unveiling of a memorial at Tonypandy Library in honour of the Welsh volunteer Harry Dobson (a marble plaque and photograph of Dobson in brigade uniform).

117 MML, IBMA, Box A-12, File Fx, letters from Madge Moxley to Mrs F.

Edwards, 18 January, 16 February, and 3 April 1951; cutting in minute book of the Fox memorial committee; E. P. Thompson to the editor of the *Halifax Courier and Guardian*, 1 May 1950. Mike Freeman, "A footnote on Fox", *Bulletin of the Marx Memorial Library*, 142, Autumn 2005, p. 32.

Chapter 8 *My country right or left*

I would like to express my gratitude to Patricia Langdon-Davies's for her hospitality during my visit to Sant Feliu de Guíxols, and for allowing me to consult the private papers of her late husband. I would also like to thank the late Robin Langdon-Davies and Dr Miquel Berga for their kind assistance during my research.

1 John Langdon-Davies papers, in private possession of the Langdon-Davies family (hence "JLD papers"), unpublished manuscript, p. 15.
2 *The Times*, 6 December 1971.
3 For instance, the artist William Townsend describes being drawn into an animated discussion in a London café between Langdon-Davies (a "big young man with tangled hair") and Tom Wintringham about the Soviet invasion of Finland (Forge, *Townsend journals*, entry for 16 January 1940, pp. 58–9).
4 See, for instance, *A Short History of Women* (Viking Press, New York, 1927) and *Sex, Sin and Sanctity* (London, Gollancz, 1954).
5 The best-known examples occur in Virginia Woolf, *A Room of One's Own* (1928/1945 edition), p. 110 and George Orwell's *Homage to Catalonia* (see above p. 151). A Catalan translation of *Dancing Catalans* was published in the late 1990s.
6 John Langdon-Davies, *Gatherings from Catalonia* (Cassell, London, 1953), p. v.
7 John Langdon-Davies, *Behind the Spanish Barricades* (Secker & Warburg, London, 1936), p. 143.
8 This book was published, in the United States, under the pseudonym of "Thomas Dent" (John Day, New York, 1934). It reflects somewhat elliptically on Langdon-Davies's boyhood in Zululand (where his father ran a school), his education in Britain, and his jailing for conscientious objection during the First World War. It ends with his first marriage.
9 This journal is reproduced in Miquel Berga, "Catalunya i la guerra civil; en la vida i l'obra ed John Langdon-Davies", PhD thesis, Universitat Autònoma ed Barcelona (1988), pp. 96–238.
10 I have found only the following few references in Wilfrid Roberts's papers, MRC, University of Warwick: Mss 308/3/MI, Roberts to Langdon-Davies, 19 October 1937; Mss 308/3/NJ, Molly Miller to Roberts, 14 October 1937.
11 This paragraph draws heavily on Miquel Berga, *John Langdon-Davies (1897–1971); una Biografia Anglo-Catalana* (Editorial Pòrtic, Barcelona, 1991), pp. 43–50.
12 Berga, *John Langdon-Davies*, p. 13.

13 "A private party for American girls during the summer of 1927: from John and Constance Langdon-Davies", original brochure in the private papers of Robin Langdon-Davies.

14 Langdon-Davies, *Spanish barricades*, p. 170.

15 John Langdon-Davies, *Dancing Catalans* (Jonathan Cape, London, 1929), pp. 43, 34 and 209.

16 JLD papers, Ramon Casanova to JLD, 10 December 1924.

17 Langdon-Davies, *Dancing Catalans*, p. 155.

18 Horace Sharp, President of Epsom DLP to Langdon-Davies, 20 February 1924 (in the papers of Robin Langdon-Davies).

19 Langdon-Davies, *Dancing Catalans*, pp. 11–13.

20 John Langdon-Davies, "The country of Quixotes", *The Listener*, 10 June 1931, pp. 969–70. The analogy with Ireland was not an accurate one as the autonomy eventually achieved under the 1932 statute was far from the virtually complete independence acquired by the Irish Free State in 1921–2.

21 On his return Robin Langdon-Davies published an article entitled "War in Spain" in *Siesta* (a school magazine), 3 December 1936 pp. 5–7. See also his handwritten diary of his visit to Spain in the R. H. Langdon-Davies papers, Imperial War Museum archive, 91/6/1. He can be seen, standing in front of a burned-out church, in photograph 32 of *Spanish barricades*.

22 Viscount Cecil, speaking on 26 November 1936 (*House of Lords debates*, 5th series, vol. CIII, col. 451).

23 Frederic Warburg, *An Occupation for Gentlemen* (Hutchinson, London, 1959), p. 193. Warburg added that his publication of *Spanish barricades* "filled the Communists with joy" as it was "ideal propaganda" (p. 202).

24 See Fyrth, *The signal*, pp. 169–71.

25 Journal, April 1950, in Berga, PhD thesis, pp. 98–9.

26 Berga, *John Langdon-Davies*, p. 137.

27 *Daily Worker*, 13 October 1936.

28 The *Daily Worker* records Langdon-Davies – "star press man back from Spain" – as speaking to seven meetings between 12 September and 8 October 1936. Langdon-Davies was, however, soon eclipsed on these platforms by the return to Britain of the *Daily Worker's* own correspondent Frank Pitcairn (Claud Cockburn). At a meeting at Shoreditch town hall, for instance, Langdon-Davies merely "filled out the picture" following Pitcairn's speech (*Daily Worker*, 29 September 1936).

29 On 26 March 1939 this committee staged a fund-raising production of Lorca's *Marriage of Blood*, translated by Langdon-Davies at the Savoy Theatre (see the flyer in the uncatalogued papers of Ewan Phillips, Tate Gallery Archive).

30 John Strachey papers, in the possession of Elizabeth Al Qadhi, "1936" Box. An undated list of projected Left Book Club choices included a suggestion for a book on "Lessons from Spain" by, amongst others, Langdon-Davies and Frank Jellinek. This commission was eventually given to Jellinek (*The Spanish Civil War*, Left Book Club, London, 1938).

31 See correspondence in JLD papers. Hugh Thomas's defence was that Arthur Koestler had identified Langdon-Davies as a Communist in *The Invisible Writing* (Collins, London, 1954), p. 323. It is worth noting that Langdon-Davies himself falsely described the scientist Joseph Needham as a Communist in a draft of his *Russia puts the clock back* (Gollancz, London, 1949). (See JLD papers, H. H. Dale to JLD, 8 March 1949). He corrected the final text to state that Needham was a "communoid biologist" and "sympathetic to Communism" (pp. 119 and 30).

32 JLD papers, Ms of autobiography; see Wilfrid Roberts' comment in Fyrth, *The signal*, p. 212.

33 John Langdon-Davies, *Fifth Column* (J. Murray, London, 1940), p. 49.

34 Journal, April 1950, in Berga, PhD thesis, p. 103.

35 JLD papers, 21 July 1938, Langdon-Davies to Palme Dutt. See Langdon-Davies's book *Air Raid* (G. Routledge, London, 1938) and the detailed riposte by Haldane in his *ARP* (Left Book Club, 1938), pp. 284–93.

36 *News Chronicle*, 28 May 1936.

37 *News Chronicle*, 13 May, 9 June and 15 June 1936.

38 Langdon-Davies, *Spanish barricades*, p. 174. See also pp. 175–7 for the text of Langdon-Davies's interview with Companys.

39 Langdon-Davies, *Spanish barricades*, p. 27. In October 1934 the Spanish Left had planned a general rising to protest the inclusion of three members of the right-wing CEDA in the centre-right government.

40 Langdon-Davies, *Spanish barricades*, p. 78.

41 Langdon-Davies, *Spanish barricades*, p. 145.

42 Langdon-Davies, *Spanish barricades*, p. 303.

43 Langdon-Davies, *Spanish barricades*, p. 197.

44 *Daily Worker*, 21 May 1938, cited in Cunningham, *Spanish front*, p. 305.

45 Langdon-Davies, *Gatherings*, p. 180.

46 JLD papers, unpublished ms, pp. 80 and 101. The POUM is barely mentioned in *Spanish barricades*, apart from some rather mocking references on pp. 169 and 170.

47 Langdon-Davies, *Spanish barricades*, p. vii.

48 Langdon-Davies, *Spanish barricades*, p. 121.

49 Langdon-Davies, *Spanish barricades*, p. 155.

50 According to a recent study, more than 50 per cent of the 8,352 assassinated in Catalonia during the civil war had been killed by 30 September 1936 (Santos Julia *et al.*, *Víctimas de la Guerra Civil* (Temas de Hoy, Madrid, 1999), p. 73. (I am grateful to Julius Ruiz for his advice on this point). See TNA, FO 371, 20537, W 10719/62/41, Horace Seymour to Norman King (Consul-General in Barcelona), 5 September 1936. King, admittedly no friend of the Republic, commented that "when one finds people like Langdon-Davies deliberately misrepresenting conditions one cannot help wondering as to his motive. The only conclusion one can draw is that he and other communistic minded people wish to introduce into England the same earthly paradise they find in Spain" (TNA, FO 371/20539,

W11537/62/41, King to Walter Roberts, 11 September 1936). *Spanish barricades*, p. 154, shows how Langdon-Davies calculated this figure.

51   Langdon-Davies, *Spanish barricades*, p. 185.

52   Langdon-Davies, *Spanish barricades*, chapter V.

53   *Daily Worker*, 12 September 1936.

54   Langdon-Davies's original remarks are in *Spanish barricades*, p. 111, and the actionable comments were in *The Tablet*, 2 January 1937 and the *Catholic Herald*, 8 January 1937. See *The Times*, 18 March 1937 for an account of the case. See also JLD papers, 22 February 1937, R. A. Llewellyn to Mr Thompson (*Catholic Herald*).

55   John Langdon-Davies, *The Spanish Church and Politics* (Watts & Co, London, 1937), p. 2.

56   Autobiographical fragment written in the 1960s, Berga, PhD thesis, p. 217.

57   This significant document was written in late 1937 and revised by Langdon-Davies in the 1960s. A Catalan translation, edited by Miquel Berga, was published in 1987 (*La Setmana Tragica de 1937,* Ediciones 62, Barcelona, 1937).

58   JLD papers, unpublished ms., p. 80.

59   Langdon-Davies composed a very detailed account of these events in a letter to his wife on 3–4 May: this reference is to p. 9. The original is in the JLD papers; extracts are reproduced in *La setmana tragica*, pp. 162–66.

60   See Tom Buchanan, "Three lives of *Homage to Catalonia*", *The Library*, 7th series, 3, 3, September 2002, pp. 302–14.

61   Orwell, *Homage to Catalonia* (1938/1989 edition), pp. 235–8. The whole question of Orwell's criticism of Langdon-Davies's comments on the May events has been closely debated in recent years: see Miquel Berga, "George Orwell in his centenary year: a Catalan perspective" (The Anglo-Catalan Society, 2003), and John Palmer *et al.*, "Setting the record straight on John Langdon-Davies". The lecture is available on the website of the Anglo-Catalan Society, along with the subsequent contributions and some original documentary source material.

62   See, in particular, Helen Graham, *The Spanish Republic at War, 1936–1939* (Cambridge University Press, Cambridge, 2003) and "'Against the state': a genealogy of the Barcelona May Days", *European History Quarterly*, 29, 4, October 1999, pp. 485–542.

63   *New Leader*, 22 October 1937; *Daily Worker*, 18 October 1937.

64   In July 1938 Negrin told Julian Zugazagoitia that "I am not fighting this war so a stupid, provincial separatism can sprout up again in Barcelona . . . " (Graham, *The Spanish republic at war*, p. 254).

65   John Langdon-Davies, "The struggle for anti-fascist unity in Spain", *The Labour Monthly*, vol. 19, October 1937, pp. 609–20.

66   Langdon-Davies, *Spanish barricades*, pp. 158–64; JLD papers, unpublished manuscript, pp. 51–9.

67   JLD papers, John to Robin Langdon-Davies, 10 April 1940.

68   John Langdon-Davies, *Finland; The first total war* (G. Routledge, London, 1940), p. 1.

69 The full letter is reprinted in Berga, *John Langdon-Davies*, pp. 189–95.

70 Journal, April 1950, in Berga, PhD thesis, pp. 103–4.

71 See chapter 10.

72 Langdon-Davies, *Fifth column*, p. 9.

73 JLD papers, Langdon-Davies to Lt Col G. A. Anstee, 13 February 1943; see S. P. MacKenzie, *The Home Guard* (Oxford University Press, Oxford, 1995), pp. 74–6.

74 JLD papers, Langdon-Davies to Col. Peter Shortt, 22 December 1941.

75 JLD papers, Langdon-Davies to Hugh Vere Hodge, 31 May 1949.

76 It was also an opportunity for Langdon-Davies to renew his contest with Haldane.

77 JLD papers, Langdon-Davies to Julian Huxley, 11 July 1949.

78 Journal, 12 June 1951, in Berga PhD thesis, pp. 186–9.

79 There is a copy of Langdon-Davies's printed circular note in the *New Statesman* papers, University of Sussex, file 13/7; Langdon-Davies, *Gatherings*, p. ix.

80 Patricia Langdon-Davies, "Paella on Sundays", typescript, 1992.

81 Langdon-Davies, *Gatherings*, pp. viii–ix.

82 JLD papers, Ramon Casanova to Langdon-Davies, 25 May 1947; author's interview with Robin Langdon-Davies, Bristol, 9 June 2000. (Robin Langdon-Davies was citing his correspondence with Casanova in the late 1960s).

83 Letter to the author from Patricia Langdon-Davies, 27 September 2003.

84 JLD papers, 23 May 1961, JLD to Eyre and Spottiswood (written in the context of Hugh Thomas's attribution of Communist Party membership, see above p. 147).

85 Journal entry for 27 June 1950, in Berga, PhD thesis p. 126.

86 Langdon-Davies, *Gatherings*, pp. 161, 150, 173–5, and 136.

87 Langdon-Davies, *Gatherings*, p. v.

88 Langdon-Davies, *Gatherings*, p. 59.

89 Journal reference for 28 May 1951, in Berga, PhD thesis, pp. 174–5; see also Langdon-Davies, *Gatherings*, pp. 110–11.

90 Although see the warning of a potential "explosion" in Barcelona in his last book: *Spain* (Batsford, London, 1971), p. 185.

91 " . . . it is indeed pleasant for a man to sit and loaf with his soul, to watch life from his study window, judiciously, without getting excited . . . There have been times in the history of the world when a man could be content with nothing more than this, and it is to be hoped that such times will come again. But they are not now." (*A short history of the future*, p. 3).

92 Journal, April 1950, in Berga, PhD thesis, pp. 100–2, and 108–9.

Chapter 9 *Spain rediscovered*

1 Giles Romilly, "Dona Nobis Pacem", *New Statesman*, vol. 37, 950, 21 May 1949, pp. 523–4. Two further articles appeared in the editions of 28 May 1949, pp. 551–2, and 4 June 1949, and pp. 580–1. Romilly, a journalist and novelist, lived a troubled life and died in 1967.

2 MML IBMA, Box 40, File B, 1 January 1947, Nan Green to Roddy MacFarquhar (the volunteer in question was Bill Rowe).

3 However, there are other examples of British volunteers returning to Spain, such as the artist Paul Hogarth (*Daily Worker*, 20 December 1949) or Nan Green, who joined a women's delegation to visit female political prisoners in 1946. Archie Cochrane attended a cardiology conference in Barcelona in 1954, driving there in his Jaguar, but only felt that he had properly "returned" to Spain when he was able to revisit the sites occupied by the British medical unit in 1978 (Bosch, *Back to the front*, pp. 69 and 232–9). Laurie Lee revisited Spain in the early 1950s and it should be noted that his travel book *A Rose for Winter* (1955; 1971 edition, Penguin, Harmondsworth) long pre-dated his published accounts of his Spanish Civil War experiences (*As I Walked Out One Midsummer Morning* (1969; 1971 edition, Penguin, Harmondsworth) and *A Moment of War* (Penguin, Harmondsworth, 1991)).

4 For an excellent overview see Carolina Labarta, "British Foreign Policy towards Spain, 1950–1961" (D.Phil., Oxford, 1999).

5 Cited in Labarta, D.Phil. thesis, pp. 201–2.

6 For example, a poll of June 1968 asked respondents "If somebody asked you about going for a holiday, would your advice be to stay at home or to go to . . . ". For Spain the result was "Go", 41 per cent and "Stay at home", 47 per cent, while the corresponding figures for France were 26 per cent and 65 per cent. A poll of May 1975 asked to what extent certain countries could be trusted as an ally in case of war. For Spain, 2 per cent answered "a great deal" and 51 per cent "not at all". However, these figures were very similar to those for Italy and Greece which, unlike Spain, were both NATO allies. George H. Gallup (ed.), *Gallup International Public Opinion Polls; Great Britain, 1937–75, Vol II*, pp. 996 and 1411.

7 Constance Babington Smith, *Rose Macaulay* (Collins, London, 1972), p. 176.

8 Gerald Brenan, *The Face of Spain* (1950; 1987, Penguin, London), p. 9.

9 See Jonathan Gathorne-Hardy, *Gerald Brenan: the Interior Castle* (1992; 1994 edition, Sinclair- Stevenson, London); for an excellent first-hand account of Brenan's experiences in Spain during the Civil War see Gamel Woolsey's *Death's Other Kingdom* (1939; 1988, Virago, London).

10 Notably *Southern Baroque Art* (Grant Richards, London, 1924) and *Spanish Baroque Art* (Duckworth, London, 1931).

11 Sarah Bradford, *Sacheverell Sitwell: Splendours and Miseries* (Sinclair-Stevenson, London, 1993), p. 337.

12 Jeremy Treglown, *V. S. Pritchett: A Working Life* (Chatto & Windus, London, 2004), p. 72.

13 *Authors Take Sides on the Spanish War* (1937). Pritchett's reply had been both characteristic and more subtle: the lesson that he drew from the Civil War was the "innate simplicity and nobility of the uncorrupted common people".

14 University of Sussex, Leonard Woolf papers, D6, Brenan to Woolf, 26 October 1943.

15 Gathorne-Hardy, *Brenan*, p. 350.

16 Brenan, *Face of Spain*, p. 73.

17 Brenan, *Face of Spain*, p. 9.

18 Brenan, *Face of Spain*, p. 71 and 67.

19 Sitwell, *Spain* (Batsford, London, 1950), pp. 49–50.

20 Rose Macaulay to her sister Jean, 25 August 1947, cited in Constance Babington Smith (ed.), *Letters to a Sister from Rose Macaulay* (Atheneum, New York, 1964), pp. 133–4. Kravchenko's book had been published in 1947 (Robert Hale, London) and caused remarkable interest. The journalist Alexander Werth wrote of the "Kravchenko-Koestler era" in post-war France (*France, 1940–1955* (Readers Union, London, 1958), p. 363).

21 Brenan, *Face of Spain*, p. 27

22 Paul O'Prey (ed.), *In Broken Images: Selected letters of Robert Graves, 1914–46* (Hutchinson, London, 1982), p. 343 (from a letter of 15 April 1946 to Lynette Roberts).

23 Norman Lewis, *Voices of the Old Sea* (1984; 1996 edition, Picador, London), Foreword. Lewis had travelled in Spain in 1934, but came to regard his *Spanish Adventure* (H. Holt, New York, 1935) with deep embarrassment.

24 Sitwell, *Spain*, pp. 60–1.

25 Brenan, *Face of Spain*, p. 16.

26 See Treglown, *Pritchett*, pp. 70 and 268 fn. 31.

27 V. S. Pritchett, *The Spanish Temper* (Chatto & Windus, London, 1954), pp. 8, 13, 146–7, 149, and 210.

28 Brenan, *Face of Spain*, p. 221.

29 Brenan, *South from Granada*, p. x.

30 Lewis, *Voices*, Foreword.

31 Rose Macaulay, *Fabled Shore: From the Pyrenees to Portugal* (1949; 1950 edition, Readers Union, London), pp. 47–8. In a letter written at this time she suggested that the Spanish had less "progressive energy" (Babington Smith, *Rose Macaulay*, p. 178).

32 Sitwell, *Spain*, p. 94.

33 Pritchett, *Spanish temper*, p. 189; Langdon-Davies, *Gatherings*, p. 112.

34 Macaulay, *Fabled shore*, pp. 72 and 32.

35 Brenan, *Face of Spain*, pp. 169 and 134.

36 Sitwell, *Spain*, p. 129.

37 Pritchett, *Spanish temper*, p. 71; Brenan, *Face of Spain*, p. 76.

38 Macaulay, *Fabled shore*, pp. 40–1. She wrote that she was often greeted by a "long shrill cat-call, reminiscent of a pig having its throat cut"; Babington Smith, *Macaulay*, p. 177. It has to be said that the sight of a woman in her late 60s driving alone, changing tyres on remote roads, and sometimes sleeping beside her car on a lilo would have probably raised eyebrows at this time even in less traditional cultures.

39 Langdon-Davies, *Gatherings*, p. 54.

40 Macaulay, *Fabled shore*, pp. 55–6.

41 JLD papers, 29 May 1952, Macaulay to Langdon-Davies.

42 Langdon-Davies, *Gatherings*, p. 27.

43 Macaulay, *Fabled shore*, p. 174.

44 It should be noted that Lewis's earlier novel *The Day of the Fox* (1955; 1960 edition, Penguin, Harmondsworth) also draws heavily on his observations of the fishing villages of the Costa Brava.

45 Pritchett, *Spanish temper*, p. 94; Brenan, *Face of Spain*, p. 13 (Brenan had served on the Western Front in World War One).

46 Langdon-Davies, *Gatherings*, p. 6.

47 Paul O'Prey (ed.), *Between Moon and Moon; Selected letters of Robert Graves, 1946–1972* (Hutchinson, London, 1982), p. 28 (letter of 29 June 1946 to Alan Hodge).

48 Brenan, *Face of Spain*, p. 166.

49 Julian Pitt-Rivers, *The People of the Sierra* (Weidenfeld & Nicolson, London, 1954), p. 15. Initially the identity of the village was disguised as "Alcala de la Sierra". Pitt-Rivers was adamant that his book contributed nothing "to controversies regarding Spanish politics" (p. xv).

50 Geoffrey Brereton, *New Statesman*, 16 October 1954, p. 478.

51 *The Times*, 12 June 1950.

52 Macaulay to Rev. John Hamilton Cowper Johnson, 19 November 1951, in C. Babington Smith (ed), *Letters to a Friend from Rose Macaulay, 1950–1952* (Collins, London, 1961), p. 225.

53 Macaulay, *Letters to a friend*, p. 105, Rose Macaulay to Rev. Johnson 27 March 1951; Macaulay, *Letters to a sister*, p. 134, 25 August 1947, Rose Macaulay to Jean Macaulay.

54 Pritchett, *Spanish temper*, pp. 85–6.

55 According to Gathorne-Hardy Brenan, who had been keen to return to live in Spain since 1943, deliberately avoided any direct criticism of Franco (Gathorne-Hardy, *Brenan*, p. 377 fn.; p. 390 fn).

56 Brenan, *Face of Spain*, p. 14.

57 Basil Davidson, "Spanish Journey III", *New Statesman*, 16 December 1950, p. 619.

58 Romilly, *New Statesman*, 4 June 1949, pp. 580–1.

59 In addition to those listed above, one should also note the complete absence of any coverage of Northern Spain.

60 Gathorne-Hardy, *Brenan*, pp. 389–90.

61 An honourable exception was James Morris's *Spain* (Faber & Faber, London, 1964) which blended a travelogue with reflections on Spanish politics and recent history.

62 Anthony Carson, *A Train to Tarragona* (Methuen, London, 1957) and *Poor Man's Mimosa* (Methuen, London, 1962). See also his shorter pieces in the *New Statesman*, such as 20 February 1960 and 19 March 1960.

63 H. V. Morton, *A Stranger in Spain* (Methuen, London, 1955), p. 7. This view was attributed to an "interview" with an anonymous Spaniard.

64 NMLH, CPGB papers, EC40, 10 November 1948.

65 Eleanor Eagle, "Visit to Barcelona", *New Statesman*, 30 October 1948, p. 369.

66 Aneurin Bevan, *In Place of Fear* (Heinemann, London, 1952), p. 43

67 See Tom Buchanan, "'The truth will set you free . . . ': The making of Amnesty International", *Journal of Contemporary History*, 37, 4, 2002, pp. 575–97.

68 Appeal for Amnesty in Spain, *From Burgos jail* (London, 1964), p. 1.

69 See chapter 10.

70 Cited in Sue Wright, "Sun, sea, sand and self-expression – mass tourism as an individual experience", in Hartmut Berghoff *et al.*, *The Making of Modern Tourism: The Cultural History of the British Experience, 1600–2000* (Palgrave, Basingstoke, 2002), pp. 192–3

71 For an excellent introduction to these issues see M. Barke, J. Towner and M. T. Newton (eds.), *Tourism in Spain: Critical Issues* (CAB International, Wallingford, 1996).

72 Letter from "Republican" in *New Statesman*, 14 February 1969, p. 225.

73 V. Bote Gómez and M. Thea Sinclair, "Tourism demand and supply in Spain", in Barke *et al.*, *Tourism in Spain*, pp. 68–9. These figures originate with the Ministry of Industry, Commerce and Tourism. France provided by far the largest number of foreign visitors to Spain. In 1975 for the first time German visitors outnumbered those from Britain.

74 *Parl Debs*, vol. 786, col. 339, 11 July 1969, written answer by William Rodgers.

75 See Barke *et al*, *Tourism in Spain*, pp. 235 and 269.

76 Susan Barton, *Working-class organizations and popular tourism, 1840–1970* (Manchester University Press, Manchester, 2005), p. 202.

77 Aylmer Vallance, "Created Travel", *New Statesman*, 6 February 1954, pp. 151–2.

78 MRC, Mss 292/946/2, "Holiday in Spain", undated typescript by Betty Hainworth. She was surprised to find that Spain was not the "police-ridden country with controls everywhere" that she had expected.

79 Nigel Nicolson (ed.), *Harold Nicolson: diaries and letters, 1945–62* (Collins, London, 1968), pp. 302–3 and p. 310. It should be noted, however, that in 1953 Nicolson had written that his wife wanted to visit Spain but that "I have a strange and eccentric objection to visiting a country ruled by a man who established his dictatorship by using foreign and native troops against his own countrymen" (letter to John Langdon-Davies of 9 July 1953 in JLD papers).

80 *New Statesman*, 9 October 1954, pp. 429–30. Hobsbawm made a number of visits to Spain during the 1950s (see his autobiography *Interesting Times: A Twentieth-Century Life* (Abacus edition, 2003), pp. 342–5.)

81 *New Statesman*, 31 March 1956, pp. 308–10, see the comments by Anthony Carson, V. S. Pritchett and John Raymond.

82 See NMLH, Labour party archive, correspondence in LP/ID Box 5 (1946) and Box 9 (1947); *Daily Worker*, 2 January 1953.

83 Although see above, p. 155, for the generally repressive ambience.

84 Christ Church, Oxford, Tom Driberg papers, C21, 13 June 1958, Cunard

to Driberg (writing from Sant Feliu de Guixols). Cunard was, however, told by the Spanish police that she could not renew her visa.

85 "Gulliver" in *New Statesman*, 23 February 1957, p. 244.

86 *New Statesman*, 21 September 1962, pp. 361–2.

87 *Daily Worker*, 28 April 1960. Russell also served in The International Brigades.

88 *Daily Worker*, 22 April 1963.

89 *Daily Worker*, 31 December 1965; for earlier examples see also *Daily Worker* 17 March 1965 and *Tribune*, 10 June 1963.

90 Tom Driberg, *Ruling Passions* (Cape, London, 1977), p. 118.

91 NMLH, Manchester, CP/CENT/INT/29/01, 25 April 1963, CPGB to Harry Bourne, Midlands District. (Bourne was a former International Brigade volunteer).

92 *The Guardian*, 6 April 1970.

93 *Morning Star*, 11 July 1969.

94 MRC, Mss 292D, Box 2435, correspondence between Feather and Mr V. C. Brodie, 29 December 1970 and 12 February 1971.

95 *Morning Star*, 10 June 1968.

96 Roger Bray and Vladimir Raitz, *Flight to the Sun: The Story of the Holiday Revolution* (Continuum, London, 2001), p. 157.

97 *Parl.Debs*, vol. 784, col. 961, 9 June 1969. Prime Minister Harold Wilson subsequently noted that Stewart had offered no "official advice" for tourists to avoid Spain (*Parl. Debs*, vol. 787, written answers col. 192–3, 17 July 1969.)

98 *Daily Worker*, 22 October 1964.

99 Viz Sue Wright's project on the early package tourists, in Berghoff, *Modern tourism*, pp. 192–4.

Chapter 10   *The Spanish Civil War in British politics since 1939*

1 University of Sussex, Leonard Woolf papers, IL8, 4 April 1967, Esslin to Woolf. Within the BBC, Esslin's comment was that "[I] don't think it can stand up as a *play* today". (Radio Plays index card, BBC Written Archives Centre, Caversham: I am grateful to Trish Hayes for sending me this reference).

2 For the politics of opposition to the Franco regime after 1939 see Tom Buchanan, "Receding triumph: British opposition to the Franco regime, 1945–59", *Twentieth Century British History*, 12, 2, 2001, pp. 163–84, and "Holding the line: the political strategy of the International Brigade Association", *Labour History Review*, 66:3, winter 2001, pp. 294–312. See also Bill Alexander, *No to Franco: The Struggle Never Stopped, 1939–1975* (Oval Printshop, London, 1992).

3 The phrase was coined by General Mola during the Nationalist advance on Madrid. It was popularised in Britain during the invasion scare of 1940, not least by John Langdon-Davies in his book *Fifth column*.

4 Q. Hogg, *The Left was Never Right* (Faber & Faber, London, 1945), pp.

156–8. There is, of course, a substantial scholarly literature which supports the view taken by many at the time that Britain's support for Non-Intervention was, in effect, an intervention against the Republican side (see Moradiellos, *La perfidia de albión*.)

5   *The Times,* 16 June 1964.

6   But see above p. 187.

7   Carter, *Blunt*, p. 179.

8   Don Carson, 1949 *TUC Conference Report* p. 371.

9   *Daily Worker*, 30 January 1951.

10 Nancy Farrie of North Wales, in *Morning Star*, 3 November 1969. See above p. 136.

11 It was, for instance, not proscribed by the Labour party. For the IBA see Buchanan, "Holding the line".

12 Nan Green, *Small beer*, p. 112; Corkill and Rawnsley, *The road to Spain*, p. 68.

13 MML IBMA, B-3, SIN/6, Sinclair-Loutit to Jim Fyrth, 18 November 1985 (emphasis in original). This sentence is reproduced in Fyrth, *The signal*, p. 91, although without identifying the author and without the qualification contained in the first nine words cited here.

14 *New Statesman* 20 April 1962, pp. 555–6.

15 British Library of Political and Economic Science, London, Ernest Davies papers, 3/24, unpublished typescript on Spain, p. 3. Davies served as a junior Foreign Office minister in 1950–1, and by the late 1950s was heavily involved in support for the democratic opposition within Spain.

16 See Buchanan, "Three Lives of *Homage to Catalonia*".

17 See Buchanan, *The Spanish Civil War and the British labour movement*.

18 Amnesty International archives, oral history project, Benenson's 1983 typescript bound with interview transcript, p. 1.

19 Lee, *My life with Nye*, pp. 147–8.

20 Francis King and George Matthews (eds.), *About Turn* (Lawrence & Wishart, London, 1990), p. 74.

21 King and Matthews, *About turn*, p. 194 (the speaker was George Allison).

22 18 November 1939, Pollitt to Central Committee, cited in John Attfield and Stephen Williams, *1939: The Communist Party and the War* (Lawrence & Wishart, London, 1984), p. 168.

23 Cited in Kevin Morgan, *Against Fascism and War* (Manchester University Press, Manchester, 1989), p. 57.

24 Attfield and Williams, *1939*, p. 183. Pollitt was heavily defeated by the Labour candidate, by 966 votes to 14,343.

25 Rankin, *Telegram from Guernica*, p. 169.

26 *News Chronicle*, 27 March 1940. For similar sentiments see Langdon-Davies, *Finland*.

27 MML, IBMA, Box 40, File A.

28 MML, IBMA Box 40, File A, IBA circular, 29 February 1940.

29 MRC, Mss 292/948.7/4.

30 See correspondence in MRC, Mss 292/948.7/4.

31 MRC, Mss 292/948.7/4, 7 March 1940.
32 Ibid. (My emphasis). Some in the Labour Party found this difficult to swallow. The agent of Coventry Labour Party wrote to Philip Noel-Baker: "are you quite sure that we '*always* supported' arms for Spain" (CCA, NBKR 9/65, George Hodgkinson to Noel-Baker, 11 April 1940).
33 Memorandum of 22 May 1941, cited in Purcell, *The last English revolutionary*, p. 156.
34 *Picture Post*, 21 September 1940, cited in S. P. Mackenzie, *The Home Guard* (Oxford University Press, Oxford, 1995), p. 71.
35 Mackenzie, *Home Guard*, p. 70.
36 Norman Mackenzie, cited in Purcell, *The last English revolutionary*, p. 186.
37 Victor Gollancz (ed.), *The Betrayal of the Left* (Gollancz, London, 1941), pp. 53 and 61–2.
38 Harrison, *Good to be alive*, p. 49 (citing a letter from Jack Brent describing the February 1944 commemoration of the battle of the Jarama).
39 NLS, Tom Murray papers, Acc 9083, Box 4/1.
40 TUC, Mss 292C/946/2, 2 October 1940, Davson to Leah Manning,
41 Cassius, *The Trial of Mussolini* (Gollancz, London, 1943), pp. 66 and 80–1.
42 *Daily Herald*, 18 June 1945; MML, IBMA, D-3, File A/22–23, Nan Green's circular of 23 June 1945.
43 *Daily Worker*, 18 July 1956.
44 Jim Fyrth, "Labour's bright morning – and afternoon", in Fyrth (ed.), *Labour's High Noon* (Lawrence & Wishart, London, 1993), p. 271.
45 See Buchanan, "Holding the line".
46 *Labour Party Conference Report*, 1950, p. 78. While the contemporary political message was clear, this was, in historical terms, a weak, confused and misleading argument.
47 *TUC Conference Report*, 1950, pp. 410–11.
48 *The Times*, 17 June 1943.
49 *Daily Worker*, 13 September 1950, letter from Eddie Lawther.
50 *Daily Worker*, 25 March, 1946.
51 *Daily Worker*, 28 September 1953.
52 *Daily Worker*, 23 and 30 January 1951; Douglas Hyde, *I Believed* (William Heinemann, London, 1950), p. 60.
53 Bob Darke, *The Communist Technique in Britain* (Collins, London, 1953), pp. 37–8, 82 and 93; see also his articles in *Picture Post*, 20 September 1952, pp. 14–17 and 27 September 1952, pp. 35–40; *Daily Worker*, 3 October 1952. It is not clear why Kerrigan was singled out for attack by Darke.
54 *Parl Debs*, vol. 545, col. 1483, 7 November 1955. Macmillan was speaking as Foreign Secretary during the parliamentary debate on the two spies who had, in fact, defected in 1951.
55 *Daily Worker*, 8 November 1955. Of course, some British veterans of the Spanish Civil War *did* subsequently spy for the Soviet Union, including Alexander Foote, Oliver Green and David Springhall.
56 *The Times*, 15 May 1953.

57 The phrase appears to have been coined by Weintraub, *The last great cause*, although Weintraub notes its use by Professor Mark Schorer ten years earlier (p. 314).

58 Jack Lindsay, *After the 'Thirties: The Novel in Britain and its Future* (Lawrence &Wishart, London, 1956), pp. 64–5. In an interesting sign of the times after Khrushchev's denunciation of Stalin in February 1956, J. R. Campbell's review in the *Daily Worker* (21 June 1956) criticised Lindsay for his evasive comments about Communist policy in 1939–41.

59 Walter Allen in the *New Statesman*, 14 June 1958, p. 769.

60 MML, IBMA, Box 38, file B/9, Nan Green to J. Campbell, 4 March 1946.

61 *The Times*, 24 January 1948.

62 Arthur Clegg, *Aid China: A Memoir of a Forgotten Campaign* (Beijing, Foreign Language Press, 2003).

63 The relationship between China and the British left is the focus of my current research.

64 John Osborne, *Look Back in Anger* (1956), pp. 57 and 84.

65 Kingsley Amis, *Socialism and the Intellectuals* (Fabian Society, London, 1957), pp. 6, 11 and 9.

66 *New Statesman*, 12 January 1957, pp. 35–6.

67 *The Times*, 2 January 1957.

68 "Critic" in the *New Statesman*, 17 November 1956, p. 614.

69 *The Times*, 20 November 1956, citing David Price MP.

70 *Daily Worker*, 17 November 1956. Robeson had been an extremely prominent supporter of the Republic during the Civil War (see above, p. 92).

71 *Daily Worker*, 24 July 1965.

72 Edward Heath, *The Course of my Life* (Hodder & Stoughton, London, 1998), p. 52.

73 Cecil Woolf and John Bagguley (eds), *Authors Take Sides on Vietnam* (Owen, London, 1967), pp. xii, 59 and 57. The twenty five were: Mulk Raj Anand, W. H. Auden, George Barker, Kay Boyle, Fenner Brockway, Margaret Cole, David Garnett, Geoffrey Grigson, Storm Jameson, Eric Linklater, Hugh MacDiarmid, Ethel Mannin, Naomi Mitchison, Raymond Mortimer, D. N. Pritt, Herbert Read, Stephen Spender, Christina Stead, Sylvia Townsend Warner, Rex Warner, Leonard Woolf, Vera Brittain, Vyvyan Holland, Alec Waugh and Edmund Blunden. In addition, a number of writers active in the 1930s who did not take part in the 1937 collection did contribute their views on Vietnam: these included Kingsley Martin, Gerald Brenan and Malcolm Muggeridge.

74 NMLH, CPGB archive, CP/CENT/INT/29 101, 5 May 1965, John Mahon to "Johnnie" (presumably the party leader, John Gollan).

75 *Morning Star*, 27 November 1967.

76 Bodleian library, Oxford, Dorothy Hodgkin papers, Ms. Eng.c.5690, Box G 127, 1979 typescript by Joan McMichael entitled "The Work of the British Medical Aid Committee for Vietnam", p. 1.

77 See the comments by Avis Hutt and Charles Lefton in *Joan McMichael-*

Askins: Her Life and Work, a pamphlet of tributes published following a memorial meeting at Conway Hall, 2 November 1989, pp. 8 and 12. Both had known her in Spanish Medical Aid.

78 King and Matthews, *About turn*, p. 190 (the speaker was George Allison).

79 *Daily Worker*, 11 January and 17 February 1950. These were Peter Kerrigan, Bob Cooney, Don Renton, Bill Alexander, John Mahon, Jeff Mildwater, Jack Coward, Wogan Phillips and Bert Ramelson.

80 MML, IBMA, Box 41, A, correspondence between J. V. Keen and Nan Green, 27 October 1947 and 31 October 1947.

81 See, for instance, Josie McLellan, *Antifascism and Memory in East Germany: Remembering the International Brigades, 1945–1989* (Oxford University Press, Oxford, 2004), pp. 57–63. In 1956 a number of former British volunteers attended a reunion in Warsaw and were uncertain how to respond to the many Polish veterans who had only just emerged from Soviet prison camps (Alison Macleod, *The Death of Uncle Joe* (Merlin Press, Woodbridge, 1997), p. 228).

82 *Daily Worker*, 31 January 1950.

83 Francis Beckett, *Enemy Within: The Rise and Fall of the British Communist Party* (1995; 1998 edition, Merlin Press, Woodbridge), p. 163; obituary by Richard Baxell, *The Guardian*, 14 July 2000.

84 *New Statesman*, 28 April 1961, p. 670.

85 *Daily Worker*, 12 March 1959.

86 See Jack Jones, *Union Man* (Collins, London, 1980) pp. 317–20.

87 *The Times*, 30 July 1954 (S. Silverman) and 6 July 1954 (G. Bing); *The Times*, 16 June 1964. As recently as 2000 the *Guardian* journalist Ian Aitken castigated "Butler's lies" during the Civil War (*The Guardian*, 10 November 2000). Aitken's father had served in the International Brigades as a senior Political Commissar.

88 *Daily Worker*, 24 May 1961; *New Statesman*, 26 May 1961, p. 817.

89 *Daily Worker*, 4 July 1964.

90 MML IBMA, Box 40, file A/22, IBA circular, 1971.

91 See Buchanan, *Britain and the Spanish Civil War*, p. 201

92 *New Statesman*, 8 August 2005, pp. 16–17. Pilger was speaking at the annual memorial meeting to mark the outbreak of the Civil War on London's South Bank.

93 *The Times*, 31 October 1972; Stuart Christie, *Granny made me an Anarchist* (Scribner, London, 2004), pp. 39–44 and 120.

94 *The Guardian*, 12 October 1993. Davison was jailed in 1985 for his part in the murder of three Israelis in Cyprus.

95 *The Guardian*, 10 November 2000 (and correspondence in 11, 13 and 14 November).

Select Bibliography

Aldgate, Anthony, *Cinema and History: British Newsreels and the Spanish Civil War* (Scolar, London, 1979).

Alexander, Bill, *British Volunteers for Liberty; Spain, 1936–39* (Lawrence & Wishart, London, 1982).

——, *No to Franco: The Struggle Never Stopped* (Oval Printshop, London, 1992).

Alpert, Michael, "Humanitarianism and politics in the British response to the Spanish Civil War, 1936–1939", *European History Quarterly*, 14, 4, October 1984.

Ball, Stuart, "The politics of appeasement: The fall of the Duchess of Atholl and the Kinross and West Perth by-election, December 1938", *Scottish Historical Review*, vol. LXIX, 187, April 1990.

Baxell, Richard, *British Volunteers in the Spanish Civil War: The British Battalion of the International Brigades, 1936–1939* (Routledge, London, 2004)

Beckett, Francis, *Enemy Within: The Rise and Fall of the British Communist Party* (1998 edition, Merlin Press, Woodbridge).

Bell, Adrian, *Only for Three Months; The Basque Children in Exile* (Mousehold Press, Norwich, 1996).

Brome, Vincent, *The International Brigades* (Heinemann, London, 1965).

Brothers, Caroline, *War and Photography: A Cultural History* (Routledge, London, 1996).

Buchanan, Tom, *The Spanish Civil War and the British Labour Movement* (Cambridge University Press, Cambridge, 1991).

——, *Britain and the Spanish Civil War,* (Cambridge University Press, Cambridge, 1997).

——, "Britain's Popular Front? Aid Spain and the British Labour Movement", *History Workshop Journal*, 31, Spring 1991, 60–73.

——, "Anti-fascism and democracy in the 1930s", *European History Quarterly*, 32, 1, January 2002, 39–57.

——, "The Republic besieged? British banks and the Spanish Civil War: 1936–1939", in Edwin Green, *et al.* (eds.), *Crisis and renewal in Twentieth Century Banking* (Ashgate, Aldershot, 2004), 87–103.

——, "Three lives of *Homage to Catalonia*", *The Library*, 7th series, 3, 3, September 2002, 302–14.

——, "Edge of darkness: British 'front-line' diplomacy in the Spanish Civil War, 1936–7", *Contemporary European History*, 12, 3, 2003, 279–303.

——, "Holding the Line: The Political Strategy of the International Brigade Association", *Labour History Review*, 66: 3, Winter 2001, pp. 163–84.

Cable, James, *The Royal Navy and the Siege of Bilbao* (Cambridge University Press, Cambridge, 1979).

Cook, Judith, *Apprentices of Freedom* (Quartet, London, 1979).

Corkill, David, and Rawnsley, Stuart, *The Road to Spain: Anti-Fascists at War, 1936–39* (Borderline Press, Dunfermline, 1981).

Cunningham, Valentine, *The Penguin book of Spanish Civil War Verse* (Penguin, Harmondsworth, 1980).

——, *Spanish Front: Writers on the Civil War* (Oxford University Press, Oxford, 1986).

Dowse, Robert, *Left in the Centre: the Independent Labour Party, 1893–1940* (Longmans, London, 1966).

Edwards, Jill, *The British Government and the Spanish Civil War* (Macmillan, London, 1979).

Fleay, C. and Sanders, M. L., "The Labour Spain Committee: Labour Party policy and the Spanish Civil War", *The Historical Journal*, 27, 4, 1985.

Ford, Hugh D., *A Poet's War: British Poets and the Spanish Civil War* (University of Pennsylvania Press, Philadelphia, 1965).

Francis, Hywel, *Miners against Fascism: Wales and the Spanish Civil War* (Lawrence & Wishart, London, 1984).

——, "'Say nothing and leave in the middle of the night'; The Spanish Civil War revisited", *History Workshop Journal*, 32, Autumn 1991, 69–76.

Fyrth, Jim, *The Signal was Spain: The Aid Spain Movement in Britain, 1936–1939* (Lawrence & Wishart, London, 1986).

—— "The Aid to Spain Movement in Britain, 1936–1939", *History Workshop Journal*, 35, 1993, 153–64.

Fyrth, Jim, and Alexander, Sally, *Women's Voices from the Spanish Civil War* (Lawrence & Wishart, London, 1991).

Gathorne-Hardy, Jonathan, *Gerald Brenan: The Interior Castle* (Sinclair-Stevenson, London, 1994 edition).

Hart, Stephen M., *No Pasaran! Art, Literature and the Spanish Civil War* (Tamesis Books, London, 1988).

Hopkins, James K., *Into the Heart of the Fire: The British in the Spanish Civil War* (Stanford University Press, Stanford, 1998).

Hoskins, Katharine, *Today the Struggle: Literature and Politics in England during the Spanish Civil War* (University of Texas, Austin, 1969).

Howson, Gerald, *Arms for Spain: The Untold Story of the Spanish Civil War* (John Murray, London, 1998).

Jackson, Angela, *British Women and the Spanish Civil War* (Routledge, London, 2003).

Keene, Judith, *Fighting for Franco: International Volunteers in Nationalist Spain during the Spanish Civil War, 1936–39* (Leicester University Press, London, 2001).

Knightley, Phillip, *The First Casualty: From the Crimea to Vietnam – The War Correspondent as Hero, Propagandist and Myth Maker* (Quartet, London, 1982).

Legaretta, Dorothy, *The Guernica Generation: Basque Refugee Children of the Spanish Civil War* (University of Nevada Press, Reno, 1984).

Little, Douglas, *Malevolent Neutrality: the United States, Great Britain and the Origins of the Spanish Civil War* (Ithaca, NY, 1985).

MacDougall, Ian, *Voices from the Spanish Civil War: Personal Recollections of Scottish Volunteers in Republican Spain, 1936–39* (Polygon, Edinburgh, 1986).

Moradiellos, Enrique, *Neutralidad Benévola: El Gobierno Británico y la Insurección Militar Español de 1936* (Pentalfa Ediciones, Oviedo, 1990).

——, *La Perfidia de Albión: El Gobierno Británico y la Guerra Civil Española* (Siglo veintiuno editors, Madrid, 1996).

Morgan, Kevin, *Against Fascism and War: Ruptures and Continuities in British Communist Politics, 1935–41* (Manchester University Press, Manchester, 1989).

——, *Harry Pollitt* (Manchester University Press, Manchester, 1993).

Morris, Lynda, and Radford, Robert, *AIA: The story of the Artists International Association* (Museum of Modern Art, Oxford, 1983).

Preston, Paul, *Doves of War: Four Women of Spain* (HarperCollins, London, 2002).

Purcell, Hugh, *The Last English Revolutionary: Tom Wintringham, 1898–1949* (Sutton, Stroud, 2004).

Rankin, Nick, *Telegram from Guernica: The Extraordinary Life of George Steer, War Correspondent* (Faber and Faber, London, 2003).

Rickaby, Tony, "Artists International", *History Workshop Journal*, 6, autumn 1978, 154–68.

Rust, William, *Britons in Spain: The History of the British Battalion of the XVth International Brigade* (Lawrence & Wishart, London, 1939).

Saville, John, "The Aid for Spain Movement, 1936–1939", *Dictionary of Labour Biography*, vol. IX (Macmillan, Basingstoke, 1993).

Shelden, Michael, *Orwell: The Authorised Biography* (Heinemann, London, 1991).

Southworth, Herbert R, *Guernica! Guernica! A Study of Journalism, Diplomacy, Propaganda and History* (University of California Press, Berkeley, 1977).

Stansky, Peter and Abrahams, William, *Journey to the Frontier. Julian Bell and John Cornford: Their Lives and the 1930s* (Constable, London, 1966).

——, *Orwell: The Transformation* (Paladin, Aylesbury, 1979).

Stradling, Robert, *Cardiff and the Spanish Civil War* (Butetown History and Arts Centre, Cardiff, 1996).

——, *Brother against Brother; Experiences of a British Volunteer in the Spanish Civil War* (Sutton, Stroud, 1998).

——, *The Irish and the Spanish Civil War* (Manchester University Press, Manchester, 1999).

——, *History and Legend: Writing the International Brigades* (University of Wales Press, Cardiff, 2003).

——, *Wales and the Spanish Civil War: The Dragon's Dearest Cause?* (University of Wales Press, Cardiff, 2004).

Thwaites, Peter, "The Independent Labour Party contingent in the Spanish Civil War", *Imperial War Museum Review*, 2, 1987, 509–61.

Toynbee, Philip (ed.), *The Distant Drum: Reflections on the Spanish Civil War* (Sidgwick & Jackson, London, 1976).

Watkins, K. W., *Britain Divided: The Effect of the Spanish Civil War on British Political Opinion* (Thomas Nelson, London, 1963).

Weintraub, Stanley, *The Last Great Cause: The Intellectuals and the Spanish Civil War* (W. H. Allen, London, 1968).

Williams, Colin, *et al.*, *Memorials of the Spanish Civil War* (Sutton, Stroud, 1996).

Index